Walrasian Economics

To understand the various strands of general equilibrium theory, why it has taken the forms it has since the time of Léon Walras, and appreciate fully a view of the present state of general equilibrium theorizing, it is essential to understand his work and examine its influence. The first section of this book accordingly examines the foundations of Walras's work, including his philosophical and methodological approaches to economic modeling, his views on human nature, and the basic components of his general equilibrium models. The second section examines how the influence of his ideas has been manifested in the work of his successors, surveying the models of theorists such as H. L. Moore, Vilfredo Pareto, Knut Wicksell, Gustav Cassel, Abraham Wald, John von Neumann, J. R. Hicks, Kenneth Arrow, and Gérard Debreu. The book also provides a bibliography (relating to Chapter 11) of recent models of many types regarding which their constructors explicitly acknowledge Walras's influence.

Donald A. Walker is University Professor and Professor of Economics Emeritus at Indiana University of Pennsylvania. He is the author of *Walras's Market Models* (Cambridge University Press, 1996), *Advances in General Equilibrium Theory* (1997), and many articles and reviews in professional journals, chapters in collections, and entries in handbooks and encyclopedias. Professor Walker is the editor of, among other works, William Jaffé's *Essays on Walras* (Cambridge University Press, 1983), *Money and Markets: Essays by Robert W. Clower* (Cambridge University Press, 1984), *Equilibrium* (2000), *The Legacy of Léon Walras* (2001), and, with J.-P. Potier, *La Correspondance entre Aline Walras et William Jaffé* (2004). He was president of the History of Economics Society in 1987–88, editor of the *Journal of the History of Economic Thought* from 1989–99, and the first president of the International Walras Society, 1997–2000.

Walrasian Economics

Donald A. Walker

Indiana University of Pennsylvania

CAMBRIDGE UNIVERSITY PRESS
Cambridge, New York, Melbourne, Madrid, Cape Town,
Singapore, São Paulo, Delhi, Tokyo, Mexico City

Cambridge University Press
32 Avenue of the Americas, New York, NY 10013-2473, USA

www.cambridge.org
Information on this title: www.cambridge.org/9780521394086

First published 2006
First paperback edition 2011

A catalog record for this publication is available from the British Library

Library of Congress Cataloging in Publication data

Walker, Donald A. (Donald Anthony), 1934–
Walrasian economics / Donald A. Walker.
  p. cm.
Includes bibliographical references and index.
ISBN-13: 978-0-521-85855-7 (hardback)
ISBN-10: 0-521-85855-0 (hardback)
1. Walras, Léon, 1834–1910. 2. Equilibrium (Economics) 3. Economics.
I. Title.
HB105.W3W35 2006
339.501 – dc22   2005028592

ISBN 978-0-521-85855-7 Hardback
ISBN 978-0-521-39408-6 Paperback

To Patricia, Valerie, and Anthony

Contents

Preface

To understand the various strands of general equilibrium theory and why it has taken the forms that it has since the time of Léon Walras, and to achieve a view of the present state of general equilibrium theorizing and the directions it appears to be taking, it is essential to understand Walras's work and examine its influence. In *Walras's Market Models* (1996), I considered the technical details of his economic models in great detail, but something more must be done to achieve a fully rounded view of his economic contributions and a truly productive use of a knowledge of them. The first section of the present book accordingly examines the foundations of his work, which were the essence of his heritage. These were his philosophical and methodological approaches to economic modeling, his views on human nature, and the basic components of his general equilibium models, considered from the point of view of what is interesting about them in light of the subsequent influence of his work. The second section examines how Walras's influence has been manifested in the theorizing of his successors, surveying the models of economists such as H. L. Moore, Vilfredo Pareto, Knut Wicksell, Gustav Cassel, Abraham Wald, John von Neumann, J. R. Hicks, Kenneth Arrow, and Gérard Debreu. Thus this book and *Walras's Market Models* are complementary. Taken together, they provide a well-rounded statement of Walrasian economics (that is to say, the economics of Walras and the scholars who came after him who used his ideas), so it is my hope they will be studied together.

I gratefully acknowledge benefiting from the comments made on an earlier draft of Chapters 1, 2, 3, and 4 by Jan van Daal, Jean-Pierre Potier, and Deborah Redman, and the comments of two anonymous referees. My thanks also go to Scott Parris and Peter Katsirubas for their technical expertise and willingness to accommodate my concerns in the preparation of the book. Any deficiencies of the final version are my responsibility.

I wish to thank the publishers for the following permissions:

"Bibliography of the Writings of Léon Walras," 1st ed., *History of Political Economy, 19* (4), 1987, 667–702. Permission granted by Duke University Press to reprint this publication, with changes.

"Some Comments on Léon Walras's Health and Productivity," *Journal of the History of Economic Thought, 21* (4), 1999, 437–48. Permission granted by the History of Economics Society and the editor to reprint, with changes, material drawn from this publication.

D.A.W.

Indiana, January 2005

Introduction

An overview of the objectives of the book

This book is about Walrasian economics, meaning the economics of Léon Walras and the economics in which other scholars have used his ideas. It has two general objectives. One is to present an accurate account of the foundations and basic components of Walras's models of general economic equilibration and equilibrium.[1] The other is to trace the influence of that legacy on his contemporaries and successors. It will be understood that when reference is made in this book to his "legacy," the word is used to mean his legacy of economic theorizing, not of his normative ideas.

In treating the subject, I have made an effort to reach an audience wider than general equilibrium specialists. I have therefore explained some theoretical propositions that are elementary knowledge to general equilibrium specialists but not to some students and not to some economists who concentrate on other fields of research. The book is as self-contained as is possible with subject matters that are infinitely extendable in various detailed respects. Virtually all the material in this book is new research, undertaken specifically for it, but treatments in greater depth of a few of the topics, notably a few of the topics taken up in Chapters 5 and 6, are given in Walker 1996.

---

[1] Walras emphasized that his model dealt with the first aspect as well as the second (239, 1889, 2, p. 364; 1889, 2, p. 370; 1891, 2, p. 434; 1895, 2, p. 630), but normally, except for purposes of emphasis, it will be referred to, as he did, simply as one of general equilibrium. By contrast, some economists' general equilibrium models deal only with equilibrium and not with equilibration, and the context of the discussion will make that clear.

The style of the citations of Walras's writings (as they appear, for example, in the first sentence of this note) is explained in the last part of this introduction.

1

Léon Walras and his economics

A biographical sketch

Walras's biography is an oft-told tale,[2] so here will be given only a brief sketch of his life. He was, of course, the founder of the modern theory of general economic equilibrium. He was born on December 16, 1834, in Evreux, France, and christened Marie Esprit Léon. He had an excellent education during the period 1844 to 1854, covering such subjects as logic, philosophy, ethics, history, physical sciences, chemistry, mechanics, elementary mathematics, geometry, and calculus (Dockès and Potier 2001, pp. 14–16). After his *lycée* education, however, he failed the entrance examinations for the Ecole Polytechnique, and did not have high enough grades to be retained in the program at the Ecole impériale des Mines. Responding to his predominant interests at that time, he abandoned the plan of becoming an engineer in 1856. He began the pursuit of a literary career and, in fact, published a novel (2, 1858) and a short story (7, 1859). In 1859, however, he began the fulfillment of a promise to his father, Auguste Walras, to give up his literary pursuits in order to devote himself to the study of social science.

Of course, Walras had to earn a living for himself and his family, so during the years 1860 to 1870 he worked first as a journalist, then worked in a bank and a railroad office, became managing director of a cooperative association bank, and worked for another bank. During this time he undertook economic research. That was a subject to which he devoted himself for many years, so it is not surprising that the degree of his technical sophistication and the character and quality of his theoretical work changed. His first phase of intellectual activity in regard to economic theory, beginning in 1859 and continuing until 1872, consisted largely of journalistic applications of his knowledge of existing theory and was experimental in regard to his original ideas.[3] Walras's participation in a conference on taxation in Lausanne in 1860 (27, 1861) and his publication of a book on property and justice in that year (15, 1860) – one that mainly set forth the ideas of his father – are examples of his interest in economic topics. Among those ideas was the argument that the state should own all land because land is not produced as the result of the activity of any economic agent and because its value is given

---

[2] Walras's autobiography is listed as entry 240 in Chapter 8. His antecedents and early life are the subjects of Jaffé 1984. Other details about his life, both private and professional, are given in Jaffé 1935, Walker 1970, Walker 1987, Walker 1996, and Potier and Walker 2004. Many of those details are mentioned and others added to them by Pierre Dockès and Jean-Pierre Potier in the most complete biography of Walras yet written (249.V, pp. IX–XCIV).

[3] See the entries for the years 1861–1871 in the definitive bibliography (Chapter 8).

to it by the growth of population and of the economy. Walras also wrote many analyses of then-current economic problems, notably contributing articles to the journals *La Presse, L'Indépendant de la Moselle, Journal des Economistes*, and *Le Travail*, and giving and publishing public lectures on his ideas about an ideal society. Those writings can be seen to be his early efforts to adopt an analytical approach to the study of practical economic issues, an approach that he refined in later years.

Moreover, at the start and again toward the end of that period, Walras began to use mathematics in the construction of rudimentary models dealing with exchange (16, 1860; 91, 1869; 95, 1871). He relates in his autobibliography: "The idea of creating mathematical economics, that I had announced in my letter offering my services to the Council of State of Vaud, never ceased to occupy my mind after 1860" (239, 1893, *1*, p. 5). He did not, however, have an adequate foundation in mathematics and lacked some of the concepts that he needed to establish the foundations of a theory of supply and demand and of the interrelationships of markets. Nothing that he wrote during that phase of his career can be considered a valuable contribution to economic theory.

Walras's 1860 paper on taxation drew him to the attention of Louis Ruchonnet, a Swiss statesman. Ten years later, Ruchonnet recommended successfully that Walras be offered an appointment, despite his lack of formal credentials in economics, at the Académie (subsequently Université) de Lausanne. Walras began his duties there as a professor without tenure in 1870, and the next year his appointment became permanent. His subsequent attempts to obtain a position in a French university were rebuffed – for, after all, he still lacked the necessary educational credentials and, moreover, he was an exponent of mathematical economics, which was regarded unfavorably by the academic establishment. He therefore remained at Lausanne for his entire academic career. He retired in 1892, and died on January 5, 1910, in Clarens, Switzerland.

Influences on Walras

It should be recalled when reading the cursory statements here about links between Walras's ideas and those of his predecessors that this book is concerned with his theories and his influence on other economists and not with the influence of other scholars upon him. Nevertheless, it is interesting to note briefly his intellectual predecessors and contributions of theirs that helped him in conceiving and constructing his general equilibrium model. Although the ideas of a number of scholars were important in preparing him for that achievement, Walras declared ungenerously that "the only two men who produced previous works which have aided me are ... A.-A. Walras, my father, and Mr. Cournot" (239, 1874, *1*,

p. 397). It is quite true that his father influenced a number of Léon's philosophical and economic ideas. Auguste was a secondary school administrator whose writings on economics, whose library of books on the topic, and whose belief that economics could be transformed into a mathematical discipline were all important in the formation of Walras's thought. Auguste had tried to make some progress on the question of the determination of prices, and bequeathed that problem to his son, along with an interest in utility and scarcity as elements that should be used in its solution. Auguste provided a number of concepts that were given an important place in Léon's economic models, providing him with "points of departure or foundations for the establishment of the general theory [sic] of economic equilibrium" (239, 1903, *3*, 217). These included a concept of marginal utility, the distinction between durable goods and those that are used only once, a classification of economic resources, a treatment of productive factors as different kinds of capital that yield services, and an aspect of the concept of a numeraire.

As for Antoine-Augustin Cournot (1810–1877), Walras expressed very early in his career (30, 1863) his debt to that eminent scientist. Admiring as Walras did René Descartes' analytical approach, and regarding mathematical economics as being in the same class of scientific achievements as Descartes' geometry (118, 1876, p. 367), Walras wrote that he was deeply impressed when, in 1853, he found a concrete expression of that approach in Cournot's work (1838). He learned from Cournot that some aspects of economics could in fact be expressed in mathematical terms, specifically with the use of calculus (239, 1874, *1*, pp. 366, 398, 421), which pointed him down the route that he should travel to achieve the objective of mathematizing economics. He wrote that he "saw, from that time on, that economics would not be a true science until the day on which the theory of value in exchange would be established . . . by means of the application of the calculus of functions" (213, 1905, p. 1, column 2). In 1853 he began to study geometry, calculus, and mechanics as they were presented in the works of Descartes, Isaac Newton, and J. L. Lagrange (240, 1893, in 239, *1*, p. 2).

In specific regard to the mathematization of economics, Walras credited Cournot with introducing him to the idea that the demand of each individual for any commodity can be mathematically expressed (240, 1893, in 239, *1*, p. 5), and to the mathematical theory of monopoly (123, 1877, p. 376; § 376, p. 659; 239, 1877, *1*, p. 535). He expressed his indebtedness to Cournot again at the end of his career. Looking back on it, he commented that he wanted to acknowledge that Cournot's application of mathematics to economics "has had, on the direction of my ideas and of my work, a particular influence" (213, 1905, p. 1, columns 1–2).

Despite his acknowledging only the influence of his father and Cournot, and although he had many original thoughts on the functioning and interdependence of all parts of the market system, Walras's ideas benefited from a variety of contributions by other scholars. For example in 1758, François Quesnay had constructed a rudimentary scheme of the relationships that he thought existed between different parts of an economic system. That was suggestive to writers that preceded Walras and perhaps to him also, although he criticized the absence in it of any notion of a theory of prices – that is, of the functioning of markets (123, 1877, pp. 328–29; § 341, pp. 605–6). Jean Baptiste Say, whose writings were frequently mentioned by Walras, emphasized in the early 1800s that the production and consumption sides of markets are interrelated, a relationship that is fundamental in Walras's economic models. Say also developed a theory of the entrepreneur that must have provided a stimulus to Walras's thought, although Walras was critical of certain aspects of Say's theory (Walker 1996, pp. 281–82). Achylle Nicolas Isnard's 1781 treatise (see Jaffé 1969, p. 20, n. 8) probably provided Walras with some ideas, inasmuch as Isnard devised a mathematical model of exchange, used mathematics in his treatment of production and capital, and defined a numeraire in precisely the way that Walras subsequently did (Jaffé 1969; Klotz 1994).

The physicist Louis Poinsot, in his *Eléments de statique* (1803), developed a model of general equilibrium of the phenomena in a physical system that Walras declared was an important source of inspiration for his theory of general economic equilibrium (239, 1901, *3*, p. 148). "I opened the Statique of Poinsot one evening" in 1853, he wrote, "and that theory of equilibrium achieved through the linking and unlinking of forces and of connected elements seemed to me so luminous and so straightforward that I read half of it in one sitting. The next day, I finished off the second half" (ibid.). Poinsot's systems of equations treating the physical universe, Walras wrote, showed him the methods by which he could treat the economic universe. In actuality, he must have been aware that a great many previous scholars had argued that the Newtonian approach to physical science – namely, analyzing the mutual determination of the values of the atomistic variables in a system – should be emulated in the social sciences.

It was certainly true, nevertheless, that Poinsot's method was suggestive to Walras in specific and detailed respects. His aim became the construction of

…a new science: the science of economic forces analogous to the science of astronomical forces. I cite astronomy because it is in fact the type of science like which, sooner or later, the theory of social wealth ought to become. In both there are natural facts, in the sense that they are and remain superior to social conventions and that they impose themselves on the human will; laws equally natural and consequently necessary, some of principal importance, few in number, the others secondary, quite numerous, varied and complex; facts and laws suitable for an extensive and fruitful application of calculus and mathematical formulas. The analogy is complete and striking (239, 1862, *1*, pp. 119–20).

Achieving a consensual understanding of Walras's legacy

Past interpretations of specific parts of Walras's legacy: Walras's fertile mind delved into subjects that have remained pertinent, and it did so in suggestive ways that led successive generations of economists to turn to his writings. These later generations interpreted many aspects of his work in the same way, but inasmuch as they had somewhat different knowledge, experiences, interests, theoretical views, and methodological predilections, they arrived at different interpretations and evaluations of some particular aspects of his theories. In fact, some scholars introduced their articles by stating that other scholars have erroneous views on the part of his legacy they were about to examine (see, for example, Burgenmeier 1994, Witteloostuijn and Maks 1988, Walker 1990, Witteloostuijn and Maks 1990, Currie and Steedman 1990, Koppl 1992, Burgenmeier 1994). Many of the ostensible disagreements arise because the authors believe they are discussing the same subject when in reality they actually are focusing upon different ideas presented by Walras under the same name at different phases of his career. Some differences of opinion reflect different views about the degree of importance that should be attached to one or another part of his writings. Other disagreements concern the meaning or logical quality of one and the same group of passages in Walras's writings viewed from essentially the same frame of reference, suggesting the possibility that some of the interpretations are demonstrably false.

However, the majority of the disagreements, and the most significant ones, do not stem from those causes. Walrasian scholars, past and present, have been highly capable economists, skilled in the exercise of their particular professional specialties. Their disagreements have a deeper cause than their abilities, educations, interests, and intellectual experiences as academic economists – which are, after all, very similar. It is that they have concentrated upon only some of his passages, and have unknowingly neglected others that must also be considered in order to assemble the full context necessary to understand correctly the meaning of any of the relevant passages. This matter is illustrated in a particularly striking way by the materials assembled in Chapters 1, 2, and 3 that reveal that there has been a neglect of not merely an isolated comment or two in which Walras argued in favor of empiricism, but of passage after passage and of page after page on that topic, many of which are in his major theoretical publications.

The approach taken in this book: The approach taken here therefore follows the advice of François Bompaire. It is Bompaire to whom credit must be given for having been the first to declare that an understanding of Walras's theories (and Cournot's and Vilfredo Pareto's as well) requires a study of all his scholarly writings, not just his models and equations. Bompaire gave a detailed literary exposition of Walras's general equilibrium economics as it relates to a laissez-faire competitive economy, and examined Walras's equations. Regarding not only Walras but Cournot and Pareto as well, however, he emphasized that:

The reader should not expect to find that our study has a purely economic and mathematical character. We have studied our authors as they are, bringing together all their writings, economic, mathematical, political, sociological, philosophic, in order to attain the best possible knowledge of their true thought in regard to the good and the bad effects of the principle of liberty. (Bompaire 1931, p. 7)

A dissenting view on the value of consulting Walras's writings other than his principal theoretical models has been expressed by Michio Morishima; that view must be considered because of its denial of the value of the approach taken in this book. Regarding "the conventional concept of the history of economic thought," Morishima noted that "the aim ... is to provide realistic portraits of great economists of the past; it is then necessary for the historian to read 'collateral material such as correspondence, recorded speeches and other published works' in addition to the major work of the economist investigated, as Peach claims" (Morishima 1996, p. 92). Morishima explained, by contrast, that his own

... view of the subject of history of economic thought is very different. Its task is not to present a precise and realistic portrait of a giant in history, but to reveal hidden and concealed relationships in thought (vision and analysis) between great economists, such as Ricardo, Marx and Walras in my own case.[4]

Morishima suggested an approach that he believed is appropriate:

For this purpose, the traditional method which Peach supports is not very useful; there was no possibility of correspondence between Marx and Ricardo, or between

---

[4] Heinz Kurz and Neri Salvadori argue that David Ricardo's economics have nothing in common with the ideas of Walras. According to them, Ricardo's approach to the theory of value and distribution is in fact "extraneous to his [Walras's] way of thinking" (Kurz and Salvadori 2000, p. 982). Michio Morishima (1996) answered those writers, contending that there are important similarities of formulations and conclusions between Ricardo's and Walras's work.

Walras and Ricardo. It is almost useless to dig in the library in the hope of discovering a new document. Instead, we have to read the major works of the economists concerned as deeply as possible. . . . I believe that the history of economic thought should not degenerate into a portrait museum; it should play the role of an information centre which informs us, based on the examination of the works of the economists of the past, how their various technical ideas and perspectives are connected with each other, what their essential contributions to present-day economics are, and how useful and suggestive they are for the future development of economics (ibid.).

That is surely not a defensible position. To understand the major theoretical works of an economist as profoundly as possible, whether for their own sake or to discern their relation to the work of other economists and modern theorizing, it is useful to bring to bear all the relevant information about those works. Indeed, Morishima has also expressed the opinion that "we can only judge the full value of [Walras's] pure economics by considering it in the context of his original farsighted scheme," which, Morishima noted, included his social and applied economics (Morishima 1977, p. vii). Moreover, in the case of Walras, his correspondence with many eminent economists is available and is very useful for understanding the relation of his ideas to his predecessors' and his contemporaries', inasmuch as he discussed their work and his own in his letters and in other writings also.

In short, therefore, in order to understand Walras's legacy, the part of this book that is devoted directly to his ideas will draw not only on his accounts of the behavior of the real economy of his day and on his work on general equilibration and equilibrium, but also on his philosophical and methodological ideas, his views about human nature, his methodology, relevant passages in his books on social and applied economics, his jottings, and his correspondence.

The foundations of a consensus: This book seeks to systematize the aspects of that legacy and thus to construct the foundations for a wider consensus on Walras's work than now exists; it capitalizes on the broad agreement that exists about many important Walrasian matters. All economists now recognize, of course, that his conception of general equilibrium is his most important contribution, even though the agreement is qualified because we do not all have the same understanding of what that conception is. There is also general agreement about the characteristics of specific aspects of his work: about his 1889 model of exchange in a temporarily isolated freely competitive market, for example, along with his theory of consumer demand and his treatment of the economics of the firm. This book validates the realization by modern Walrasian scholars that his contributions have a much wider range, diversity, and richness than was thought to be the case in previous years, a realization that enables the introduction here of new and wider perspectives on Walras's theoretical legacy. The book puts into place the last major necessary rectification of the interpretation of his scientific economic thought, namely an accurate and balanced account of his philosophical and methodological views, one that recognizes and meticulously documents the very extensive empiricist aspects of his philosophy and methodology. With that rectification, and with the exposition of his views on human nature, the analysis of the major components of his mature comprehensive model, the characterization of his written pledges sketch, and the emphasis upon the structure and functioning of his models rather than upon his equation systems, the major part of the heuristic scheme falls into place and a new interpretative synthesis of his economic theorizing is achieved. The synthesis provides a truly rich, more complete, and coherent picture of Walras's contributions and thus provides the foundation for a consensus on the character of his legacy.

Walras's legacy

The initial model: Walras's second phase of theoretical activity, his period of high creativity and maximum theoretical prolificacy, spanned the period 1872 to 1877.[5] It was during those years that he developed his initial comprehensive model of general equilibrium. The starting point of his investigations was his realization that the quantity that an individual demands of a commodity does not depend just on its own price, as Cournot had postulated, but also on the price of other commodities and on the income of the consumer (239, *1*, p. 5), and (Walras added)

---

[5] For Walras, this phase came toward the end of the fourth decade of his life, after the period that Joseph A. Schumpeter called "the decade of sacred fertility" of a scientist (Schumpeter 1951, p. 87). Schumpeter apparently arrived at that thesis by his studies of scientists' professional lives. In presenting Eugen von Böhm-Bawerk as an example that illustrates his thesis, however, Schumpeter credited the Nobel Laureate chemist and philosopher Wilhelm Ostwald (1853–1932) with the development of the "theory of the fundamental importance, for the scientist, of the years following upon the termination of physical growth" (Schumpeter 1925 in 1964, p. 373; 1954, p. 388). J. M. Keynes's thesis on this matter poses the same threat to the self-esteem of a high proportion of scientists at any given time. He also believed that the years before thirty are the creative ones for a scientist, and thus would have interpreted Ostwald's proposition as referring to the decade that comes right after the end of physical growth. W. S. Jevons, Keynes wrote, did his creative work in his twenties, "at an age when the powers of pure originality are at their highest..." (Keynes 1936 in 1956, p. 128; and see Keynes 1925/1930, in ibid., pp. 115–16). For Schumpeter and Keynes, therefore, Walras's contributions were made long after what they considered to be normally the creative period.

on his wealth or purchasing power (239, 1877, *1*, p. 535). Another decisive event in the development of Walras's initial model was his learning from Antoine Paul Piccard, a colleague at the Académie de Lausanne, a way of deriving an individual's demand function for a commodity from his utility function (239, 1872, *1*, pp. 309–11). That construction provided Walras with a way of introducing scientifically the utility-maximizing motive for economic behavior in markets and the essential utility-maximizing condition of individual equilibrium.

By 1872, armed with those ideas, Walras was ready to begin his period of great creativity and to flesh out his conception of general equilibrium in a functioning model. This he did in four memoirs (124, 1877), the substance and much of the wording of which appear in the *Eléments d'économie politique pure* (106, 1874; 123, 1877), a treatise that he made the principal vehicle for the expression of his legacy in economic theory. Thus Walras not only expressed the belief that all economic phenomena are interrelated (which had been done by many economists before him), he also specified their interrelations, offered an account of their disequilibrium behavior, and described their conditions of equilibrium. His initial model will not be discussed directly in this book because it has not directly been part of his legacy. That distinction was accorded to his later models. That is not to say that the initial model was not important. It was his brilliant expression of pure originality, and he was careful to preserve the parts of it that were valuable – the majority of it – incorporating them into the model that will now be introduced.

The mature comprehensive model: In Walras's subsequent period of maturity as a theorist, lasting from 1877 to about the middle of the 1890s, he prepared the greatest edition of the *Eléments*, the second (176, 1889), in which he presented his mature comprehensive model of general economic equilibration and equilibrium.[6] In that edition he improved the realism and coherence of his work, refined and extended his concepts and theoretical tools, and introduced calculus. The mature model is a model of exchange, production and consumption of consumer commodities, savings and production and pricing of durable capital goods, markets for loans, and the role of money generally. In the chapters on Walras's

---

[6] Schumpeter maintained that the work done by a scientist after conceiving the ideas of his creative period was a development and refinement of them (Schumpeter 1951, p. 87). Keynes similarly contended, referring specifically to Jevons, that "The last third of Jevons's life after he was thirty was mainly devoted to the elucidation and amplification of what in essence he had already discovered" (Keynes 1936 1956, p. 128). Thus Walras exemplifies that aspect of their theses by having spent his years after 1877 developing, refining, and extending the ideas in his initial model.

ideas that pre-dated the fourth edition of the *Eléments* (210, 1900), the unqualified word "model" used in reference to his ideas means the mature comprehensive model. When the plural word "models" is used in reference to his ideas, it is to draw attention to the sub-models that constitute the mature comprehensive model, such as his models of the consumer, of the entrepreneur, and of capital formation.

The purpose of the chapters in Part I is to provide the reader with the guidelines and context that are necessary for an understanding of the complex strands of Walras's legacy. Section I explains the building blocks of his mature system of economic thought. These are his philosophy and methodology, treated in Chapters 1, 2, and 3; his view of human nature, treated in Chapter 4; and the ideas about the structure and functioning of competitive markets that he incorporated into his mature comprehensive model, treated in Chapter 5.

The written pledges sketch: The characteristics of Walras's theorizing during his last intellectual phase are taken up in Section II of Part I. That phase, which began around 1896, was one of decline. His output of theoretical and other work had begun to diminish long before that year, but soon afterwards his powers of concentration and analysis weakened rapidly, and the lessening of his productivity and creativity became more marked.[7] In 1899 he produced an incomplete model, a sketch of a virtual process of equilibration, intended to eliminate the path dependency of equilibrium that was generated by the disequilibrium transactions and disequilibrium production in his mature comprehensive model. He believed this could be accomplished by the device of written pledges to supply goods and services, as described and analyzed in Chapter 6. Walras's realization that a virtual adjustment process would make it possible to have a model that is not path dependent was the second major part of his legacy.

Walras's final phase could be said to have included the years from 1900 to his death in 1910, or they could be viewed as a period of repose, for after 1899 he wrote not another word of theory and very little of anything else. Thus as a contributor to economic theory, he bloomed late – at the age of thirty-seven or thirty-eight – and faded early, writing less each decade after 1877, and writing little and adding even less of

---

[7] Schumpeter remarked that Walras's "creative period roughly coincides with his tenure of professional office (1870–1892)" (Schumpeter 1954, p. 828). Schumpeter was in this case using the word "creative" in a wider sense than when he was discussing a scholar's period of sacred creativity, namely using it in the wider sense of a period of appreciable scholarly authorship. His comment makes it evident that he correctly perceived the deterioration in Walras's abilities after 1892.

value after he was sixty, and nothing at all in the way of theoretical contributions during the last eleven years of his life, as is demonstrated in a methodical and quantitative way in the last part of Chapter 6.

Walras's influence upon other economists

Opinions about the most important aspects of Walras's legacy

There have been significant changes in what have been considered to be the most important and influential aspects of Walras's legacy.[8] For many economists just sixty or seventy years ago, Walras was considered notable mainly for having developed marginal utility theory. J. R. Hicks wrote that "his position with Jevons and Menger as one of the independent discoverers of the Marginal Utility principle is generally regarded as Léon Walras's chief title to fame; and this no doubt justly enough" (Hicks 1934, p. 338). In the words of George Stigler, Walras "is best known as one of the discoverers of the theory of subjective value" (Stigler 1941, p. 228). Those statements do not mean that their authors always agreed with the popular judgment. Stigler was quite clear that Walras's "fundamental contribution" (ibid., p. 229), his "greatest contribution" (ibid., p. 242), was "the concept of general equilibrium" (ibid., p. 229).[9] Hicks also in effect dissented from the popular notion and his

[8] It certainly cannot be said that historians of economic thought, including some theoreticians acting in that capacity, have neglected Walras's writings. Nor can it be said that the part of that literature that is in English has been neglected by the editors and publishers of volumes of collected works. A collection of nineteen essays written between 1935 and 1980 by William Jaffé and edited by the present author (Jaffé 1983) treats the genesis and development of many of Walras's ideas, the meaning of his work, and his place in the history of economic thought. A collection of twenty-five articles dating from the period 1931 to 1989 was prepared by Mark Blaug (1992). John C. Wood (1993) edited a three-volume collection of sixty-eight articles, many of them duplicating ones in the earlier collections. The present author edited a two-volume collection (2001) of 65 articles mainly written after 1990, 54 of which were newly collected, in accordance with the policy of the publisher not to include ones that appear in previous collections unless it were absolutely essential to do so in order to give coherence to a particular section of the volumes. A considerable number of the articles, particularly in the first three collections mentioned, are of mainly historical interest. It is instructive, however, to read older opinions about Walras's contributions, because some of them were expressed by eminent economists, and some of them were sometimes read by economic theorists, who, indeed, on occasion thereby became acquainted with misrepresentations of Walras's ideas and incorporated them in that form into their own work.

[9] It was not, however, as Stigler would have it, "one of the few times in the history of post-Smithian economics that a fundamentally new idea has emerged" (Stigler 1941, p. 229), inasmuch as the idea is to be found in the works of a number of Walras's predecessors.

own statement in other passages, as will be seen in Chapter 10. J. A. Schumpeter did not make the popular misjudgment, writing as early as the time of Walras's death, that "the theory of economic equilibrium is Walras's claim to immortality . . . ," although Schumpeter also believed that "the foundation stone of his structure" was "the marginal utility concept" (Schumpeter 1910 in 1951, pp. 76–77). William Jaffé agreed that the theory of general equilibrium was Walras's greatest contribution, but diverged from Schumpeter's view in pointing out that Walras arrived at his conception of general equilibrium before he developed his theory of marginal utility and demand (Jaffé 1972, p. 396; 1976, p. 513).

Walras himself was quite clear in his own mind that the theory of general equilibration and equilibrium was his major legacy. For example, when a correspondent praised his theory of money, Walras thanked him but added:

I must state that that theory is not the one that I most cherish. The theory that I would above all be happy and proud to see awarded the description of being "one of the greatest scientific efforts of the epoch," is the theory of the mutual determination of the prices of products and of productive services (rent, wages, and interest), based on the conception of the entrepreneur as an economic type distinct from the landlord, the worker, and the capitalist, and on the conception of the two markets for products and of services (239, 1887, 2, 213).

As recently as the 1960s, Walras was known by economists such as Jaffé primarily as being concerned with static analysis and specifically for having been the first theorist to develop a system of static equations of general economic equilibrium. Such economists portrayed Walras's general equilibrium models as being static, virtual, and timeless (Jaffé 1981, p. 328; in Jaffé 1983, p. 259). Indeed, some economists portray his models in that way today (Rebeyrol 1999, 2002; Bridel 1997). In this book it is emphasized that Walras did in fact develop, as is implicit in his foregoing remark and as he often claimed explicitly, a "dynamic theory" of "the demonstration of the realization of that equilibrium by the play of the rise and the fall of prices until the equality of effective supply and demand" is reached (239, 1895, 2, p. 630).

Walras also predicted that his general equilibrium theory would be influential. He was confident that he had laid the foundations for future theoretical studies, and that there would not be fundamental changes in economic theory that would displace his work. He declared repeatedly that he had correctly described the economy in his model and that the role of his successors would be to fill in the missing parts and to refine it (239, 1891, 2, pp. 434–35; 239, 2, 1892, p. 499; 189, 1892, in 191, 1896, p. 477; 249.VIII, appendix I, § 10, p. 705). Walras knew that he had priority regarding the development of general equilibrium theory but, he explained, "It seemed to me that in taking up for the first time the general problem of economic equilibrium, I should limit myself to trying to give *very broad outlines* of its solution, and leave to another generation of economist-mathematicians the task of correcting the details and filling in all the empty parts" (239, 1892, 2, p. 409). "I have never claimed," he wrote, "to have finished the entire body of economic theory all by myself, but only to have sketched it. Serious and capable people, first, will recognize that I have succeeded in making that sketch, and second, will finish the picture" (239, 1891, 2, pp. 434–35). That, in a general sense, is what happened, as will be seen; the two parts of Walras's theoretical legacy – the mature comprehensive model and the written pledges sketch – strongly influenced all later general equilibrium modeling.

Walras considered his theoretical legacy to be a positive body of work, as he emphasized in mentioning Pareto and Enrico Barone as examples of serious and capable people. He was aware that they disagreed strongly with his normative views in general and his views about an ideal economic system in particular and would never consider completing them, but he noted that they had already begun the work of adding to his positive economic model:

MM. Pareto and Barone . . . do not claim to refute me by proving that I have not completed pure mathematical economics all by myself, and they do not set themselves the task of redoing what I have done. They take the science at the point to which I have brought it and left it, forming the goal of continuing it after me; and they thereby reach important, new, complete, and definitive results (239, 1895, 2, p. 655).

Walras's contemporaries and immediate successors

The research into general equilibrium theory and applications of it that have benefited from Walras's ideas are truly the measures of the magnitude of his influence. Those studies are examined in Part II. One of the strands of competitive general equilibrium theorizing was the investigation of non-virtual economic systems that stemmed from Walras's mature comprehensive model. Chapter 9 shows how the ideas he set forth there were used by his contemporaries and immediate successors. The most important of them in regard to the Walrasian line of theorization were Vilfredo Pareto (1848–1923), Knut Wicksell (1851–1926), Enrico Barone (1859–1924), Henry L. Moore (1869–1958), and Joseph A. Schumpeter (1883–1950).[10] That strand went into a period of

---

[10] Many of Walras's themes were developed by Irving Fisher (1867–1947), as for example in his doctoral dissertation, in which he constructed a general economic equilibrium model replete with an equation system. Nevertheless, Fisher stated that the original source of his inspiration in regard to "marginal utility and mathematical

quiescence during the 1930s, was pursued with renewed vigor in the form of general equilibrium treatments of Keynesian economics, cultivated in microeconomic research after 1960, and is flourishing at present in the types of models listed in the first part of the bibliography for Chapter 11.

Virtual competitive models, 1930–71

The second strand of post-Walras investigation, namely general equilibrium models that are virtual in disequilibrium, or, as a special case, are always in equilibrium, is examined in Chapter 10. They clearly bear the marks of the type of general equilibrium model that Walras wanted to construct in his last phase of theoretical activity. That strand dominated the field of theoretical inquiry from 1930 to 1971. The reasons for its eclipse were difficulties that were internal to the models and their lack of relation to real economic processes. Those matters are discussed toward the end of Chapter 10.

Summary and concluding remarks

Chapter 11 begins with a brief summary of Walras's legacy in the field of positive economic theorizing. The chapter then notes recent uses of his ideas in theoretical models regarding which their constructors explicitly

treatment in general" was W. S. Jevons. Fisher owed the notion of the symmetry of supply and demand and of a rate of flow of a commodity to Rudolph Auspitz and Richard Lieben. He also benefited from those three economists in numerous minor respects (Fisher 1892, pp. 3–4). The true relation of Fisher's general equilibrium theorizing to Walras's is problematic. In the preface to his dissertation, Fisher wrote, regarding his presentation of general equilibrium, that

These equations are essentially those of Walras in his *Éléments d'économie politique pure*. The only fundamental differences are that I use marginal utility throughout and treat it as a function of the quantities of commodity, whereas Professor Walras makes the quantity of each commodity a function of the prices. That similar results should be obtained independently and by separate paths is certainly an argument to be weighed by those skeptical of the mathematical method. (Fisher 1892, p. 4)

Does that word "independently" mean that Fisher, a doctoral student in economics at Yale University interested in mathematical economics and therefore indubitably familiar with a wide range of the relevant economic literature, was claiming to have discovered the marginal utility principle and to have conceived of and constructed a general equilibrium model in about 1892 without having had knowledge of Walras's treatise, published in 1874 and 1877 and followed by numerous expositions and commentaries by Walras and other economists? And this despite Fisher having noted: "I have assumed that my readers are already familiar with (say) Jevons, Walras, Menger or Weiser where illustrations and explanations regarding 'final utility' abound" (ibid., p. 5)!

acknowledge that they have used Walras's ideas, and recent empirical applications of general equilibrium theory in which such acknowledgements are made. It is evident from the profusion of these recent models that Walras's legacy continues to contribute to advances in economic understanding.

The place and use of the bibliography of Walras's writings in this book

Walras's legacy is conveyed in the pages of his writings that were published during his life and in his unpublished writings. His legacy likewise has been preserved in subsequent republications and publications. The annotated list of those writings is presented in Section III. They are the record Bompaire instructs us to look at in order to form a sound exposition and interpretation of Walras's legacy. The definitive bibliography is not an appendix to the book as a whole because the book deals not only with his ideas but with the ideas of many other economists. Moreover, it is not just a bibliography but also literally the basis of his legacy, and in the annotations it presents a wealth of information about his writings and thus about his intellectual biography. It is therefore properly placed in a section under Part I. The general references, on the other hand, refer to the works of authors other than Walras who are mentioned in both the chapters on his ideas and in other chapters, so those references are properly placed separately at the end of the book. Chapter 7 introduces the definitive bibliography and Chapter 8 presents it.

It obviously would be redundant to list Walras's writings cited in this book not only in his bibliography but also in the list of references. Instead, his works or passages from his work are cited by giving, in parentheses, the entry number of the document in the definitive bibliography, the date the document was published or written, and the pagination of the cited material in the source in which it appears. It is unnecessary to note Walras's name each time one of his writings is cited; it is evident that any citation that begins with an entry number is an entry in the definitive bibliography. With its simple entry number, this method refers the reader directly to all the details of each of the cited publications, which are frequently complex, with multiple dates of delivery of papers and of publication.

With the exceptions noted below, Auguste and Léon Walras's *Œuvres économiques complètes*[11] are not cited in this book, for three reasons. First, the original publication of any of Walras's writings given in this

---

[11] This publication is described at the beginning of Chapter 7.

bibliography is the true primary source for it. The reprints of his writings differ from the original in format and pagination. For example, the reprints that Walras put into collected volumes have pagination that differs from the original; then those collected volumes have been reprinted in the *OEC* with formatting and pagination that diverges still further from the original; and then in the case of the translations of two of those collections, the formatting and the pagination diverge even further and, of course, the language is different. Second, any of Walras's economic writings can be found by consulting the index to the *OEC*. Third, the dates of publication of the volumes in the *OEC* have nothing to do with the dates when Walras wrote or published his texts. The exceptions are that the location in the *OEC* is given for economic manuscripts that are not published anywhere else, for some writings that Walras published that would be extremely difficult to find in the sources in which they originally appeared, and for cited material that appears in Walras's *Eléments d'économie politique pure*, as distinct from his other writings. As is done in this sentence in reference to the index (249.XIV), the volumes of the *OEC* are identified with their bibliographical entry number in Chapter 8, in this case 249, followed by the volume number.

In references to the *Eléments*, the edition that is cited first is the one in which the relevant material initially appeared, possibly with very minor differences of wording between it and a subsequent edition. In very many cases, the material that appears in all editions initially appeared in the first edition, either in the first part published in 1874 (106) or in the second part published in 1877 (123). All such cited material became part of the mature comprehensive model of general economic equilibrium that he presented in the second (176, 1889) and third editions (191, 1896).

The second edition of the *Eléments* is cited when reference is made to the ideas in the mature comprehensive model that do not appear in the first edition. It is not necessary to cite the third edition because its first thirty-six lessons are the same as in the second edition and have the same pagination.[12] When an edition of the *Eléments* is cited, its bibliographical entry number, its date of publication, and the pagination of the cited passage are given, followed by a semicolon, and then the relevant section number and the pagination in the *OEC* comparative edition of the *Eléments* (249.VIII).

That comparative edition is cited, with the pertinent section number, for several reasons. First, it presents the textual variations of all editions. For example, a passage in the first edition may be documented with the reference (106, 1874, p. 36; § 32, p. 59); or, if the passage initially

---

[12] The differences between the second and third editions are described under entry 192.

appeared in the second edition, with (123, 1889, pp. 106–109; §§ 83–84, pp. 121–25). It will be noted that, to avoid useless repetition, the entry number and volume number of the comparative edition are not given. The use of the section symbol indicates that reference is being made to it. The only instances in which there is no section symbol for that edition is when the passage appears in one of Walras's introductions to the *Eléments*, because his introductions do not have numbered sections. Second, the section number in the comparative edition enables passages that are in the fourth (210) and fifth (224) editions of the *Eléments* to be located there, because they have the same section numbers as the comparative edition. Third, the section numbers in the comparative edition make it easy to find an alternative to my English translation of a passage in the *Eléments*, or an English translation of a passage that I summarize, to be located in entry 245, which is a translation of the fifth edition. Fourth, the comparative edition is cited in addition to the original sources of the material because it is a readily available standard presentation of Walras's treatise. The citations of it recognize the possibility that the reader will wish to consult the French version or to read what Walras wrote in the passages that surround the one that is cited.

More than one edition may be cited in front of the reference to the comparative edition; for example, both 123, 1877 and 176, 1889. That is done because the material first appears in the 1877 edition, but Walras changed it appreciably or added to it appreciably in the 1889 edition. The body of the text of the *OEC* comparative edition is the fifth edition of the *Eléments*. If the comparative edition is not cited after an earlier edition, that is because Walras eliminated the relevant material from the fourth and fifth editions so that the pagination of the comparative edition does not reflect that material, or because Walras changed it so much that it would not be proper to suggest that it is part of those editions. The variations of all the editions of the *Eléments* are reprinted in the pages of the comparative edition, but in a variety of ways that, in many instances, make it difficult to cite where they appear. Sometimes they are part of the text but placed within crochets, sometimes reproduced as separate pages, and sometimes as footnotes.

In a further effort to simplify the citations, the name of Walras's correspondents are not given, nor is the number of the letter in entry 239. That information is irrelevant for an account of what Walras was asserting and irrelevant for an understanding of the passages that are quoted or mentioned. Moreover, that information is unnecessary to locate the source of the cited material, inasmuch as the volume and page number of entry 239 suffice for that. To further simplify the citations, the date of the day on which Walras wrote a letter has been omitted, inasmuch as that information is of no significance for the purposes of this book, but the year in which the letter was written is given in order to indicate its general chronological position. The exceptions to this practice appear in Chapter 6 in the treatment of Walras's health, where the precise dating of his sequence of letters is of interest.

It is an accepted convention, adopted in this book, that quoted material can be capitalized and punctuated in a way that improves readability and helps the reader, without indicating such changes with brackets, as long as no change in meaning occurs. This is done to avoid the unattractive and cumbersome use of brackets and the insertion of a capital letter or lower-case letter that the author did not write. An example is the translation of a sentence that Walras wrote beginning with a capitalized initial word. The sentence appears in the text as "Walras wrote that 'it is like this that things happen in the real world'", not: "Walras wrote that '[i]t is like this that things happen in the real world.'" Finally, regarding italicized words in quotations, it will be understood that they always appear in italics in the original unless it is explicitly stated that the emphasis is added in this book.

PART I

Walras's ideas

The foundations of Walras's mature comprehensive model

CHAPTER 1

General philosophy and methodology

I. Introduction

There was a rationalist side to Walras's philosophical and methodological thought and, in a certain sense and in certain limited respects, an idealist side, but he was also a realist[1] and an empiricist. He had the latter attributes in the sense that he contended, first, that there is an objective reality independent of ideas about it – there is the personal reality and there is *"la réalité impersonnelle"* (82, 1868, columns 210, 214, in 194, 1896, pp. 109, 119), "the reality of physical phenomena" (79, 1867, column 185, in ibid., p. 89); second, that concepts should reflect reality, and that theories regarding all aspects of experience that are amenable to scientific thought should be grounded firmly on empirical knowledge; and third, that both the assumptions and the conclusions of theories should be compared with reality and rejected or modified in the light of new empirical evidence. In Chapters 2 and 3 it will be shown that Walras made those contentions regarding the special case of economic science and the even more special case of his mature comprehensive model of general equilibration and equilibrium. It should be emphasized that Chapters 1, 2, and 3 are expositions of Walras's views. They do not judge them. They do not consider whether he was right or wrong in holding his views, nor whether he or other nineteenth-century scholars' opinions on scientific method accurately reflected how science is done or should be done, nor whether his terminology regarding "realism" or "empirical knowledge" or other philosophical and methodological matters was consistent with modern usage or appropriate in the light of modern conceptions. His definitions of terms are explained and made evident by the context in which they are discussed.

---

[1] In the terminology of philosophers, "realism" was a Platonic doctrine of the reality of ideas, of which things and beings are only the reflection. Realism was also the name of the medieval doctrine that universals are more real than perceptions of objects, and of the doctrine that names denote the essences of things named. Those definitions differ from the use of the word in reference to Walras.

To understand the ideas of a scholar it is necessary to focus upon the sense of the preponderance of his writings, and thus to discern his core system of thought. It is then possible to interpret his statements properly, identify statements he made that are inconsistent with his core thought, and relegate these to the category of irrelevant anomalies rather than falling into the error of using them as the basis of an unrepresentative exegetical edifice. In the present study, Bompaire's advice, explained in the Introduction to this book, is followed. That course makes it evident that the realist, empiricist, idealist, and rationalist aspects of Walras's thought formed a coherent and unified philosophical and methodological system, expressed many times, and that his exceedingly few statements that seemingly contradict that system are isolated fragments that lie outside of it. It will be shown that he developed his system of thought as a synthesis in opposition to extreme or exclusive empiricism and extreme or exclusive rationalism.

II. Some antecedents and contemporaries

Methodological tradition

In focusing on these matters, it will be seen that Walras's philosophical and methodological views were much richer than has been supposed. It will also be seen that although his views were rich, they were not original. The reader who is familiar with the history of Continental and British philosophy and methodology will be struck by the fact that virtually any idea Walras had on those topics can be found in the writings of scholars who preceded him. Whether he studied the writings of any particular scientist or not, ideas that he shared in common with his predecessors were widely disseminated in Western culture many years before his time, and he drew liberally from a rich spectrum of Western thought. It is therefore not surprising that some of his ideas can be traced back, in a general sense, to the seventeenth (Dockès 1996, p. 33) or eighteenth centuries, as for example to the ideas of René Descartes (1596–1650) and Isaac Newton (1642–1727). The same can be said of the views of any nineteenth-century scholar, such as the Newtonian aspects of the outlook of John Stuart Mill (1806–1873). For some of his empiricist ideas, Walras drew upon the philosophical school that owed much to John Locke (1632–1704), whose writings were in his library. He also owed empiricist ideas to Etienne Vacherot (1809–1897) (Debs 2004), a philosopher who, contrary to the beliefs of some scholars, was not the partisan of unalloyed idealism that he has been portrayed to be. Some other contemporaries by whom Walras was influenced or to whose ideas he reacted were Antoine-Augustin Cournot (1801–1877), Pierre-Joseph Proudhon (1809–1865), J. S. Mill (1806–1873), and Victor Cousin (1792–1867).

Walras and Descartes

Like many nineteenth-century French scholars, Walras subscribed to a number of René Descartes' views (114, 1875, in 249.VII, pp. 307–14; Jolinck and Daal 1989[2]; Koppl 1992). There is also a striking analogy between the history of interpretation of the philosophical thought of Descartes and the interpretation of Walras's ideas put forth in this book. Just as thorough research has exploded the myths about Descartes' ideas, so also does thorough research provide a balanced understanding of Walras's epistemology and methodology. In characterizing Descartes' ideas, I cannot improve upon Deborah Redman's excellent exposition and contributions to recent Cartesian scholarship (Redman 1997, pp. 21–35), so I will summarize the principal relevant points that she makes. The truth of the assertions about Walras's ideas is demonstrated in this and other chapters in Section I.

Descartes contended that there are aspects of science that are more fundamental than mathematical propositions. He wanted to determine the principle that provides a secure foundation for the use of mathematics in a science, and concluded that the principle is that mathematics must be based on a clear understanding of the structure and patterns of the relevant subject matter (ibid., p. 27). Walras similarly believed that mathematics cannot be justified in economics unless it is erected on a realistic foundation. Furthermore, we now realize that, for Descartes, "the demonstrations that make all fields of inquiry scientific are not exclusively mathematical deductions, but any method of showing and explaining the evidence, including a wide variety of deductive and inductive procedures and analogy" (ibid., p. 29); the same was true of Walras's thought. In Descartes' work – and in all of Walras's – no inconsistency is alleged to exist between the rational and the empirical aspects of theorization. Descartes "understood the role of experience – that it is the source of principles and basic concepts in physical science and that observation and experiment" are necessary (ibid., p. 31), and so did Walras. Descartes "acknowledged that 'there are

---

[2] Albert Jolink and Jan van Daal (1989) have pointed out that Walras's conception of the use of mathematics in theoretical work was influenced by Descartes' *Mathesis Universalis*. Other influences in that regard are well known and have been noted in this book, such as the work of Poinsot and Cournot.

two ways of arriving at a knowledge of things – through experience and through deduction'" (Descartes, quoted in ibid., p. 31), and so did Walras.

Like other philosophers and scientists in the seventeenth and eighteenth centuries, by the "geometric method" Descartes meant not only deduction as in geometry, but also the methods of pure mechanics and the exact natural sciences; by the word "deduction" he meant not only the deductive process in logic and mathematics, but also "inferential procedures such as induction and arguments by analogy" (ibid., p. 29) – in short, "any reasoning process by which we argue from whatever evidence is available for the credibility of a given conclusion" (Clarke 1991, p. 241). Thus when Descartes wrote that the way of arriving at truth is to use the process of deduction – the "rational" method – he was "simply making an argument for providing as much evidence as possible to support a conclusion" (Redman 1997, p. 29). It will be seen that Walras also maintained that deduction involves induction, and that conclusions should be supported by evidence.

Descartes' expression of the need for experimental procedures is "almost Baconian in its emphasis" (Gewirtz 1941, p. 88). His recognition of that need stemmed from his actual practice as a physicist – the parallel of the many studies of current economic problems made by Walras during his journalistic phase and subsequently. "As a result, Descartes ends up qualifying his theory of natural philosophy to such an extent that it brings him somewhat closer to the Aristotelian position he was fighting" (Redman 1997, pp. 30–31). In Walras's case, he began at the place that Descartes eventually reached, recognizing at the very beginning of his career the importance of empiricism in his statements of the fundamental principles of knowledge and scientific method, as well, of course, as in his empirical investigations.

Descartes' ambiguities, inconsistencies, and modifications of his views, like Walras's, will doubtless continue to fuel controversies, but, "Of this much, however, the philosophy and history of science is certain: The characterization of Descartes as an archrationalist who did not appreciate the experimental side of science is a false representation of Descartes as scientist and philosopher" (ibid., p. 33). Exactly the same can be said of Walras.

The archrationalism thesis

Walras stated in one place that the deductive phase of scientific construction in the physico-mathematical sciences does not have recourse to infusions of new empirical considerations, and when it is completed, those sciences "re-enter the experiential realm after that, not to confirm,

but to apply their conclusions" (106, 1874, p. 32; § 30, p. 53). He made
a similar statement about the specific field of geometry, as will be seen.
Some scholars have relied on those statements and upon one that he
made about economic theory (see Chapter 2) to support their opinion
that Walras believed that science is a wholly "deductive system whose
assumptions need not be true and whose propositions do not have to
be confirmed by data before being applied" (Pokorny 1978, p. 391).
According to Pascal Bridel, "There cannot therefore be any question, in
[Walras's] epistemology, of comparison of models to reality or verification of models by reference to reality, either on the level of assumptions
or of conclusions" (Bridel 1990, p. 183, as paraphrased approvingly in
Lendjel 1997, p. 71; see Bridel 1997, p. 142).

Then how do those scholars believe Walras establishes and judges the
truth of assumptions and conclusions? The answer according to Eméric
Lendjel is that Walras's writings "bear witness . . . to an explicit choice
of a rationalist epistemology, consciously adopted along with its implications, according to which the truth of an assertion is not established by
experience but by the exercise of reason" (Lendjel 1997, p. 49). Bridel's
and Lendjel's contentions on those matters will be called the *archrationalism thesis*, and the word "archrationalist" will be used to mean
someone who espouses the epistemology they describe, or to indicate
a theory or model that exemplifies it. In the accounts of the writers in
question, therefore, Walras was an archrationalist: Neither his assumptions, nor the "facts" entering into his models, nor his conclusions, nor
the verification of those elements refer to reality. His theoretical work is
detached from empirical considerations.

In this and in the following two chapters it will be shown that those
characterizations of Walras's philosophical orientation and his ideas
about scientific method are not tenable. The scholars who have made
them have neglected Bompaire's advice, despite the fact that they have
repeated it by declaring that, in order to understand Walras's general
equilibrium model, everything he wrote must be taken into consideration (for example, Bridel 1998, p. 232). The lesson of the history of
Cartesian heuristics is that scholars must examine received views critically in the light of the evidence. The application of that lesson to the
case of Walras's work results in shaking off the common but incorrect
notion that he did not appreciate the experimental side of theoretical
formulation and testing.

Walras and J. S. Mill

Mill was an enormously influential philosopher and the preeminent
economist during the period of the 1840s until his death in 1873, and

his ideas continued to be a part of Western intellectual tradition long after that. In this and the following three chapters Walras's ideas will sometimes be considered in connection with Mill's, and the similarity – often striking – of the language they used in discussing methodological matters will sometimes be noted. This is not done to suggest that he necessarily paraphrased Mill, or always agreed with him, or even that he was familiar with all the passages in Mill's work that are quoted. It is done to show, by comparing the two scholars' ideas, that Walras studied and subscribed to the major nineteenth-century strands of scientific methodological opinion, which were well-represented in Mill's writings. It is done to show that, in general respects, Walras thoroughly assimilated and reflected the mainstream philosophical and methodological thought of his time.[3] It is also done to show that, even if Walras drew heavily upon French traditions in those regards, he and Mill had many points of contact with, and in common with, the scholarship of a wide international intellectual community. Mill was certainly part of that community. He had a residence in France, was fluent in French, and was thoroughly familiar with French philosophical traditions.

Walras's statements that the sciences use deduction and that they "re-enter the experiential realm . . . not to confirm but to *apply* their conclusions" (106, 1874, p. 32; § 30, p. 53; emphasis added) were not novel. They were similar to views that had been expressed, in similar words, by Mill in his influential essay on economic methodology (Mill 1836/1844), and it is likely that Walras was aware of that. Mill contended:

By the method *à priori* we mean (what has commonly been meant) reasoning from an assumed hypothesis; which is not a practice confined to mathematics, but is of the essence of all science which admits of general reasoning at all. To verify the hypothesis itself *à posteriori*, that is, to examine whether the facts of any actual case are in accordance with it, is no part of the business of science at all, but of the *application* of science" (ibid., p. 143).

In the same way that proponents of the archrationalism thesis characterize Walras's sentence as archrationalism, so also have those sentences of Mill's been alleged to enunciate the "apparent position that the basic economic theory is impervious to predictive failure" (Hollander and Peart 1999, p. 369). In the light of the passage, Samuel Hollander and Sandra Peart remark, it is "scarcely surprising to find it commonly alleged that

---

[3] The truth of this assertion is not obviated by Walras's deprecating comments about Mill as a philosopher and as an economist, reminiscent of W. S. Jevons's strictures. Incidentally, those comments did not prevent Walras from invoking Mill's authority to support his own views when he found it advantageous to do so (for example, 239, 1891, 2, p. 434).

Mill denied to verification the role of testing, and conceivably of modifying theory . . . " (ibid., p. 371).[4]

Hollander and Peart disagree with that allegation and proceed to demonstrate that Mill made "clear allowances" in both "principle and practice for the improvement of theory in the light of empirical evidence" (ibid., p. 395), as will be shown to be true also of Walras. Hollander and Peart do not, however, do justice to their thesis, for their characterization of Mill's statement is an evident misreading of it. It is perfectly understandable why he contended in that particular passage that confirmation of conclusions is not part of science. It was because there, like Walras in his sentence, Mill was *defining* "science" as a process of deduction and, at the time of writing that particular passage, he did not regard testing as part of a deductive process. Nevertheless, he did not say that the validity of theories is not tested by empirical evidence. On the contrary, in that passage he said it *is* tested, and in that way, but he called that process "applications," and, in truth, the only way theories are tested is by applying them. The applications reconnect the theory with reality and often produce results that necessitate the modification of its assumptions.

There are numerous writings in which Mill insisted on the necessity of verification of theories, writings that are very similar to ones penned by Walras. For example, Mill contended regarding social science that:

The conclusions of theory cannot be trusted, unless confirmed by observation; nor those of observation, unless they can be affiliated to theory, by deducing them from the laws of human nature, and from a close analysis of the circumstances of the particular situation. It is the accordance of these two kinds of evidence separately taken – the coincidence of *à priori* reasoning and specific experience – which forms the only sufficient ground for the principles of any science so "immersed in matter," dealing with such complex and concrete phenomena. (Mill 1981–1991, *8*, p. 874)

In the same vein, he argued regarding all sciences that:

We cannot, therefore, too carefully endeavor to verify our theory, by comparing, in the particular cases to which we have access, the results which it would have led us to predict, with the most trustworthy accounts we can obtain of those which have been actually realized. The discrepancy between our anticipations and the actual fact is often the only circumstance which would have drawn our attention to some important disturbing cause which we had overlooked. (ibid., *4*, p. 332)

---

[4] Similarly, Mark Blaug interprets Mill as believing that "We never test the validity of theories, because the conclusions are true as one aspect of human behavior, by virtue of the assumptions, which in turn are true by virtue of being based on self-evident facts of human experience" (Blaug 1992, p. 68).

Mill even dropped his distinction between deduction as science and verification as part of applications, and defined deduction as including not only induction but also verification. Asserting that "deduction" is a "mode of investigation," he argued that it "consists of three operations: the first, one of direct induction; the second, of ratiocination; the third, of *verification*" (Mill 1981–1991, 7, p. 454; emphasis added).

Those phrases of Mill's – the combination of reason and experience, the comparison of theories with facts – are leitmotifs in Walras's writings. Abundant quotations in this book will show that, just like Mill, Walras contradicted his own statement about sciences not confirming theories experientially, bringing his definition of science into accordance with Mill's mature views on the deductive mode of investigation. Indeed, Walras's statement that, after the deductive phase of inquiry, "the physical sciences properly speaking" reconnect with experiential reality "not to confirm but to apply their conclusions" (106, 1874, p. 32; § 30, p. 53) does not make sense. Walras was perfectly aware that to apply or attempt to apply conclusions is to confirm or refute them, and he knew, as his statement indicates, that they are applied or revealed to be inapplicable by connecting them with reality. The statement was also totally inconsistent with his assertions that the physical sciences are experimental. He knew and affirmed many times, as will be seen, that testing the validity of conclusions is standard scientific method, that in sciences such as physics, biology, and chemistry, experiments are devised to determine if assumptions, conclusions, and predictions are valid. Like Mill in his mature work, Walras did not exclude empirical research – observation, experimental procedures in the case of some sciences, and induction – from "pure science"; on the contrary, he argued that it is an essential part of it. Remarking on the obvious, he noted as an example that to design machinery using the principles of pure mechanics is not pure science (114, July 1879, pp. 15–16), but he asserted that empirical research to establish the principles of a pure science and to evaluate its conclusions is scientific activity, as will be seen.

III. Concrete particular facts versus essences

Regarding all intellectual activity, Walras insisted on the necessity of clearly distinguishing positive and normative studies. "With time, and thanks to sustained efforts, the human intellect determines at the same time, with ever increasing certainty, in the order of natural facts, what is; and, in the order of ethical facts, what ought to be" (21, 1861, in Walras 249.VII, p. 143). When he discussed a theory of science, he had reference to what is, to a positive body of knowledge. He contended, furthermore, that "a theory of science in general is indispensable for constructing social science theory, economic theory, or the theory of any other particular science" (9, 1860, p. 197, n. 1). Accordingly, "the right and the duty of the economist is, before all and with care, to construct the philosophy of science" (106, 1874, p. 10; §8, p. 32). He maintained that science is both experimental and rational, so a philosophy of science must be "both experimental and rational" (9, 1860, p. 197, n. 1; 205, 1898, p. 453).

To give proper weight to the role of the "experimental" component in Walras's view of science and its place in his modeling, his treatment of facts must be examined. He has been portrayed by some writers as defining facts in a fashion that is unlike the ordinary perception of the meaning of that term. They contend that he adhered to a rationalist epistemology, which they contrast with an empiricist epistemology, and which they allege indicates that he did not believe that hypotheses should be based on facts. According to Pascal Bridel, "Walras does not accumulate details in order to build up realistic hypotheses: for him, ideal types are purely abstract phenomena" (Bridel 1997, p. 142). Thus some writers contend that he did not intend that the components of his model have referents in "une réalité sensible" and that it did not (Lendjel 1997, p. 81; and see Koppl 1992, Rebeyrol 1999, Tatti 2000, Huck 2001, Bridel and Huck 2002). "When L. Walras employs the word *fact*, it is not in the ordinary sense. He draws a contrast between 'bodies,' which are material and changeable, and 'facts,' which are the substance of things in its ideal permanence" (Dockès 1996, 25–26). For those writers it therefore appears that when Walras referred to "facts," such as competition and exchange, he did not, to use Lendjel's words, mean "real facts" but "genres," "species," or "essences" (Lendjel 1997, p. 75; see Chapter 2). The degree of representativeness of that view of Walras's use of the word "fact" will now be examined.

It is true that Walras stated that "in the world there are two orders of real manifestations of matter: bodies and phenomena, or, if one wishes, beings and facts" (9, 1860, p. 196; and see 1874, p. 18; § 16, p. 39), and that "bodies are temporary; facts endure" (108, 1874, p. 18; § 16, p. 39). For "bodies," the word "beings" can be substituted, and for "phenomena," the word "facts" can be substituted. In those passages, he declared that bodies are the same thing as beings and are temporary, and that phenomena are the same thing as facts and endure. Nevertheless, he frequently did not employ those words in those senses. For example, in extensive writings penned a few months before the 1860 passage just quoted, Walras presented very different definitions of them. He wrote:

I call *bodies* every instance that is limited in extent.
I call *properties* the characteristics of a body.
I call *phenomena* every instance that is limited in duration.
I call *circumstances* the characteristics of a phenomenon. (4, 1859, p. 30)

Therefore phenomena, that is, facts, are not enduring. Having thus defined his terms, Walras explained that both bodies (beings) and phenomena (facts) are real, concrete, and specific:

Reality is thus shared by two classes of real and concrete individual instances, – 1st bodies possessing properties: a certain *block of marble* that is there on my table, having certain dimensions, color . . . – a certain *oak tree* in my courtyard, of a certain height, having a certain number of branches, planted at such-and-such a date. . . . A certain *man* that, at this moment, goes by in the street, with such-and-such a name. . . . – 2nd phenomena accompanied by circumstances: a certain *fall* that happened to an object, lasting a certain number of seconds. . . . A certain *desire* that I heard expressed the other day by such-and-such a person that I know. . . . – The *slavery* of blacks in certain provinces of the south of the United States of America. (4, 1859, p. 31)

The distinction Walras made in those passages is therefore not between "bodies or beings" that are temporary and "phenomena or facts" that endure. Instead, quite the reverse: Bodies or beings are concrete particular things or persons; phenomena or facts are events, emotions, and institutions, which are transitory and many of which are even ephemeral.

Walras went on repeatedly to make it clear that he perceived individual facts to be exactly the same as most scholars and non-academics consider them to be today, and used the unqualified word "fact" in the ordinary modern sense; that is, to refer to particular concrete real things, persons, processes, events, and situations. He did so when he criticized those who "do not know how to distinguish between an idea and a fact," between "l'idéal et la réalité" (51, no. 6, December 31, 1866, col. 183; in 194, 1896, p. 15). He did so when he argued that "if it is necessary and sufficient, in order for a science to exist, that it rest upon a vast ensemble of *specific* facts, then social science will exist" (15, 1860, p. VIII; emphasis added). He did so when he described "elementary phenomena." They exist in reality and they are not ideas: "The intellect that observes them forms the idea of them and the ideas are expressed by words" (4, 1859, p. 8). He did so when he referred to "all the individual and concrete facts in society; that is to say, a social phenomenon occurring in reality" that "could immediately be identified, attached to a cause equally individual and concrete . . ." (15, 1860, p. IX). Those sentences provide another example of Walras's practice of using the terms "*individual and concrete* facts" and "phenomena" to mean the same thing, that is to say, material and changeable bodies, instead of saying, on the one hand, that bodies are material and changeable, and, on the other, that facts or phenomena are the substance of things in its ideal permanence.

Walras's habitual usages of terms also appear in his definitions of natural facts and humanistic facts, the latter including industrial and ethical facts. Natural facts have their origin in the blind and ineluctable forces of nature. Humanistic facts have their source in the exercise of the free will of humans. Humanistic industrial facts consist of relations between persons and things so arranged as to subordinate the uses of things to the objectives of persons (106, 1874, p. 18; p. 35, and § 17, p. 39). Industrial techniques and economic production are complementary examples of those types of facts (ibid., p. 38; § 34, p. 61). Humanistic ethical facts consist of relations of people with people (ibid., p. 13; p. 35). It will be noted that in that scheme of classification, Walras again used the term "facts" to mean material and changeable bodies, such as industrial techniques and economic production, as well as changeable "relations."

Walras further explained the nature of ordinary facts by noting the difference between them and theories in this way: "In good French, a fact is one thing, and the theory of the fact, that is to say the study of its nature, of its causes, of its consequences, and of its laws, is another thing" (108, 1874, p. 333). By "a fact" in that passage Walras did not mean "essences" or some esoteric philosophical notion; he meant, in good clear ordinary language, real things and events, as is indicated by the example he used to illustrate the difference: "In good French, to identify and report facts, for example the facts of credit, to say what credit operations are conducted today, to say how credit was organized by the Jews, by the Phoenicians, the Carthaginians, in the Middle Ages, is to undertake statistical studies; it is to establish the history of credit, it is to produce a work of scholarship" (ibid.). Those cannot be considered examples of an idealist notion of the meaning of the word "facts." There are hundreds of other examples in his journalistic writings, in his studies of real economic problems and policies, and in his theoretical writings of his treating the things, persons, relationships, events, and processes of the real world as facts in exactly the same way as academics and non-academics alike do today.

IV. General facts

Walras also defined what he called "general facts," and did so in just the same way as his predecessors did and as is done today in scientific contexts. John F. W. Herschel, for example, a scientist who was very influential during the period 1830 to 1860, explained that laws apply not to individual facts, but to general facts: "When we have amassed a great store of such general facts, they become the objects of another and higher species of classification, and are themselves included in laws which, as they dispose of groups, not individuals, have a far superior degree of generality" (Herschel 1831, §§ 94–95, p. 102). "Science," Walras similarly explained, "constructs the theory of general facts or groups of particular facts; that is to say, it indicates their nature, their causes, their consequences, formulating their laws" (239, 1901, *3*, p. 162). A general fact is therefore not a metaphysical concept; it is the term Herschel and Walras used for "a general subject matter." Examples of "general facts," Walras wrote, are vegetation, a natural fact studied by a natural science; property, an ethical fact studied by moral science; and civilization, a historical fact studied by historical science (9, 1860, p. 196; 15, 1860, p. 4). There is nothing metaphysical or purely conceptual about vegetation, property, or civilization.

Like Herschel and many others, Walras indicated how general facts are obtained, thus presenting the standard scientific view of one facet of the connection between theories and reality. General facts are, as the adjective indicates, generalizations, built upon observations of individual facts: "When dealing with a series of individual facts between which there are resemblances and differences, the scientific intellect eliminates all of the qualities that are specific to each of the facts, gathers together the qualities that are common to all or to several of the facts, and forms a species" (9, 1860, p. 196; 15, 1860, p. 4). What Herschel called "higher species of classification" were then identified by Walras: "In operating on a certain number of species in the same way that the scientific mind has already operated on a certain number of individual facts, a genus is attained. And so forth," attaining progressively higher levels of generality (ibid.). In the botanical realm, for example, progressively more general facts are pin oak trees, oak trees, hard-wood trees, deciduous trees, trees, and vegetation. Facts, at different levels of generality, become the bases of hypotheses (ibid., p. 197; 15, 1860, p. 5).

Thus, Herschel and Walras were describing an aspect of the process of induction, made possible by means of observation and classification of individual real facts. Walras affirmed that general facts established by scientific methods are universal, permanent, and irreducible abstractions of which the concrete cases are particular manifestations (9, 1860, p. 196; 15, 1860, p. 4). For example, he would have said dendrological science identifies deciduous trees. The trees are a fact and not a theory. Any particular deciduous tree has a finite life: Ultimately it disappears, but deciduous trees endure as a class, each particular instance exemplifying the characteristics identified in the scientific description of the general fact.

V. Pure sciences

Subject matter

As part of his effort to construct a philosophy of science, Walras undertook a classification of scientific disciplines according to their subject matter and methods. He altered it from time to time, defining and classifying sciences in somewhat different ways. All the numerous variations he presented[5] are not the concern of this chapter, which is rather to provide a picture of Walras's general outlook to aid in understanding his views on the methods of the sciences and their relation to reality. The purpose of that picture, in turn, is to aid in understanding his view of the nature, methods, and uses of economic science (Chapter 2).

Reminiscent of J. S. Mill's statement that "science takes cognizance of a *phenomenon*, and endeavors to discover its *law*" (Mill 1981–1991, 4, p. 312), Walras asserted that "science is conducted, not with bodies but with phenomena, for which bodies are the theater. Facts, laws, relationships, these are the object of science" (9, 1860, p. 196; and see 1874, p. 18; § 16, p. 39). In that early passage, Walras used the words "phenomena" and "facts" to mean "general facts." Thus any pure science formulates theories about the general facts of the real world, for example, theories of the properties and behavior common to all vegetation, theories that explain how deciduous trees function, theories about the properties common to all oak trees, theories about how they have become differentiated into many varieties. Walras illustrated the approach taken by scientific inquiry with his example of the treatment of the individual real and concrete facts of credit. "To reason about these facts" – how credit was organized by the Jews, the Carthaginians, and so on – is to identify and consider the general fact of credit, the aspects of credit that are common to all of its particular manifestations in different cultures at different times. To reason about these facts is to move to the theoretical plane of discourse: "to explain the nature of credit, to enumerate the kinds of credit, to demonstrate the rules of credit, that would be to construct the theory of credit, that would be to produce a work of science..." (108, 1874, p. 333). With the passage of time, Walras increasingly and ultimately almost exclusively used the unqualified words "the facts" to mean real concrete individual facts, and had little or no occasion to mention general facts directly or by implication.

Walras explained that a distinguishing characteristic of a pure *natural* science is that it studies the natural facts mentioned above, "the facts and relationships that have their origin in the play of the ineluctable forces of

[5] These have been given a detailed exposition by Jean-Pierre Potier (1994).

nature" (141, August 1879, p. 246). He stated in 1879 that the pure natural sciences include "mathematics, physics, chemistry, natural history,
anthropology" (ibid.), and during the period 1879 to 1896, he classified
mathematics and economic theory also as pure natural sciences (see the
references given in Potier 1994, p. 235; and see 249.XIII, p. 563). All
those sciences use abstractions drawn from reality and have conclusions
that are connected to it. In 1898, Walras repositioned mathematics in
his scheme by identifying it as a tool, and made some other changes
in his classification, arguing that the pure natural sciences result from
"the application of *mathematics* to *physics, chemistry*, and vegetal and
animal *physiology*" (205, 1898, p. 452). In Walras's terminology, an
abstract science therefore turns out to be a pure science that is a method
or technique that is applied to various subject matters that are likewise
called pure sciences.

There are also pure *moral* sciences. They study, via the identification
of the characteristics of general facts, the individual humanistic facts
mentioned above, "the facts and relationships that have their source in
the exercise of the free will of men" (141, August 1879, p. 246). In 1879,
Walras identified those sciences as "the history of human activity in all
its forms: languages and literatures, religions, art, science, industry, customs, law, war, politics" (ibid.). In an elaboration that Walras introduced
in 1898, he stated that the pure moral sciences result from the application
of cœnonics, by which Walras meant the theory of social behavior (198,
1897, p. 1019), and economic theory "to *psychology, history, sociology,
geography, statistics*" (205, 1898, p. 452).

Methods

Walras contended in his early work that "there are two species of
sciences, those that are *a priori* and those that are experimental
[d'expérience]." The former apply "the principle of *necessity* or *contradiction*"; the latter apply "the principle of *order* and of *causality*" (14,
1860, in 249.VII, p. 58; and see 15, 1860, p. XIII; see Chapter 2). If by
the first parts of those sentences he meant that there are *a priori* sciences
that do not have empirical components and connections, that was an idea
that he subsequently rejected, as will be seen. Indeed, in the light of his
other statements on abstract sciences, he probably meant, like Mill, that
"the method *à priori*" is "a mixed method of induction and ratiocination" (Mill 1836/1844, p. 143). In any case, Walras retained the notion
that experimental sciences compare theories to reality. Following the
ideas of the American sociologist Franklin H. Giddings (1896, pp. 47–
50), Walras manifested that notion in his discussion of three types of

science, considered from the point of view of their relation to reality – namely concrete, abstract, and pure sciences (205, 1898, pp. 449–51). According to Walras, they all have empirical components. Among the "orders of facts" is "sensory experience, that is to say the ideas by which we attain cognizance of the subject by the intermediation of the senses" (82, 1868, column 208, in 194, 1896, p. 105).

Concrete sciences deal with empirical data; they are experimental and identify particular facts. As for the abstract sciences, Walras made it clear by the following line of reasoning that he believed they also have empirical components. Their abstract quality does not mean that they are not founded on reality. On the contrary, Walras contended, they are so founded because, in Giddings's words, "the abstract sciences are not abstractions from nothing. They are abstractions from concrete phenomena" (Giddings 1896, p. 50). As Walras put it:

It is certain that the physico-mathematical sciences, like the mathematical sciences properly speaking, leave the empirical realm as soon as they have drawn their types from it. From these real types, they abstract ideal types that they define; and, on the basis of these definitions, they build *a prioria priori* all the scaffolding of their theorems and proofs (106, 1874, p. 32; § 30, p. 53).

Walras was maintaining, like all scholars before him, that those sciences draw their basic components from reality. Like Thomas Hobbes, whose writings were in his library, and a host of other scholars, Walras was arguing that after the facts have been ascertained, those sciences follow the deductive method.

Turning to the third type of science, Walras asserted that each pure science results from the application of an abstract science to a concrete one, and consequently has empirical foundations. "All pure science is constructed from the point of view of *pure truth*, both rational *and experimental*" (ibid., p. 453; emphasis added to the last two words). All the pure sciences therefore use both empirical and rational methods, induction and deduction. The pure *natural* sciences deal with an objective external reality, and are positive, observational, and experimental. The "natural world is scrutinized by the senses in order to make it the object of pure natural science" (205, 1898, p. 492). He identified one of the "orders of facts" as being "sensory experience, that is to say the ideas by which we comprehend the subject by the intermediation of the senses" (82, 1868, column 208, in 194, 1896, p. 105). "Science is organized so as to maintain the physical, chemical, botanical and physiological facts distinct and separate in order to study them *experimentally*" (203, 1898, p. 1; in 205, p. 491; emphasis added). According to Walras, writing during the period 1893 to 1895, "The constancy of moral laws attests to the existence of the absolute personal reality, just as the constancy of natural laws attests to the existence of the absolute external reality" (205, 1898, p. 493).

The pure natural sciences use "the method of induction and deduction" (151, July 1879, p. 15). They result "from the association, on the most extensive possible scale, of deduction with induction, of reasoning with experience" (205, 1898, p. 468). "Reasoning" was, for Walras, somewhat broader than "deduction," because "reasoning" includes not only logical thinking to form conclusions and inferences but also the formulation of concepts and assumptions. Induction is the use of real facts, known by experiencing them, to form generalizations, and "the method of induction and deduction . . . is the true scientific method" (151, July 1879, p. 26). Induction, "the new method," has replaced speculation (ibid., p. 28), and the deductive aspect of reasoning is based on facts. Deduction therefore involves induction. Moreover, induction involves deduction:

Perhaps it is well for it to be noted in passing that the method called induction is both induction and deduction; there is no science that does not have recourse to reasoning as well as to observation and experience to establish the relations and the laws of the facts with which it is concerned. But, that having been said, it is incontestable that there has been a marvelous development of the physical and natural sciences and consequently of industry since the adoption of the new method (141, July 1879, p. 28).

The process of empirical investigation and discovery

Walras expressed his rejection of archrationalism in his definition of facts, in his treatment of the nature and methods of concrete, abstract, pure, and applied science, and in the methods that he used in his own work. He also manifested that rejection by drawing important distinctions between, first, what happens during the process of scientific discovery, of finding real facts, forming abstractions, and identifying general facts; second, the formulation of assumptions and hypotheses; third, the subsequent deductive procedure; and fourth, the process of testing assumptions and conclusions.

According to Walras, "Facts occur before ideas and principles are formed. Practice comes before theory, and above all, before there is a finished, perfect, definitive theory" (ibid.). Walras there expressed three notions. First, individual facts are not concepts or ideas; they are not "essences"; they are not scientific creations. They are generated and experienced in the course of daily life. Second, facts precede theories. Third, theories are the results of a formative process; they do not spring full grown from the mind of their creator. As the author of several sequentially improved theoretical "tentatives" (16, 1860; 91, 1869; 95, 1871), of many other pages of scribbled attempts that preceded the *Eléments* (106, 123), of emendations of the latter undertaken even when it was in the stage of proofs, and of the extensive revisions in the second edition, Walras was well aware of that. Thus, when he declared that deduction – the rational aspect of theorizing – is used in working out the structure and conclusions of a science (106, 1874, p, 32; § 30, p. 53), he was not describing the process of investigation and discovery, that is, the process of identifying facts, striving to arrive at satisfactory abstractions, and formulating assumptions. When he referred to "deduction," he meant the interpretation of the inductively obtained hypothesis, the procedure of drawing its consequences and implications, thus obtaining the temporarily finished structure of a theory or model. To Walras, "deductive" describes the form and logical characteristics of the interpretation.

In the journalistic, experimental, creative, and mature phases of his career, Walras was opposed in principle to making assumptions that are contrary to fact, which he regarded as a matter that is different from making simplifying assumptions. Reinforcing the idea that the components of theories must be drawn from reality, Walras explained that:

In effect, we assume:

1st that the world of ideas and of the ideal are the proper object and the true field of theory and of science. – (The following first being understood, namely that no ideas and no ideal situation are admissible in theories and in science except on the condition that they are drawn, by understanding and reasoning, from the facts and the reality that experience furnishes) (51, December 31, 1866, column 180, and in 194, 1896, p. 10).

Of course, by "the world of ideas and of the ideal" Walras did not mean "the best possible" or "the situation that he would like to see brought into being."[6] He meant the theoretical plane of positive scientific discourse about the reality that actually exists. In those contexts, his idealism consisted of following the scientific method of the use of abstractions. It can be confusing that, in contrast, he sometimes used the word "ideal" to mean a state of affairs that he liked, as will be seen.

Walras divulged more about the stage of empirical investigation and discovery in his consideration of how science studies general facts. In this connection, he left no doubt as to his philosophical position: "Reality is the totality of everything that exists. Reality is a fact: it is the fact of

---

[6] Nor, when Walras used the words "ideal" and "idealism" was he espousing the opinion that the objects of external perception, in their intrinsic nature or as perceived, consist of ideas, the doctrine called "Platonic idealism."

Existence. The fact of existence is a *general* fact which is manifested in all places and at all times, which is *universal* and *permanent*" (4, 1859, p. 6). The science that studies it is ontology. In order to develop that or any science, general facts must be studied, and, "It seems to me," he wrote, "that to construct logically the theory of a general, universal, permanent fact, it is simply necessary to pose and answer the following five questions regarding that fact" (ibid.). In Walras's words, these are:

1st What is the nature of the fact?
2nd What are its origins? In other words: what is its cause?
3rd Into how many principal species is it divided?
4th What are the *laws* that it follows, either in its most general form, or in its principal species?
5th What consequences does it entail? In other words, what are its *effects*? (4, 1860, p. 6; and in 9, 1860, p. 196; and in 15, 1860, p. 5).

Walras went on to state that "to each of these five questions there are corresponding methical procedures that lead to their solutions. All these questions being answered, the science is constructed; the theory of the general fact is achieved . . . " (9, 1860, p. 197; 15, 1860, p. 5).

Use of individual facts as the basis of assumptions and to evaluate conclusions

What, Walras asked, are "the principal methical procedures that lead to the solution of the questions that have been posed?" He answered that they are "*observation, experiments, inductions, hypotheses*" (ibid.). For the second of these Walras wrote the French word "*expérience.*" In some contexts in his writings that word has the same meaning as the word "experience" that appears in English sentences like, "All knowledge comes from experience," or "Visiting the Grand Canyon is a wonderful experience." *Expérience* does not, however, have that meaning in Walras's methodological writings. It is evident that, because he preceded that word with "observation," he did not redundantly mean experience in the sense of obtaining knowledge by observation. He meant knowledge obtained by the active involvement of the researcher in working with the empirical subject matter, and that is best translated, in this case, by "experiments." Elsewhere Walras was more explicit and described sciences as "*expérimentales*," using that word in the same sense as the English "experimental" to refer to sciences like chemistry or physics that conduct laboratory-style experiments. He was referring to such sciences when he asserted that "pure natural science" studies physical, vegetal, chemical, and physiological facts "experimentally" (203, 1898, p. 1; in

205, p. 491). He was using the word "experimental" to mean "founded on and tested by empirical data."

According to Walras's statement, the procedures of observation, experimentation, and induction are the methods by which the hypotheses of a theory and, if it has been constructed logically, therefore its conclusions, are made consonant with reality, and they are also the methods by which the theory is tested. The methods involve the interaction of a theory with the facts with which it deals, in such fashion that, in the course of developing it, its assumptions and conclusions are repeatedly tested by observations and experiments, and its assumptions altered if necessary in the light of the empirical information. The closer the assumptions and conclusions are to observations and experience, the more reliable they are.

It is clear that Walras did not subscribe to what is called today the hypothetico-deductive method.[7] A brief common definition that bears on this subject distinguishes, "*Experimental science*, which uses scientific experiments (opposed to *abstract science*, hypothetico-deductive)" (Robert 2002, p. 1001). In its pure form, the latter method does not rely upon induction to arrive at a hypothesis; instead, a hypothesis is made creatively, perhaps as a hunch or an intuition. It is used to deduce various possible facts and is then tested by examining empirical evidence to see whether those facts obtain in reality. If the predicted facts are actually observed, then the hypothesis is at least tentatively confirmed. That method is therefore one of conjectures that are confirmed or refuted by empirical evidence. Incidentally, there is no discussion here of issues such as observations being consistent with false hypotheses, the non-confirmation of inductions by subsequently observed particular facts, the methodological aspects of verifying hypotheses about unobservable phenomena, and so forth, because Walras did not consider them.

The foregoing citations of Walras's writings have shown that, in contrast to hypothetico-deductive methodology, he believed hypotheses should be based on inductions, and thus on facts carefully accumulated by observation and experimentation. He emphasized the experimental foundations of the hypotheses made in abstract sciences: "It is perhaps the most delicate point, in the physico-mathematic sciences, to borrow in this way from reality the experimental data on which the intellect then establishes the series of rational deductions" (103, 1874, p. 10).

---

[7] "In the Bacon-Mill tradition, induction was assumed to be both a method of discovery and a method of proof of scientific laws. Today the doctrine that scientific hypotheses are discovered by induction is known as inductivism. This view is opposed by the hypothetico-deductive (HD) conception of science: scientific statements and theories are *free creations*, hypotheses, that are tested by deducing empirical propositions from them" (Niiniluoto 1998, p. 248, emphasis added; and see Hands 1998, p. 376).

The theory or model into which the hypotheses are incorporated is elaborated as a deductive structure, a process that is not experimental. The final outcomes of the structure are deductions that are predictions of possible facts. If further observation and experimentation determine that they materialize in reality, Walras regarded them as confirming it. To illustrate this, he gave the example of the planet Neptune. Observations detected irregularities of the movement of Uranus. The hypothesis of the existence of Neptune was based on those observations because Newton's system required the existence of that planet to explain the irregularities. That hypothesis could not be verified at the time it was made. "What completed the facts by finding the planet Neptune? Reasoning without experience" (239, 1893, 2, p. 573, n. 8). Walras did not really mean "finding," which would have contradicted "reasoning without experience," because "finding" something is to experience it. He meant "hypothesizing" the existence of the planet on the basis of the factual evidence of the irregularities. Subsequently, the hypothesis was confirmed experientially to be accurate by finding the planet. In fact, it "is proved by experience, and therefore, it is true for everyone, and for everyone to the same degree, that each planet moves around the sun in a plane orbit of which the vector rays make equal areas in equal lengths of time" (85, 1868, column 274, in 194, 1896, pp. 148–49). The reasoning to which Walras referred was not the use of innate knowledge nor a hunch; it was the deduction of the implications of the Newtonian model of the universe, which was ultimately based on observations and the other aspects of the process of construction of theories that Walras described in the ways indicated earlier in this chapter.

Reaffirming that theories about general subject matters must be tested by reference to individual facts, and thereby contradicting once more his own statement about the non-confirmation of hypotheses and conclusions quoted at the beginning of this chapter, Walras noted that "in opposition to erroneous hypotheses" in the physical and natural sciences, "simple everyday facts are provided by experience in the physical and natural realms *and are used to refute them*" (jotting by Walras, in Potier 1994, pp. 253–54; emphasis added). "Simple everyday facts," he thought, are not concepts, genres or essences; they are individual facts that exist in the "réalité sensible." Theories are also refuted by the facts identified by historical studies, although the evidence is difficult to obtain: "How much more difficult it is in regard to historical studies to have recourse to reality against science! What are the facts in that field of study that are tortured by false hypotheses?" (ibid., p. 254). Thus hypotheses should be "true," reflective of the facts in the relevant domain. Walras affirmed his belief that "without a doubt, [reasoning] and science cannot be in contradiction with experience and facts" (239, 1893, *2*, p. 573, n. 8). In the same way, flatly contradicting yet again the archrationalism thesis, Walras declared that science uses facts to find laws, expressing them with equations: "It is in this way that the physico-mathematical sciences formulate rationally laws *that are confirmed by experience*" (239, 1901, *3*, p. 162; emphasis added).

VI. Applied sciences

If it were true that Walras did not believe that models can be compared with empirical information, he ought to have thought that they cannot be used for policy applications, because such uses would require the models to be compared to reality. According to Walras, however, applications of the theoretical conclusions of sciences are indeed made in order to understand real particular situations, phenomena, and problems and to guide the formulation of actions and policies. Changes suggested by a policy must be applied to real conditions, and determining whether the policy is efficacious requires comparing theoretical conclusions with its real outcomes. Walras had the same opinion as Mill, who pointed out that if a science is not to be useless, "practical rules must be capable of being founded on it," and an "art would not be an art, unless it were founded upon a scientific knowledge of the properties of the subject-matter..." (Mill 1836/1844, p. 124). Walras likewise argued that a theory can be used in the formulation of policies designed to alter real situations only if it has correctly identified their fundamental features and structural characteristics (239, 1874, *1*, p. 443; 141, July 1879, pp. 15–22). Pure science, he wrote, is thereby enabled to be the basis of applied science and practice. He remarked that "it is only foolish people who need results in order to understand the significance of pure science. Any scientist worthy of that name saw the beauty of Newton's system without thinking that it would be of use in helping to navigate a boat in the sea" (239, *2*, 1893, p. 573, n. 8). Nevertheless, "The physical and natural sciences have industry as their ultimate goal" (141, July 1879, p. 16).

Accordingly, Walras identified applied science as another aspect of all disciplines. Agreeing with Mill's affirmation that "science is a collection of truths; art, a body of rules, or directions for conduct" (Mill 1836/1844, p. 124), Walras used the same language to describe applied science, writing that one of its branches is applied *natural* science, which furnishes "rules for the conduct of persons with respect to impersonal things" (141, August 1879, p. 246). It is both "rational and experimental" (205, 1898, p. 453). It considers what ought to be from the viewpoint of expediency, usefulness, and material well-being (ibid.). Examples are agricultural technology, industrial technology, and medicine (141, August 1879, p. 246).

The other branch is applied *ethical* science, which furnishes rules "for the conduct of persons with respect to each other" (ibid.). It considers what ought to be from the viewpoint of what is equitable and just in relation to the phenomena that result from the exercise of human will (106, 1874, pp. 16–17; § 15, pp. 38–39). Examples are individual and social ethics (141, August 1879, p. 246). Following the teachings of many scholars, including Victor Cousin, whose ideas in turn reflected the influence of Immanuel Kant (see Rebeyrol 1999, pp. 14–17), Walras believed that, like the rules of applied science, propositions regarding ethics, or what ought to be, should be founded on a scientific basis; that is, on the basis of a theory or model that accurately reflects the relevant aspects of reality. He probably also read that notion in the work of a philosopher in many respects different from Kant, namely John Locke (Redman 1997, pp. 68–69; see Chapter 4 of the present book). Walras contended that applied ethical science is "exclusively rational" (205, 1898, p. 453), but he also declared that, as is true of other sciences, individual facts are essential for it: "It is easy to recognize that the method of deduction, when exercised on a considerable accumulation of facts gathered beforehand by observation of humanity and society, gives birth to the finest and most fruitful social ethics, but, when it operates in a vacuum, produces only completely vain and ridiculous utopias" (141, August 1879, p. 238). That would appear to be contradictory were it not for Walras's conviction that rational thought contains empirical components. In short, the operations of erecting the finished structure of applied ethical science are deductive, but its assumptions are based on empirical observations of society and human nature.

Finally, Walras identified "industry"– the actual practice in everyday life of the rules of usefulness, practicability, and convenience furnished by applied natural science – as distinct from the study of them; and "mores" – the actual practice in everyday life of the principles and rules of applied moral science – as distinct from the study of them (205, pp. 453, 458). In Walras's lexicon, mores are the manner of functioning of the institutions of property, the family, and government.

Walras deduced far-reaching consequences from his classification of studies, as, for example, in his portrayal of the situation of German scholars in the nineteenth century. They distinguished between only the theoretical side of political science and the practical one. That was a consequence, he believed, of their lack of an adequate philosophy of science. They would otherwise have been led to the distinction between pure science and applied science, and the distinction between natural science and moral science (141, August 1879, pp. 229–30). That would have greatly strengthened their theoretical work. They would also have devised reasonable practical arrangements, such as appropriate administrative placement of the programs in German universities, avoiding incongruities like the teaching of both constitutional policy and the processes of animal births in the division of administrative and financial sciences (ibid., p. 245).

VII. The real and the ideal

Real and ideal types

The notion of real and ideal types is a recurrent theme in Walras's methodological writings and it has an important place in his economic modeling. Real types, according to Walras, are phenomena identified by scientists who study concrete reality. The real types must be properly identified and accurately described so as to give a true representation of it. Ideal types are abstracted from real types and are defined neglecting perturbations, transitory conditions, and unimportant variations found in particular cases (123, 1877, p. 267; § 222, pp. 334–35). They are therefore free of the idiosyncrasies of specific empirical instances of a phenomenon (106, 1874, p. 32; § 30, p. 53). Walras's use of the term "ideal types" is an instance of his use of philosophical terminology in a way that differed from traditional meanings. His "ideal types" are, of course, actually nothing other than "scientific abstractions" used, he believed, as the basis of chains of deductive reasoning.

Similarly, Walras chose to use the words "perfect," "permanent," and "universal" in reference to scientific abstractions. That was in the terminological tradition of scholars who, like Descartes and Locke, used those adjectives in reference to geometry. What Walras meant, however, is the same as what a modern scientist means when he says simply that he has formulated an abstraction. Geometrical forms, he stated, are ideal types; and those ideal "types are the proper object of pure geometry. – (I understand well that there are no ideal types that are admissible, in social science as in pure geometry, except those drawn by the understanding from the real types that experience furnishes.)" (51, December 31, 1866, columns 181–82, and in 194, 1896, p. 12). Thus when Walras stated that an ideal type is perfect, he was not really saying anything more than that it has the properties that the scientist defines it to have, whereas the more or less similar phenomena found in reality do not have exactly those properties, or have those properties but also have unimportant additional features. He gave the following examples to illustrate this obvious matter (106, 1874, p. 32; § 30, p. 53). The concept of a circle as defined in plane geometry is perfectly round, will exist as long as humanity has concepts, and is the same in all cultures and epochs in which circles are contemplated. Empirical phenomena that are circular, however, are approximately round, each particular case being flawed or deviating in some respect from the form of a perfect circle and being more or less transitory. In any empirical circumference, Walras continued, the radii are not all exactly equal to each other. Likewise, in any actual triangle drawn by a human, the sum of the angles is not exactly equal to the sum of two right angles. The exact properties of the geometric forms therefore cannot be proven by empirical measurements of their similar real counterparts. Walras thus emphasized in that passage as in others that there are propositions that are developed on the basis of pure reasoning that cannot be verified by experience in the sense of empirical measurements and experiments, but that are logical according to the rules of the system of logic. In those reflections, Walras was arguing along the same lines as J. S. Mill, who had observed that "the conclusions of geometry are not strictly true of such lines, angles, and figures, as human hands can construct. But no one, therefore, contends that the conclusions of geometry are of no utility. . . . No mathematician ever thought that his definition of a line corresponded to an actual line" (Mill 1836/1844, p. 145).

The history of civilizations shows that Walras was not accurate in stating that real geometrical types are easily obtained from observation of reality – "furnished immediately by experience" (51, December 31, 1866, column 182; and in 194, 1896, p. 13). Nor was he accurate in contending that ideal geometrical types are relatively easily obtained, as compared with ideal types in the social sciences, by an "immediate" a posteriori synthesis of experience (ibid.). It took many centuries for the development of constructions such as cycloids, epicycloids, roulettes, deltoids, astroids, involutes, logarithmic and parabolic spirals, not to mention three-dimensional forms such as hyperboloids of one sheet, hyperbolic paraboloids and quadratic cylinders; most societies did not develop them at all. Furthermore, those forms did not, for the most part, have real counterparts in nature but were rather internal developments in the fields of geometry and related mathematics. In Walras's defense, however, it should be noted that he realized, as indicated by his listing of great scientific thinkers of the past, that scientific bodies of knowledge like mechanics and astronomy have required many years of the labor of many scientists (210, 1900, p. XX; p. 22).

Walras's view of geometrical forms also illustrates his thesis that abstract and pure sciences are connected to reality not only by their basing ideal types on real types, but also in regard to the empirical confirmation of their conclusions. In 1874, he wrote regarding those forms that "reality does not confirm these definitions and demonstrations; it permits only a rich application of them" (106, 1874, p. 32). That sentence would appear to provide some evidence that the archrationalism thesis may have some validity in reference to Walras's view of mathematics, but in fact it did not represent his considered conclusion about even that specific aspect of science. Regarding the geometrical definitions, he emphasized that they must be based on real types drawn from reality (51, December 31, 1866, column 182; and in 194, 1896, p. 13), as has just been seen. Regarding both definitions and demonstrations, he rewrote his 1874 sentence sometime during the period 1896 to 1899 to reflect his rejection of the opinion that reality does not confirm them: "It is *only approximately*," he asserted, "that reality confirms these definitions and demonstrations; but it permits a very rich application of them" (210, 1900, p. 30; p. 53; emphasis added). Thus reality does confirm them if they are true, although it does so approximately; the exact properties of geometric forms, for example, are confirmed approximately by empirical forms. If that were not the case, the geometrical or other concept or theory would not be applicable. It would have to remain part of a contrived logical structure, a sort of intellectual game, or it would have to be reformulated. Indeed, Walras allowed, approximate confirmation is all that empirical tests can ever provide for theories (see 239, *3*, p. 183, n. 2; Chapter 2). Part of his wording, however, was not well chosen, inasmuch as he referred to approximate confirmation and application in the foregoing quotation as though the degree of fruitfulness of the definitions and demonstrations is somewhat independent of the confirmations. In fact, he frequently expressed the opinion that numerous, diverse, and successful – what he called "rich" – applications of the definitions and demonstrations *are* confirmations of them.

Walras added that some physical functions, unlike geometric forms, can be deduced from scientific knowledge without immediate recourse to empirical information, but experience confirms them. Regarding a function f(t) expressing velocity, "Thanks to the mathematical method, we can arrive at it by pure reasoning, without the help of experience, which subsequently intervenes to confirm, if one wishes, but not to verify the result" (249.VII, p. 251) – a distinction without a difference. All of the dozens of other quotations in this book that bear on the issue make it clear that in the contexts in which he employed them, Walras used the verbs "to confirm" and "to verify" as exact synonyms, as indeed they are in similar contexts in ordinary and scholarly usage in English and in French.[8] For example, he explained that "since we are unable to review all the social facts to find in them always the persistent agreement of material interests and Justice, we are simply going to put before us the fact of society and the principal social facts and, with respect to each of them, verify the exactitude of our principle in several rapid lines that will be easy to interpret" (249.XIII, p. 175). Again, he declared that consideration of a curve had "the advantage of indicating a proper method of experimentation to establish by direct experience the reality of the law [of gravity], if one did not know it, or of verifying it if one had discovered it by another means" (176, 1889, p. 15; in 249.VII, p. 251). So, the law is verified by experimentation.

Similarly, Walras evaluated Malthus's theory by verifying it: "an increase in the quantity of capital goods properly speaking, one which precedes and exceeds the increase in the number of persons, [occurs] in order to compensate for the constancy of the amount of land. Here the theory of Malthus on population and subsistence levels is verified" (249. XI, p. 500). Regarding his analysis of the different effects on the level of rents of industries producing necessities and of luxury goods industries, he remarked: "Let an effort be made to verify seriously this assertion, and one will be convinced of the essential difference in the economic conditions in which the two varieties of industries in question operate" (12, 1860, in 249.VII, pp. 99–100), and then went on to evaluate the statistics that bear on the issue.

---

[8] The dictionary translation of the first meaning of "*vérifier*" is "to check," and the second, which is the relevant one for the contexts of this book, is: "(=*confirmer, prouver*) [+*affirmation, fait*], to establish the truth of, to confirm (the truth of), to prove to be true; [*axiome*] to establish *ou* confirm the truth of; [+*témoignage*] to establish the truth *ou* veracity *(frm)* of, to confirm, [+*soupçons, conjecture*] to bear out, to confirm; [+*hypothèse, théorie*] to bear out, to confirm, to prove" (Collins Robert 2002, p. 1070). In English, the first or principal meaning of "To confirm" is "1. To support or establish the certainty or validity of; verify" (American Heritage Dictionary 1991, p. 308). "To verify" is "1. To prove the truth of by the presentation of evidence or testimony; substantiate. 2. To determine or test the truth or accuracy of, as by comparison, investigation, or reference: conduct experiments to verify a hypothesis" (ibid., p. 1343; and see Robert 2002, pp. 509, 2756). Those are exactly the senses in which Walras used "to confirm," "confirmation," and "to verify." In fact, there are few instances in which he used the word "verify" and still fewer in which he used "verification," and in some of those, the context was such that he meant "to check," as when he referred to dates at which he and another writer had published books, and being uncertain, wrote "(Verify these dates)" (249.XIII, p. 536), and as when he wrote "*Vérifier Éléments*, 2ᵉ édition" (ibid., p. 550), and wrote, regarding inventories of goods, "*la vérification, le conditionnement, l'arrimage, la bonne conservation et la réexpédition de toutes sortes de marchandises*" (249.XII p. 621).

Imagination

Walras's remarks about the imagination are not illuminating. He used the words "representations of the imagination" to describe concepts on several occasions, as for example in an undated jotting[9] regarding the notion of "perfect circles" (249.XIII, p. 557), despite his identifying perfect circles elsewhere as abstractions from real types, as has just been seen. In 1868 (82, 1868, cols. 211–12; and in 1886, pp. 110–14), he contended that "perceptions of the imagination" are not abstractions. Being "nothing more than collections of sensations or of feelings," any "attempt at abstraction made in regard to them would only end up in annihilating them, without producing any idea" (ibid., col. 212; 1886, p. 113). In an article written five years before his death, however, he took the opposite position:

I will say only that [Cournot] greatly contributed to convincing me that all the sciences (mathematical, physical, or other) are based on *concepts* (names, diagrams, matter, forces, etc.) without metaphysical significance, which are nothing other than *representations of the imagination or mental syntheses*, but which are nonetheless the indispensable base on which these sciences erect their edifice of facts and of relationships that are very truly objective. (213, 1905, p. 1, column 1; and in 237, 1962, p. 61; emphasis added)

Compounding the confusion, in making those retrospective comments Walras forgot that he had asserted that the bases of scientific constructions are ideal types based upon real types that are identified as existing in reality, not representations of the imagination. Perhaps, however, in the foregoing quotation he meant no more than that the representations are categories that are used to identify and classify the objective facts; that is, are used to erect a scientific edifice with those facts. He used the word "imagination" in the ordinary sense when he attributed great scientific discoveries and erroneous notions to its action (jotting, 1909, 249.XIII, p. 619), and when he declared that it is as necessary for the scholar, the engineer, the economist, and the politician as for the artist in order to have aspirations that transcend what exists at present (198, 1897 in 205, 1898, p. 271). He also used the word "imagination" in the sense of Etienne Vacherot (1858), without defining it clearly, to indicate a subjective sort of cognition that adds unity to what is perceived or that aids in forming perceptions (90, 1868 in 249.IX, p. 98). "Exterior and inward personal perceptions constitute the domain of a first intellectual faculty, the imagination; let us investigate how these perceptions of the

---

[9] This matter is further discussed in Chapter 4, where it is again noted that the jottings are not adequate nor reliable support for the view that Walras believed concepts are created by the imagination.

imagination are formed in the mind by means of external and internal experience" (253, in 249.XII, p. 129). Information is transmitted through the senses and hence processed by the brain, so what is experienced is "in part, a product of the imagination" (205, 1898, p. 493). It has been seen that a fundamental tenet of Walras's philosophical and methodological system was that ideal types are firmly based on real types that are drawn precisely and scrupulously from real facts, so it was an aberration for him to declare on two occasions that ideal types are products of the imagination without precise correlation to real phenomena, albeit related to them (see Chapter 3).

Idealism and realism

Walras described himself at different times as having different opinions about idealism and realism. In this regard, William Jaffé was far from making sweeping and shallow generalizations. He gave a carefully qualified accurate description of Walras's relation to idealism. Jaffé would not say that Walras was an idealist, allowing only that he "leaned toward" it, and not for long, but only "in his early youth" (Jaffé 1980, p. 349, n.). Nevertheless, the passage that Jaffé quoted to support that description does not do so, and his misuse of it must be added to the list of misinterpretations of Walras's thought. In the passage in question, which evidently dates from early in his career, Walras declared: "I am an idealist," but he went on to explain in his next sentence that by the word "idealist" in that particular passage he meant that he was ideal*istic*, which is a very different matter. He was not using the word "idealist" in its epistemological sense but in the sense that, like Jesus, he had noble aspirations for the future of humanity despite their impracticality and the consequent difficulties in the way of their realization. He railed against accepting facts as masters and as laws, and complained that "empiricism triumphant reigns supreme," by which he meant that the harsh realities of the facts of the existing social and economic situation should not stifle hopes and dreams of changing it:

I am an idealist. I believe that ideas transform the world into their image and that the ideals conceived by a man, by a school of thought, impose themselves on human affairs. I believe that the world has taken eighteen centuries to try – without success – to realize the ideals of Jesus and the first Apostles. I believe that the world will take another eighteen or perhaps twenty centuries to try, without better success, to realize the ideals conceived by the men of '89 – ideals seen more clearly by us and clarified by our successors. . . . It is possible that my ideal is narrowly conceived. It is less so, however, than one would be led to believe by the imperfect rendition of it given by my words. However that may be, I take refuge in my ideal. It is my sanctuary against the invasion of brute facts.... [10]

Walras was there using the words "idealism" and "ideals" in the normative sense to mean a liking for a state of affairs that he wanted to see come into existence.

Turning to the question of *epistemological* idealism at about the same time as writing that passage, Walras stated, in explanation of his ontological views, that he was neither an epistemological idealist nor a realist. Epistemological idealism is not normative; it is a positive doctrine regarding the nature of knowledge – whether pleasant or distasteful, desired or disliked – and how it is obtained. He contrasted the positions, first, of an idealist, second, of a realist, and, he wrote, "thirdly" (to emphasize the distinction) of himself. He was, he explained, "nothing, for the moment, but a sincere man" (4, 1859, p. 3). Walras argued, with literary flourishes, that common sense should rule on ontological questions. "You, Realists, you do not want to hear any discussion of Beauty, nor to know what it is. But will you therefore deny the light of day? The idea of Beauty is universally understood. You, on the other hand, you Idealists, you are scarcely more sensible. Why be contemptuous of bourgeois people and of Reality, and want to speak only of princesses and viscounts?" (ibid., p. 5).

Syntheses of doctrines and methods

Walras asserted that he wanted to create a reconciliation and synthesis of rationalism and empiricism and believed that he had done so in both principle and in practice. Scholars who believe that is not so have neglected and denied the existence of his writings in favor of the synthesis. They have argued that the idea that he wanted such a fusion, and consequently that he believed that theories should be realistic and judged by their consonance with reality, is a confusion of methodological and ontological aspects of his thought (Lendjel 1997). They describe his epistemology and his work as "idealist" (Koppl 1995; Dockès 1999, p. 20; Tatti 2000, p. 17), not recognizing the limited sense in which he stated that was true nor noting the realist aspect of his thought. One such writer alleged that *if* Walras entertained the idea of the synthesis at all, it was not to effectuate it, but merely to *glimpse* that it may be *possible*. Moreover,

[10] The jotting in Walras's handwriting is in my possession. It is published in 249.XIII, p. 551. Another English translation is given in Jaffé 1980, p. 533, n. 14; reprinted in Jaffé 1983, p. 349, n. 14.

that scholar has argued, if Walras had done so, it would have been from the perspective of a metaphysical synthesis of concepts and reality rather than from that of a methodological synthesis concerned with constructing and improving theories: "If Walras glimpsed the possibility of a fusion of concepts and reality, it is not so much from the perspective of verification but from a metaphysical perspective" (Lendjel 1997, p. 74).

In contrast to those notions, by following Bompaire's advice it will become evident that there is no confusion of Walras's methodology and ontology in the contention that he wanted to achieve a synthesis or in the other aspects of the exposition presented in this chapter. Walras described himself in his creative phase as both an idealist and a realist, asserting that he had achieved a synthesis of those two doctrines. That, with a recognition of the domains to which he applied those words and with proper interpretations of them, is a correct characterization of his orientation during his creative and mature theoretical phases. In this connection, it is important for an understanding of his philosophical and methodological positions to note, as has been abundantly documented above, that by his idealism he did not mean that he believed there is knowledge that consists of innate ideas, conceived independently of experience.

It is also crucial to recognize that his reference to his idealist and realist views and to their synthesis was made with respect to the domains of applied economics and policy. He declared: "I have been very occupied by the study of these questions and I have reached a resolution of the question of idealism and of realism by a synthesis that seems to me more and more felicitous and fertile as time passes. That synthesis rests on the distinction between science and policy applications. I am an idealist in regard to science; I am a realist in regard to applications" (239, 1874, *1*, p. 444). He then explained in a similar passage that by "science" he meant *applied* science, and by "policy applications," he meant practice. He made this clear by stating that, in his system of thought, "the distinction between the Ideal and the Real" did not relate to *pure* science contrasted with "the Real," but to the distinction between *applied* economic science (the theory of the art of producing wealth) and policy applications (the practice of that art) (239, 1877, *1*, p. 542):

I call *applied* science the theory of an art, and consequently, *applied economic theory* the theory of the art of producing wealth. With respect to the practice of an art, it deals only with what I call policy; it is not therefore between pure science and applied science but between applied economic theory and policy that the distinction between the Ideal and the Real is to be made (ibid.).

Reinforcing the point that pure science is not involved in that distinction, Walras went on to say that "with respect to my pure economic theory, it studies purely and simply the fact of the determination of prices . . ." (ibid.). Thus, in the context of the foregoing remarks, when he referred to "the Ideal" he certainly did not mean that pure science is or could be a representation of what is thought to be good or desirable conditions of the physical and social worlds. Applied science, however, *does* deal with "the Ideal" in the sense of that which is "desirable"; applied science is prescriptive; it formulates rules of conduct to achieve the goal of efficiency.

Walras also claimed to have made another type of synthesis, one relating exclusively to the content of pure science. That was the synthesis of rationalism and empiricism (239, 1874, *1*, p. 374). His idea of that synthesis was a central thrust and unifying principle of his organized system of philosophical and methodological thought, clearly and steadily seen, articulated, and carried out by him. He affirmed that his epistemological views and the pure scientific work that they shaped had not only rational but also empirical components. As has been seen, his fusion of rationalism and empiricism called for theories that are based upon realistic foundations and that use deduction to reach realistic conclusions. Believing as he did in the value of reconciling differences of approach and method and the possibility of doing so, Walras wanted his epistemological position regarding the activity of engaging in pure scientific research and its content to be viewed as effectuating that fusion. He rejected again the idealism that maintains there are innate ideas: "When the idealism of Hegel came on the scene with the aim of creating the physical and moral world *a priori*, the moment was ripe for a reaction in favor of experience" (ibid., pp. 373–74). The "true place of the intellect" is the rational method, that is, deduction, which must be synthesized with empiricism:

Now that empiricism runs unchecked, it would be an excellent idea to proclaim the true place of the intellect and for there to be a reconciliation of these great methods: the experimental method and the rational method. And what field would be better chosen for that synthesis than that of the social sciences. . . . As for me, my keenest desire is to see that beautiful philosophic and scientific synthesis in action and my dearest ambition is to take part in it (ibid., p. 374).

The synthesis provides a balance of methods: "It is as narrowly exclusive to want to do away with the rational method and thereby privilege the experimental method as to do away with the experimental method and thereby privilege the rational method . . ." (253, in 249.XII, p. 206).

VIII. Conclusion

Walras did not merely glimpse the possibility of the syntheses of reality and concepts, of realism and idealism in regard to applied science and policy, of the experimental and the rational methods in pure science, of induction and deduction. He stated that his point of view and his synthesis of rational and experimental also were, to use the word he used to describe the synthesis in the foregoing quotation, "scientific" (ibid.). Far from being an archrationalist, Walras espoused a systematic and coherent system of philosophical and methodological thought of which those syntheses were integral and important parts. Whether he called a science abstract or pure, or both, as in the case of economic theory and geometry, his view of the matter was that in either case it has not only rational but also empirical components. "Experience nourishes and supports reason, and reason sheds light on and guides experience . . . " (79, 1867, column 185, in 194, 1896, p. 94). He did not say that the construction of abstract and pure sciences is a rational process and that their applications are experimental. He asserted that they use both rational and experimental methods in the construction of their theories. In order for a fact to be given scientific status, "it must be both real and rational; it is necessary that observation and experience establish that the fact exists and that it exists in such and such a manner, and that reasoning shows that it cannot fail to exist and that it cannot exist in any other manner under normal conditions" (154, 1880/1881, in 194, 1896, p. 338). Prior to the last phase of his career, he consistently argued that general facts, real types, ideal types, assumptions, and hypotheses should be drawn from the facts furnished by experience, that deduction is used to interpret hypotheses, and that experiments and observation are used to evaluate conclusions. He recognized that deduction is not discovery of new knowledge but is instead a process of interpreting empirical knowledge and of arriving at an understanding of its implications. Walras did not, therefore, subscribe to the view that science does not verify its hypotheses by reference to facts. Nor was there a place in his organized system of philosophic and methodological thought for his own isolated and internally contradictory statement that the physico-mathematical sciences do not consult reality for confirmation (106, 1874, p. 32; § 30, p. 53; see above).

Walras thought that valid theories and facts cannot be contradictory. That means that assumptions must be compared with the facts on which they are based, and must be modified if they are not consistent with them. Once deduced, he believed, the conclusions of theories and models must be tested by reference to the facts that they are intended to explain or predict, and modified if they are not consistent with them. In most disciplines, he noted, and particularly in the social sciences, those activities are not simple acts, but rather a difficult and often lengthy process. They require repeated comparisons of the formative assumptions with reality, and progressive modification and reformulation of them and of their conclusions in accordance with additional and improved empirical knowledge arising from research and from attempts at their scientific and practical applications. Theories, Walras asserted, are therefore refuted or achieve a degree of probability of confirmation by reference to empirical evidence. The process of theoretical formulation and testing continues until the evidence leads the theorist to believe that he has arrived at sound representations and explanations of reality.

Thus Walras's statements to the effect that he was a Platonist, that he was an idealist, and that, in his normative economics, he conceived idealistically of an ideal society do not mean that he was not also a realist or that he did not try to understand and model human behavior in the real world. Notwithstanding some of his purely terminological idiosyncrasies, Walras was squarely in the methodological tradition of nineteenth-century scientists. There were, of course, variations of detail in that tradition, from which he chose some aspects and rejected others, but in general respects, he was a scholar of his own time, which indeed no philosopher or scientist can escape being.

CHAPTER 2

Economic philosophy and methodology

In this chapter and the following one Walras's economic philosophy and methodology are discussed. They are special aspects of the general philosophical and methodological views that he developed during the creative and mature phases of his theoretical activity. He drew most of his ideas about economic philosophy and methodology from the work of his predecessors, including his father, J.-B. Say, J. S. Mill, A.-A. Cournot, and others mentioned in Chapter 1, and from Pelegrino Rossi (Diemer 2002) and Jules Dupuit (ibid). In regard to the specific features of his economic theorizing, Walras's beliefs about economic science were the same as those of many other important economists, such as those mentioned above, in the respects that will be indicated in this chapter. He tried to implement the methodological ideas of nineteenth-century physical scientists – which were not the same thing as their mechanics or their physics.[1] They, of course, were indebted for many of their methodological ideas to the scientists of previous periods. Whatever their origins, Walras's methodological practices, his use of mathematics, and his modeling techniques were far in advance of anything that economists in centuries previous to his own could have imagined.

---

[1] Philip Mirowski (1989) believes that Walras not only wanted to see the methods of the physical science used in economics, which is true, but also believes that Walras drew upon specific concepts of nineteenth-century physics and particularly its mechanics subdivision in order to construct his economic models. Other scholars offer a more convincing analysis. Albert Jolink (1993) indicates that Mirowski's account of Walras's ideas about physics and their relation to his economics is distorted in such a way as to seem to support Mirowski's thesis but that Walras's work does not in fact do so. Jolink and Jan van Daal (1989) show persuasively that Walras's use of mechanical analogies did not result from a knowledge of or misunderstanding of nineteenth-century physics. He first constructed his models following the general methodological precepts of the physical scientists of his time – induction, mathematization, deduction – and then subsequently tried to find analogies between his constructions and specific physics concepts (ibid.).

Walras's ideas about how to undertake economic theorizing, implemented in his mature comprehensive model of general equilibration and equilibrium, constitute a system of economic methodological thought designed to achieve his goal of understanding the economy of his time. The system can be seen to be constituted of a carefully reasoned logical sequence of steps. For purposes of clarity, his six principal steps are outlined first, with subsequent appropriate discussion and documentation. First, Walras believed that the economy is an objective reality. Second, he advocated and followed procedures by which it should be studied, namely observation, experimentation, induction, abstraction of ideal types, hypothesizing, deduction, and verification. Third, his study of the real economy convinced him that the vast majority of markets were freely competitive. Fourth, he wanted his mature comprehensive model to reflect that reality, so he had to abstract the features of freely competitive markets from the real economy and assume them to prevail throughout his model economy. Fifth, he contended that his model could be made to reflect reality in progressively greater detail by incorporating additional components drawn from the real economy, and that doing so would enhance the model's applicability to the solution of real economic problems. Sixth, he indicated the criteria and the methods by which theories and models should be judged, and evaluated the results of the foregoing steps.

I. The first step: Assertion of objective economic reality and the corresponding positive nature of economic theory

Objective economic reality

Walras believed that every aspect of the world, and hence the economy, is an objective reality (as documented in Chapter 1). He wrote that he wanted to "distinguish . . . humanity, society, the individual, the real state, in a word, social reality," and he identified each of the ideal types based on those real phenomena (51, 1866, columns 181–82, in 193, pp. 12–13). For example, economics, both positive and normative, "exists; it exists not only in the ideal realm of the mind, but also in the reality of things" (76, 1867, column 145, in 194, 1886, p. 59). The subjects of economic studies are in the real world: "Let us now cast our eyes around us," he exhorted his readers. "We will see that there are in reality two distinct markets: a *market for productive services* and a *market for products*" (152, 1880, in 249.VII, p. 437). Of course, when he referred to reality, he meant his perception of it. He recognized that different theoreticians may experience the real economy from different perspectives and may therefore have "divergences in their conceptions of economic phenomena" (239, 2, 1901, p. 176).

The corresponding positive character of economic theory

Walras was concerned with the definition and classification of the various aspects of economic studies (106, 1874, pp. 3–44; §§ 1–39, pp. 25–66). Applying his general methodological distinction of positive and normative studies to the specific field of economic studies, a distinction that was a foundation of his work, he identified three economic subject matters (15, 1860, p. XVI; 89, 1868, in 194, 1896, p. 31; 106, 1874, p. 22; § 20, pp. 42–43). These deal respectively with "the true, the useful, and the just"; that is to say, they are respectively positive, utilitarian, and normative (239, 1862, 1, p. 120). He undertook his examination of economics from that "triple point of view" (ibid.). Moreover, declaring (like his predecessors) that, "Economics is a science" (9, 1860, p. 196), Walras contended that, like every particular scientific discipline, it has the various aspects discussed in Chapter 1: that is, briefly, pure science, applied science, and practice. The branch of economics that establishes what is true, Walras asserted, is the first of those subject matters, namely pure economic theory. He announced early in his career his intention to study it and to develop a rigorous analysis and synthesis of real economic and social phenomena. This he would do by examining the nature, laws, causes, and results of social wealth; industrial activities; and the distribution of income (239, 1862, 1, p. 120). The economic theorizing should be conducted along the lines of the physico-mathematical sciences. The Physiocrats, and J.-B. Say, David Ricardo, and J. S. Mill, he pointed out, considered that economics was that kind of a science. The deficiency found in their work is that they tried to use verbal reasoning in connections where only mathematics could lead to a successful analysis (114, 1875, in 249.VII, pp. 304–5).

Walras put the central core of his creative and mature work on economic theory into his treatise, the *Eléments d'économie politique pure* (106, 1874; 123, 1877; 176, 1889). Some writers, like William Jaffé (1977), have contended that the *Eléments* describes a utopia, constructed in part with features that Walras took from his knowledge of the real economy, but a normative scheme nonetheless. Most economists, however, have noted his desire, expressed in the *Eléments* and elsewhere (as documented in Walker 1984), to devise a positive model, or without discussion have regarded that objective as self-evident. Referring to passages that belong to the mature comprehensive model, they have analyzed Walras's general equilibrium theory from the point of view that it is an attempt to understand the real economy of his time.[2] Moreover, readers of Walras's many descriptive and analytical studies of empirical subjects (see Chapter 8) have perforce recognized that he had an evident concern with economic reality.

Given his belief in the objective reality of the economy and his desire to analyze it as it is, Walras naturally asserted that his model of it is positive. Economic theory, he maintained, should be constructed by "abstracting from all considerations of material advantage or of justice" (239, 1873, *1*, p. 345). When he stated, for example, that the price of a commodity rises or falls in accordance with the conditions of supply and demand in its market, he was "taking note of an observed truth entirely and absolutely independent of any considerations of either usefulness or equity" (90, 1868, in 194, 1896, p. 30). His "system of pure economic theory" consists of "an exposition of the mechanism of free competition from a purely objective point of view" (239, 1894, *2*, p. 624, n. 5). "My model," he declared, "concludes nothing in favor of nor against that regime, and I think it is necessary to abstract theory completely from the ethical point of view" (239, 1877, *1*, p. 542). In this way, when the time comes to introduce it, Walras asserted, "the field of study will be found to be free of and unburdened by any preconception" (ibid.). Thus he intended that his economic theory, as expressed in the *Eléments*, be free of normative considerations, and he believed that it is.

Pure economic theory could not, in Walras's view, be otherwise than free of normative considerations, because when he made those statements and when he constructed his initial and mature models of general equilibrium, he considered economic theory to be a pure natural science, like physics or chemistry, dealing with objective reality. Before 1896, Walras did not place economic theory among the moral sciences, because he believed it was concerned with phenomena that are not influenced by free will. He called economic theory an abstract science, and a pure science (205, 1898, p. 454). It will be recalled that Walras also specified that economic theory and cœnonics are applied to disciplines such as history and sociology to generate the pure moral sciences (Chapter 1). The

---

[2] For example, Kuenne 1961, Howitt 1973, Morishima 1977, Walker 1984, Brems 1986, Witteloostuijn and Maks 1988, Gijsel 1989, Negishi 1989, Currie and Steedman 1990, Witteloostuijn and Maks 1990, Ingrao and Israel 1990, Syll 1993, Hilton 1995, Herland 1996, Morishima 1996, Walker 1996, Potier 1998, Rebeyrol 1998.

status of economics in that presentation results in a convoluted account of its relation to other disciplines. Inasmuch as he had argued that his pure economic science results from the application of mathematics to economic studies, it is unconvincing that he then treated pure economics, like mathematics, as one of the methods-and-techniques sciences that are applied to various fields, thus generating "psychology, history, sociology," and so on.

Support for the idea that economics is a natural science can be found in the writings of previous scholars such as John Locke, who believed that the laws of human nature "are like the laws that govern the movements of planets," and "that economic relations are similar to natural phenomena" (Redman 1997, p. 69), just as Walras declared in his comparison of economic theory to astronomy (see Introduction and following text). Walras's basis for his view was that he reasoned that in freely competitive markets there is a given supply and a competitive pricing process of such character that the price of each commodity is determined independently of the wishes of any of the participants. Wheat, for example, has a price because it is useful and limited in amount, "two natural circumstances" (106, 1874, p. 29; § 28, p. 50). Its price "does not result from the will of the seller, nor the will of the buyer, nor from an agreement between the two." They would each like a more favorable price than the one determined by the market, but, under the given circumstances, wheat is worth neither more nor less (ibid.).

Walras's claim that his economic theory is positive is supported by his treatment of economic facts. According to the idealism thesis, "when Walras speaks of the 'fact' of free competition, of the 'fact' of exchange, or of the 'fact' of the transformation of services into products, he was not referring, as Walker would have it, to real facts, but to 'genres,' to 'species,' or to 'essences'" (Lendjel 1997, p. 75). How Walras treated facts with respect to science in general has been described in Chapter 1. His treatment of the special case of economic facts will now be considered, and it will become evident that the idealism thesis is in contradiction to what Walras meant by the word "fact" in the contexts in which he was referring to the real economy, and specifically in reference to free competition, exchange, and the transformation of services.

To stress the character of some economic facts, Walras used the word "natural." The relation of utility to something from which it is derived "is a natural fact in the sense that it depends on the nature of our needs being such and such and on the nature of things being able or not to satisfy them more or less" (15, 1860, p. XV). Value in exchange therefore "has the character of a natural fact" (106, 1874, p. 29; § 28, p. 50) and has its place, like all subject matters in which free will does not play a part, in the category of the natural sciences:

> The fact of value in exchange is a natural and ineluctable fact; since, although it is generated partially as a result of the presence of mankind on the earth, it is above all generated as a result of the limitation of the quantity of useful things, and should be considered just as independent of our psychological liberty as are the facts of gravity, of vegetation, etc. (9, 1860, p. 201).

> Among the economic facts are found the fact of value in exchange and the fact of exchange which are essentially natural facts just like the facts of heat, of illnesses. They are the primitive and direct object of political economy, a natural science as completely independent of justice as is physics or pathology (15, 1860, p. XV).

Using the methods of the physical sciences, the economic theorist studies the natural facts, including quantitative relationships, that are manifested in exchange in freely competitive markets. It is obvious that by "economic facts" such as competitive markets and exchange, Walras meant ordinary "primitive" – that is, basic, fundamental, and intellectually unprocessed – matters of everyday life, like plants, heat, and illnesses, not "genres," "essences," or transcendental entities.

Believing that his economic theory establishes what is true, and in accordance with his general methodological tenets, Walras did not, in his mature phase of theoretical activity, make assumptions that he thought were contrary to fact. That is not to say that he did not make assumptions he believed could simplify without distorting the results. In his mature comprehensive economic model, he assumed, for example, that there are no disequilibrium transactions during a market day, although he knew there were. He described that, however, as "a hypothesis no scientific mind will hesitate to concede to the theoretician" (239, 1895, 2, p. 630), thereby indicating his (erroneous) belief that the assumption in question was not really contrary to the facts but was rather a simplification that clarified the essential features of the process of price formation in a freely competitive market. His use of abstraction and simplification in relation to free competition will be discussed shortly, and his use of them in regard to utility will be discussed in Chapter 4.

The aspects of objective reality treated by economic theory

Walras's definition of his pure economic theory as being the study of exchange and value in exchange (91, 1869–70, in 249.XI, p. 343) appears to be narrow. It appears to be a statement that it is the theory of pure exchange. In 1877, for example, he described the aspect of economic theory that he had chosen to emphasize in his own work in this way: "With respect to my economic theory, it studies purely and simply the fact of the determination of prices or the ratios of exchange under a hypothetical regime of absolute free competition" (239, 1877, *1*, p. 542). On various occasions he repeated that definition (for example, 176, 1889, p. XII; 249.VIII, p. 11). How should it be interpreted? There are two questions to consider. One is the implications of the last six words of the quotation. The other question is what the statement indicates about Walras's belief about the scope of economic theory.

Some scholars have interpreted those six words to mean that his model was not concerned with the real economy of his day. They argue that the model is a fiction because the nineteenth-century economy was not characterized throughout by absolute free competition; and "hypothetical," they believe, means that the model is a sort of imaginative creation without realistic referents:

Put in another way, Walras, contradicting the evidence provided by observation, imagines a fictional world constituted by a vast market composed of special markets governed by free competition; and the preface of the second edition of the *Eléments* (1889) specifies completely explicitly that "pure economic theory is essentially the theory of the determination of prices under a hypothetical regime of free competition." (1874, p. 11).[3] The consequences of that unrealistic (non réaliste) hypothesis – competition – are that the *Eléments* constitutes a pure theory, like pure mechanics, that cannot claim any descriptive realism (Diemer and Lallement 2004, p. 6).[4]

The meaning of "hypothetical" is "that which is of the nature of a hypothesis," and a hypothesis is a proposition intended to characterize or explain phenomena. Was Walras using the word "hypothetical" to refer to an imaginary or fictional notion or to a hypothesis based on facts. In the latter case, to what degree did Walras believe his hypothesis about free competition was so based and what did he claim was the quality of its empirical foundations?

As a brief preview of this matter, Walras's explanation of the specific wording of the statement will be examined. It will be seen that the

[3] That sentence is not found on page 11 or anywhere else in the first edition. The authors meant page 11 of bibliographical entry 249.VIII. The sentence appears on page XII of the second edition (176, 1889), with the difference that the last three words are actually "absolute free competition."

[4] The authors go on to assert that, "In order to prevent any ambiguity and all possible errors of interpretation, Léon Walras, in his article "Une branche nouvelle de la mathématique" (1876), recalled the necessity of clearly distinguishing three different things regarding competition: the observable facts, the ideal type, and the normative doctrine" (Diemer and Lallement 2004, p. 6). It is true that Walras recalled that necessity in his 1876 article, but his intention in doing so was to guard against just such an interpretation of his writings as is made by Diemer and Lallement. The conclusion of Chapter 3 shows that he intended his 1876 statements to make clear that he believed his model was about economic reality.

meaning of his statement is quite otherwise than the foregoing long quotation asserts. This was made clear by his contentions about the economy, about methodology and scientific hypotheses, and about the characteristics of his model and its relation to the real economy. By a "hypothetical" regime he did not mean a non-existent regime but rather an "assumed" one – assumed because of the realism of that assumption. He meant an abstraction and generalization based upon observations of the real economy and used to make deductions about it that are verified by reference to it. He had converted the economic theory of "a hypothetical regime of absolute free competition [into] an exact science and one of the most beautiful of all the exact sciences" (239, 1888, 2, p. 251.). There was not, so far as Walras was concerned, any such thing as an exact natural science that is a fiction. He explained that hypotheses could be more or less conjectural and realistic, and claimed that his hypothesis was on the more realistic end of the scale. Indeed, he declared, although he did not presume to claim that his theory of general economic equilibrium was as great as Newton's, he was as glad to have produced it as he would have been to have produced Darwin's. The hypothesis of a freely competitive equilibrium system, Walras continued, is less conjectural and more firmly based on facts than Darwin's and it is at least as important as Darwin's in respect of being practical knowledge about the real world:

It is less hypothetical and more definitive, and inspires at least as lively an interest; for it is of at least as much importance to us to know how the prices and the quantities of commodities to be produced and to be exchanged tend to determine themselves naturally, as to know if we descend from monkeys or if we are a distinct species (ibid.).

Walras stated that his own hypothesis was drawn "scrupulously" from real markets:

Definition of the market and of competition; effective demand curves

Before all, it is necessary to define with precision the mechanism of the free competition that we assume governs our market. For that, let us go to a free market and see how it functions. Let us, for example, go into a wheat market, and let us take note scrupulously of the operations that are conducted there. It is perhaps the most delicate point, in the physico-mathematic sciences, to borrow in this way from reality the experimental data on which the intellect then establishes the series of rational deductions (103, 1874, p. 10).[5]

---

[5] See Chapter 1, where the last sentence of the quotation is also used. Walras added the title in the republications of the text, first in italics, as shown here, and subsequently in roman capitals. See the annotation of entry 103.

"Let us recall, moreover, that it is always a matter here, not of posing and solving in reality in any given case the problem in question, but exclusively a matter of conceiving scientifically the nature of the problem that generates itself and that solves itself empirically on the market" (176, 1889, p. 134; § 110, p. 161). In the light of statements like that, of which there are many, it cannot reasonably be supposed that Walras's reference to a "hypothetical regime" means that he was asserting that his model did not capture the essentials of real competitive markets. The words "unrealistic" and "fictional" are used by Diemer and Lallement, but Walras did not use those words or share their view. He wrote: "I continue to believe that my conception of the equilibrium of production is not a *fiction* but an *abstraction* . . ." (239, 1893, *2*, p. 598; emphasis in the original), and declared that his model was "very much in conformity with reality" (239, 1879, *1*, p. 628, n. 3).

As for the scope that Walras believed his theory to have, a first matter to consider, in relation to his other writings, is his assertion in the foregoing statement that economic theory studies the determination of price or the ratios of exchange. In partial explanation of his model, Walras characterized pure economic theory, in a passage that he wrote in 1872 and republished in subsequent years, as, "The Theory of Value in Exchange or *Theory of Social Wealth*." In the rest of that particular passage, he relegated "The Theory of Industry or *Theory of the Production* of Social Wealth" to the domain of "Applied economics" (98, 1872, in 249.XI, p. 419). Pure economic theory studies, "The totality of all things, material or immaterial, which are susceptible of having a price. . . . That is why economic theory is also *the theory of social wealth*" (176, 1889, pp. XII–XIII; p. 11). The totality of such things includes durable goods, primary materials, non-durable consumer goods and services, and the services of labor, natural resources, and capital goods. Thus Walras's definition of value in exchange as the same subject matter as social wealth indicates the broad significance that he attached to economic value, giving a much wider perspective to the meaning of studying ratios of exchange.

Walras's statement classifying "the theory of production" as applied economics did not clarify his meaning, but his subsequent definitions are clear and broader in scope. He stated that pure economic theory does not deal exclusively with the exchange of commodities that are already produced and on the market. It is rather "the pure and simple study of the natural and necessary effects of free competition in regard to *production* and exchange" (239, 1873, *1*, p. 345; emphasis added). Again, he specified that his "system of pure economic theory" reveals, "from a purely objective point of view, the mechanism of free competition in regard to exchange and production" (239, 1894, *2*, p. 624, n. 5), that pure economic theory first establishes the theory of exchange and then the theory of production, setting them forth in systems of equations (114, 1875, in 249.VII, pp. 298–304). Thus Walras referred to the whole class of effects of free competition and included production as well as exchange in pure theory, and, of course, a large part of the *Eléments* deals precisely with the theory of production. Indeed, in one place he referred only to production, writing that the goal that he set himself in his "pure economic theory in mathematical form was to present and explain, for the first time, the mechanism of production by reducing it to its essential elements" (180, 1892, in 191, 1896, p. 477; 210, 1900, p. 479; appendix I, § 10, p. 705). Walras therefore included in his pure theory such matters as an analysis of what happens to production functions and to the average cost of production during the process of adjustment of prices, services hired, rates of production and consumption, and quantities exchanged. He called what happens during that process a "tatonnement," a word meaning reiterated hesitant efforts to find something – in the case of the economy, to find equilibrium. Clearly, in considering these matters, Walras was not dealing with what he considered to be fictional and unrealistic elements. He also indicated the breadth of his definition, insisting as it does on the effects of free competition, by classifying a central part of his welfare economics as pure theory, namely his attempts to demonstrate that freely competitive markets generate a relative maximum of utility for society (123, 1877, p. 305; §§ 263–64, pp. 423–25).

II. The second step: The methods by which knowledge of the real economy is obtained

Observation, experience, and experiments
in economic theorization

Toward the end of his life Walras claimed that he had drawn his ideas "not from other books but from my brain," thus failing on that occasion as on numerous others to acknowledge his many debts to his predecessors. He then went on to state that he followed the "Meth[od] of reasoning and not of experimentation" (249.XIII, p. 560). The vast preponderance of the evidence will now be considered. In contradiction to that jotting, Walras developed and subscribed to a system of thought that fully recognized the place not only of reasoning but also of obtaining and using empirical knowledge in constructing economic theory, and he stressed that he drew upon such knowledge. In fact, in the rest of this jotting he contended that empirical knowledge is half of scientific method. He wrote that he was "not contemptuous of facts and experience, but that is only the half of it (Germans, French sociologists)." Indeed, in this jotting he was primarily interested in emphasizing the use of reason as the method that is indispensable when considering justice and "interests" – concern for material welfare (ibid.). Even when describing social ethics as an a priori discipline, he asserted that its assumptions are based on experience (249.XIII, p. 569).

According to Walras, there are economic hypotheses similar to some of the functions of physical science (Chapter 1) that are formulated on the basis of the previous state of the science, and therefore without being directly based upon a new collection of facts. "Proceeding in economic theory by the same means as in physics, we will arrive at the same results, of which the most important will be to link together economic relations and laws, in such a fashion that, certain of these relations and these laws being given by experience, the others are deduced by reasoning" (249.VI, p. 257). Experience shows that an economic relation exists; reasoning explains it. For example, "The fact of surplus value of land rent in a progressive society" is "well established by experience and well explained by reasoning . . ." (163, 1885, p. 80). "The first of these conditions of scientific truth is that the matter in question rest on a demonstration either rational or experimental . . ." (85, 1868, column 274, in 194, 1896, pp. 148–49). "The *law of the variation of equilibrium prices* is similarly expressed purely and simply by noting that, in accordance with observation and experience, when the utility of the commodity increases or its quantity diminishes, the price rises; that when the utility decreases or the quantity increases, the price falls. This law is demonstrated by making clear why and how this happens" (249.VI, p. 436). Whether the foundations are the existing science or new empirical knowledge, the hypotheses and the conclusions deduced from them are subjected to the test of confirmation or refutation by empirical evidence.

J. S. Mill contended that, "The backward state of the Moral Sciences can only be remedied by applying to them the methods of Physical Science, duly extended and generalised" (Mill 1981–1991, *8*, p. 833), and specifically that "the methods of physical science" are "the proper models for political economy" (Mill 1981–1991, *1*, p. 173). Agreeing with that view (14, July 1879, p. 15), Walras declared that the methods of pure economic theory include "observation" and "expérience" (239, 1885, *2*, p. 64; and see, for example, 9, 1860, p. 197; and see below). His argument that scientific methods should be used is an argument that economic theory should deal with reality. By the first of those French words, used in application specifically to economic science, Walras meant exactly what the same word in English means in scientific contexts, namely scrutiny of real phenomena. There is no doubt that he always thought that economic science is observational in that sense. He believed that economics, unlike some sciences, deals only with observable external facts and observable personal subjective facts (106, 1874, p. 103; § 102, p. 146; 198, 1897, in 205, p. 270), which he called "natural facts." Thus he did not consider the methodological problems that arise in connection with the testing of theories about unobservables. Illustrating the meaning of "observational," he asserted in an early essay that, for example, the detailed description of the techniques of modern industry – empirical knowledge, obtained by observation – lays foundations "of unshakable solidity" for economics (21, 1861, in Walras 249.VII, p. 141). The economic researcher follows scientific methods to establish and document the accuracy of observations, but he has a neutral role in that process.

Walras's use of the word "expérience" in economic research contexts is the same as in his discussions of science in general (Chapter 1). If he had used only that word to describe economic method, there may be some reason to regard it as meaning "empirical studies" or something else less categorical than experimentation. His precise wording, however, was that the methods of economic theory include "observation ou expérience la plus rigoureuse" (239, 1885, 2, p. 64), thereby differentiating the two methods as he did in the quotation in the next paragraph of this chapter, and indicating that the latter term alludes to a second aspect of economic research. That aspect, in that context, does not have the meaning of the English word "experience," which cannot be rigorous. The French "expérience la plus rigoureuse" instead indicates that the researcher enters actively into the situation of interest, handling and interpreting economic facts with careful scientific methods, identifying real types that are important, using them to form abstractions, isolating the true characteristics of the variables, tracing their effects in order to uncover causal relationships, and testing the verisimilitude of assumptions and conclusions. In short, the word "expérience" in Walras's economic writings in the context under discussion, just as in his discussions of his general philosophical and methodological views, translates as "empirical research techniques." The use of those techniques is also the meaning of Walras's term "experimental."

Walras argued in one place that economics is observational but not experimental in the sense of the laboratory sciences when he criticized economists who contended that economics is "experimental" but who, in actuality, did not have a clear idea of what a science is or what an experiment is (198, 1897 in 205, 1898, p. 270). He explained that

...economics can be an observational science but not an experimental one. Mechanics, physics, chemistry, physiology experiment. Because of the

impersonal nature of the facts that they study, they can isolate specific facts
and make them occur, a hundred percent of the time, in a relation to other facts.
By induction, they arrive at the judgment that the relation is a physical or natural
law. Economics does not experiment; it observes personal facts (ibid.).

It is clear that in that particular statement, Walras regarded observation
and experimentation as different forms of research, and that by the latter
he was referring to controlled experiments, usages that should be borne
in mind in the following discussion.

In 1861, however, Walras asserted, contradicting the passage just
quoted, that, "Economics is an experimental science..." (27, 1861,
p. 92). It has been suggested that he expressed that view when under
the influence of his father (see Potier 1994, p. 256), as though he held
it temporarily and not as a basic conviction. In fact, Walras repeated
it during his entire career. By "experimental science" he did not mean
controlled laboratory experiments. He meant, as he stated in the rest of
the sentence, that "it observes natural facts with the greatest rigor, discovering their order and relationships" (27, 1861, p. 92). Determining
causal relationships – "order and relationships" – is a principal objective
of experiments, so he used that phrase to evoke that activity. Detecting
those relationships is a principal objective of observation. Walras was
preserving the difference between "experimental" and "observational"
and was stating, over the course of the two clauses of his sentence, that
economics employs both methods.

There are many other passage in which Walras asserted unambigu-
ously that economic theory is experimental in the active participatory
sense of that adjective. It has been seen in Chapter 1 that, for most of
his career, he classified economic theory along with physics, chemistry,
and biology as a pure natural science. He used the words "experimental" and "observational" in reference to natural sciences, as when he
wrote about "the *experimental* sciences which, through the observation
of facts attain, by induction or by hypothesizing, progressively more
profound knowledge of laws and relationships" (15, 1860, p. XIII). It is
probable that in that passage he meant, not that observational sciences
by convention can be called experimental, but that scientists conduct
experiments and observe the results. After 1896 he described economic
theory as a pure *moral* science, thus asserting before and after that date
that it is a pure science, and contended that, "All pure science is done
from the point of view of *pure truth*, rational *and experimental*" (205,
1898, p. 453; emphasis added to the last two words).

Walras remarked that a certain scholar made a faulty distinction
when he described physical and natural sciences as observational, and

physiology and social science as experimental, but Walras did not mean that social science is not experimental. He contended rather that the natural sciences are not only observational but also experimental and that social science is not only experimental but also observational (249.XIII, p. 558). He argued that, "The physical and natural sc.[iences] properly speaking are just as experimental as physiology. Physiology will also be both rational and experimental. *Social science, id*" (ibid.; emphasis added.). The Latin *idem*, meaning "the same," indicates his belief that economics, as a social science, is also not only rational but also experimental in the sense that the physical and natural sciences are. For example, it determines that the "intrinsic value of land is a scientific fact from the points of view of reasoning and of experience" (215, 1907, in 249.VII, p. 471). Then in 1900, Walras summed up his views on this matter by declaring that, "It is now very certain that political economy is, like astronomy, like mechanics, a science that is both experimental and rational" (210, 1900, p. XX; p. 22). Walras's declaration implies that he thought that economics has empirical bases and is tested empirically.

Walras's assertions about the methods of economics make it evident in yet another way that he rejected the archrationalism thesis. He maintained that, as he practiced it, economic science is like all the other pure sciences in using observations and experiments. He affirmed that it does so in order to attain knowledge of reality and that those methods are undertaken precisely in order to compare assumptions and conclusions with reality. The theories and models developed in the experimental sciences, of which he declared economics is one, *are* compared to reality. Those sciences apply the criterion of "the conformity of theory with perceived reality [de l'ordre pensé avec l'ordre perçu], or the principle of *order* and of *causality*" (14, 1860, in 249.VII, p. 58; and see 15, 1860, p. XIII), and they apply that criterion by using observation and experimentation. Thus he believed that in regard to their relation to reality; that is, in regard to the ontological status that he conceived their subjects matters to have, all the pure sciences are the same. According to Walras, they all, including economics, deal in a scientific way with "une réalité sensible," not in a metaphysical way with a metaphysical realm, which is indeed explicit in his view that they are all experimental or observational or both. Whatever nuances he placed on the words *"experience," "*experimental," and "observational," it is clear that by using them to describe the methods of economic science, he was doing so to indicate that it is empirically based and empirically verified. Walras therefore contended that he arrived at his model of a "hypothetical regime of absolute free competition" by using the correct scientific methods of observation of the real economy and by experimentation to arrive at his abstractions.

To summarize: First, Walras believed that knowledge of reality is obtained by sensory experience and thus he dissented from the view that knowledge that is certain comes from innate ideas, referring to "the natural world that is scrutinized by the senses in order to make it the object of pure natural science" (203, 1898, in 205, p. 492; see Potier 1994, p. 268; Chapter 1). Second, he believed that all the pure sciences not only have a rational aspect but are also experimental or observational or both. An attribution to him of the opinion that pure economic science does not compare its assumptions or conclusions with reality is therefore contradictory to his thought. That attribution would imply that Walras had a separate epistemological and methodological outlook with respect to just one of the pure sciences, namely economics; that he believed that economic activities in the real world, alone of all the subjects treated by science, are ontologically different and are not scrutinized by the senses to make them the object of pure economic theory; and that pure economic theory, alone of all the sciences, is neither observational nor experimental. The archrationalism thesis cannot be true unless Walras thought that all pure sciences are empirically based, deal with reality, and are compared to it, except the pure science of economics. That, it has just been shown, is contradictory to what he believed.

III. The third step: Recognition of the near-ubiquity of freely competitive markets in the real economy

Walras's main objective as an economic theorist was to understand the behavior of the markets that functioned in the economy of his time, and he therefore studied what he considered to be the two major types, namely monopoly and freely competitive markets. He did not integrate monopoly and freely competitive markets into a single model, nor did he want to do so. "To be logical, it is necessary to proceed from the general case to the particular case, and not from the particular case to the general case, as would be done by a physicist who, in order to observe the sun, carefully chooses an overcast period instead of taking advantage of a cloudless sky" (106, 1874, p. 51; with changes in 176, 1889, p. 70; § 43, p. 73). The "secret of science is to bring the general case to the foreground and to relegate particular cases and exceptions to the background..." (239, 1891, 2, p. 434). Applying that general scientific method to economics, he contended that the methodologically correct procedure is to put aside the special cases that he considered imperfectly competitive markets to be, and to analyze the characteristics of the majority of markets (1874, p. 49; § 41, p. 71; 1877, p. 267; § 222, pp. 334–35).

What were the majority? What was his idea of the character of the real economy of his day? Walras surveyed it and concluded that it was principally, first, one in which there was private ownership of economic resources and other commodities; second, a market economy; and third, one in which "free competition in regard to exchange is the almost universal regime" (239, 1891, 2, pp. 434–35). It is true, his observations led him to recognize, that production and exchange in the real economy are subjected to legal and administrative regulations, and are influenced by custom. The regulations are becoming less important, but the force of custom remains (114, 1875, in 249.VII, p. 298). Nevertheless, free competition is "the principal mode, practiced on all markets with more or less precision and therefore with less or more frictions" (239, 1895, 2, p. 630). He reinforced the clarity of the meaning of those statements by drawing an analogy between the subjects studied by physical scientists and economists. The mathematics, he observed, may not be understood by everyone, but we would all agree that Newton and Laplace had described "the world of astronomic facts conforming to the principle of gravity." Walras was writing about the real cosmos, about what those scientists and he believed was a valid description of it. Then, writing about the ordinary facts of the real economy, he went on to ask: "Why not accept in the same way the description of the world of economic facts conforming to the principle of free competition?" (123, 1877, p. 365; § 370, p. 651).

If Walras had tried to deal with the frictions and particular modes of behavior that are found in imperfectly competitive markets as well as the behavior of highly competitive markets in the same model, he would have found it impossible to achieve the goal of constructing a comprehensive model of an entire economic system. His subject matter would have been too complicated for him to analyze with his mathematical skills or even with the most advanced mathematical techniques that were available (123, 1877, p. 267; 176, 1889, p. 252; § 222, pp. 334–35).

IV. The fourth step: The construction of a freely competitive model

The assumption that the markets in the model
are freely competitive

Walras wanted his mature economic model to reflect the fundamental characteristics of the real economy. That is demonstrated in all aspects of his theorizing, because the way he treated each topic is an expression in one particular respect or another of the parts and implications of his system of scientific thought, and that system rests on connections between theory and reality. His views about the real economy and scientific methodology led Walras to the fourth step in his construction of his system of economic theorizing, namely to making the assumption that all the markets in his model are freely competitive. He recognized the complex facts of reality, he explained, but in a scientific investigation of the determination of the relation of the market for products to the market of services and of the equilibrium prices of those commodities, the soundest procedure is to assume their markets are regulated by free competition alone (114, 1875, in 249.VII, p. 298). "I prefer," Walras wrote, "for my part, to start with unlimited competition, which is the general case, to arrive finally at monopoly, which is a special case ..." (176, 1889, p. 499; § 381, p. 665). Explaining this matter further, Walras wrote: "I have reduced the economic mechanism to its most essential elements by abstracting from all the accessory complications" (239, 1892, 2, pp. 509–10). Regarding competition, Walras repeated he had "as a first step, reduced that mechanism to its essential elements" (239, 1894, 2, p. 624, n. 5).

By the economic mechanism, he was referring to the real economy that his observation and empirical research presented to him. He was identifying the fundamental aspects of the economy, not taking the first step toward constructing a fiction or a utopia. He contemplated that empirical totality and then arrived at his model by a subtractive and extractive process; that is, by abstracting elements of that totality, discarding those that were not essential parts of its structure and functioning. In contrast, when a writer makes up a fictional or utopian economy, he undertakes an additive process, conceiving of one component after another, many of them fictional, and putting them into a model. Of course, a positive model does not spring forth fully formed from the mind of the theoretician, and thus in discussing the history of the process of its formation, the assembling and articulation of its parts is referred to as "constructing" the model. By contemplating the finished system and comparing it to the reality to which it is related, however, it becomes clear that its parts are simplified extractions from a complex reality.

The functioning of freely competitive markets, Walras argued, is then seen to determine simultaneously the rate of production and prices of products, and the rate of production and prices of productive services. Explaining and demonstrating this is the object of pure economic theory (114, 1875, in 249.VII, p. 298). "In the question of the tatonnement, for example, I take the almost universal mode of free competition in exchange" and the associated phenomenon of Walrasian pricing, which is the changing of the price in the same direction as the sign of the market excess demand (239, 1891, 2, p. 434). It is for the same reasons that Walras's assumption of free competition was adopted by all general equilibrium theorists for decades, and is still used in many models.

Real referents of the components of the model

It has been alleged that to suppose that Walras wanted to develop a model that would explain the real economy of his day is an error occasioned by an inability to distinguish between his real types and his ideal types. Walras, it has been contended, did not intend the ideal types in his model to have referents in the real economy of his day and they did not (Koppl 1995, Lendjel 1997, Huck 2001, Bridel and Huck 2002). Those characterizations of Walras's philosophical and methodological outlook in general and of his economic model in particular are not defensible, as has been indicated in the foregoing exposition of his approval of empirical methods and components of economic science and his conclusions regarding the character of the economy of his day, and as will now be made clear in an examination of his real and ideal economic types.

The manner by which Walras arrived at his economic abstractions demonstrates that he habitually referred to economic facts as being individual concrete facts of the real economy, that he explained how they are apprehended and organized so as to identify real types, that the ideal types that he used as components of his model are based on real types, and that he therefore established the connections between the ideal types and the real economy. As Walras phrased matters, the components of his model are ideal types based on real types and are therefore firmly connected to reality. "No one," he wrote,

> ... can prevent us from defining, that is, drawing by abstraction from experience, the ideas of social wealth, capital and income, productive services and products, proprietors, workers, and capitalists, entrepreneurs, the market and of prices; the idea of humans in society, of their division of labor, of their quality of being reasonable and free. Now, on the foundation of those ideas, we can, we should, establish the theory of production and that of the distribution of the social wealth among the people in the society (89, 1868, in 194, 1896, p. 187).

"As in geometry," he said, "the only ideal types admissible in social science are those that are extracted by the understanding from the real types that experience furnishes" (251 in 249.XII, p. 166).

> Just as, in taking up the problem of the mathematical determination of the prices of products, we have had to define with precision the mechanism of free competition in regard to exchange, similarly in taking up the problem of the mathematical determination of the prices of productive services, we have to examine carefully *the facts and experience to obtain from them the exact notion of the mechanism of free competition* in regard to production (123, 1877, p. 222; § 178, p. 276; emphasis added).

Thus Walras drew the mature model's basic components from the reality
that he perceived, which, as has been seen, was the near-ubiquity of free
competition. His conviction about economic reality explains why he
constructed a model of a freely competitive economy, and makes clear
that he did not do so to construct a hypothetical in the sense of a fictional
model (see Diemer and Lallement 2004), or a utopia whose conditions
necessitated the operation of that type of system (see Jaffé 1977).

Induction and deduction

It has been shown that Walras believed that induction – using empirical
information, gained by experimentation and observation, as the basis
of assumptions, hypotheses, and scientific laws – is an important part
of investigation in all science. Therefore he believed that the process of
induction is a crucially important aspect of *economic* science. It is true
that he wrote in 1896 that social science is "an abstract and deductive
science as much as and more so than the mechanics of material forces"
(194, 1896, p. VI). "Economics," in particular, "is incontestably, in any
case, a science that is not only abstract and deductive, but also mathematical" (205, 1898, p. 450).[6] In the foregoing sentences, however, Walras
was, of course, referring to the *deductive phase* of theorizing; he was
not asserting that social science does not rest on empirical knowledge
and is not tested by it.

On the contrary, like the other social sciences, Walras contended, economics must be cultivated by scholars of general culture who are "accus-
tomed to handling, at the same time, induction and deduction, reasoning
and experience" (210, 1900, p. XX; p. 22). Studying the physical and
natural sciences gives the social scientist "the habit of using the method
of induction and deduction that is the true scientific method" (141, July
1879, p. 26). Walras commented regarding that habit: "Is it not permitted to believe that the same method which has so well succeeded in the
physical and natural sciences would have equally good results in the
moral and political sciences . . .?" (ibid., p. 15). Adopting the method of
using both induction and deduction,

> . . . pure economic theory should draw from experience the real types of exchange,
> supply, demand, market, capital goods, incomes, productive services, products.
> From these real types, theory should abstract ideal types by a process of definition,
> and reason on the latter . . . (106, 1874, p. 32; § 30, p. 53).

---

[6] Mill was another example of the many economists who contended that social science
is deductive and abstract and that "political economy, too, was Newtonian because of
its deductive, abstract nature" (Redman 1997, p. 325).

The word "real" in that quotation perfectly describes the types in question. It indicates that Walras believed they exist in the real economy and are apprehended through experience of it; they are facts in the ordinary sense of the word, not "essences." Most of Walras's references to facts are references to real concrete individual facts; only the intellectually processed facts he called ideal types are abstractions that describe what is common to groups of similar real facts and essential to them only in that sense. Another example of his meaning of the word "ideal" is his statement that "this state of equilibrium of production is, like the state of equilibrium of exchange, an ideal and not a real state" (123, 1877, p. 231; § 188, p. 283). Walras did not mean "ideal" in the sense of a normative goal; he meant a state envisaged through scientific abstraction that would be reached if the parameters identified in the model were actually to remain constant for a sufficient period of real time. Because the ideal types in his mature comprehensive general equilibrium model are based upon real types, the ideal types rest on an empirical foundation. They have referents in "une réalité sensible," and that, for Walras, is their justification.

Thus Walras was not following arcane philosophical directives in his choice of methods to construct his economic models. Scientific thinking, he observed, requires that subjective elements be discarded in order to leave in our perceptions only what is objective or absolute (205, 1898, p. 492). Neither metaphysical nor fanciful, his procedure and his descriptions of it embody the manifestly accurate perception that the concepts used in scientific theories, and thus the theories themselves, are idealizations of real situations, events, and things. As Giddings remarked (see Chapter 1), abstractions are not abstractions from nothing; they are taken from reality. The ideal economic types are therefore idealizations in the sense that they are, like perfect circles, free of the irrelevant idiosyncrasies and perturbing events and forces that affect corresponding particular real instances of the phenomena. That is what Walras meant when he wrote that he had reduced the economic mechanism to its most essential elements. "The world is not perfect. Perfection is a pure idea. The relation of perfection to imperfection is the relation of the ideal to reality" (249.XIII, p. 560). The ideal types found in Walras's mature comprehensive model of economic equilibrium do not differ in character and purpose from those used by economists and scientists in other fields. Like scientists in all disciplines, in order to obtain his economic abstractions (his ideal types), Walras stripped away from his portrayals of empirical economic phenomena (his real types) the aspects that were not relevant for his model. He then expressed the results in scientific form.

Walras thought that the task of obtaining economic ideal types is arduous. In the social sciences, he asserted, there is a lengthy process of interplay of scientific reasoning and the reality with which it deals: "The real type in the theory of society is not immediately furnished by experience, and the ideal type can be drawn from it only by means of an *a posteriori* synthesis that is very long and very laborious" (51, December 31, 1866, column 182; and in 194, 1896, p. 13; and see 15, 1860, p. XIII). The process involves repeated comparisons of the formative scientific abstraction with the real type found in reality, improvement of perceptions of real types by continued observation of facts and experimentation, and consequent repeated modifications of the abstraction. "In regard to the economic and social sciences, the ideal types must be sought with difficulty in a complex amalgamated mass of data; there is, we would say, a problem of complexity. It is therefore necessary to make an empirical effort of decomposition or analysis and of reconstruction and synthesis in order to obtain the real types and attain the ideal types" (Dockès 1996, pp. 59–60). Walras would have thought that this is a good description of the processes by which all scientists arrive at their abstractions.

Real referents of the components of the model in practice

Comparing Walras's knowledge of the facts of the economy of his day with the ideal types in his models renders it objectively ascertainable that his ideal types have real referents, that is, the components of his mature comprehensive model correspond to elements in the real markets he described in many writings. That could not be otherwise than the case because he abstracted the former from the latter. To suggest that Walras did not think that the masses of empirical detail about actual markets he provided in his writings are ordinary facts would be ludicrous. He was not writing about some metaphysical intellectual construction, but about the real world, the "réalité sensible."

Some examples, selected from literally hundreds that appear in his writings, will illustrate this matter. He provided abundant information about his knowledge of the institutions and behavior of real competitive markets. Among many others, he discussed commodity exchanges, grain markets, fish markets, (106, 1874, pp. 48–49; § 41, pp. 70–71; 249.XII, passim in pp. 445–714), and the institutions, participants, rules, types of securities, and different sorts of operations on the Paris Bourse (13, 1860; 65, 1867; 147, 1880; 249.XII, pp. 671–80; 249.XII, p. 890, n. 21). In those real freely competitive organized markets, Walras noted, prices are determined by the forces of supply and demand without collusion

and are changed by buyers and sellers in the same direction as the sign of
the market excess demand, which is what Walras meant by the term "free
competition" (106, 1874, p. 50; § 42, pp. 71–72). He likewise asserted
that the workings of free competition also occur in many real unorganized
competitive markets (106, 1874, pp. 48–49; § 41, pp. 70–71).

The ideal types in his model – bonds, brokers, criers, buyers, sellers,
prices, supply, demand, the physical setting of the markets – are therefore, via real types, abstractions from his knowledge of real markets. He
used those ideal types, together with a few simplifying conditions, to
obtain his model of an organized market, "le marché type" (147, March
1880, p. 460; 147, April 1880, p. 78; Walker 2000b) that he assumed in
all his theoretical formulations of freely competitive markets. He was
not like those economists, he declared, who

... have not furnished the definition of either the mechanism of free competition,
or of the diverse elements of that mechanism. They have not extracted from experience, by observation and abstraction, the types of these elements: the *market,
demand, supply*, the *raising of prices*, the *lowering of prices*, the *equilibrium
price, products*, the *productive services: labor*, the *services of land*, the *services
of capital goods*, the *services of the entrepreneur*, etc. (114, 1875, in 249.VII,
p. 301).

In that passage, as in many others, it is patently obvious that Walras
was saying that the real economy is characterized by a system of freely
competitive markets; that he abstracted its features to obtain the ideal
types that are in his model; and that those ideal types therefore have a
one-to-one correspondence with elements in the real economy. Thus he
not only said that economic science should base its ideal types on real
phenomena, he did precisely that in his theoretical work. It is clear that
on the occasions when he described his work as dealing with a "hypothetical" regime of competition, he did not mean that its hypotheses were
not drawn from reality.

Again, examining in his model the impact of the substitution of a
commodity in place of one whose price has risen, Walras remarked that
the behavior "is what is seen every day" (106, 1874, p. 154; § 152, p. 238).
In order to construct his purely competitive model of the capital market,
he declared that "it is necessary to borrow some decisive circumstances
from reality and from experience" (123, 1877, p. 302; § 269, p. 434).
In one analysis he temporarily assumed that capital is lent in kind, but
then, indicating from whence he obtained his ideas about the savings of
capitalists, noted that "in the real world, capital is lent in money, for the
reason that it is in this form that the capitalist accumulates his capital
by saving (123, 1877, p. 252; § 208, p. 313). As for the problem of
the determination of the price of a commodity money, his geometrical

method solves it "as it is done, in the real world, by the tatonnements that are very well represented" by his diagram (176, 1889, pp. 385–86; § 283, pp. 483–84).

Walras's procedure is also illustrated by his treatment of market imperfections. He preferred free competition for most economic activities in his ideal society and in the real economy, but he recognized that it was not the only real market structure. Indicating his interest in the empirical situation, Walras pointed out that "whatever is said, or seems to be said, quite frequently by economists, free competition is not the only possible form of organization of economic activity; there are others, such as regulation, tariffs, economic privileges, monopolies, etc." (123, 1877, p. 369; § 371, p. 655). He identified the characteristics of industries that he considered to be natural monopolies – in particular, the economics of railroads – and set forth a model of their behavior in order to analyze their pricing and output policies (115, 1875). His model of monopoly is an ideal economic type; it uses concepts abstracted from real monopolies (123, 1877, pp. 377–85; § 370–84, pp. 660–68). Although Walras knew that the quantity demanded of any monopoly's product is influenced, however slightly, by the actions of other firms, to obtain the ideal demand function for his model monopoly, he assumed that the disturbing influences of their pricing and output policies do not exist. Real monopolies, Walras would have said, therefore imperfectly resemble the ideal pure monopoly found in economic theory.

Fictional versus real types

Some of the components of Walras's constructions are not ideal types because they are not abstractions, not idealizations, not based on real types found in the real economy. They are fictions. This is clear in general but obscured in some instances by Walras's terminological inconsistency. In a few cases, he used the word "imaginary" to refer to fictions. In others, he used it merely to indicate that creative mental activity enters into the scientific formulation of ideal types that, as abstractions, do not have precisely the features of particular real instances (Chapter 1). In a few cases, he described ideal economic types as imaginary. In others, he described imaginary components as ideal. Regarding the net income commodity, for example, he wrote that he had imagined it – that to produce its effect, "it will be sufficient to imagine" it; but he also wrote that it is an "ideal commodity" (210, 1900, p. 250; § 242, p. 359).

Despite those terminological variations, the fictional components and the ideal economic types in Walras's writings are easily distinguished.

He had no choice but to use the ideal economic types that appear in his mature model, whether he approved of them or not, because they were based on important elements of the real economy. The fictional components were not. Like the fictional written pledges made by suppliers and the fictional perpetual net income commodity, they appear in the theorizing that Walras introduced in the fourth edition of the *Eléments*, abandoning the aim of realism. Fictional components also appear in abundance in Walras's writings about his "ideal society."

Walras used the fictional components because he liked them, and he was aware that in matters of policy it is necessary "not to lose one's head, to keep oneself free of illusions, and not to believe that one's desires are realities" (141, July 1879, p. 5, in 249.VII, p. 377). His ideal society did not actually exist, but he believed it would be achieved by implementing the reforms that he recommended. In referring to it, he was dealing with a normative conception, and therefore when he used the word "ideal" in connection with it, he did so in the sense of "desirable" or "the best." Its institutions, economic agents, and rules of economic life are the ones that he desired, and the justice and social utility to which he referred were his notions of the meaning of those terms. Obviously "the" social ideal, which he regarded as "perfection in regard to justice and social utility" (Dockès 1994, p. 280), is in reality *his* social ideal, an elevation of his personal preferences to the level of what he considered to be universally valid metaphysical principles.

There is an evident contrast between the fictional situation in Walras's ideal society in which all natural monopolies are owned by the state and the real situation in the nineteenth-century European and American economies. Privately owned monopolies existed in the real economy and were important, so Walras had to recognize them in his economic theorizing, but he chose not to put them into his ideal society. Natural monopolies are there owned by the state. Similarly, the institution of the possession of land by private individuals existed in the real economy and it was an important institution, so Walras had to abstract it and feature it in his economic model. In contrast, he did not put it into the "'rational society' that is in conformity with the ideal society of his youth" (Dockès 1994, p. 322; Dockès 1996, p. 221). Into the ideal society, he put the fictional condition that all land is owned by the state; the private ownership of land and therefore landlords do not exist there. In the same way, he provided theoretical analyses of taxation policies in the real economy, but for his ideal society he chose the fictional condition that there are no taxes, along with the fictional condition that the state supports itself exclusively with the rents that it charges for the use of land.

Realism and applications

Walras's mature comprehensive model diverges from reality in the respect that it includes only freely competitive markets (and in some other ways), but he nevertheless asserted or implied many times that it was realistic. He meant that in the sense that it provided an understanding of the real economy of his day and was applicable to the solution of real economic problems. Walras was greatly concerned with those matters. During his journalistic phase and his entire subsequent career, he analyzed a wide variety of empirical economic situations. When he started work on the *Eléments*, he declared that one of his major objectives was to construct a model of general equilibrium in order to understand and evaluate the consequences of free competition, to devise sound policies to encourage it, and to enable the evaluation of alternative forms of economic organization in activities in which it does not work (123, 1877, pp. 267–68; 176, 1889, p. 254; § 223, pp. 335–36). After he finished his treatise, he demonstrated that he had succeeded in developing empirically useful theoretical constructions by applying them to the analysis of such matters as the Paris Bourse, banking, agriculture, monetary policy in Europe and India, and railroads. "I have shown," he wrote, "by its application to a single question (that of money) how the new method permits an improvement over the old solutions. I will show the same thing in regard to credit, speculation, [property, income tax] etc., in the *Eléments d'économie politique appliquée* and in the *Eléments d'économie sociale*" (239, 1889, 2, 364–65).[7] At the end of his life, Walras declared that he had worked during his entire career to develop theories that were applicable to real problems (Walras 1909, pp. 581–83), "to put the 'social question' onto its true basis and, if possible, to solve it scientifically" (ibid., pp. 580–81). In other words, he believed his work was realistic; that was why his "economic theory," he contended, "provides us the means of achieving in actual practice both justice and economic objectives" (ibid., p. 583).

V. The fifth step: Introduction of more empirically derived detail

The fifth step Walras took in the development of his model was to assert that once he had presented the essential elements of the economy in it,

---

[7] It will be observed that Walras used the word *Eléments* in that passage. Subsequently, of course, he chose the word *Etudes*.

it could be made progressively less abstract, and thus to correspond in progressively greater detail to reality, by incorporating additional conditions drawn from the real economy and from other aspects of society. Walras explained that it was possible to do that because the fundamental structure of his model was "sufficiently in conformity with reality" (239, 1895, 2, p. 629). The idea he expressed there is that a theory will not be valid or useful unless it has that quality; and, of course, determining whether that is the case requires comparing its assumptions and conclusions with reality. Its verisimilitude made it possible for additional empirically derived material – "secondary elements," as he called them – to be introduced into it. That, he wrote, allows economic questions to be studied in mathematical form in any degree of detail that is desired (ibid.).

The secondary elements, according to Walras, *should* be added: "It is appropriate to introduce into [my] conception one by one all the complications that reality presents" (239, 1894, 2, p. 624, n. 5). He was referring to economic details and psychological and sociological elements that he had excluded from his abstract economic model (239, 1875, 1, p. 435; Chapter 3). In the same sense, he wrote that "we should pass from the assumption of an annual periodic market to that of a permanent market; that is to say from the static to the dynamic state." Why should that be done? Walras's answer was, "in order to bring us closer and closer to the reality of things" (123, 1877, p. 310; § 322, p. 579). He was again advocating that a progressively more detailed correspondence of a model to the real economy should be achieved and thus again manifesting his belief that theories should be judged by reference to the degree of their consonance with reality. Moreover, Walras indicated that in order to undertake applications of economic theory, it is essential to take into account the findings of other disciplines (141, July 1879, pp. 16–17). "Economic theory is only the theory of social wealth. To pass from it to applied economics and social economics, it is necessary to introduce into the picture the physiological, psychological, individual, and moral aspects of human nature. You must believe that is something I know well how to take into account" (239, 1874, 1, p. 366). He vehemently rejected the charge that he tried to apply pure theory directly without considering the aspects of society and individual behavior studied by other disciplines: "On the contrary. To give directions about the distribution and production of social wealth by men in society, I have taken care to develop the *general theory of society* and to combine the principles with those of the *theory of social wealth*" (239, 1901, 3, 173). Thus although he was on occasion (ibid.; 249.XIII, pp. 567, 568) critical of

Pareto's method of successive approximations as it referred to achieving progressively more realistic theoretical formulations (Chapter 9), he agreed with the aspect of it that called for the involvement of disciplines in addition to pure economic theory in the analysis and solution of real problems.

CHAPTER 3

Methods of evaluation of economic theory

I. The sixth step: Criteria for evaluations

In Chapter 2 it was shown that Walras was guided by his philosophical and methodological views about economic theorizing in the steps that shaped the development of his mature comprehensive economic model. His sixth step was to develop the criteria he believed were valid for judging the results of the preceding steps in his system of thought and for judging the work of other economists, and to make those judgments.

Walras contended that all economic models (once it is established that they are logical) should be judged by comparing their assumptions, structure, contents, and conclusions with the real economy. He declared, therefore, that his own model should be evaluated by comparing it with the reality from which he abstracted it. His statements cited in Chapter 2 to the effect that his mature model of general equilibrium is in conformity with reality are such comparisons. His belief in the necessity of evaluating theoretical work and the criteria that he believed should be used to make the judgments were consequences of his intellectual orientation, part of his organized philosophical and methodological system.

Theorizing and reality

There is an interesting passage in the *Eléments* (quoted in Chapter 1) in which Walras declares that theory should find real types in the real world, base ideal types upon them, and then build the structure of scientific reasoning on the latter, to which he adds the remark, "not returning to reality until the science has been constructed and doing so in order to make applications. We will thus have, on an ideal market, ideal prices that will be in a rigorous relation with ideal demand and ideal supply" (106, 1874, p. 32; § 30, p. 53). Is that, as has been claimed (Bridel 1990, p. 183; Lendjel 1997, p. 70), evidence supporting the opinion that Walras's "rationalistic approach . . . excludes any confrontation of the results of pure economics with reality for validation" (Bridel 1997, p. 142)?

85

In fact, there are four ideas in that passage. The first is an insistence upon the necessity of basing the building blocks of a theory on empirical knowledge, which is an explicit assertion of the necessity of constructing a realistic theory. The only way to determine if a real economic type – and hence an ideal economic type – is a proper representation of reality is to compare it to the real economy. The second is the implication that economic science is elaborated as a deductive process. In that regard Walras was naturally aware that a given deductive chain is a closed system. New empirical data differing from the original set would lead to new assumptions, which naturally must be introduced at the level of assumptions. Obviously, the new components contained in the new assumptions cannot properly be introduced into the middle of a chain of deductive reasoning based on the old set of components. Thus in making his statement about economic theory "not returning to reality until the science has been constructed," Walras was referring to the working out of the deductive structure once a given set of ideal types and assumptions has been formulated. It was elsewhere that he described the phase of laborious abstraction, formulation, comparison of the basic components and assumptions with reality, and reformulation of them. It was elsewhere that he referred to the phase of comparing the conclusions of the theory to the facts, and to the phase of introducing more detail into it. The third idea in the passage is that theories should be applied, and that means that they must "return to reality," and that implies that they must be realistic. The fourth idea, expressed in the terminology of ideal types, unfashionable today, is that the elements, relationships, and functioning of economic models are clearly defined and precise, an affirmation that, using modern terminology, any modern theoretician would apply to his own models. Thus, far from supporting the notion that Walras was an archrationalist, the passage contradicts it.

There is nevertheless a sentence in which Walras ostensibly contradicted his view of the necessity of empirically testing economic theory. He was reacting to a passage in which Cournot wrote that economic theory, like mathematics, allows and stimulates "the control of reasoning by experience in all the parts that are susceptible of scientific treatment" (Cournot 1863, p. 16). Walras jotted at the bottom of the page on which that statement appears that economic theory *"n' attend pas des confirmations de l' expérience"* (Walras undated, in Potier 1994, p. 242, where Cournot is also quoted). He meant that economic theory does not need to be confirmed by experience, that the use of it does not need to await confirmation by experience.

Walras's jotting is not representative of his thought. First, it makes no sense internally. He did not think that economic theory would be developed and then neglected, that it would have no uses in reference to the real economic past, present, or future. Indeed, his sentence, like all his writings, indicates his view that economic theory is used. To use it, however, is to apply it, and to apply it *is* to confirm it or contradict it by experience. Second, the jotting is incompatible with Walras's philosophical and methodological system of thought. He affirmed on many occasions his belief that economic theories are confirmed (or refuted) by empirical information and that if the theories are to be used for applications, confirmation is necessary. He granted, however, that some economic hypotheses cannot be confirmed because the phenomena to which they refer are not measurable. His expression of those opinions was part of his organized system of economic philosophy and methodology, whereas his jotting in Cournot's book is a poorly conceived fragment that lies outside of that system and is incompatible with it. This will now be demonstrated in yet another way, namely by showing how Walras believed that assumptions and conclusions should be evaluated and how he actually judged examples of them found in the works of various economists, including his own.

Logical experiments and historical evidence

Walras was fully aware that it may be difficult to determine whether a particular real phenomenon exists under the conditions assumed in a model. He knew that if a particular fact of the real economy contradicts a conclusion of a model, it may not be because the model is wrong but because the conditions assumed to be constant or not to exist in the model are violated in reality by exogenous events and unknown endogenous influences. "If reasoning on the one hand, and observation and experience on the other hand, are contradictory, it is necessary to try to bring them into agreement if it is desired to elaborate the science with the use of the fact in question; but if the reasoning is correct, it is not destroyed by that contradiction, because possibly it is the fact that should be either more accurately identified or explained by exceptional circumstances" (154, 1880/1881, in 194, 1896, p. 338). He pointed out that, "In practice, that determination," namely of the causes of changes of variables in the real economy, "could be more or less difficult" (106, 1874, p. 103; § 102, p. 146), even with respect to impersonal facts such as the quantities of commodities held by economic agents (ibid.). Economic theory not only deals with such "external" experiences (203, 1898, p. 1), but, unlike the physical sciences, it also "observes personal facts" (198, 1897 in 205, 1898, p. 270) – "intimate reality" (203, 1898, p. 1; in 205, 1898, p. 492). Personal facts are experienced by economic agents, and pose an even greater problem because a given set of personal facts is "always associated with other personal facts" so that economic theory "can never say with certainty" if the set occurs *because of* the other facts or *although* the other facts are present (198, 1897 in 205, 1898, p. 270).

Walras therefore conducted logical experiments: "It follows that, in this field, deduction must always come to the aid of induction" (104, 1874, in 205, 1898, p. 251). Regarding the determination of cause and effect in empirical situations, "that determination could be more or less difficult; but nothing forces us to declare that it is impossible in theory" (106, 1874, p. 103; § 102, pp. 146–47). The outcomes of the deductive phase of his modeling are the conclusions of his analysis. In his comparative static logical experiments, for example, he varied the quantities of commodities held by the participants, or their utility functions, and deduced the consequences for the equilibrium prices (for example, 106, 1874, pp. 134–37; 176, 1889, pp. 159–63; §§ 137–38, pp. 209–14. 176, 1889, pp. 127–28; § 103, pp. 149, 151. 106, 1874, p. 104; § 103, p. 151. 123, 1877, p. 294; 176, 1889, p. 309; § 265, p. 430).

Walras then compared the conclusions about both impersonal and personal economic facts with reality. His means of doing so was observation of them. Even at the beginning of his career, when he first identified "natural facts" as the subject matter of economics, he declared that "it observes" them "with the greatest rigor" (27, 1861, p. 92). It is true, he recognized, that in some cases, "Science pronounces truths that experience is unable to confirm," an example of which, according to Walras, is the proportionality of prices to marginal utilities (239, 1893, 2, p. 573, n. 8), but in that instance by "experience" he meant objective quantitative methods. He thought that the proportionality, like all the facts studied by economics, is nevertheless observable. Like satisfaction, he believed, it is observable by introspection.

Employing the laboratory of historical experience, Walras explained that economists find periods in which, first, the constants in the model are constants or nearly so in reality and in which, second, the interesting variable changed. The consequences of the change are then traced in the historical record. "The case can even be recognized in which the prime cause of a variation of a price draws itself, so to speak, to the attention of the observers" (106, 1874, p. 103; § 102, p. 147). An example, Walras pointed out, would be the rise of the price of a commodity just when a remarkable feature of the commodity is discovered or an accident destroys part of the supply of it. "One cannot do otherwise than connect one or the other of those events with the rise that occurred" (ibid.). Insofar as it is a question of examining statistical data, however, observation is not an easy process because the data may be erroneous or not complete and therefore only approximately representative of the real situation (104, 1874, in 205, 1898, p. 251). Additional examples of Walras's use of historical evidence are given in the following section.

Walras's evaluations of his own model

Limitations of space dictate that only a few of Walras's evaluations of the assumptions and conclusions of his model can be given here, but they nevertheless constitute convincing evidence of his methodological beliefs and, like his applied economics, demonstrate that he regarded his model as dealing with the economy.

In discussing the behavior that establishes the existence of individual supply and demand functions, Walras wrote that "it is like this that things happen in the real world" (106, 1874, p. 152; § 151, p. 235); and after further explanations, he repeated that assertion (ibid.). Likewise, the settlement of financial claims between, for example, Brussels, Amsterdam, and Frankfurt, is done in a market that acts as a vast clearinghouse, thus manifesting in the real economy "the law of supply and demand which regulates all these exchanges" (106, 1874, p. 208; § 316, p. 538). Why did Walras choose to put in his model the condition that entrepreneurs purchase productive services in the country in which they sell their products? He did so, he wrote, because "it conforms to reality," and that was his evaluation of the scientific worth of the condition[1] (123, 1877, p. 258; 176, 1889, p. 243). He wanted to judge his analysis of speculative finance, and he did so in this way: "In conclusion, it remains to take a look *at the facts* surrounding [that activity] in order to find in them, if possible, *confirmation* of our ideas" (147, April 1880, p. 85; emphasis added). He proceeded to examine the empirical evidence in great detail. Walras stated as an abstract theoretical proposition, as a first approximation, that the offer of services by each worker is a function of the prices of all services and products. Thus he used an ideal type, but cautioned that "the economist should not be dupe of his abstractions" (198, 1897, in 205, 1898, p. 275), by which he meant that the theorist must evaluate his theories by examining reality. He proceeded to compare the proposition with the conditions found in the real economy, and showed that it is true in some occupations but not realizable in others (ibid.).

---

[1] Walras had written "assumption" in 1877 but replaced it with "condition" in 1889, implying a less abstract relation to reality. He also changed the last part of the sentence. He eliminated the passage in the fourth edition (see 249.VIII, p. 322).

Walras compared his theory of prices and incomes to the empirical evidence regarding the historical course of those variables, and judged his theory favorably because it arrived "at the reality of things" (104, 1874, in 205, p. 257). Similarly, he evaluated the validity of two conclusions of his theory by comparing them with reality: "This second conclusion seems to me, like the first, perfectly in conformity with the surrounding facts" (ibid., p. 251). He called upon empirical evidence, upon a real fact, to explain apparent exceptions, namely "the fact which has already been sufficiently described by me ... " (ibid.). He evaluated his theoretical classification of the elements of social wealth – landed, personal, and artificial capital – and of the payments for their services, by comparing his theory with the facts: It is, he wrote, the only classification that "conforms to the nature of things and that is justified by the comparative history of political economy and of modern industry" (21, 1861, in 249.VII, p. 142). He decided to study a particular aspect of monetary behavior because, "In the real world [Dans la réalité], that use of a commodity as money has a certain influence on its value ... " (106, 1874, p. 150; § 150, p. 228). He judged by an empirical consideration the justification of his assuming that money is used, as has been seen (Chapter 2), asserting that he was thereby adopting "the hypothesis conforming to the reality of things" (106, 1874, p. 149; § 149, p. 227). He evaluated his notion of something that is both a numeraire and money in this way: By using that notion, "we bring ourselves more and more closely to the reality of things" because money is also the numeraire in the real economy (106, 1874, p. 151; and, referring only to the numeraire, in 210, 1900, p. 157; § 151, p. 233). His concept represents the matter "as it takes place in reality" (249.XI, p. 493).

As for the solutions of his system of equations of general equilibrium, Walras compared them with the real economy. That is how he judged the scientific worth of the system: "The sequence of events in the real economy constitutes the empirical solution of this system of equations" (123, 1877, p. 365; § 370, p. 651). He believed (erroneously, as will be seen in Chapter 5), that "the result of the flow of the interrelated phenomena of reality is truly the empirical solution" of his system of general equilibrium equations (123, 1877, p. 365; § p. 651), and asserted many times that his model of tatonnement was realistic (Chapter 5, and see Walker 1996, Chapters 12, 13, 14). He developed theories of pricing of products and services, of the rate of net income and the pricing of landed, personal, and capital factors of production, and of money prices. Separately considered, these are "all abstract theories, but which," he wrote in judging their value by the criterion of their realism, "upon interpenetrating each other, put us, by means of a methodical synthesis, into full reality" (210, 1900, p. 172; § 164, p. 254). His compared his mature comprehensive model of general equilibrium with the real economy and concluded, as noted in Chapter 2 in another context, that it was "very much in conformity with reality" (239, 1879, *1*, p. 628, n. 3), "the image" of the economy of his time (179, 1891, p. 47; 191, 1896, pp. 469–70; appendix I, § 4, p. 698). He insisted on "la vraisemblance et la plausibilité" – the *verisimilitude* and the *plausibility* of his economic theory (239, 1888, *2*, p. 251). Verisimilitude is the quality of appearing to be true or real. That was the case, he explained, because the model contains components such as a market, supply, demand, a pricing process, and equilibrium prices of services and products; and, he continued, "these *concepts*, it should be emphasized, are rigorously in conformity with the *facts*, with observation, with experience. Indeed, thanks to the intervention of money, the two markets, for services and for products, are perfectly distinct in the reality of things, as they are from the viewpoint of science" (ibid., p. 230; p. 282; emphasis added). Walras was at pains in that passage as elsewhere to indicate by the juxtaposition of the two italicized words that they have distinct meanings. "Concepts" in that context are ideal types; "the facts" are features of the real economy. There are, for example, the facts of the real markets for services and for products, and there is Walras's model of those markets, which contains idealizations of them. Likewise, he judged his model of price formation by comparing it with reality: It was a scientific way of "taking note of an *observed truth*" (90, 1868, in 194, 1896, p. 30; emphasis added). He supported his analyses of product differentiation, price discrimination, and monopolistic practices by references to empirical conditions (123, 1877, pp. 384–85; § 384, p. 667). He compared to real markets his assumption in a theoretical situation that all of the supply of a good is offered at whatever price it may bring: "This case, so simple, is in reality extremely frequent..." (106, 1874, p. 155; § 153, p. 239).

Yet another example is Walras's discussion of the consequences of certain firms increasing their production above the average quantity for the industry. Those firms will make profits, whereas firms that produce less than the average will make losses and go bankrupt. Thus the consequence of "fixed costs has the enormous importance that it condemns small entrepreneurs to disappear beneath the big entrepreneurs and that it leads free competition to end up in monopoly." Walras then asserted: "Very well, if my theory concludes that such a process occurs, it is a true theory – because that process certainly happens" (239, 1891, letter 1027, n. 7). Thus Walras described an empirical process, compared his theory with it, stated that his theory identified that process, and then asserted that the reason his theory is true is that its conclusion is

verified by the empirical evidence. If it had not been, he would have had
to change the theory to bring it into consonance with reality. He continued by asserting that "free competition is not self-sustaining; there must
be an exterior power that maintains it. I will undertake to establish in
applied economics the consequences of that truth of economic theory.
In the meantime, in the domain of economic theory, I will not go beyond
my data" (ibid.). Walras was writing about the real economy of his day,
about a theory based on the fact, as he believed it to be, that free competition in the real economy is not self-sustaining, about a process that
"certainly happens," not some metaphysical supposition. He was dealing
in his theory with a "réalité sensible," the tendency in the real world for
freely competitive industries to become increasingly concentrated, not
with a hypothetical or ideal situation, and asserted that he intended, for
the bases of his theorizing, to stick to the factual information of which
he had knowledge.

Walras evaluated his theory of capital in the same way. It has been
seen that he claimed that he drew its assumptions "from reality and
from experience," thus comparing them with reality (123, 1877, p. 302;
§ 269, p. 434). He then did the same for the finished structure: It "is
precisely what a theory of that nature should be: the faithful expression
and exact explanation of the phenomena of reality" (176, 1889, p. XXII;
p. 19), a statement that he modified to read "an abstract expression and
rational explanation of the phenomena of reality" (191, 1896, p. XXII;
p. 19). Chapter 1 has shown that by "phenomena" in such a context he
meant concrete individual facts. The machinery, buildings, and producers' goods he discussed in his theory of capital cannot be supposed to
be anything else. The "fact of the division of labor" is not a theory or an
abstract concept. "It is a fact the evident existence of which is immediately apparent from a glance at society" (106, 1874, p. 36; § 32, p. 59).
Likewise, Walras compared his modeling of why money is held with
the real monetary economy and judged that the model reflected it: "This
conception conforms to reality, but is rendered rigorous by means of
scientific reasoning" (210, 1900, p. 300; § 273, p. 443). That conformity
was his justification of his modeling. As compared to barter, Walras
chose to adopt "the assumption of the intervention of money, which is,
when all is said and done, closer to the reality of things. ... In the reality
of things, the producer of wheat sells his wheat for money, the producer
of coffee does the same thing; and with the money obtained thereby, the
former buys coffee, the other buys wheat. That is what we are going to
assume here" (106, 1874, p. 149; § 149, p. 227). Judging his monetary
theory by comparing with the facts its conclusion about the relation of
the quantity of precious metal and its utility, he wrote: "And, in fact,

that is truly what happens, as demonstrated by experience" (123, 1877, p. 186; 176, 1889, p. 463). In the same vein, he declared that his modeling of the holding of assets reflects real economic behavior because, "In reality, in a functioning society, a consumer, landlord, worker or capitalist knows very approximately" what he needs to hold (ibid.). Economic theory must explain the real economy, as, for example, the case of differentials in the prices of foodstuffs in industrial and in agricultural centers. Comparing his theory to the facts, "We thus see that we have arrived, quite easily, by reasoning and theorizing at the reality of things" (104, 1874, in 205, 1898, p. 257). He compared his treatment of accounting and inventory control with the facts and concluded "that our theory of production is well-founded on the nature of things" (123, 1877, p. 235; § 191, p. 289). His definitions dealing with the accounting practices of the firm are "established theoretically and practically" (1877, p. 244; § 198, p. 297). Walras presented a model with fixed coefficients of production, but he judged it by reference to the real situation, and declared that "in reality they are not" and that he would take that into consideration (123, 1877, p. 249; § 2204, p. 305). Supporting the verisimilitude of his theory, Walras noted that different parcels of "land can have, as we will see that they have in reality," greatly differing marginal utilities and value (123, 1877, p. 219; § 174, p. 270). Walras did not want to assume that very large emissions of currency be made because he judged that that supposition "is not in conformity with the reality of things," and that "is why we assume an emission" on a much smaller scale (148, 1879, in 205, 1898, p. 355).

In summary, Walras believed that his mature comprehensive model was a realistic abstraction, not a fiction. Friedrich von Wieser agreed with him:

> It does not copy nature, but gives us a simplified representation of it, which is no misrepresentation, but such as to sharpen our vision in view of the complexities of reality. [It is] like the ideal picture which the geographer draws on his map, as a means, not to deception, but to more effective guidance, he meanwhile assuming that they who are to profit by the map will know how to read it, i.e. to interpret it in accordance with nature (Wieser 1891, p. 108).

Walras's evaluations of the theories of other economists

It will now be shown that Walras demonstrated in yet another way his belief that the assumptions and conclusions of theories should be evaluated by reference to their consonance or dissonance with reality, namely by confronting the theories of other economists with empirical evidence. One example is his examination of David Ricardo's theory of rent.

Walras considered the proposition that infinitely small increments of capital result in an infinitely small reduction in the rate of production. "Of course this might not be true," he remarked, "but until it is shown that this case is the general case or the exception, not by arbitrary assumptions, but by observations drawn from experience, we have the right to reason theoretically on the basis of the former" supposition (123, 1877, pp. 342–43). He was contending that the empirical evidence should determine whether Ricardo's assumption can be judged to be true or untrue, and hence be retained or rejected. He kept that wording for twenty-three years, and then, in 1900, modified it to read: "...the general case, by reasoning or by experience..." (210, 1900, p. 404; § 354, pp. 624–25). Thus he allowed that reasoning – logical thinking to form conclusions or inferences – could be used, which would have to be done on the basis of the evidence and to establish the logical soundness of the argument. He continued nevertheless to indicate that experience – that is, new empirical research – should be undertaken to determine if the proposition is consonant with reality. In another instance, he evaluated in this way the "hypothesis of the English school that value depends upon labor": "The observation of facts formally contradicts that hypothesis" (15, 1860, p. L). What was Bastiat's cardinal fault regarding the English school? It was not illogical qualities of his reasoning. It was that he "wanted to make others accept those consequences that were the most contrary to the reality of the facts" (106, 1874, p. 160; § 160, p. 249). Walras judged T. R. Malthus's theory about the potential rate of increase of population by noting that "it is an estimate that is less than, rather than greater than, is true in reality" (123, 1877, p. 317; § 328, p. 593). He was comparing the theory to the facts, and evaluating it by reference to them. He followed the same method regarding Malthus's contentions about the rate of increase of the means of subsistence: They "are not founded in either reason or experience" (ibid., p. 317; § 328, p. 594). The error of Condillac and J.-B. Say in regard to utility was that their definition of utility is too broad. This can be seen by examining the facts: "It attributes value to things that, in reality, do not have it" (106, 1874, p. 157; § 157, p. 245).

Walras noted that it suffices to compare J. S. Mill's second and third categories of commodities with the real economy to see that they "cannot be infinitely multiplied" (ibid., p. 337; § 349, p. 616). The English economists have a formula for the determination of the average rate of wages, "but is it so determined in reality?" (ibid., p. 357; § 365, p. 643). An examination of the facts of the economy reveals that it is not (ibid., pp. 357–58; § 365, pp. 643–44). Walras's criticism of the English economists' analysis of special productive services is based on a comparison of the real economy with their classifications. Examples of real occupations, he asserted, such as the services of artists, singers, doctors, and surgeons, refute their analysis. Walras also confronted their analysis with the facts that different products come from different types of land, that grapes are grown on some types and wheat on others, but that the land could nevertheless be used to produce alternative crops (ibid., pp. 334–35; § 347, pp. 613–14). A comparison of the Physiocratic theory with the real facts shows that it is erroneous because it failed to recognize that the income from the land in towns is a true net product of industry and commerce (ibid., pp. 327–28; § p. 605). The Physiocrats' conclusion about the economic behavior of the sterile class is wrong. How did Walras arrive at that judgment? Was it because he discovered logical faults in the deductive structure of the theory? No, it is wrong because it "violate[s] the reality of the facts" (123, 1877, p. 326; § 338, p. 604). Walras argued that "it is therefore observation and experience that confounds and ruins the hypothesis of Rousseau and of all the XVIIIth century of the existence of the *state of nature* anterior to and superior to the *social state*, at least from the economic point of view, the only one that we are concerned with here" (253, in 249.XII, p. 121). With the assumption of trading bodies, Jevons "abandons the realm of reality and places himself on the terrain of fictitious means." Walras preferred to stay with what is realistic: "Wanting to remain, so far as we are concerned, on the former grounds, we cannot accept Jevons's formula" except for a special case (176, 1889, p. 190; § 163, pp. 252–53). Likewise, Walras believed that he had refuted the English theory of interest by following the same procedure – that is, not by proving that it is illogical but by finding that it conflicted with the situation in the real economy. "It is very certain that, in the reality of things, a given individual can have two or three" roles (123, 1877, p. 228; § 184, p. 280), and a realistic approach must recognize that the roles are distinct. The English theory, he argued, fails to distinguish between the entrepreneur and the capitalist, economic agents who are clearly different in reality. Some entrepreneurs borrow the funds that they need for their firms and therefore are obviously not capitalists, and there are many capitalists who are not entrepreneurs (123, 1877, p. 359; § 366, p. 645). Walras clearly thought that he had not failed to make the distinction, that the entrepreneur in *his* model was correctly based on the entrepreneur found in the real economy.[2] J. S. Mill's theory that concluded that the system

---

[2] It has been contended by one analyst that "the entrepreneur is not a real personage in [Walras's] epistemology." He is "an ideal type and an analytical principle ... " (Lendjel 1997, pp. 78–79). That provides another example of the consequences of neglecting

of tenant farmership was beneficial appears wrong in the light of casual empirical data, and, Walras wrote, "some facts, more precise and more general, will make it apparent how the results of experience agree with the conclusions of [my] theory" (254, in 249.XII, p. 557). Walras judged the conclusions of applied economic science by the same criterion. For example, contemporary applied science "reduces to the formula '*Do nothing!*' Unfortunately that conception receives from reality every day, under our very eyes, overwhelming refutations" (169, 1886, in 205, 1898, p. 124).

What more clear and eloquent statements of the interplay of theoretical economics and empirical evidence through time could Walras have made than in the following passages?

Industry must furnish facts to economics; economics must accept these facts, generalize them, draw laws from them, and from these laws, deduce rules for the use of industry. In a time when occupations become more and more specialized, when the division of labor is unlimited, it is more essential than ever to maintain the communication of practice to theory, of theory to practice, of facts to principles, of principles to facts; otherwise intelligence and consciousness go to one side, material activity to another, and the harmonious unity of human destiny which alone creates its energy finds itself, for the time being, disrupted. Industrialists are assuredly wrong to be disdainful of economic teachings: by being so, they condemn themselves to routine activities and light-heartedly place themselves in unfavorable conditions of production and of sales; but the economists are even more ill-advised to not fix their eyes attentively on industrial developments: it is by so doing that they narrow the scope of science instead of enlarging it, going backwards when it is necessary to go forwards, closing themselves up in antiquated systems and, neglecting the great problems, linger on questions of detail which they often do not even succeed in understanding (21, 1861, in 249.VII, pp. 151–52).

Similarly, "We have seen how modern industry had served the theory of value in exchange by introducing into reality [dans la réalité des choses] all the kinds of social wealth, and in constraining science, in a way, to recognize, to enumerate, to describe those kinds successively; how modern industry had served the theory of property in the same way . . . " (21, 1861, in 249.VII, p. 149).

When Walras wrote about the facts that industry must furnish to economics and "the influence of industry on economic theory" (ibid., p. 137), it is evident he was referring to ordinary industrial facts, not to abstractions, concepts, or "essences." The same is true of his remarks

the link between ideal types in Walras's economic model and the economy of his day. It is true that the entrepreneur in the model is an ideal type, but it has the quality of ideality – abstractness and generality – precisely because Walras abstracted it from a real type, namely real entrepreneurs.

about industrial practice as the basis of theory, and the application of accounting procedures to agricultural production:

We have here a striking example of the manner in which theory and practice should aid one another; for it is certain that industrial practices, expressed by accounting methods, can successfully serve to establish the theory of production; and it is equally certain that that theory, once it is established, can serve no less felicitously to express agricultural practices by means of accounting methods (123, 1877, p. 238; § 194, p. 293).

Walras was certainly not glimpsing a metaphysical relation between economic theory and industrial reality.

II. Applications of economic theory

Rationale of applications

Walras realized that applications of pure economic theory to normative or applied matters may involve considerations drawn from psychology, sociology, political science, and other studies (Chapters 2, 4). It might be thought that applications therefore do not test his basic economic model but rather a wider, policy-oriented construction; or it might be thought that there is a difference between testing hypotheses and testing the basic model. Walras did not agree with those views. He thought that if applications showed that a wider economic model is true, then they showed that its pure theoretical core – the basic model – is also true, and he thought that tests of its hypotheses are tests of it.

Walras believed that economic theory can be applied to practical problems – that, indeed, it "is a prerequisite for any economic and social applications" (239, 1874, *1*, p. 443; and see 205, 1898, p. 454). Rejecting archrationalism, therefore, Walras recognized that theory has to be realistic in order to reveal the aspects of the economy that are susceptible to manipulation by policies, and to explain the functioning of the economy so that policies could be designed that could modify it. Theorizing about land use, for example, must satisfy "both reason and experience." To achieve that, land use must be studied closely to ascertain its real characteristics; if these are supposed "arbitrarily, without relation to reality, the resulting science is pointless, without any possible application" (249.XI, p. 362). One can construct a science for its own sake, Walras noted, and make no practical use of it, "But one will see that these truths of pure economic theory provide the solutions to the most important, strongly debated and least clear problems of applied and social economics" (106, 1874, p. 32; § 30, pp. 53–54).

Social economics

Acting upon his methodological conviction, Walras used his positive economic theory as a basis for policies to achieve his notion of social and economic justice. He introduced a normative scheme in the field of argumentation, utopian speculation, and prescription that he called social economics (194, 1896). Policies should be based on sound theory. For example, so long as economists are content purely and simply to proclaim laissez-faire, laissez-passer as a sacrosanct dogma, their attacks on the socialists are no better founded than the opinionated proclamations of the socialists themselves (114, 1875, in 249.VII, p. 303). Walras observed that in order to have a basis for preferring one type of market structure rather than another and to devise sound economic policies, or simply "out of scientific curiosity," "it would be necessary to study the natural and necessary effects of the various different possible forms of organization of society" (123, 1877, p. 369; § 371, p. 656).

Walras believed that the policies he recommended would establish the proper functions of the individual and of the state, and solve the "social problem," namely the problem of the poverty of the working class (see Jaffé 1980, p. 532, n. 10; and Jaffé 1983, p. 347, n. 10). The policies included the purchase of all land by the state, state ownership of natural monopolies, laws to ensure the continued existence of freely competitive markets, a respect for individual ownership of non-land property and private income, and the abolition of income taxes (194, 1896). Thus his recommendations constitute an extensive program of reformulation of economic institutions.[3]

Applied economics

Walras also wanted to improve the functioning of the real economy, which led him to applied economics, the third subject matter in his aforementioned well-known triad of economic studies. Applied economics is, he explained, an applied natural science dealing with the relationships between people, not as moral beings, but in their role as workers performing tasks and thus having relationships to things. It is

---

[3] Walras's opinions about a preferred society were strongly influenced by the philosophical outlook of the scholars of his century, which was naturally in turn influenced by the ideas of previous scholars. His father's notions about natural law, derived from Hugo Grotius and Samuel von Pufendorf (Jaffé 1977, p. 29, and Jaffé 1983, p. 103), led Léon to believe that there are inherently true principles of economic justice that spring necessarily from the nature of things and of economic interrelationships. He adopted Etienne Vacherot's opinion that taxation is unjust and Victor Cousin's belief that differing socioeconomic interests can be reconciled.

concerned with material well-being and expediency. In the majority of his economic writings – approximately 60 percent (Chapters 6, 8) – Walras used economic theory to explain the workings of the economy, to discover features of the economy upon which policies can operate to solve empirical problems, and to predict the results of parametric and structural changes. Applied economics seeks "the most favorable conditions for *agriculture, industry, commerce*, and *credit*, or *the theory of the production of wealth*" (74, 1867, column 115, in 194, 1896, p. 30). It "enunciates the rules of usefulness" (205, 1898, p. 453) and "prescribes the rules of conduct" (141, August 1879, p. 246) to achieve economic efficiency. For example, maximizing the output of the economic system increases material well-being; applied economics is concerned with how to achieve that outcome.

Economic theory can and should be the scientific basis of policies. Walras deplored, in the work of contemporary economists, "the divorce, more and more marked, between economic theory and concrete reality" (220, 1910, p. 1, column 4, in 239.VII, p. 516). Developing and applying pure economic theory is the way to arrive at practical answers to economic problems (141, July 1879, pp. 15–22).[4] For example, because it is not self-evident, according to Walras, that the consequences of free competition are the most desirable for society, one of the purposes of pure theory is to furnish the analytical means for applied economics to inquire into whether free competition promotes the general welfare. Applied economics is thereby enabled to study the effects of free competition in agriculture, industry, trade and credit (114, 1875, in 249.VII, p. 301). It is because of the lack of a clear distinction between pure theory and applied theory and the lack of a rigorous analysis of the

---

[4] Peter de Gijsel (1989) notes Walras's assertions that his general equilibrium theory provided the positive analytical basis necessary for his policy formulations, which justified in Walras's mind the term "scientific socialism" as a description of his approach to remedying the ills of society. Roger Koppl (1995) believes that Walras paradoxically thought that his general equilibrium model was both positive and normative, although Koppl was unable to point to any statement of Walras's to that effect. Koppl tries to support his thesis by taking the indirect route of maintaining that a resolution of the paradox that he alleges exists is made possible by an understanding of the ideas of Etienne Vacherot, who argued in favor of the reconciliation or synthesis of seemingly contradictory doctrines. Koppl contends that Walras, influenced by that notion, effectuated a synthesis of positive and normative ideas in his *Eléments*. Using a special definition that makes "normative ideas" hardly distinguishable from "positive ideas," Koppl maintains that Walras considered all sciences to be such a synthesis, which directly contradicts what Walras wrote many times (Chapter 1). Nevertheless, as is true of other writers and ultimately setting aside his own thesis, Koppl regards Walras's general equilibrium model as a positive foundation, dealing with what *is*, for his explicitly normative conceptions of states of affairs that did not exist but that he thought *should* exist.

principle of free competition that political economy was mired, according to Walras, in so unsatisfactory a state. It is obvious, Walras remarked, that applied mechanics, for example, cannot be undertaken without a prior development of pure mechanics, but it has not always been as clearly seen that the practical fields of knowledge "such as natural law, agricultural, industrial, commercial, and financial economics, are preceded and governed by an entire group of pure sciences, namely metaphysical and humanistic philosophy, human physiology and psychology, history, criticism, pure economic theory" (ibid., pp. 15–16). Thus "applied economics and social economics, which dominate politics and business, are themselves dominated by pure economic theory, philosophy, and historical studies" (ibid., p. 17). It "is necessary to know the natural properties of social wealth. We cannot command value in exchange, as is true of gravity, except by obeying them. From this follows the necessity of constructing pure economic theory" just as applied mechanics necessitates pure mechanics (239, 1874, *1*, p. 443; and see 198, 1897 in 205, 1898, p. 271). In regard to the social and economic order – the organization of industry and property – Walras noted that it could be altered. To do so, however, a theoretical analysis of the real economic situation must be undertaken. Only in that way can theory be of use in the development of applied science, which is necessary for the wise guidance of actual practice (ibid.; 141, July 1879, pp. 15–17). It follows that economic theory must itself be sound, and to achieve that condition, Walras followed other nineteenth-century scholars – like J. S. Mill, John Herschel, and Auguste Comte – in believing that it was necessary to apply scientific methods to it.

As other examples of real problems that need to be studied with the aid of realistic theory, Walras considered whether mines, railroads, and the emission of bank notes should be in private hands (ibid., pp. 18–20). Similarly, he examined the use of a commodity money in the real economy, asking whether it is a good idea to have a unique or a double monetary standard. That cannot be known without answering "a prior question of pure science," thereby learning the effects of the two types of standard (ibid., p. 18). In that connection, Walras illustrated the differences between economic theory, applied economics, and practice in this way:

– How does the double use of a commodity as a commodity properly speaking and as a medium of exchange as money contribute to the total value of that commodity? That is a question of economic theory. *– Is it appropriate to have two monetary metals or only one? And, in the latter case, should it be gold or silver?* That is a question of applied economics. Finally, *in a given country, at a given time, where there is the double monetary standard of gold and silver, if silver is demonetized,*

what will be the probable influence of that policy on prices? That is a question of practical economic policy (114 1875; 249.VII, p. 305).

It must be admitted that in this particular example, what Walras called applied economics and what he called practical economic policy appear to be virtually the same type of approach, one of predicting the results of the adoption of a policy.

The usefulness or expediency of economic policies does not establish their justice or injustice (106, 1874, p. 16; § 15, p. 38; 1898, p. 458), as Walras showed with an example: If "commodities are sold at high prices to the rich and cheaply to the poor . . . there will be a great increase in effective utility," which would be expedient. Normative considerations, however, reveal that the goal to strive for is not simply maximum economic welfare, but "the maximum material well-being *compatible with justice*. The fact that you may be hungrier than me does not confer upon you, in and of itself, the right to eat my dinner" (239, 1885, *2*, p. 50).

Nevertheless, the objective of both expedient and just policies is to change the real situation in accordance with goals, and that takes time and sustained effort. Walras expressed that obvious matter in the philosophical terminology of which he was fond. He also, confusingly, used the word "theory" in a few passages to mean "a normative scheme." For example, he wrote that in the realm of applied social science and practice, "It is an essential point of my doctrine that no economic and social theory can be put immediately and completely into practice, and that true, certain and definitive progress always consists in a slow and patient routing of reality towards the ideal" (239, 1902, *3*, p. 201). This is the case because economic life takes place and has certain well-entrenched features that develop prior to and hence independently of policies to reform the economy. "Money is minted; railroads are constructed; mines are exploited; bank notes are issued; wealth is distributed among individuals; the state is supported by the income tax. In such conditions, the facts arise outside of principles and are contrary to them; practice is unlinked with and even contradictory to theory." If policymakers come to believe that those features should be modified to achieve various social goals, "Then, later, it is necessary to align the facts with the principles, to make practice conform to theory" (141, July 1879, p. 28); that is, conform to the normative scheme. As is true of many others, these passages provide more examples of instances in which what Walras meant by "the facts," in this case minting money, constructing railroads, exploiting mines, and so forth, are not intellectual constructions – indeed, are not anything other than features of the real economy.

Walras would have been happy, he said, to see questions of normative and applied economics examined in a journal "consecrated to *practical questions*" (239, 1902, *3*, p. 202). Institutions, such as the property system, should be established not only "rationally" but "experimentally" (ibid.). He wanted ideal*istic* tendencies to be tempered by a recognition of what is pragmatically feasible, and practical policies, which introduce a normative goal, to be based on sound positive theory:

> We people of the Latin race are reproached for being to an excessive degree theoreticians and idealists; and that reproach is well-founded: our revolution, our socialism proves that. Let us therefore become practical and realistic. I would very much like that to happen, basing our practical policies on a serious theory and leading our reality toward a high ideal of justice and material well-being (ibid.).

III. Applications and evaluation of mathematics in economics

Justification

Whatever reservations Auguste Walras may have had about the use of mathematics in economics, his declaration that "economic theory is a mathematical science" (Auguste Walras 1831, p. 278), and that knowledgeable persons "rightly expect to see it one day ranked among the mathematical sciences" (ibid., p. 284), was the aspect of his ideas on the subject that caught Léon's attention and that became firmly rooted in his mind. He therefore developed the method of using mathematics to describe and analyze some of the features of his general equilibrium model and to formulate and examine many real economic problems – and did so without formal training in economic modeling, without having taken more than a few mathematics courses, and lacking the company of other similarly inclined economists. That method was one of his major legacies. He was its principal proponent in the nineteenth century and was directly responsible for it being used by his immediate successors and indirectly responsible for its use by mainstream economic modelers down to the present day. He expressed his belief that he was bequeathing the mathematical method and a positive body of scientific work to future generations of economists.[5] "I have not," he wrote, "the least doubt about the future of my method and even of my doctrine, but I know that success of this sort does not become clearly apparent until after the death of the author" (239, 1904, *3*, pp. 250–51).

---

[5] He was not suggesting, as he had done very early in his career (239, 1859, *1*, 35–39), that subsequent generations should subscribe to and refine his scheme for a just society.

Walras thought that the opponents of mathematical economics do not have a defensible case. To support their belief that the application of mathematics to scientific subject matter is in general impossible, they would have to show that Descartes, Newton, Fourrier, Ampère, Horn, Clausius, Zeuner, and Tyndall were wrong in applying mathematics to mechanics, astronomy, physics, and chemistry. That, Walras commented ironically, would be difficult to prove (114, 1875, in 249.VII, p. 325). Alternatively, if they grant that those applications were possible and were made, then to sustain their position against the use of mathematics in economics they would have to show that economics is not a science of quantitative relations between variables. He contended they cannot do that because economics unequivocally is, to a large degree, such a science (ibid.), "a new branch of mathematics" (ibid., p. 291). It is, he stated or implied, a physico-mathematical discipline (106, 1874, p. 31; § 30, p. 53; 114, 1875, in 249.VII, p. 304). He later came to believe that economics is a psychico-mathematical discipline (205, 1898, p. 464), then reverted to contending that it is "entirely like the physico-mathematic sciences" (210, 1900, p. 29; § 30, p. 52), and then still later stated once more that it is a psychico-mathematical discipline (219, 1909, p. 2). He was careful to qualify that by saying, "Of course, it is understood that we are not speaking of doing violence to the nature of things by treating qualitative facts at all costs as quantitative facts" (114, 1875, in 249.VII, p. 329). Moreover, "Without a doubt, and even in that essentially abstract, general and theoretical activity of analysis, there is a point at which mathematical operations should be halted in recognition of the multiplicity and diversity of individual preferences and idiosyncrasies, and of the fact of free will" (103, 1874, p. 102).

In Walras's opinion, inasmuch as many aspects of reality can be symbolized mathematically and inasmuch as mathematics enables more precise deductions than does the literary method, the rational or deductive phase of theorizing attains its clearest and most efficient form in mathematical formulations (ibid., pp. 328–29). "The employment of the language, of the method, of mathematical truths has no goal but that of pursuing a more rigorous, more penetrating analysis than that which is permitted by ordinary language" and thus obtains more exact conclusions (239, 1874, *1*, p. 371). He argued that "the legitimacy and the utility of the use of mathematics in economics has been principally demonstrated to me by its results, that is to say by the complete clarification of theory [formerly] wholly obscure: for example, the theory of value" (239, 1897, *1*, p. 742). Walras predicted that the algebraic and geometric representation of fundamental economic variables was destined to transform political economy just as it had transformed mechanics (114, 1875, in 249.VII, pp. 310–11), and he continued until the end of his life to insist upon the parallels of economic theory with the mathematical formulations of pure mechanics (219, 1909; 249.XI, annex III, pp. 625–50).

One objection to mathematical economics, Walras noted, is that the general public cannot understand it. Nevertheless, the use of mathematics in economics should not be abandoned on that account, because it is essential for the theoretical study of many questions and because of the important practical respects in which it is useful (114, 1875, in 249.VII, p. 328). Walras exhorted his readers to rejoice in the mathematization of the parts of economics that can appropriately be treated in that way (114, 1875, in 249.VII, p. 329). Even though the mathematical theorems and proofs of pure economic theory may be incomprehensible to the general public, the conclusions of economic research, he contended, can be expressed in a literary fashion. Non-economists then have no difficulty in understanding them and hence in understanding the bases of policy recommendations (ibid).

Theoretical uses of mathematics

Walras examined the ways in which mathematics can be used in economic theory. In that case, the coefficients are not numeric and the mathematical functions are general (ibid., pp. 311–12). In economic theory, the "formulas not only can but must remain indeterminate, in order to remain at the same time general and permanent" (ibid., p. 306). The mathematics has "no goal other than the scientific determination of the relations between magnitudes: quantity, utility and marginal utility, demand, supply, the price of commodities" (239, 1875, *1*, p. 435), and the initial endowments of commodities and resources (114, 1875, in 249.VII, pp. 304, 312–13). Inasmuch as cardinally non-measurable variables can be treated mathematically, Walras's list, it will be noted, included utility and marginal utility. His model deals with those variables and with supply and demand, establishing, he claimed, both the existence of equilibrium and its stability:

The formulation of pure economic theory in the mathematical form is an operation which essentially ought to consist in furnishing a system of equations based upon the double condition of the maximum satisfaction of wants and of the equality of supply and demand for services and products, and to show that the mechanism of free competition leads precisely to the solution by tatonnement of that system of equations . . . (239, 1889, 2, p. 365).

"The use of the mathematical language and method," he claimed, "enabled me thus not only to demonstrate the laws of the establishment of equilibrium prices, but also" to undertake logical experiments, namely, "to demonstrate the laws of the variation of those prices, and to analyze the fact of free competition and in so doing to establish it as a principle" (123, 1877, pp. 365–66; § 370, p. 651). "Thanks to the concurrent use of the analytical formulation and of the geometric representation," he wrote, "we obtain both the idea and the image of the phenomenon of the determination of prices on the market in the case of the exchange of several commodities for each other; and, in achieving that, in my view, we at last possess the theory" (179, 1891, p. 8; appendix I, § 4, pp. 698–99).

Equations based on economic reality

Walras asserted that not only the verbal components of his model had real referents, but the symbols and relations in his equations did also. He was fully aware that mathematics can be used improperly, deluding the economic theoretician into thinking that he is achieving a more precise description of reality than is achieved with words, when in fact he is distorting it. That defect of economic modeling, Walras explained, results from using mathematical symbols and equations that do not have referents in "the economic phenomenon" (239, 1897, 2, p. 727) – the functioning of the real economy – a procedure that he vigorously opposed. He stated: "I believe it is essential" to focus on the real economy and by "proceeding in that way to avoid that great stumbling block to the application of mathematics to economics, namely of putting something other than economic reality into the equations" (ibid., p. 728). His model, he declared, has

...the advantage of noting mathematically all the phases of the economic phenomenon: prices cried at random – demands at these prices – supplies corresponding to demands – raising or lowering of prices in accordance with the excess of quantity demanded over quantity supplied or of quantity supplied over quantity demanded, and, finally, exchange at equilibrium prices (ibid., pp. 727–28).

Continuing with that theme, he indicated that the equations and their associated theories or models are not the same thing:

I find one thing very striking. It is that the economists who are mediocre mathematicians, like Jevons, have produced very worthwhile theories, while the mathematicians who are not very good economists, like Edgeworth, Auspitz and Lieben, say many foolish things. From that, I conclude that it is essential to establish the foundations of economic theory very solidly before building mathematical constructions on the foundations that are called upon to support them (239, 1890, 2, p. 404).

What makes a theory "foolish," Walras was explaining, is its failure to be based on realistic foundations. It is ironic that, despite his methodological convictions and his efforts, successful in many respects, to develop a realistic, mature economic model, he did not build his equation system upon that foundation insofar as that system did not take account of the dynamics of the tatonnements in his model, as will be seen in Chapters 5 and 6.

Walras described himself as one of the economists who did not have a high degree of mathematical skill. Advanced mathematical analysis is necessary but, he confessed, "I am, for my part, not much at ease with it. I have studied treatises on the infinitesimal calculus and I can read works in which calculus is used, but, not having had much occasion to practice differentiation and integration, I am embarrassed at trying to use them myself" (239, 1892, 2, p. 510). That did not disturb him. He believed that, for an economist, the acquisition of mathematical proficiency is a matter of secondary importance, the knowledge of economic reality being primary. He complained that criticisms of his use of mathematics had been made by persons who had not read his work, and asserted that if they were to study it, they would see that his economic equations differed from his knowledge of the entities and functioning of the real economy, and that he wanted the equations to symbolize the latter. Anyone who reads his articles on money would recognize immediately, he wrote to Jean Cheysson, an engineer and economist, that, "I am as far as possible from engaging in what you call *purely mathematical abstractions and speculations*; that I am much more an economist than a mathematician; and that I have never had recourse to mathematics except to give *true expression to facts and to economic relationships* that are essentially quantitative, but *are always taken from observation or the most rigorously conducted experimentation*" (239, 1885, 2, p. 64; emphasis added to the last twelve words).

Walras emphasized again that the mathematical symbols and relations used in economic theories should correspond to real entities and relations. He called "upon experience for the notions of products and of productive services," and so forth, and then expressed "mathematically the quantities possessed" (114, 1875, in 249.VII, p. 314).

All these operations: choice of variables and of functions, adoption of notations that are both simple and expressive; the use, as Descartes said, of geometrical methods to "better consider particular relationships and to represent them more distinctly to the imagination and to the senses"; the use of algebraic methods to "retain them in the mind or to understand several of them at the same time"; employment of the method of deduction or of synthesis; these are difficult operations for the success of which the essential thing is not so much having some fairly elementary mathematical knowledge *but rather being in possession of economic data that are always carefully drawn from experience* (ibid., emphasis added).

The equations are not the model; they are the mathematical expression of some of its features; and the essential thing is to get the model right because mathematical expressions of an erroneous model are of no value. "I have," he wrote, "been able to develop all this theory, although very unaccomplished as a mathematician, in my capacity as a good economist, because the mathematical difficulties are insignificant and only the economic difficulties are serious" (239, 1897, *2*, p. 728).

Mathematics and applications

Exploring the limitations of mathematics in connection with establishing truth, Walras observed that it is possible to use mathematics in applied economics only because equations can have real referents. The equations could not otherwise have empirically derived numerical coefficients. Applications, however, are restricted by the nature of the subject matter (114, 1875, in 249.VII, p. 315). Regarding marginal utility functions, for example, it is impossible to replace theoretical ones with ones containing empirically derived numerical coefficients because utility is not quantitatively measurable (ibid.). The use of mathematics is also restricted with respect to measurable magnitudes by the limitations of the available statistical techniques and data. During Walras's lifetime, those limitations made it difficult to establish statistical demand and supply functions, but he speculated that improvements of methods and data would one day enable that to be done reasonably accurately (ibid.). Indeed, he remarked, there were many economic phenomena for which numerically specified functions could be established immediately for the purpose of practical applications. That was true regarding actuarial matters (ibid., p. 327). Likewise, such questions as the imposition of a tax or an import duty could be studied using empirical equations, thereby enabling the impact of those changes on various variables to be determined quantitatively (ibid., p. 317). To answer the third question posed above regarding the demonetization of silver, numerical calculations could be used in that case (ibid., pp. 306, 328). Such calculations would provide information that would enable the formulation of economic policies that have sound theoretical foundations (ibid., pp. 316–17). It may even transpire, he argued, that "the application of mathematics to economics will one day include the substitution, in certain given cases, of computations in place of the mechanism of the raising and lowering of prices on the market" (239, 1874, *1*, p. 374). In all those considerations, it is patently evident that Walras was asserting that his model had referents in the real economy. It could not otherwise have been applied to the functioning of real markets and especially not to the determination of prices by mathematical operations on empirical supply and demand functions.

Walras believed that, like geometrical figures, mathematical reasoning can be only approximately confirmed empirically. Emile Bouvier expressed Walras's view in this way: "To the objection that mathematical economists disagree among themselves regarding their own mathematical results, L. W. had conceded the point and rested his case on the observation that the question was never one of finding absolute truth, but of whether mathematics could help the economist arrive at a better approximation to it" (Jaffé summarizing Bouvier 1901, in 239, *3*, p. 183, n. 2).

Walras was also aware that the use of mathematics can be unproductive, adding nothing to economic knowledge. Employing mathematics for its own sake, he observed, results in sterile exercises. He remarked that "our pure mathematicians, who are nothing more than integrating machines, give me the impression of being constricted intellects" (239, 1901, *3*, p. 149). He believed that he had avoided that trap by linking mathematics and literary analysis, thereby creating a new and worthwhile mode of discourse. He wanted words to be used to describe the institutional, technological, procedural, and behavioral foundations of economic models, and mathematics to be used, where possible, to analyze economic interactions and deduce their outcomes. Economic theory and applied economics should be developed by "men with minds and a culture that are at the same time scientific and literary; for only then will they be subject to the true scientific method" (141, July 1879, p. 27). He praised that type of synthesis in the work of one of his correspondents: "By causing a mathematical theory of economics to be taught and thus restoring the intimate alliance of science with letters, you will perhaps save French intellectual creativity from decadence" (239, 1901, *3*, p. 149).

IV. Confirmation of hypotheses and conclusions by experience

In accordance with those considerations, Walras insisted that economic theories and models had to meet two tests. One is the test of reason – that is, to use sound thinking in forming inductions and assumptions and sound logic in deducing conclusions. The other is the test of realism. At every juncture, he turned to reality as the basis of his hypotheses

and as the criterion of the verisimilitude of his conclusions, and he criticized other economists' theories that he considered to be deficient in
those regards. Thus to Walras, reasoning had an empirical connection
not only at the stage of empirical verification but also at the level of
its foundations, inasmuch as it should be properly exercised on facts
to form inductions that correctly represent and generalize them. His
synthesis of the experiential and rational methods in economic theorizing, his applications of theory to real problems, his comparisons of the
assumptions and conclusions of his theories to reality, and his evaluation
of the theories of other economists by comparing them to the facts, all
reflect the realist side of his intellectual orientation. To emphasize the
truth of those remarks, it is worth recalling his words: Theories formulate the laws of "general *facts* or groups of *particular facts*" and use a
deductive structure of equations; and "it is in this way that the physico-
mathematical sciences" – which economic theory is "entirely like" (210,
1900, p. 29; § 30, p. 52) – "rationally formulate laws *that are confirmed
by experience*" (239, 1901, *3*, p. 162; emphasis added). Regarding a
conclusion of his theory about the results of free trade, Walras asserted:
"That rational indication is confirmed by experience" (197, 1895/1897,
in 205, 1898, p. 293), and declared that "observation and experience
confirm it" (205, 1898, 261). Similarly, "economic theory demonstrates
à priori and economic history confirms *à posteriori*" the effects of the
evolution of economies (ibid., p. 474). "In a progressive economy land
rent rises, a circumstance that is "demonstrated by reasoning and confirmed by experience" (218, 1909, in 249.VII, p. 513). Walras's theory
indicates that the price of land should rise, and the fact that it has done so
"furnishes us a striking experimental confirmation of our theory" (154,
1880/1881, in 194, 1896, p. 304; and in 249.XI, p. 233). According to his
theory, the true character of the land registry is exclusively fiscal and the
record shows that "history is a striking confirmation by experience of the
predictions of the theory" (102, 1873, in 194, 1896, p. 400). Regarding
"the fact that *the land tax is not a tax on income but a co-ownership
of land by the state* . . . we have constructed, in economic theory, an *a
priori* and rational proof of this fact; we add here that the *a posteriori* or
experimental proof is found in all the pages of history" (253, in 249.XII,
p. 371; and see 102, 1873, in 194, 1896, p. 407).

   We "do not have to fear," Walras reassured his readers, "that the
confirmations of experience are not joined to the indications of reason"
in the matter of the French monetary system (205, 1898, p. 110). With
respect to the volume of legal tender bank notes, "Experience agrees also
with reasoning regarding the necessity of having a mandatory circulation to avoid catastrophes" (254, in 249.XII, p. 647). "Science properly

speaking has fulfilled its proper function, in a country in which it is believed that good principles are the basis of fruitful applications and that there are no contradictions between theory and practice, when science has determined those principles. ... If the principles are not respected, there is only error, confusion, disorder; and that is what the history of the railroads would prove, in case of need, by way of confirmation ... " (205, 1898, p. 232). The liberty of the trade in cereals provides "an admirable experimental confirmation of the truths that economics establishes a priori" (254, in 249.XII, p. 598). Regarding the system of corporations and regulation of them, "The examination that we will undertake shortly of that system will add the confirmation of the experimental proof to the demonstration by reasoning that we are making here of the superiority of the system of liberty of work and trade" (ibid., p. 475). "Economic history is infinitely precious"; it furnishes economic theorists "either with points of departure" for theoretical formulations – the empirical bases of hypotheses – "or with empirical confirmations" of theories – empirical tests of their validity – once they have been developed (198, 1897, in 205, 1898, pp. 270–71). To test his ideas about financial speculation, Walras noted that "to finish [the study of it], it remains for us to take a look at the *facts* surrounding it in order to find, if possible, the *confirmation* of our ideas" (147, April 1880, p. 85; emphasis added). Regarding Jevons's theory of business cycles, "Posterior observations have not only confirmed the reality and the regularity of the phenomenon in question, but also established that they are not national but rather international or universal" (205, 1898, p. 135). "The mechanism of commercial credit institutions is of a degree of perfection so well demonstrated by science and so well confirmed by experience that there is no reason why it would not serve as an exact and durable model for industrial credit institutions" (70, 1867, pp. 1744–45). Emphasizing once more the importance of empirical confirmations of conclusions, Walras affirmed that "justice is confirmed by its concordance with material interests; rational material interests are confirmed by experience; and *until that confirmation is obtained, science is not definitively achieved*" (198, 1897 in 205, 1898, p. 270; emphasis added). Of course, it must always be remembered that, according to Walras, theories, which arrive by rational deduction at conclusions, have their bases in factual considerations.

V. Conclusion

Walras wanted to understand the behavior of the market system in the economy of his time. Consequently, his principal objective as an economist, during his mature phase of theoretical activity, was to construct a model of general equilibration and equilibrium whose elements were drawn, as he said, "scrupulously" from reality. He contended that using them enabled him, through a process of deduction, analysis, and empirical verification, to develop an abstract but accurate representation of the real economy of his day, and therefore one that reflected and predicted its outcomes. In Chapter 2 and in this chapter, an account has been given of the methods by which he thought he had achieved that objective.

Walras neatly summarized three aspects of a competitive economy and its study in the following way (114, 1875, in 249.VII, p. 298). There is "the fact of free competition as it exists in more or less imperfect conditions." That was his characterization of the ordinary facts of the real economy of his day, identified in Chapter 2 as the third step in his system of economic thought. Next, there is "the idea or the conception of absolute free competition as it could possibly exist, excluding any intervention of notions of utility or equity." That is his positive model, identified in Chapter 2 as the fourth step of his system of thought. It incorporates ideal economic types, free of the frictions and imperfectly competitive elements that characterize some real markets. It is also the modern conception of perfect competition. Lastly, there is "the principle of free competition as it should be constituted so as to satisfy those notions." That is his applied and normative economics, concerned respectively with utility and equity.[6] It is also exemplified in the work of Vilfredo Pareto and A. C. Pigou, and in the new welfare economics and the work of many modern economists.

The adherents of the archrationalism and idealism theses have concentrated on Walras's fourth step, his "conception of absolute free competition," developing a special interpretation of it that neglects the third step, and thus neglects the connection that Walras insisted it had with competition in the real economy. Jaffé, in his later years, concentrated on the normative aspect and did not believe that Walras had worked on the third and fourth steps. The truth is that Walras paid attention to all the aspects of the study of competition and made clear the ways in which he thought they were different and were related, declaring that "there is too much simplification. All these operations are necessary. Consider free competition as a fact, as a concept, and as an economic and ethical principle" (249.XIII, p. 560).

This chapter and the two preceding chapters have shown, among other things, first, that when Walras referred to economic facts he meant

---

[6] An excellent treatment of how Walras passed from one to another of these four concepts is given in Arena and Ragni 1994.

"real facts"; second, that the components of his model were intended by him to have referents in the real economy; and third, that according to Walras, again with respect specifically to economic propositions, the truth of an assertion is established by logically correct reasoning and by experience; in other words, that his philosophical and methodological system requires comparison of models to reality in order to verify or falsify them, on both the levels of assumption and conclusion. In the light of the unambiguous and abundant evidence presented in this book, contentions to the contrary seem very strange. If Walras's name were not invoked in connection with them, it would be impossible to believe they were written about him, so strongly do they contrast with the letter and the spirit of his work. Walras emphasized in his creative and mature intellectual phases that he was not an archrationalist in either principle or practice with respect to his own theorizing or his evaluations of it, or with respect to the criteria that he used to evaluate the work of others.

CHAPTER 4

Human nature

I. Introduction

Walras's treatment of the general characteristics of human nature was an application of his general philosophy and methodology to that aspect of reality. His treatment of human nature in relation to economic situations was an application of his *economic* philosophy and methodology to that specific aspect of reality. His ideas on both of these matters had many similarities with the ideas of scholars who preceded him, but he is more responsible than anyone else for a particular conception of human nature being imprinted indelibly on neoclassical economics and on the vast majority of all modern economic models. It is interesting, therefore, to study his ideas about human nature in general, and to examine how he arrived at his conception of an economic agent and his justification for it.

Walras's ideas about human nature have been studied by a number of writers,[1] but there are some respects in which our knowledge of and understanding of his ideas can be deepened, and this chapter undertakes to do that. The numerous aspects of Walras's ideas considered here include his recognition that human nature has many different facets, his difficulties in dealing with the notion of free will, his identification of real and ideal types regarding human nature, the contrast between his knowledge of human nature and his concept of economic man, and his use of the latter in a series of steps of reasonings about the functioning of his economic model.

Among other benefits, the results of the inquiry contribute to a fuller comprehension of Walras's approach to modeling economic behavior and aid in an assessment of the scientific value of his models. He has been thought to have had virtually the same ideas about consumer demand and exchange as did W. S. Jevons and Carl Menger.[2] The study presented

---

[1] See especially Dockès 1996 and the references given in that book.

[2] J. A. Schumpeter accepted that judgment in a general way but observed that "the agreement of his results with those of Menger and Jevons is as striking as the differences in their starting points and methods" (Schumpeter 1910 in 1951, p. 77). Friedrich

here of Walras's ideas on human nature provides the basis for judging his similarity or otherwise to those economists on those subjects. The study also enables a comparison of his concept of human nature with the ideas on that topic of other neoclassical economists, such as H.-H. Gossen and Alfred Marshall, and with the ideas of modern economists.

Fortunately, it is not necessary to infer Walras's conception of human nature, because he discussed the subject explicitly and at length. He did so at the beginning of his career as an economist in his work "Recherche de l'idéal social" (1867–1868, in 90, 1868), an important source for this chapter. He evidently retained the ideas expressed there, inasmuch as he republished it (194, 1896, pp. 25–147) without changes when he was 62 years old. Another important source is his "Esquisse d'une doctrine économique et sociale" (205, 1898, pp. 449–95), where the ideas he expressed on the subject were unquestionably his mature ones, because he wrote that text during the period 1893–1895. Three other important sources for this chapter are his *Eléments d'économie politique pure*, his correspondence (239), and some of his jottings.[3]

II. Aspects of human nature

Distinction between animal and human nature

Like the other parts of his economics, Walras's treatment of human nature was the outcome of his observations and vicarious knowledge of both external and internal aspects of human behavior (203, 1898, p. 1). According to him, to understand human nature it is necessary first of all to recognize the distinction between the characteristics shared by humans and animals, and those reserved exclusively for the former. That enables the identification of specifically human behavior. Walras noted that a line

Hayek repeated that observation, writing that "their work is so clearly distinct in general character and background that the most interesting problem is really how so different routes should have led to such similar results" (Hayek 1934, p. 394). William Jaffé (1976), however, developed the argument that the ideas of the three economists on demand were significantly different, thus initiating a durable controversy. The controversy is reviewed and reconsidered in a recent article by Philippe Fontaine (1998). From a different point of view, Roger Koppl (1995) arrived at the conclusion that Walras should not be considered a typical neoclassical economist.

[3] Most of Walras's jottings cited in this chapter are undated. I originally used typescripts and photocopies of Aline Walras's transcriptions of them, identifying them by the collection in which they are kept. Since I wrote this chapter, however, Walras's jottings were published in 249.XIII, pp. 509–622. Inasmuch as the originals are not readily accessible, I have located most of the cited jottings in that source and have referred to it. If I was unable to find the jotting there, I have cited the collection in which it is found; for example, the Fonds Lyon. The collections are described in the introduction to the published version (ibid., pp. 503–8).

of demarcation exists between the physical characteristics of humans on the one hand and their intellectual and ethical characteristics on the other. On one side of that line, a person's physiological and psychological life is on a purely animal plane; on the other, it is distinctively human (90, 1868, in 194, 1896, p. 101). It was not with the physical but with the moral aspects of human nature that Walras was concerned.

Multiple facets

In any specific respect, Walras of course recognized that there are differences in behavior in different societies and times, that humans in all societies reveal themselves as such in a variety of ways. As everyone does, he knew that there are differences in the personality of different individuals, that different persons experience different sentiments, passions, outlooks, and attitudes and are motivated in contrasting ways (249.XIII, pp. 519–66, passim). He noted "the sadness of humans and their melancholy" (ibid., 1862, p. 589). Some people are "perfectly snobbish" (ibid., p. 546; and see p. 515). Some try to increase their wealth and improve their social position at the expense of others, and some are obsequious if they find that being so is useful for obtaining favors (ibid., p. 524). Some persons use force and treachery to appropriate wealth (106, 1874, p. 40; § 35, p. 62). There is flattery, intrigue (249.XIII, p. 515; and see p. 521, no. 19), trickery, honesty, vanity, pride (ibid., p. 616), and avarice (ibid. p. 529). There is "unintelligence and ill-will. Stupidity and jealousy" (ibid., p. 614). Some individuals "are incapable, lazy, spendthrift"; others "are skilled, hardworking, and economical" (205, 1898, p. 473). There is intolerance, mediocrity, and foolishness (249.XIII, pp. 614, 620). Some individuals undertake the necessary tasks of life, while others depend upon the generosity of others (205, 1898, p. 473). "The world is full of people" who do their duty "too much or too little" (jotting, Fonds Lyon). Walras also observed that humans are "artistic, scholarly, moral, and industrious, and therefore sociable and progressive" (194, 1896, p. 190).

Malleability

Did Walras believe that human nature is "eternal and everywhere identical" (Dockès 1996, p. 31)? He did not, if by that is meant that a person's nature is fixed, innate, and independent of his personal history, society, and culture. Human nature, he believed, is malleable. Behavior changes in a given society over time and differs from one society to another according to the conditions that form the personalities of its members

(194, 1896, pp. 189). There are "differences relative to place and time" (ibid.). Sadness and melancholy, for example, are not intrinsic features of human nature but rather "an effect of the iniquity of social laws, that, plunging some into insurmountable poverty and others into excessive wealth, do not furnish anyone the conditions of true happiness, which actually consist of material and moral well-being achieved by work" (249.XIII, 1862, p. 589).

According to Walras (writing in an era when instinct psychology was widely accepted), a part of human behavior is influenced by instincts. That, he believed, is the part dominated by the sensations and sentiments that have their source in self-love (194, 1896, p. 107)). He also emphasized, however, that humans are not ruled exclusively by instincts. They experience "a class of *disinterested emotions* unknown to animals" and can therefore behave in ways that are not selfish (ibid.). In explaining some of the respects in which human behavior transcends instinctive behavior, Walras evidenced again his belief that human nature is malleable. His basic position was that human nature can be modified because it has the non-instinctive components and because humans can control their instincts. For example, religion can change human nature. "No one," he declared, "should believe that I misjudge the role of Christian spiritualism in human behavior. I understand that role, and I admire it. The spiritual aspect of behavior has raised persons and citizens above the animal level by the struggle of the free and responsible personality against instinct; the moral human being has created himself through Christianity" (249.XIII, p. 588). Through the "renovation of society we will arrive at the renovation of individuals" (ibid., p. 581). Scientific knowledge and reasoning can also change human characteristics: "astronomy . . . has done the most to draw up mankind from its cowering state afflicted by fear, and to raise it to the rank of a being that understands and dominates the physical universe" (ibid., p. 577).

Walras noted that the abilities and accomplishments of human beings are not the automatic results of innate characteristics. The fact that a person may be born with a high degree of intelligence, for example, does not guarantee that he or she will create important scientific or artistic works, which rather are the products of effort and study (jotting, Fonds Lyon). The full development of human faculties comes about "through the effort that is required by the difficulty of making a living, and in consequence, through hardship" (249.XIII, 1862, p. 589). In this context, Walras added the curious remark that "nature gives us intelligence," but "we give ourselves talent and genius by an effort of free will" (ibid., p. 583), an idea that is contrary to the truth. Talents and genius are inherent characteristics of people who are so endowed, and, in recognition of that fact, Walras elsewhere mentioned "talent...received...as an inborn characteristic and not acquired through energy, persistence and work" (249.XIII, 1862, p. 589).

Essential unity in behavior

Despite his remarks about the diversity of the aspects of human nature, Walras thought that "underlying the differences relative to places and times, there is an essential unity" in human nature (194, 1896, p. 189). He must have encountered that idea in many of his readings. David Hume, for example, asserted:

It is universally acknowledged that there is a great uniformity among the actions of men, in all nations and ages, and that human nature remains still the same, in its principles and operations. The same motives always produce the same actions: The same events follow from the same causes (Hume 1777/1975, p. 83).[4]

Walras thus shared to a significant degree the belief of the writers of the Scottish Enlightenment "that certain human traits were timeless and uniform and thus could be anticipated or predicted" (Redman 1997, p. 186). Walras had reference to general propensities, drawing his knowledge of them from his experiences and his readings. He concentrated his attention on the behavior of people in Western societies but also mentioned others. He declared that in "all times and in all places" – among which he referred to Africa, India, and Tahiti as well as European countries – "you will find humans associated with humans and will find them more or less likely to be concerned with that which is beautiful, that which is true, that which is useful, and that which is good" (194, 1896, p. 121). They "have economic and ethical relationships with each other" (ibid., p. 126). "All these statements are truths of observation and of experience. It is observation that teaches us that humans are never found in a solitary state, without relationships with other humans" (253, in 249.XII, p. 120).

According to Walras, other universal aspects of human nature are an esthetic sense, revealed in artistic efforts and poetry, and a capacity for reasoning and understanding, expressed in language and science. Yet another is the exercise of free will in the development of the institutional arrangements of private property, the family, and government (205, 1898, pp. 457–58; 194, 1896, pp. 101–2, 104). Walras discussed at length

---

[4] If Walras studied the books he owned, he must have become familiar with Hume's philosophical notions. They are discussed in the works of many philosophers and numerous histories of philosophical thought that were in his library.

the facets of civilization – science, art, industry, and so on – that are expressions of human nature. "All aspects of human physiology and of human psychology," he declared, are manifested in an aptitude for the division of labor and in the personality of humans (194, 1896, p. 128). The "essential unity" is therefore manifested in the exercise of human faculties in art, science, industry, and ethics (ibid., p. 189).

These considerations reveal the dual character of Walras's account of human nature. He remarked upon the existence of differences in personalities, genetically transmitted characteristics, and motivations. Those are differences in the nature of humans. It turns out, therefore, that he was making a distinction between human nature as manifested in a certain class of traits he believed to be shared by all humans, and other traits of human nature that vary from one person to another. To say that some of those behavioral traits are part of human nature and others are not would not be tenable, so Walras wisely chose to say that there is an essential unity in human nature, rather than to make the stronger categorical statement that it is everywhere and in all epochs identical. That allowed him to maintain that there are similarities on the general level of motivations, interests, and preoccupations, and also differences in the nature of individuals in specific respects.

III. Free will

Walras took several positions on the question of whether or not free will is an aspect of human nature. One such position was that humans have freedom of choice. "Pure materialism," he asserted, "is absurd. Not to see in the life of humanity, in the work of society, in history, and in progress anything more than an exercise of physical functions and a series of physiological facts" is an error (249.XIII, p. 591). "Determinism is metaphysics, not science" (ibid., p. 599). He contended that "there is in the universe a force which knows itself and possesses itself: that is human willpower" (106, 1874, p. 18; § 16, p. 39). In their economic activities, humans "do not obey the blind inevitability of natural forces, but rather the motivations of human will" (194, 1896, p. 124). It "is free to be exercised in the realm of production as in the realm of the distribution of social wealth" (106, 1874, p. 38; § 34, p. 61) and "is aware of being exercised and can act in several ways" (106, 1874, p. 19; § 17, p. 40). It is "a force that is clairvoyant and free" (106, 1874, p. 18; § 17, p. 39; and see 194, 1896, p. 141).[5]

---

[5] See Potier 1994, pp. 227, 229, 235, 249, 267–68, where that idea of Walras's is emphasized.

Nevertheless, Walras took another position on the issue of free will. He thought that the universe obeys the laws of cause and effect, and accordingly he subscribed to the opinion that free will is "the inevitable *illusion* of a being who is at the same time a product and an agent [an effect and a cause], and who is aware of himself as a cause, but not as an effect" (Edmond Schérer quoted in 205, 1898, p. 451; the words in brackets were inserted by Walras; emphasis added). Accepting that notion with some reservations (249.XIII, pp. 562, 569), Walras described the "experimental fact of the 'illusion of human liberty' as a fact of unique importance" (205, 1898, p. 452). In one instance, seemingly not wishing to commit himself definitively on the matter, he identified "the fact of freedom or of its illusion" as one that is indispensable for understanding the sciences (ibid., p. 453).

That did not solve the problem for Walras. He continued to be troubled by what he believed to be the seeming incompatibility of the ideas of free will versus determinism, and returned to the subject numerous times, arguing in favor of one or the other of the views or trying to reconcile them.

First, he proclaimed that free will is not an empirical fact but a notion, a creation of the mind intended to describe and explain the apparent liberty of choice. In this respect, Walras was influenced by Etienne Vacherot's view that experience is a synthesis of objective and subjective elements, and accepted Vacherot's opinion that a subjective element is contributed not only by the mind but also by "the imagination" (205, 1898, p. 460). Accordingly, Walras contended in a youthful jotting, persons with free will, "moral person[s], workers dividing tasks" are "representations of the imagination" rather than unintellectualized phenomena that are objectively present in the universe ((249.XIII, p. 557)). Repeating his phrase about the imagination, he wrote that the concept of humanity possessing free will is one of the "ideal types, perfect, absolute, precisely because they are creations of the mind, not without a relation to reality, but without a correlative object in reality. *Perfect circle, free will*, two representations of the imagination" (ibid.).[6]

Second, in his phase of intellectual maturity as a theoretician, Walras adopted the contrary point of view that the existence of free will is an empirical fact: "I have always taken the fact of the free will of mankind as fact of experience" – not a concept or an essence – "without giving it either more metaphysical value or less scientific value than the facts of

---

[6] Walras used the words "representations of the imagination" again in connection with science toward the end of his life, but in that instance made no mention of free will (213, 1905, p. 1, column 1; and in 237, 1962, p. 61; see Chapter 1).

vegetation and of life" (194, 1896, p. VI; and see 249.XIII, p. 562). He praised the ancient Greeks for recognizing "the facts of experience in all their diversity, and among them, the fact of the free will of humanity . . ." (ibid.).

Those two approaches of Walras's to the problem were uncharacteristically ill-assorted. Not much weight can be given to the youthful jotting just quoted, however, inasmuch as Walras maintained categorically in writings published in his subsequent mature intellectual period, as has just been seen, that free will is "a fact of experience." He used the word "fact" in the modern sense as something found in objective reality. Furthermore, the jotting is unconvincing as an argument that free will is a creation of the imagination, because it also concedes that free will does have a relation to reality, which implies that it has a referent in reality. Moreover, Walras affirmed even in his earliest writings that the bases of scientific constructions are ideal types drawn from real types identified as existing in reality, and are not creations of the imagination (see Chapter 1). Indeed, Walras argued in his mature intellectual period that perfect circles have referents in reality, namely the imperfect real circles from which they are abstracted as idealizations (106, 1874, p. 32; § 30, p. 53). Perhaps in his youthful note he simply wanted to say that the representations of the imagination are categories that are used to identify and classify objective facts, that is, used to erect a scientific edifice.

Third, Walras claimed that the problem of free will versus determinism is resolved by identifying a crucial difference between the physical world and the moral activities of humanity. The former, he maintained, is subject to the law of causality. Things and natural forces "do not have the awareness of acting, and even less than that are they able to act otherwise than they do" (106, 1874, p. 19; § 17, p. 40). They are "blind and inevitable" (106, 1874, p. 19; § 17, p. 39). Humans, on the other hand, are not subject to that law. A human "is a free and reasonable being, that is to say a *moral person*, as distinct from all the other beings which, not having reason nor being free, are only *things*" (194, 1896, p. 33). What is a moral person? Walras defined him and her by their characteristics: "a superior awareness that links a human to his destiny, a superior intelligence which enables him to understand it, free will which permits him to involve himself with it; these are the three faculties which cause a human to be a moral person" (194, 1896, p. 141). Walras added that

. . . in the presence of the action of causes which impinge upon him and the reactions which his faculties call into being, a human raises himself progressively above that action and that reaction by the awareness of his unity, of his identity. He dominates his emotions and his ideas and he dominates his decisions. He is aware of himself, he knows himself and he possesses himself. He has an objective and he pursues it, but he does so knowing that he has an objective and that his obligation is to pursue it (ibid., p. 115).

Walras repeated that it is for those reasons that "we say that a human being achieves a clairvoyant and free destiny, and that he is not a thing but a person" (ibid.). A problematic aspect of Walras's third line of reasoning is that it reduces to an assertion that free will exists without disposing of the notion that the phenomena that make up the universe, among which are human beings, obey causal laws.

Fourth, Walras decided to preserve the notions of both free will and determinism with respect to human behavior. His effort to do this took the form of maintaining that although free will exists, it is not operative with respect to all human behavior, that perhaps no more than 30 or 40 percent of human decisions are free. Humans are able to tread only a narrow path of volitional liberty, a path bounded on each side by strictly causally determined phenomena. "Perhaps that force," the free will of a human being, "does not know itself and does not possess itself as much as it supposes" (106, 1874, pp. 18–19; § 17, p. 39). The freedom of choice of humans is subject to "a superior determining principle. Their liberty consists only of making their conduct conform to the demands of the principle that reflective thought enables them to identify" (194, 1896, p. 124; 1990, p. 110). That is the principle of utility or of concern for material well being (ibid.).

Walras then repeated, with some variations of language (ibid.), that whereas things and natural forces are subject to the law of causality, the decisions of humans are not completely subject to it. The problem that he struggled with was not vanquished by that argument, however. It is a supposition, not a scientific demonstration. If a person's decisions are responses to events and situations, either exterior to or within the person, and are influenced by personal, social, and biological history as recorded by the individual's physiological structure, and if the decisions are the manifestations on the conscious plane of a series of chemical and electrical cellular processes that produce neurological changes and cerebral effects, why would the decisions not all be strictly determined consequences; that is, the consequences of causes?

Economists used to wrestle with the question of the relation of free will specifically to economic science, and they produced different answers. In Karl Marx's opinion, for example, free will makes it impossible to achieve a scientific study of much of social and economic behavior. Sound methodology, he believed, restricts the domain of science to the study of mechanical causation and hence makes it impossible to explain free teleological behavior scientifically (Marx 1858, p. 46; 1867, *1*, p. 10). J. S. Mill, on the other hand, thought that human behavior is causally determined, so he had no difficulty in coming to the conclusion that social science, including economic science, is possible (Mill 1981–1991, *8*, pp. 835, 898).

In the light of those considerations, Walras finally adopted a position about reality that, he believed, resolved apparent contradictions between the ideas of the autonomy of human will and determinism so far as concerns economic science. Like Marx, he regarded pure economic theory as applying to the domain of causal relationships, and the domain of free will as lying outside of economic science, but he also believed that a great deal of social and economic behavior is amenable to scientific analysis. Walras therefore disagreed with critics who declared that his economic models were invalidated by the operation of free will. They argue that *"one of the factors in the determination of the price in free competition is human free will, whose decisions cannot be predicted mathematically"* (176, 1889, p. 252; § 222, p. 334). The critics were incompetent, he contended, to pronounce on that matter: "What a type! The cretin of the Institute [of France], the gentleman with the rosette of the Legion of Honor, accumulating fourteen academic appointments, knowing beyond that neither a word of psychology nor of mathematics, who says to you that '*human free will does not allow itself to be put into an equation*'" (249.XIII, p. 533).

Walras responded that the criticism is based on an incomprehension of what he did with mathematics in his model. It may be, he conceded, that the force of free will, which is exercised regarding various matters prior to the formation of prices, cannot be expressed mathematically. He granted that "mathematical operations" in economic theorization can be pursued only up to the point at which they "should be halted in recognition of . . . the fact of free will" (103, 1874, p. 10). Mathematical economists are not upset by that circumstance, however, because it does not invalidate what they are doing (114, 1875, in 249.VII, p. 326). Walras pointed out that "we have never tried to predict mathematically the decisions made by humans with free will; we have tried only to express their effects mathematically" (103, 1874, p. 10).

Free will, Walras contended, may act in the economic decisions made during pre-market behavior, but once those decisions have been made, market processes unfold independently of them and hence independently of the agents' will. In an economic model, he argued, it is irrelevant whether preferences are expressions of free will or deterministic forces. He explained that economists put the question of free will aside, in order to investigate the economic effects of preferences described by utility curves. People may have no influence over the utility derived from commodities, or limitless influence, or a limited degree of influence, but, he contended, those possibilities have no relevance for his scientific method "because that method only comes into play exactly at the moment when the influence of individual preferences, idiosyncrasies, and free will ceases" (114, 1875, in 249.VII, p. 326). No matter how they are determined, he pointed out, the utility curves and hence the demand curves are what they are. When they change, the effect is that prices change. That is discovered and explained by economic theory, which is therefore

... focused completely, not on human free will, but on its effects. Does the degree of freedom of will prevent its effects from obeying natural and mathematical laws? Not at all. Whether or not you are free to throw a stone, something that you are certainly not free to do is to cause that stone, once you have thrown it, to fall otherwise than in obedience to the law of gravity. It is just the same in that regard for value as for gravity (ibid.).

Furthermore, Walras pointed out, the existence of free will would not render predictions of behavior impossible. Aggregates of people follow some uniform and hence statistically predictable patterns of behavior, and individual behavior is predictable with respect to such uniformities of it as exist. Those who oppose mathematical economics in the belief that it is incompatible with free will are inconsistent because they use birth-rate and suicide-rate curves and make predictions based upon them, even though free will appears to operate in individuals' decisions about having children and committing suicide:

It is argued that the transformation of social science into a mathematical science transforms human beings into machines, etc., etc. ... But truly, it is we ourselves who thus learn, not without astonishment, that birth and death rates completely escape the influence of human will. We believe we are at least as free to marry or not, to prolong our lives by a healthy life style or abbreviate them by bad habits, as to exist without houses, without furniture, without clothing and without food. We believe we are even free to commit suicide, if we so choose, which does not prevent statistics from indicating that there is, on average, only a certain percentage of us who will use the liberty to do so. This reveals clearly enough that even the effects of the free will of humanity are not entirely outside of the purview of prediction and calculation (114, 1875, in 249.VII, p. 327; and see 249.XIII, pp. 534–35).

Walras finally abandoned further consideration of the problem and thereby arrived at a position that is scientifically superior to that of either Marx or Mill. He did not want to base his economics on the notion of the existence or the absence of free will. He declared that whether free will is accepted as a fact or considered to be an illusion is of little importance. "Scientifically," he maintained, to say that free will is the illusion of a being who is aware of himself as a cause but not as an effect, "is to say nothing" (205, 1898, p. 451). Natural scientists are not constrained in their research by the question of free will and engineers build dams without thinking about it. Economists and politicians are not intellectually paralyzed by the problem of its existence or nonexistence and can similarly design models and apply economic policies without worrying about whether or not their activities are the uncontrollable unfoldings of a determinate universe (ibid.). In accordance with the principle that economic science does not need to consider the questions raised by the issue of free will or the illusion of it, and should not do so, Walras declared that "for my part, I used the needs [utility] curves as facts [on which I base my reasoning] without investigating the influences that the nature of things and human will could respectively have" (239, 1874, *1*, p. 435). "All social science can be based on the fact of moral personality without knowing what free will is" (249.XIII, p. 557). Economic science, Walras correctly concluded, can exist regarding much of economic behavior whether there is free will or not.

IV. Society and the individual

Critique of individualism

Walras's idea of a human being shows that he did not belong without reservation to the school of individualist thought, if by that school is meant the belief that the characteristics of society are without exception the products of the motives and ideas of individuals. He asked: "Is it thus also in the individual, or in the group, that the force is found which at times throws nations off the path of progress and into political reactions, and at times precipitates them into war and revolutions?" He answered: "We believe it is only by making abstractions that it is possible to conceive of either the individual without the state or of the state without the individual, and that humans in society, individuals in the state, is the only reality" (194, 1896, p. 91). Concrete unintellectualized reality in those regards is constituted of individuals who are integral parts of society. Humans function in a societal context, so the influence of the latter upon individuals must be taken into account.

The lives of all persons in a society are made interdependent by the activities they undertake to satisfy their needs (106, 1874, p. 36; § 32, p. 59). The division of labor implies the interdependence of workers, and indeed the aptitude of humans to undertake work in that way enables them to earn their livelihood and is therefore the condition that makes possible their existence (ibid.). Likewise, with respect to private property, a subject to which he devoted much thought, Walras maintained that the appropriation of things "depends, it is well understood, not upon each of us in particular, but on all of us in general. It is a fact of human life that has its origin not in the individual will of each person, but in the collective activity of the entire society" (106, 1874, p. 39; § 35, p. 62). Walras's account of the history of appropriation does not, however, represent it as originally being a consequence of "collective activity" and certainly not of cooperation. The division of wealth at the beginning of civilization, he contended, was determined by "force, trickery and chance, although nevertheless not totally divorced from rational conditions. The bravest, the most vigorous, the most able, the most fortunate have obtained the largest part, and the others have had the rest, that is to say nothing or very little" (106, 1874, p. 40; § 35, p. 62). Even so, Walras believed that the manner in which objects are appropriated depends on the stage of development of the society and that societies have evolved in the direction of a distribution of wealth based upon principle (ibid.).

Human nature as the basis of social phenomena

Despite those considerations, Walras subscribed to methodological individualism insofar as he thought that some aspects of human nature are not formed by social interactions but are instead fundamental in the sense that they give rise to various forms of social behavior. That view is a foundation for Walras's opinion that humans manifest the same general features in all societies at all times. There are, he contended, three inherent characteristics of human nature that influence the character of society: "*human will, need,* and *wants*" (205, 1898, p. 451). These are "the causes of the moral and economic activity of humanity" (ibid.), and as such must be studied in order to understand it.

Contending again that aspects of human nature influence society rather than the other way around, Walras sought in the former what he called the principle of the distinction between art and science, and the principle of the distinction between industry and custom (194, 1896, p. 128). Likewise, he believed it is "in the study of human nature that we must look for the principle" of the concordance between art and science, and the concordance between industry and custom (ibid.). Additionally, human nature determines certain important features of history: "There will be antagonism or harmony in human destiny depending upon whether there is antagonism or harmony within human nature" (ibid.). To decide which of those alternatives exist,

Let us therefore return to the question of human nature: to physiological nature, that is to say to the aptitude for the division of labor, and to psychological nature, that is to say to amicable and beautiful love, to understanding and to reason, to free will; and let us see whether all these faculties exist like metal springs functioning in opposing ways, or like the well-organized parts of a smoothly operating mechanism (ibid.).

The bases of human nature and therefore of human behavior are to be found in the nature of the human brain and body.

V. Deductions about society from an understanding of the general features of human nature

A theme found in the writings of many scholars is that the characteristics of society and hence social science can be deduced from an understanding of human nature. For example, the eighteenth-century Scottish scholars, including Adam Smith, "proposed to arrive at a knowledge of human nature by using empirical methods in the spirit of Bacon and Newton. ... With certain principles of human nature established, predictable outcomes, conduct, and behavior could be deduced as typical or natural" (Redman 1997, p. 114). Through "a study of human nature, philosophers could identify key customs and institutions on which to build a science of man" (ibid., p. 113). It has been seen in Chapter 1 that J. S. Mill also believed that there are invariable laws of human nature, and that discovering them made possible a science of society. He had the Newtonian goal of formulating "secondary laws of a science of society derivable from the simplest primary laws of human nature" (ibid., p. 325): "The conclusions of theory cannot be trusted," he asserted, "unless confirmed by observation; nor those of observation, unless they can be affiliated to theory, by *deducing them from the laws of human nature*, and from a close analysis of the circumstances of the particular situation" (Mill 1981–1991, 8, p. 874; emphasis added).

Walras was squarely in that tradition. He believed that inasmuch as there are aspects of human nature that shape the development of society, it is possible to deduce the characteristics of society from the characteristics of human nature. Therefore, to establish the principal features of the structure and functioning of society and the economy, he argued, the first thing that has to be done is to construct an accurate definition of a human being (194, 1896, p. 122); in other words, to achieve an understanding of human nature. The way to do that is to use empirical research methods to examine real human behavior and then to abstract the definition from reality: "Thus, to develop the economic or moral theory of society in general, and to develop it in an a priori and rational fashion, it is first necessary to obtain the definition of a human by abstraction from experience" (194, 1896, p. 189). "The human, not the human-animal, but the human properly speaking who is the theatre of humanistic facts, has been revealed to us both by external or physiological experience and by internal or psychological experience" (82, 1868, column 214, in 194, 1896, p. 119). Walras accordingly observed human behavior in the real world, identified the important features that were common to different individuals, and discarded their idiosyncratic features. "We are therefore," he declared, "in possession of a definition of the ideal human extracted with care from a correct analysis of the real human" (194, 1896, p. 122). Comparing his definition with the reality from which he drew it, he asked regarding it: "Do we depart from observation and experience?" and he answered: "No" (ibid., p. 189). He asserted again that he had arrived at the definition "without leaving the realm of either observation or experience, raising ourselves above reality only by scientific abstraction" (ibid., p. 190). Walras declared that "from that experimental definition, it remains only to deduce, by a series of analytic judgments, all the theorems of social science" (ibid., p. 122), "experimental" meaning "founded on empirical information."

Walras also joined the long list of his predecessors who appealed to natural law and the moral character of humans in order to reach sound scientific knowledge. As John Locke viewed this matter:

Natural law, the will of God, is a body of rules conforming to rational nature. In order to show that rules of moral obligation could be derived from nature (i.e., human nature), ethics had to be demonstrable. And the demonstrability of moral principles, thought Locke, is analogous to the demonstrability of mathematical principles: while in mathematics reasoning starts with properties of figures and numbers, in ethics it begins with the idea of man as a rational creature. (Locke's view explained in Redman 1997, pp. 68–69; see Locke 1954, p. 54.)

In the same manner, Walras argued that scholars could "examine carefully the scientific results that can be reached by starting with the moral personality of humans, on the grounds of the good old natural law, if only they employ a little thought and reasoning" (194, 1896, p. VII).

It is not surprising that many of the results Walras deduced from his understanding of human nature were the ones he preferred. For example, he concluded that private property, an institution of which he approved, is one of its consequences. "The appropriation of scarce things or of social wealth is a humanistic and not a natural fact: it has its origin in the exercise of human will and activity, and not in the forces of nature" (106, 1874, p. 39; § 35, p. 61). The next step in Walras's reasoning is normative. On the basis of his principles of moral philosophy, he introduced the idea that human nature is a legitimizing condition. Its consequences are morally and thus legally right: "The *right* of private property is founded on the fact of the *personality of humans*" (194, 1896, p. 33; emphasis added to "right"). In other words, humans naturally want to own things, and a rule is meet and proper if it expresses a natural proclivity, at least in the case of property rights. It is a "natural law," Walras contended, that humans own themselves and therefore their faculties; "thus a human is also, by natural law, owner of the things that are part of social wealth for which he has exchanged his labor" (ibid.).

VI. *Homo œconomicus*

Human nature in Walras's economic models

Walras brought together the results of his inquiry thus far in this way: "From the analysis of human nature and of the classification of the social world that we have established . . . , it follows that there are two groups of facts and social relations: *economic facts and economic relations*, and *moral facts* and *moral relations*" (ibid., p. 123). The economic phenomena obey and express what is useful or what is of material interest and are studied by economics, a social science. The moral phenomena obey and express the idea of justice and are studied by a moral science, which is social science properly speaking (ibid.). Walras's treatment of human nature in relation to economic phenomena will now be examined.

What is the facet of human nature that Walras extracted "from a correct analysis of the real human" (194, 1896, p. 122) and featured in his economic model in a setting drawn from a correct analysis of the real economy? He identified it by distinguishing three aspects of human nature in this way:

In fact, the person who has needs, who takes part in the division of labor and who, in order to maximize satisfaction of his needs sells services and buys products in quantities such that their marginal utilities are the reciprocals of the potentially exchangeable quantities of services and of products, l'*homo œconomicus*, is also the person who is endowed with sympathy and an esthetic sense, with understanding and with reason, with a will that is conscious and free, l'*homo ethicus*; and they are both the person living in society, cultivating art, engaging in science, following customs and undertaking industrial activities, in short, l'*homo cœnonicus* (205, 1898, p. 450).

The abstraction that Walras featured in his economic model is *homo œconomicus*, just as has been done by most economists before and after him. His use of it does not mean that he abandoned consideration of economic reality. He argued that deductions from human nature cannot be made in isolation from a situation in which humans act, and he was not interested in speculating about the consequences of human nature in artificial situations. He therefore criticized the situations and the behavior of the economic actors in the models constructed by H.-H. Gossen and W. S. Jevons. They deduced the consequences of humans who desire a "maximum of pleasure with a minimum of trouble" (163, 1885, p. 77), just as Walras did, but their deductions were irrelevant because they did not place their economic actors in a setting drawn from the real economy. Perhaps, Walras commented, matters occur as those scholars describe on Robinson Crusoe's island or in an isolated or primitive society. Nevertheless, "they do not happen like that, I will not say in our actual social and economic state, but in the abstract and ideal social and economic state which is the one about which pure economics constructs theories" (163, 1885, p. 77). That statement provides a perfect example of the meaning in Walras's writings of the word "ideal" in connection with the nature of economic models. He was not referring in that quotation to the ideal society that he preferred and that he wanted to see created. He was alluding to the idealized situation that his economic models constitute as a result of their being constructed with humans and markets abstracted from the real economy via the identification of real types in it. In his criticism of Gossen and Jevons, he was asserting that, unlike them, he was not dealing with artificial situations in which the interactions of persons in a market economy are absent, but with the real economy on the abstract level of economic theory.

Walras's *homo œconomicus* mirrored the classical economists' concept. J. S. Mill, for example, asserted that political economy "does not treat of the whole of man's nature as modified by the social state, nor of the whole conduct of man in society" (Mill 1836/1844, p. 137) – what Walras called the conduct of *homo cœnonicus*. Mill went on to say that economic theory "is concerned with him solely as a being who desires to possess wealth, and who is capable of judging of the comparative efficacy of means for obtaining that end" – the motivation and sagacity of Walras's *homo œconomicus*. Therefore economic theory "predicts only such of the phenomena of the social state as take place in consequence of the pursuit of wealth" (ibid., pp. 137–38). Mill also remarked: "Not that any political economist was ever so absurd as to suppose that mankind are really thus constituted..." (Mill 1836/1844, p. 139). Similarly, as has been shown above, Walras knew, just as everyone knows, that humans have more goals than the simple acquisition of material wealth, that human nature has many other facets. Mankind "seeks not only what is useful and materially satisfying, he seeks also truth and beauty" and justice (194, 1896, pp. 100–101). Thus, as several writers have pointed out (see, for example, Dockès 1996, p. 80), it would be incorrect and indeed, to use Mill's word, absurd to suppose that Walras believed that humans act solely as calculating mechanisms whose only objective is the maximization of utility.

Economists before and after Walras have given the same justification for the abstraction *homo œconomicus*. Mill, for example, explained that it is used in economics "because this is the mode in which science must necessarily proceed" (Mill 1836/1844, p. 139). Otherwise no general propositions could be formulated and economic science could not exist (ibid., p. 146). Economic theory deals only with the aspects of behavior in which the acquisition of wealth is the *main* motive, so assuming that to be the *only* motive in those connections, "of all hypotheses equally simple, is the nearest to the truth" (ibid.). Walras justified the abstraction *homo œconomicus* in the same ways. First, he argued that it is a necessary simplification, one without which there could not be a science of economics, and he noted that the abstraction is of great importance not only for economic theory but for applied economics also: In the latter, "we assume theoretically that humans always know their interests and seek them; and practically it is necessary to act as though that were true: it is the best way of arriving at the truth" (jotting, Fonds Lyon). Second, he justified it on empirical grounds, namely that it captures an important part of reality: "Personal material interest remains an individual's great stimulus" (205, 1898, p. 485). "Personal interest should not be completely eliminated as a human motive under the pretext that 'personal interest *is not the only motive of human beings*'" (249.XIII, 1891, p. 611). On the contrary, like Mill, he contended that it is the motive of behavior in economic contexts.

Walras rejected the charge that his use of mathematics in connection with his model made it impossible for the model to take account of certain relevant aspects of human behavior. When Charles Renouvier, for example, wrote to him that "psychological, social, and other conditions are of such a character as to introduce a difference between the predictions of mathematical economics and the establishment of economic facts," and maintained that the difference is considerable (239, 1874, *1*, p. 396), Walras replied that sound theoretical method necessitates holding those conditions in temporary abeyance. He explained that in his *Eléments d'économie politique pure*, "exclusively a work of theoretical" economics, "I believed that I could abstract from the 'psychological, social, and other conditions' of which you speak, on the grounds that they are disturbances of secondary importance" (239, 1875, *1*, p. 435). Moreover, "The economists who take issue with the right to abstract from perturbing circumstances do themselves abstract from them every day: it is a scientific necessity" (249.XIII, p. 555). Walras declared that he wanted to recognize such conditions but that he would do so only in the proper context: "It is only, it seems to me, when it comes to the point of applying numerical calculations to accurate data that the place is reached at which account of those conditions should be taken" (239, 1875, *1*, p. 435). By psychological conditions in those passages he obviously meant aspects of human nature other than those of economic man, inasmuch as the motives and sensations of economic man are psychological characteristics.

VII. Steps in Walras's economic reasoning about preferences and market behavior

Walras followed a chain of reasoning that connects the characteristics of economic man with the functioning of markets, explaining "the links between the phenomena of utility, of effective demand and supply, and of the equilibrium price" (123, 1877, p. 388; § 387, p. 671). It is very clear that in his discussion of those links he was referring to real people and the real economy, and to abstractions that he drew from them. He used his perceptions of human nature and his knowledge of the structure and procedures of real markets to establish the links between the former and the functioning of the latter, and he made his account of those matters directly a central part of his model. In regard to those links, there is therefore no distinction between his account of reality, carried out on an abstract level, and his model.

The first step

On the basis of his observation of personal facts, Walras first asserted that real persons have desires for commodities, that the satisfaction of desires generates utility, and that there is a functional relation between each commodity and utility. He featured that condition in his model: "Each transactor, in our theory, can be assumed to establish his curves of utility or need in accordance with his preferences" (176, 1889, p. 252; § 222, p. 334). Different needs are felt to have greater or lesser intensity in comparison to others, which influences the real costs that economic agents are willing to incur to procure commodities that satisfy their wants (106, 1874, p. 78; § 72, p. 105). Following the principle that science should not consider the questions raised by free will or its illusion, Walras explained that "for my part, I took the utility curves as facts [used as my starting point][7] without investigating the influence that the nature of things and free will may respectively have" (239, 1874, *1*, p. 435).

---

[7] The words in brackets are William Jaffé's effort to transcribe nearly illegible writing.

The second step

Walras then identified four properties that he believed utility to have in reality, each of which are aspects of human nature:

A. He granted that utility is not a directly cardinally measurable magnitude (114, 1875, in 249.VII, p. 315), but he nevertheless believed that it is measurable and therefore that to treat it as such was not contrary to fact. He justified that treatment in three ways. First, he explained that "for a *mathematical expression* used for the purpose of undertaking a *theoretical study* it seems to me sufficient to suppose that utility is measurable in economics by defining it as the intensity of the last want satisfied, just as it is assumed that mass is measurable in mechanics by defining it as the 'number of molecules' or the 'quantity of matter' in a physical body" (239, 1901, *3*, pp. 171–72). Second, he argued that utility can be rendered measurable, "as is done for temperature, by expressing it by an arbitrary function that always increases with it (Pareto-Poincaré). That is advantageous for a *numerical evaluation* aimed at *practical applications*" (ibid., p. 171). Therefore, "I assume," he wrote, "that there exists a scale for the measurement of the intensity of needs or of intensive utility, true not only for similar units of a given type of wealth but also for different units of the various types of wealth" (106, 1874, p. 79; § 74, p. 107). Third, he believed that once having used that assumption, he was able to dispense with it. He wrote to Henri Poincaré that:

You have made me very happy by explaining to me with the authoritativeness that you command that I was justified in representing the satisfactions of individuals by functions, even arbitrary ones, but always increasing with the satisfactions represented, on the condition of eliminating those functions, as I effectively do, as soon as I deduced from them the curves of demand and of supply together with their essential properties (239, 1901, *3*, p. 167).

B. Walras then adopted the hypothesis that the utility that a consumer derives from each commodity is independent of the amount he consumes of others (123, 1877, p. 246; § 201, p. 302; 176, 1889, p. 99; § 75, p. 111). Walras recognized, however, that "utility is not always a function of a single variable" (239, 1901, *3*, p. 172), namely of each individual commodity separately. "I have studied and made notes regarding the utility of interdependent commodities (and also of commodities that are substitutes for each other)" (239, 1892, *2*, p. 498). Nevertheless, he defended his abstraction. "But I put all that aside with the goal of simplification" (ibid., p. 499). He regarded it as a simplification that captures an aspect of consumer preferences, and pointed out that the features of the total real situation that it left out could be taken into account in a more detailed representation of reality: "It is very simple to assume that [utility] is a function of the quantities consumed of several commodities. The utilities are then proportional to the partial derivatives of the total utility function with respect to the quantities consumed of the various commodities" (ibid.).

When Walras assumed independent utilities, he did not mean that, in reality and in his model, the maximum amount of money that a consumer will pay for, say, a bottle of wine, depends only on the utility of the wine: "It depends also in part on the utility to the consumer of bread, of meat, of clothes, of furniture; for according to whether that utility increases or decreases, the maximum sacrifice that will be made in exchange for wine will diminish or increase" (123, 1877, p. 387–88; § 387, p. 670).

In technical terms, the maximum pecuniary sacrifice that a consumer is disposed to make to obtain a unit of a product is a function not only of the utility of the product, but also of the utility of all the other products that are on the market, and is also a function of the consumer's financial resources (123, 1877, p. 388; § 387, p. 671).

C. Walras initially focused on the case of continuous utility functions, putting aside, also on the grounds of a desirable simplification, the fact that some preference functions are discontinuous (239, 1901, 3, p. 172). He then explained what happened in real pricing situations if demand functions are discontinuous, and made his model reflect that condition (106, 1874, pp. 61–62, 133–34; § 52, pp. 85–87, § 133, p. 203; 1889, pp. 106–9; §§ 83–84, pp. 121–25; 1889, p. 156 and Fig. 5; § 133, pp. 203–4).

D. Walras's fourth characterization of preferences was that humans experience decreasing marginal utility, which he believed was established, like his other ideas about preferences, by observation of real interior and exterior facts: "All these successive units have, for possessor (1), an intensity of utility that decreases from the first unit, which fills the most urgent need, until the last, after the consumption of which satiation occurs" (176, 1889, p. 98; § 74, p. 107).

The third step

Walras then contended that important aspects of real human behavior are that individuals seek "*the maximum satisfaction of needs, or, the maximum effective utility*" (106, 1874, pp. 86–87; § 80, p. 116) from all the commodities they consume, and that in many cases real economic agents calculate rationally and accurately how to do so. He therefore featured that behavior in his model and assumed that other aspects of human nature are not operative. Referring to his analysis of pure exchange in real competitive markets, for example, he observed that "taking as a point of departure the utility of each of the commodities to each of the transactors, expressed by curves that are decreasing functions of the quantity consumed, I demonstrated . . . *the condition of the maximum satisfaction of needs*" (163, 1885, p. 68). Walras also believed that consumers in the real economy think about their future needs and keep stocks of commodities and money "awaiting the due dates of their rental incomes, of their wages, of their interest receipts, or in order to buy new capital goods" (210, 1900, p. 300; § 273, p. 443). Producers similarly "await the payment for the products they have sold" (210, 1900, pp. 300–301; § 273, p. 445). He therefore assumed in his model that economic man also maximizes utility by being economical and prudent.

Nevertheless, Walras's letters and jottings make it clear that, like everyone else, he was perfectly aware that humans may be shortsighted in regard to providing for their future and may make errors, be indecisive, and be unskilled at formulating efficient plans for maximizing profit and utility. He knew, like everyone else, that humans can be irrational in the sense of behaving in a way that frustrates the achievement of their own consciously held goals, and that they may act without understanding or being aware of their true motives. Walras turned to reality to evaluate his theoretical considerations. He noted that, in the real economy, complications such as imperfect abilities, imperfect knowledge, and various frictions and obstacles often prevent the complete attainment of economic plans and therefore maximum utility. Real individuals are not absolutely selfish and thus do not strive to maximize utility to the fullest possible extent, and they are not perfectly discerning, perspicacious, and wise. "The preceding reasoning," about monopolies, "is based on the hypothesis, generally accepted regarding economic questions, that private interests are both selfish and clairvoyant. But that hypothesis, we have recognized, does not conform strictly to reality. For egoists, private interests are always both; but for clairvoyant persons, matters are different" (196, 1875/1897, in 205, 1898, p. 226). "With respect to assumptions, it is very certain that it is necessary to be careful when passing from abstract theory to reality. In reality, there are frictions in the economic mechanism; and, additionally, men are neither perfectly egoistic nor perfectly clairvoyant" (239, 1901, *3*, p. 167). Walras indicated that he introduced those considerations in his applied and social economics, thereby treating a fully realistic situation (ibid.).

VIII. The consequences of the characteristics of economic man

The fourth step

Walras's identification of those consequences constituted the next link in his account. Continuing to present it as a description of what happens in the real economy and as a component of his model, he explained how the utility curves and economic conditions give rise to the specific forms of an economic agent's demand and supply functions: "Each owner of a commodity who enters the market in order to exchange a certain quantity of that commodity for a certain quantity of some other commodity has his *trading desires*, either potential or effective, susceptible of rigorous determination" (106, 1874, p. 59; § 50, p. 82). Real consumers, professional traders, and wholesale and retail merchants, he explained, add to their holdings of each commodity, or sell out of their stocks of commodities, until they hold the batch of commodities that maximizes their utility. The buying and selling may be done as a reaction of the individual to quoted prices, but "these dispositions are no less real" "in the potential and non-effective state" with respect to prices that are possible but not quoted (106, 1874, p. 60; § 50, p. 83). A person in the real economy can "predict all the possible values of p_a, from zero to infinity, and consequently determine all the corresponding values of d_a, expressing them in some manner," and therefore has a demand function (ibid.). Walras's additional characterization of demand functions, also based on observation of real behavior, was that any individual's demand for a commodity is, in principle, a function of the prices of all commodities (106, 1874, p. 111; § 110, p. 161; 123, 1877, p. 247; § 201, pp. 303–4).[8]

The fifth step

Walras's objective was to demonstrate scientifically how prices and all other economic variables are mutually determined in freely competitive markets (Chapters 2 and 5). Once having derived individual demand

---

[8] John Creedy (1999) notes that Walras's individual demand curves are not partial equilibrium constructions. In consideration of the interrelationships of commodities and their prices, Walras identified "general equilibrium" demand and supply curves. Creedy notes that those curves are treated in the work of C. F. W. Launhardt, and that they have been independently rediscovered several times. Creedy examines their derivation and suggests, in the light of their potential central role in the analysis of exchange, that they could be very useful, particularly when employed with nonlinear mathematical methods.

functions, his next step was therefore to show the part he believed they play in the functioning of real competitive markets and hence in the functioning of the markets in his model: "Having thus successively shown: 1° how current or equilibrium prices are determined by the demand curves and 2° how the demand curves themselves result from the utility and the quantity of the commodities, I revealed the relationship which links utility and the quantity of commodities to their price on the market" (163, 1885, p. 69; 194, 1896, pp. 351–52). Walras was not asserting that he created the relationship in a model by making postulates; he was stating that it exists in reality and that he *revealed* it.

Putting together his observations of the motive of utility maximization, the demand functions, and the existence of markets and their pricing procedures, Walras explained that "the condition of maximum satisfaction [is] always the determining condition of the supply of services and the demand for products and for net income" (123, 1877, p. 285; 244, 1988, p. 369). The services and products acquired by consumers

… are those which interest people in their roles as individuals freely occupying themselves with achieving their preferred personal conditions; that is to say, with the satisfaction of needs that are diverse and unequal for each of them. Each consumer calculates the number of units of services or of products such as foods, clothing, furniture, etc., that he wishes to consume. He compares the intensity of the utility, not only of similar units of a given service or product, but of different units of diverse kinds of services or products. Once the prices are cried or posted, he sees how he should allocate his income among the diverse commodities in order to obtain the greatest possible total utility. And, finally, he demands those quantities of the various products or services (115, 1875, in 196, 1897; and in 205, 1898, p. 197).

That allocation of income among the various available commodities is done in such a manner that no redistribution of it would produce a greater total amount of satisfaction (106, 1874, pp. 86–87; § 80, p. 116; 176, p. 297; § 261, pp. 407, 409, 411). The consumer does that by buying the quantity of each commodity that makes the utility received from the expenditure of a unit (a marginal amount) of money on it equal for every commodity purchased.

Walras explained that similar considerations are true of the behavior related to saving and investing. For example, with respect to the production of new capital goods, economic agents seek "the maximum effective utility of new capital goods" (175, 1889; §§ 257–58). Walras thus found "in the desire to obtain the maximum satisfaction of needs, the determining cause of the offer of productive services and of the demand for products by landowners, workers and capitalists" (106, 1877, p. 231; 176, 1889, p. 214; § 188, p. 284; and see 106, 1877, p. 284; § 244,

p. 369). The supply and demand functions, Walras maintained, are part of the real economic mechanisms of exchange, production, consumption, saving, and investment. He integrated the functions into the totality of the interdependent activities that constitute his mature comprehensive economic model of general equilibrium.

IX. Conclusion

Many scholars before and after Walras have argued that scientific methods should be applied to the study of human nature, and believed that when that was accomplished, social science could be used for the scientific solution of policy questions. Walras subscribed fully to those ideas, but early in his career he did not think that the study of social science had produced beneficial effects similar to those that astronomy had brought about in humanity's ideas about its place in the universe. He did not, however, exclude the possibility of that happening: "Perhaps constructing social science as a positive science will not produce less progress in the ethical ideas of humanity" (249.XIII, p. 557). Scientific training, he argued, is essential for that purpose. He asked rhetorically:

Would we see so many socialists or economists limiting themselves to inadequate and vague definitions of mankind and of society if they had learned to borrow from observation and experience the rigorous and precise definitions of the different minerals, types of vegetation, or animals? And would we see them so powerless to draw the series of social relations from a definition of mankind and of society, if they knew how to extract the series of geometric properties from the definitions of forms? (141, July 1879, p. 26).

By 1891, Walras had become optimistic about those matters:

It is by proving rigorously the elementary theorems of geometry and algebra, and then the resulting theorems of the calculus and mechanics in order to apply them to experimental data, that the marvels of modern industry are achieved. Let us proceed in the same way in economics, and we shall doubtless succeed in acting upon the nature of things in the economic and social realm just as we have in the physical and industrial realm (179, 1891, p. 48; and in 192, 1896, appendix I, p. 471; 249.VIII, 1988, appendix I, § 4, p. 699).

In fact, Walras thought he had achieved that goal. The method of natural scientists, he asserted, is to discover the fundamental causes of a phenomenon and by analyzing them arrive at an understanding of it (194, 1896, p. VII). By applying that approach to the study of human nature, Walras believed he had achieved an understanding of it and had used that knowledge to construct the study of economic behavior as a positive science. "Experience, by the intermediation of the concrete and inductive sciences such as physiology, psychology, history, first provides it with the definition from which positive science extracts its fundamental formula by the exercise of reasoning, and then provides the data regarding the great problems to which positive science applies that formula by using the rational method" (194, 1896, p. VII). He thought that doing so made it possible to find scientific solutions of social and economic problems, and he was convinced that he had provided precisely those sorts of solutions.

Walras described human nature as having many facets – some admirable, some deplorable – as being malleable, as differing in detailed respects from one person to another, and as having the same general characteristics in all societies in all epochs. He believed on the basis of his observations that the feature of human nature that operates in economic situations is the objective of maximizing satisfaction. He therefore abstracted the economic motive from the complex reality of human behavior and showed how it actuates the behavior of economic agents. The desire to maximize utility, he asserted, has many consequences, such as efforts to obtain income and wealth and the expenditure of income on certain kinds and amounts of commodities. Walras visualized real economic agents as acting in a setting of real market institutions and procedures, and then deduced the consequences of their supply and demand desires in that setting. In his model, he presented consumers, service suppliers, and entrepreneurs as being clairvoyant and as acting in a rational fashion to consider all available information and their preferences in order to maximize their utility, as knowing how to do so, and as predicting correctly the utility that they will derive from commodities. He summarized his modeling of the action of human nature in economic situations in this way: "From the condition of maximum effective utility is deduced rationally the *demand* function or the *effective supply* function depending upon the *price* . . . ; and from the condition of equality of supply and demand is deduced rationally the *ruling* equilibrium *price*. Thus all of economic theory can be constructed as a mathematical science" (205, 1898, p. 467). He was nevertheless cognizant of the fact that real persons are not totally egoistic and that they make mistakes of economic judgment, and he contended that he took account of those facts in his writings on social and applied economics.

Walras's treatment of *homo œconomicus* and thus of preference functions and of the principle of utility maximization was enormously influential. This was because, instead of confining his analysis to the investigation of consumption and simple exchange, he went far beyond the work of other developers of utility principles by using the principles in connection with the behavior in multiple markets of a variety of participants undertaking different economic functions. Walras's conception of economic man was therefore a foundation of his model of economic behavior, and it is for the same reasons as those advanced by him that the abstraction *homo œconomicus* has been and continues to be employed by all general equilibrium theoreticians, albeit divested of some of his contentions about preference functions.

CHAPTER 5

Basic sub-models

I. Walras's approach

The purpose of this chapter is to identify and describe the fundamental components of Walras's mature comprehensive model of general equilibration and equilibrium.[1] To convey fully their character, it will, on occasion, be necessary to analyze these components critically. The way he developed the model is in sharp contrast to his approach in his written pledges sketch (Chapter 6), which is the same as the approach of the theorists who created the modern virtual general equilibrium models.[2] The latter is typified by the work of Gérard Debreu. In his *Theory of Value* (1959), for example, Debreu constructed an equation system on the basis of a number of axioms. He did not mean for them to describe the actual behavior of real economic agents acting in a real economy. His equations are not descriptive of economic behavior, as indicated by the fact that he made no mention of the institutions, technology, spatial features, regulations, pricing procedures and conventions, and other structural characteristics of markets. Such matters, he explained, are "irrelevant for the logical development of the theory" (ibid., p. 35).

Walras, on the other hand, devoted page after page to the description of what he perceived to be the behavior of real economic agents in the setting of real markets with specific characteristics, using the techniques of observation, abstraction, and generalization discussed in previous chapters of this book. He presented that description, and his explanations of how the phenomena are generated and their consequences, as his mature comprehensive model. Thus, as was true of his treatment of economic

---

[1] These topics are treated in much greater detail in Walker 1996, but there is novel content and manner of exposition in each section of this chapter.

[2] A virtual model is one in which no economic activities occur in disequilibrium, except the quotation of prices and the manifestation of the associated desired (*ex ante*) supply and demand quantities. Trade, hiring of resources, production, consumption, savings, and all other such economic activities occur only when the general equilibrium set of prices is found, and that is when the functioning of the model becomes non-virtual. Special cases of a virtual model are ones in which use is made of oral or written pledges to trade if the price is the equilibrium price.

man, it cannot be said that Walras first described the real economy in the
Eléments and then drew upon that description to construct his model.
It is evident from his explicit assertions and from the way he presented
the material in the book that he did not think there was any difference
between his account of what he perceived to be real economic phenomena and the content of his model. There were some exceptions to
that approach. One of them – one that was not only unrealistic but that
also distorted his account – was his modeling of behavior in regard to
new capital goods, as will be seen. Other exceptions were, he believed,
simplifications that identified phenomena found in reality but dispensed
with certain related aspects that he deemed unnecessary for a model that
concentrated on the broad outlines of economic behavior, and that he
asserted could be introduced as needed (Chapters 2 and 4).

Following the procedure adopted by Alfred Marshall, many theorists
concentrated upon the analysis of entities such as an industry, a market,
a consumer, and a firm on the assumption that they are analytically temporarily independent of the rest of the economy, thus analyzing particular
equilibrium situations. Walras asserted, in contrast, that it is necessary
to consider simultaneously the interaction of all parts of the economy
in order to understand the behavior that transpires in any part of it, and
for that reason he developed general equilibrium analysis. He was the
first economist to construct a complete general equilibrium model that
included the major aspects of an economic system. Doing so required
him to examine exchange, production, consumption, investment, savings, and money, and to explain many different economic processes that
take place within each of those aspects, and he did that in ways that
were replete with useful tools, concepts, and analyses. Thus he not only
expressed the belief that all economic phenomena are interrelated, which
had been done by many economists before him, he also constructed a
model that specified the interrelations of its parts and demonstrated the
implications of the interrelations in regard to the equilibrating process
and the equilibrium values of the variables.

Walras assumed that the type of structural features and important
aspects of the pricing process found in the nineteenth-century Paris
Bourse (Walker 2000b, 2001b) characterized all the markets in his
model. On any market day, brokers pledged orally, for their own account
or for clients, to buy or sell certain quantities of a security at whatever
price was currently quoted. They called out their pledges loudly, creating what he called "the tumult of the Bourse" (106, 1874, p. 51; § 42,
p. 72). ibid.). In Walras's words, the brokers bid the price up or down
(106, 1874, p. 50; § 42, p. 72) and they "give orders." Would-be buyers "demand at that price"; would-be sellers "offer to sell at that price"

(ibid). Although in the real Bourse, irrevocable disequilibrium transactions occurred within a market day, Walras assumed they did not. He then expressed the interrelatedness of real markets in a presentation in his model of the dependence of supply and demand quantities for each commodity upon the prices of all commodities, and analyzed the formation of prices and the associated volume of sales (176, 1889, 139–41, 147; § 116, pp. 171, 173; § 123, p. 187).

Turning to the question of flows of production and consumption, Walras described the connections that he identified in the real economy among the behavior of consumers, entrepreneurs, workers, capitalists, and landlords, explained the relationships between input and output markets, described how the flows of goods and services are adjusted in the real economy, and made all those features a part of his model. He asserted that there are, for each industry, market supply functions for productive services (123, 1877, p. 255; §§ 213, p. 319; 123, 1877, p. 287; § 245, p. 371), market demand functions for outputs (123, 1877, pp. 246–47; §§ 201–2, pp. 302–4; 123, 1877, p. 287; § 245, p. 371), and market supply functions for output (123, 1877, p. 254; §§ 210–11, pp. 315–17). He made those descriptions part of his model, and from them he deduced the resulting connections among the prices and rates of output of different commodities, analyzing the pricing, production, and acquisition of productive services, primary materials, consumer commodities, and capital goods. He gave an explanation of the role of money in the economy, analyzing loan markets, cash balances, metallic currency, and fiat money (176, 1889, pp. 375–424), and made his treatment of all those phenomena a part of his model (see Marget 1931, 1935; Kuenne 1961; Walker 1970; Howitt 1973; Morishima 1977; Hall 1983; Hilton 1995).

II. The entrepreneur

Economics of the firm

Walras appears to have developed independently the modern idea of a firm's production function. He defined the coefficients of production as the quantities of each of the kinds of productive services that are used in the production of one unit of the product of a firm (123, 1877, p. 248; § 203, pp. 304–5). In much of his modeling, he assumed that the coefficients are fixed (123, 1877, p. 249; § 204, p. 305), but he also considered the case of variable coefficients in relation to general equilibrium (123, 1877, p. 249; § 204, p. 305; 123, 1877, pp. 313–15; 176, 1889, pp. 319–21, 490–92; §§ 324–25, pp. 584–86, 721–22). Similarly, in connection with the production function, he analyzed the entrepreneur's disequilibrium experiments with different combinations of inputs to maximize profit (191, 1896, pp. 490–92), and made that analysis part of his mature model. Making additionally clear that he was referring to irrevocable disequilibrium behavior, Walras explained that the experimenting entrepreneur ("l'entrepreneur qui tâtonne") "adds or decreases each productive service according to whether the value of the increment of the service is less or greater than the value of the [additional] output that the increment generates" (191, 1896, pp. 490–91). He thereby finds the minimum average cost of production "by tatonnement" (239, 1895, 2, p. 651).[3] Walras derived the equation for a firm's average cost from the production function, the prices of the inputs, and, implicitly, the firm's budget (123, 1877, pp. 248–50, 253; §§ 203–5, pp. 305–6; § 209, p. 315). He expressed the firm's supply function for output verbally and mathematically.

The marginal productivity theory of distribution sprang from Walras's work on the economics of the firm (see foregoing citations and 123, 1877, pp. 314–15; §§ 325–26, pp. 586–87), as was evident in Vilfredo Pareto's (1896/1897, 2, pp. 84–90) and Enrico Barone's (1895, 1896) sophisticated treatments of that theory.

The entrepreneur's role

Walras contended that understanding the role of the entrepreneur in the real economy is "the key to all economic theory" (239, 1887, 2, p. 212) because of the essential functions the entrepreneur undertakes. Explaining his or her behavior and its consequences, Walras contended that the entrepreneur is instrumental in the processes by which the interrelationships of economic variables are established and by which the economy moves toward equilibrium. Walras maintained that one connection between real input and output markets is established by entrepreneurs through the circumstance that the average cost of production is altered on the input side of the market by their actions and the price charged on the output side is in part a consequence of the supply they bring to market. Another connection established by entrepreneurs between those markets is that they make payments to the owners of the economic resources that they purchase and hire, and those sums are spent by their recipients on consumer commodities and capital goods properly speaking produced by the entrepreneurs (123, 1877, pp. 228–30; §§ 185–86, pp. 281–82).

---

[3] The use of different amounts of services in disequilibrium cannot take place in a virtual model. This is remarked upon here, as in other connections in this book, because the contrary belief that the mature comprehensive model is virtual has been expressed (Rebeyrol 1999, pp. 134–35; 2002, pp. 541–49).

Walras incorporated all the foregoing perceptions of the functions of real entrepreneurs and the consequences of their activities into his mature comprehensive model.

One problem in Walras's formulation is that he gave different definitions of the entrepreneur. More than once, he portrayed the entrepreneur's function as exclusively that of buying labor, land services, capital-goods services, and raw and semi-finished goods, and selling the firm's product (239, 1887, 2, p. 212; 239, 1895, 2, p. 629). When Walras took that point of view, he asserted that controlling the productive process is a managerial function and that the Walrasian entrepreneur is not a manager. Taking "part in the capacity of a director or otherwise in the operation of the transformation of services into products" is not an entrepreneurial activity (239, 1887, 2, p. 212). In Francis A. Walker's work, Walras charged, "the *entrepreneur* is totally confused with the *director of the firm*" (249.XIII, p. 565).

On the other hand, in various passages Walras described the entrepreneur as having precisely the role of directing the transformation of services into products.[4] Controlling the productive process, he combines the factors to produce consumer commodities or capital goods (123, 1877, p. 233; § 189, pp. 287–88). Using productive services, he acts "in his role as entrepreneur to transform them into products" (123, 1877, p. 246; 176, 1889, p. 229; § 201, p. 302). The entrepreneur, "having applied the productive services to the primary materials," sells the products (123, 1877, p. 233; § 189, p. 287). That is not all. As has been seen in the previous section, Walras also specified that one of the entrepreneurial functions is choosing a technology for the productive process – for example, fixed or variable coefficients of production. In the latter case, another entrepreneurial activity is experimenting with the production function by changing the proportions of the inputs to maximize output for any given cost (191, 1896, pp. 490–92). Still other entrepreneurial functions are ordering that output be diminished or increased and directing the flow of resources toward profitable lines of production and out of unprofitable ones (123, 1877, p. 231; § 188, pp. 283–84).

Walras maintained that the entrepreneur receives payment *qua* entrepreneur only for the activities of purchasing and combining the factors of production and selling the output, and only in disequilibrium. He asserted that the remuneration of the entrepreneur is profit. Profits are made when average cost is less than price. The entrepreneur makes a loss in the reverse case (123, 1877, pp. 231–32; § 188, pp. 283–85). Walras

---

[4] Claude Mouchot (2000) has pointed out that Walras stated that combining inputs to produce an output is also an entrepreneurial function.

explained the accounting practices that entrepreneurs use in real firms to gauge various aspects of their condition, and in particular, their profitability (123, 1877, pp. 233–44; §§ 189–99, pp. 287–98). It is obvious that he had reference to the economy in which there are disequilibrium transactions and disequilibrium production because, apart from the fact that there are no profits or losses in a virtual purely competitive economy, Walras indicated that he was dealing with the activities of entrepreneurs and the operations of firms in the real economy. He then asserted that his model used that treatment as one of its foundations (123, 1877, p. 235; § 191, p. 289).

Walras identified the conditions that would obtain if equilibrium were actually reached, and, mixing in his wider conception of entrepreneurial functions, explained that entrepreneurs adjust production from one disequilibrium rate to another, thereby altering average cost and price until they become equal and profit per unit of output therefore falls to zero. When that occurs in all enterprises and supply equals demand in all markets, a state of equilibrium obtains (123, 1877, pp. 228–29, 230–32; § 189, pp. 194–97). It follows, Walras asserted, that in equilibrium the entrepreneur has no income qua entrepreneur (123, 1877, p. 232; § 188, p. 284), and receives remuneration only for whatever functions he performs as a worker, including in the latter category performers of managerial functions for which they receive a salary, or as a capitalist, or as a landlord. Thus in equilibrium he subsists on wages or interest or rent, or more than one of those types of income (ibid.).

That gives rise to a second problem in Walras's treatment of the entrepreneur. The activities of buying and selling that Walras called entrepreneurial are not confined to disequilibrium. The Walrasian entrepreneur buys productive services and sells output in equilibrium also, thus contributing to the value of the output by performing those functions. His remuneration as entrepreneur should therefore continue, but profits – from which that remuneration would have to be paid – are zero. The way out of this seeming theoretical predicament, which Walras did not explore because he did not realize that it existed, is in two parts (Walker 1996, p. 299). First, it should be recognized that there are routine activities of buying and selling in both disequilibrium and equilibrium, and that for performing them the entrepreneur, in his role as a managerial worker, receives a salary. Second, some of the buying and selling decisions in disequilibrium require that the successful entrepreneur have exceptional abilities of judgment and perspicacity, because in that situation there are risks, unforeseen events in the service markets, and problems in securing supplies. The payment to the entrepreneur for making those decisions wisely is a part of the profits of the firm, and the penalty for making bad decisions is a reduction or elimination of his bonuses and stock options and, in the worst case, dismissal. In equilibrium, the demanding and risky aspects of buying and selling disappear, so the part of the entrepreneur's profit that is paid for undertaking those aspects becomes zero.

Yet another problem in Walras's exposition is that he did not specify that the entrepreneur receives payment as entrepreneur for his other entrepreneurial functions – choosing the technologies used in the firm, experimenting with the proportions of the inputs, changing the flows of resources out of unprofitable firms and into profitable ones. That oversight is easily rectified. In Walras's model, those functions are undertaken only in disequilibrium. Walras properly identified their equilibrating character. His exposition can therefore reasonably be supplemented by recognizing that the Walrasian entrepreneur receives a part of the profits of the firm for undertaking them. In equilibrium, he does not perform those functions, so his remuneration for them in that state becomes zero.

Walras was right to have said that the word "entrepreneur" should be reserved for an economic agent who is, in his entrepreneurial capacity, not a worker, a capitalist, or a landowner. He should therefore have found some word other than "entrepreneur" for the person who undertakes the routine activities of buying, producing, and selling in both disequilibrium and equilibrium, and some word other than "profit" (bénéfice) for the payment for them. "Manager," "managerial labor," and "wages of management" would have been appropriate because those payments are "under the average cost curve," a necessary payment for the services of a worker in both disequilibrium and equilibrium.

The entrepreneur and losses

Walras should also have consistently recognized that losses are borne not by the entrepreneur as such but by the owners of the firm, and that the entrepreneur is ordinarily one of them. He should have incorporated that notion into his theory of the entrepreneur. Instead he either identified it as an empirical matter of which his theory did not take account, or insinuated it, all the while stating that the entrepreneur as such bears losses: "And, in effect, is it not evident that if he [the entrepreneur] obtains for his own productive service, *in his own business*, a price that is greater or lesser than the one he would obtain elsewhere, he gains a profit or suffers a loss from the difference between those prices?" (123, 1877, p. 232; § 188, p. 285; emphasis added).

Walras evinced the recognition in question in discussing cooperative associations, whose members, he pointed out, should be envisaged separately in their double role of shareholders who are, in his words, "entrepreneur-capitalists" and also either employees in production cooperatives or clients in consumer, credit, and real estate cooperatives. As "shareholders" – capitalists – they "either bear the losses, or preferably, obtain the profits of the firm in proportion to their ownership of the capital" (205, 1898, pp. 284–85). Thus in that passage, Walras specified that in the real economy, profits are the income of capitalists and losses are borne by them.

He then made it clear that an entrepreneur must, in practice, also have the role of being an owner of something of value, and that it is only in such a capacity that he can have a negative remuneration. It is necessary, Walras wrote,

... that the entrepreneur own something that he can give up in order to cover the losses of the firm. Theoretically, it can be assumed that the entrepreneurs are nothing other than entrepreneurs; practically, matters are rarely like that. It happens as an exception that an entrepreneur whose ability and honesty are perfectly well-known obtains credit without guarantees, or, as is said, with *personal* guarantees; but, in general, the entrepreneur must be at the same time landlord or capitalist, and moreover his land or his capital goods must be employed in his firm or in another. Then, it is understood that if his firm, instead of generating profits, generates losses, the losses will be covered by the liquidation of his possessions before the capitalists' equity is reduced (205, 1898, pp. 318–19).

Evidently, if the entrepreneur in Walras's model is to bear losses, then he must also, in the model, be a capitalist.

III. Tatonnement

Equilibrium and stability of the real economy

The basis of the dynamics of Walras's mature comprehensive model was his conception of the real economy as being a system in which the equilibrating processes are incremental, irrevocable, time-consuming adjustments of prices, of the volume of irrevocable disequilibrium transactions, and of irrevocable disequilibrium production, consumption, and savings. He understood that in the real economy, prices and quantities of goods and services exchanged, produced, and consumed are always disequilibrium magnitudes from the general equilibrium perspective (123, 1877, p. 310; § 322, pp. 579–80). The real economy is always "tending toward equilibrium without ever arriving there because it cannot move along a path toward it except by tatonnements, and before the tatonnements are finished they have to begin again, following new routes, all the parameters of the problem ... having changed" (123, 1877, p. 310; § 322, p. 580).

The parameters of the real economy, according to Walras, are utility functions and the quantities of goods and services possessed by the participants (106, p. 102; § 102, p. 146), and conditions such as technology, the amount of land, and the size of the work force (123, 1877, pp. 146; § 237, p. 353). Inasmuch as many of the parameters change before equilibrium is reached, the "state of equilibrium of production is, like the state of equilibrium of exchange, an ideal state and not a real one" (123, 1877, p. 231; § 188, p. 283). In the real economy, it "never transpires that the price of products is absolutely equal to their average cost of production in productive services, nor does it ever happen that the quantities supplied and demanded of productive services or of products are absolutely equal" (ibid.). "It can happen, and in reality it happens frequently, [that] the price stays always above the average cost of production" (123, 1877, pp. 310–11; § 322, p. 580).

Walras explained that in the real economy, the variables undergo mutually interdependent adjustments in the situation that follows a change in the basic conditions, as determined by the interrelationships between excess demands for different commodities, the behavior of market participants, and the process of pricing. Prices are changed repeatedly, inducing changes in the amounts of commodities produced, supplied, and demanded at any given time. Buyers and sellers in real markets do not know the equilibrium magnitudes of prices and quantities of commodities produced and traded, and are concerned only with their own equilibrium and not the particular equilibrium of their market or of the entire economy; their activities nevertheless cause the values of the variables to move in the direction of the equilibrium magnitudes. They do so by quoting one set of prices after another in such a manner as to diminish excess demands, and through reacting to each set by producing, buying and selling, and consuming different amounts of the commodities.

In other words, the real economy cannot move in a single adjustment from an initial disequilibrium position to one of equilibrium. Nevertheless, if the adjustment processes in the real economy were not disturbed by parametric changes, it would converge, Walras maintained, to a stable equilibrium of all variables: "The operations of the raising and lowering of prices, of the increases and decreases of the quantities of commodities produced, etc., on the markets are nothing other than *the solution* by tatonnement of the equations of exchange, of production, and of capital formation" (239, 1889, 2, p. 364; emphasis added), the solution being the equilibrium set of variables. He did not arrive at the idea that the real economy is an equilibrating system by studying mathematics but by observing the economy and reflecting on it and on the ideas of other economists, and through the verbal reasoning expressed on many pages of his writings (for example, 123, 1877, pp. 222–44; §§ 189–99, pp. 287–98).

General equilibration and equilibrium of the model

Various controversies surround the nature of Walras's treatment of tatonnement. As is frequently the case in Walrasian exegesis, the major differences of opinion on the character of tatonnement have been generated by the fact that he introduced the written pledges sketch of a virtual process in the fourth edition of the *Eléments*, but nevertheless retained in contradiction to that process much of the non-virtual mature comprehensive model. For example, it has been argued (see articles cited in Walker 1996, Chapter 12) that he failed to depict disequilibrium behavior, whether in connection with stability or otherwise, that he did not construct a model of economic tatonnement, and that he was uninterested in the economic adjustment processes that characterize real competitive markets. It has been contended that he was instead concerned with a technique of mathematical iteration for the purpose of finding the solutions to the equations of a model of general equilibrium. William Jaffé, for example, expressed the view that the tatonnement in all Walras's models is a static, timeless mechanical process (Jaffé 1981). Roger Koppl believes that Walras did not model disequilibrium behavior, that he thought that "any discussion of disequilibrium falls, by necessity, outside the province of pure economics" (Koppl 1992).

There is a very different view. Drawing upon the features of Walras's mature comprehensive model, economists such as Martin Currie and Ian Steedman (1990, ch. 3) have expressed the opinion that he wanted to develop a realistic model of time-consuming economic tatonnement in a freely competitive economy. They correctly argue that he modeled a dynamic equilibrating process in real time of price formation, exchange, production, consumption, capital accumulation, and monetary adjustment. It has likewise been shown that, in his model of an oral pledges market (Walker 1996, Chapters 3, 4, 5), he devoted a great deal of attention to the equilibrating behavior of markets. He incorporated into that model a number of real trading practices, explaining who changes the price, how offers to buy and sell are made, how agents act on behalf of their clients, how the quoted price converges to equilibrium, and how it is known when the market excess demand is zero. A. van Witteloostujin and J. A. H. Maks (1988, 1990) and Michio Morishima (1996) similarly explain that the textbook presentation of Walras's theorizing in regard to statics and dynamics does him an injustice. Walras based his model, they demonstrate, on his theories of who changes prices, of iterative pricing, of entrepreneurial behavior, and of a presumed convergence of the variables to equilibrium. Rather than offering only a static theory, they point out, Walras's model moves through a dynamic sequence of adjustments.

Many economists have stated that Walras assumed that prices in his model are cried by an auctioneer (for example, Hildenbrand and Kirman 1988, pp. 102–3). Some writers believe that he assumed there is a single central market in which all commodities are traded and that it is directed by a single central auctioneer. Michio Morishima had no difficulty in discerning that Walras assumed that each commodity is sold in its own market, but Morishima developed his own original notion to the effect that Walras assumed there are many auctioneers, one in each separate market (Morishima 1977, pp. 19, 31). In fact, Walras did not mention or imply a central price quoter or decentralized price quoters in any connection.

Many economists have contended that in Walras's model the buyers and sellers are all always price takers. Claude Ménard (1990, p. 114), for example, asserts that one of the "major assumptions" of Walras's model is that entrepreneurs are always price-takers. Economists who believed that is true and who have also recognized that Walras did not mention a central price quoter have contended that models like his therefore do not contain any mechanism for the changing of prices (Arrow and Hahn 1971, pp. 266, 325). They have thereby gratuitously created for themselves a problem of how prices are changed. Arrow's solution was that pricing must either be exogenously determined in a purely competitive market, that is, conducted by a central price quoter, or that it must be done endogenously by imperfectly competitive firms (Arrow 1959, p. 43).

In fact, Walras drew from the real economy the pricing behavior he used in his mature model, and accordingly, in all his many treatments of price formation he explicitly portrayed buyers and sellers, including entrepreneurs, as quoting and changing prices in decentralized markets (see, for example, 1877, p. 229–31; §§ 185–87, pp. 281–83; complete documentation is given in Walker 1996, pp. 55–56, 85–89, 101–2, 264–66).

Walras's verbal reasoning about the equilibrium
and stability of the model

Having achieved, as he thought, an understanding of the behavior of buyers, sellers, consumers, savers, and producers of goods and services in the real economy, and having incorporated that behavior into his mature comprehensive model, Walras then examined the question of the existence, uniqueness, and stability of the model's general equilibrium. He thereby initiated the major agenda followed by general equilibrium theorists for sixty years following his death.

Regarding the stability of the mature comprehensive model, Walras declared that "the object and goal of economic theory consist above all and before all in the demonstration to which I am referring" (239, 1889, 2, p. 364), namely the explanation of how the disequilibrium behavior of a freely competitive economy would, *ceteris paribus*, lead to equilibrium. By publishing his initial results in the years 1874 to 1877, Walras became, he pointed out, the first economist to study the stability of a general equilibrium model (239, 1895, 2, p. 630). He presented his reasoning about the real economy as the equilibrating characteristics of his model (for example, 123, 1877, pp. 222–44; 176, 1889, p. 280; §§ 189–99, pp. 287–98). He did not, he remarked, represent the tatonnements in that model in the virtual way that he did in the later written pledges sketch (210, 1900, p. VIII; pp. 5, 8; see Chapter 6). Instead, he represented them "as they are made . . . *effectively*" (ibid.; emphasis added); that is, as they occur in reality, and therefore as being irrevocable adjustments of the disequilibrium variables.

By means of verbal reasoning, Walras then traced out the process of adjustment toward equilibrium in his model. On one occasion he preferred to say, responding to criticism, that stability was "probable" (176, 1889, p. 246) rather than "certain" (123, 1877, p. 261). He had reference there to a market for services in a special model in which there is no production of new capital goods nor markets for capital goods (see Walker 1996, pp. 113–154). Regarding his mature comprehensive model, however, he was convinced it is stable, on the grounds of the following reasoning. The participants do not actually trade unless the price in their market is found to be one at which the market supply and demand quantities are equal (106, 1874, p. 50; § 42, p. 71; 239, 1895, 2, p. 630; Chapter 3). If they are unequal, the price is changed in accordance with the Walrasian pricing rule (see Chapter 4). When the market-day equilibrium price is found, the traders fulfill the verbal pledges they have made at that price (ibid.). It may be, however, that the equilibrium is "imperfect" (176, 1889, p. 135; § 111, p. 161). Walras explained that the price at which the equality of supply and demand quantities occurs in any market and the transactions that take place at that price are actually disequilibrium magnitudes if either of two conditions obtains: If other markets are not in equilibrium, or if the price and the average cost of production of the commodity are not equal (123, 1877, p. 264; § 220, p. 329). If the first of those conditions obtains, he indicated, the participants in any given market, whose supplies and demands are functions of all prices, will be affected by the changes of prices in the other markets that are undergoing disequilibrium adjustments. That will have the effect of shifting the individual demand curves and hence the market demand curve in the given market either before or after the equality of supply and demand as a function of its price is reached in it. In either case, Walrasian pricing in the various markets will continue. Thus although exchange takes place only at market-day equilibrium prices, irrevocable non-virtual behavior in disequilibrium nevertheless occurs in the mature model of general equilibration and equilibrium of exchange because trade takes place in any particular market as soon as the supply and demand quantities are equal in it, although other markets are not yet in equilibrium. When their prices subsequently change, the particular market becomes disequilibrated as the participants react to those new prices. It is revealed that the trade that has occurred in the particular market was actually a disequilibrium amount from the viewpoint of the equilibrium of the system as a whole. In studying these matters, Walras became the first economist to present a model of the determination of market-day prices and of the quantities exchanged in a system of multiple interrelated markets.

The other part of the adjustment process is that the inequality of average cost and price leads to changes of supply functions. According to Walras, the rate of production of the commodity in each market and therefore its market-day (temporary) equilibrium price are progressively altered on each of a series of subsequent days until general equilibrium is reached. The aspect of the tatonnement in the real economy and in the model that takes place with respect to new quantities produced is the progressive diminution, as a result of the changes of the price in the output market and of the prices of inputs, of the difference between price and average cost of the product. The rate of output in each firm and hence of the output of the industry is changed in the same direction as the sign of that difference. The aspect of the tatonnement in the real economy and in the model that takes place with respect to the price and sales of each commodity is the increase of the quantity if the price is greater than average cost and the reverse if the price is less, and hence is the movement of the market-day equilibrium price of the commodity toward its average cost on each successive day. As those processes occur, "the system of new quantities manufactured and new prices . . . is closer to equilibrium than the previous one, and it is necessary only to continue the tatonnement in order to approach it more and more closely" (176, 1889, p. 241; § 212, p. 318).

Walras then considered the equilibrium conditions for the entire set of markets. It was in this context that he set forth Walras's law or the basis for that law, first given that name by Oskar Lange. It is curious that Lange (1942, p. 51, n. 2) cited § 116 of the 1900 edition of Walras's *Eléments* (210), and that Don Patinkin repeated, albeit rather questioningly, that citation and also offered § 122 of the first edition (106, 1874), because in neither of those places, nor in the other places mentioned in a general way by Patinkin, did Walras state the law in anything like a direct way. In fact, it was on page 256 of the first edition (123, 1877; § 213, p. 323) that he presented a version of the law, limited by the consideration that he treated only markets for productive services. Letting O be the quantity supplied, D the quantity demanded, p the price, and the various subscripts respectively indicating the services of land, personal faculties, and capital goods, the relation is:

$$(O_t - D_t)p_t + (O_p - D_p)p_p + (O_k - D_k)p_k + \cdots = 0$$

In that place, Walras presented the law as an equilibrium condition: In the general equilibrium of a multi-market freely competitive economy in which there is production, the sum of the values of all excess demand quantities for commodities is zero (assuming, he should have added, that all prices are positive), because all the excess demand quantities are zero. "Unless that equation is satisfied, it is not possible to have equilibrium" (ibid., p. 257), which indicates that the equation is not satisfied in disequilibrium. In the *Eléments*, he used primes on the terms; the equation without primes just given is exactly how Walras presented the law in 1897 (198, in 205, 1898, p. 277). There, he also asserts that the "mechanism of free competition solves" the equation, implying that it is true in equilibrium and that in disequilibrium, before the functioning of that mechanism, the sum of the values of the excess demand quantities is not zero.

Walras's additional remarks are interesting not only for the content that they add to the law, but also because they reaffirm, just two years before his adoption of the virtual written pledges sketch, his view of the real economy and of his model as being systems in which there are irrevocable disequilibrium transactions and production. He explained:

That equation permits, in itself, the affirmation that, excluding the case of a general crisis, if at a given moment the supply of certain productive services exceeds the demand for them, the demand for certain other productive services must exceed their supply (ibid.).

It appears that his implication is that the algebraic sum of the values of the excess demand quantities for all commodities is also zero in a state of disequilibrium. He went on to examine the adjustments of prices in disequilibrium and the concomitant changes in production and of the supply and demand quantities that lead those quantities to equality in the case of each service. His discussion included noting that services that are not transformable into others, as is the case with land services in relation to labor, undergo changes in prices, and that services that are usable in different ways, such as a type of labor that can be altered to perform a different task, may undergo primarily changes in their amounts in each line of production. He concluded with respect to wages that "to lead to or to maintain the equilibrium of production in regard to wages, it is necessary in the last analysis to redirect labor from firms in which wages are tending to fall towards firms in which wages are tending to rise" (ibid., p. 278).

The "state of equilibrium," Walras declared, "is the normal state in the sense that it is the one to which things tend automatically" under the conditions of "free competition in production and exchange" (123, 1877, p. 231; § 188, p. 283); that is, under the conditions that he thought obtained in the vast majority of real markets and that obtained in his model. Then "the equilibrium prices are those at which the quantities demanded and supplied of each service or product are equal, and at which, moreover, the price of each product is equal to its average cost of production" (176, 1889, p. XV; p. 13). The equilibrium prices lead each economic agent to initiate behavior that they then want to continue – buying, selling, investing, and consuming certain amounts (see for example, 123, 1877, pp. 250–51; § 206, pp. 306–7). The mutually determined sets of equilibrium prices, average costs, and quantities supplied and demanded are harmonious; they fulfill the plans of all the participants in the model. No one who could change the prevailing economic conditions wants to do so, and no one who wants to change them is able to do so.

Entrepreneurs, capitalists, and capital formation

Walras analyzed saving and investment behavior in the real economy (123, 1877, p. 284; 176, 1889, pp. 270–71, 307; § 241–42, pp. 357–63). In the course of his study of those matters, he formulated a macroeconomic savings function, being the first economist to do so. In his examination of capital accumulation, Walras discussed additional ways in which entrepreneurs connect different economic sectors and markets. Capitalists in the real economy transfer their money savings to entrepreneurs through purchasing stocks and bonds (123, 1877, pp. 302–3; 176, 1889, pp. 309–10; § 269, pp. 434–36), a process that Walras examined in studies of credit markets (205, 1898, pp. 307–36). The incomes paid to owners of economic resources by entrepreneurs are partially saved by the recipients in their role as members of households, and the savings are used by entrepreneurs in capital-goods industries to acquire raw materials and productive services in order to construct new capital goods. These are bought by capitalists and used by entrepreneurs in firms to make other capital goods properly speaking and consumer commodities (123, 1877, pp. 294–95; 176, 1889, pp. 286–87; §§ 254–55, pp. 388–91). Walras analyzed how those goods are priced and are employed in the most profitable uses, thereby resulting in an increase in levels of production of different types of commodity (123, 1877, pp. 273–311; 176, 1889, pp. 261–317; §§ 231–70, pp. 345–436). He likewise developed an explanation of the determination of the rate of net income generated by the use of capital goods, and of the determination of the market and equilibrium rates of interest (123, 1877, pp. 278–311; 176, 1889, pp. 261–312; §§ 231–71, pp. 345–436). He made his account of all those matters a part of his mature comprehensive model.

Conditions of a reprise

Walras identified a tatonnement in his model as being a complete adjustment process, beginning with a new initial disequilibrium and ending with equilibrium. Within a tatonnement, he distinguished each "reprise of tatonnement" (176, 1889, p. 280) – the several stages that occur during the course of the overall process. He had in mind an initial period of price adjustments and associated disequilibrium behavior, followed by the participants pausing and assessing their individual situations and market conditions, a recognition by some participants that they can improve their economic situation, followed by a second period and a second assessment, followed by additional periods until the equilibrium is reached. Thus each of the reprises eventuates in a temporary disequilibrium of the entire system.[5] Each such successive state is closer to the eventual general equilibrium than the previous state, and the entire tatonnement ends when equilibrium is reached.

---

[5] Witteloostujin and Maks (1988, 1990) believe that a Walrasian tatonnement in the mature model consists of a series of temporary market equilibria between which there are intertemporal disequilibria. If they had reference to the equilibrium in a particular market achieved by the equality of the quantities supplied and demanded on a market day, and the subsequent series of particular equilibrium market-day prices, that is true. It is not, however, true of the final state of each disequilibrium reprise of the general equilibrium tatonnement. Except for the last one, each reprise ends in disequilibrium, which is why it is suceeded by a new reprise.

A reprise takes place under these conditions:

It is always a question of arriving at the equilibrium of capital formation in the same manner that we arrived at the equilibrium of exchange and at the equilibrium of production, that is to say by assuming that the given conditions of the problem are invariable during all the time that the tatonnements take, except that the assumption will subsequently be made that those given conditions are variables in order to study the consequences of their variations (ibid., p. 279). . . . We must assume that, at each reprise of tatonnement, our entrepreneurs that produce products [non-durable goods] and new capital goods find, in the country, landlords, workers, and capitalists possessing the same quantities of services, having the same needs for services and products, and the same dispositions to save (ibid., p. 280).

It would have been simpler if Walras had declared that the supply functions for capital-goods services are unchanged, rather than the amounts of those services. When he wrote that the capitalists have the same quantities of services, he must have meant that the maximum potential amounts of capital-goods services are the same at the beginning of each reprise of tatonnement. He must have been referring to the capacity of the capitalists to offer services, and similarly regarding the other resource owners, because he stated that the services that are tendered on the market are functions of prices and not a fixed amount. The amounts provided change during the tatonnement as prices change (123, 1877, p. 247; 176, 1889, p. 230; § 201, p. 303). They each vary "with all the prices of all the services and products" and are determined, "after the determination of those prices, by the maximization of effective utility" (205, 1898, p. 275). If it were the case that the maximum potential amounts of capital goods services are the same, that condition, together with unchanging preferences of the capitalists, would ensure that the supply functions for capital-goods services are the same at the beginning of each reprise.

Walras asserted that disequilibrium production of non-durable goods and of net new durable capital goods occurs during each reprise of the tatonnement:

A certain rate of net income and certain prices of services being cried, and certain quantities of products and of new capital goods being produced, if this rate, these prices and these quantities are not an equilibrium rate, and are not equilibrium prices and quantities, it is necessary not only to cry another rate and other prices, but also to produce other quantities of products and of capital goods. . . .
At a rate of net income cried first at random, and then raised or lowered according to the circumstances, the entrepreneurs that produce new capital goods will fabricate certain quantities of new capital goods determined first at random and then increased or diminished quantities according to the circumstances (176, 1889, p. 280).

The net new investment that occurs during the equilibrating process changes the magnitude and composition of the capital stock. The new durable capital goods are sold during the disequilibrium phase at disequilibrium prices: Those goods, being produced "in the general tatonnement then being brought onto the capital goods market and *being sold there* in accordance with the mechanism of free competition, *would be sold at prices that differ from their average costs of production*, but are closer to being equal than the previous prices were to being equal to their average costs of production" (ibid., p. 292; emphasis added). The "average costs and prices of output being generally unequal, the entrepreneurs who produce new capital goods will make profits or losses . . ." (123, 1877, p. 295; 176, 1889, p. 289; § 256, p. 393), phenomena that do not exist in a virtual model. Those are additional robust statements of irrevocable disequilibrium production and resources allocation, and of the identity of the model with the real economy.

Another fundamental change in the situation is the redirection of resources by the entrepreneurs during the phases of the tatonnement, which alters the composition of output:

Now this tatonnement is precisely that which generates itself on the market, under the regime of free competition, when the entrepreneurs who produce new capital goods, just like those that produce products, direct resources toward the enterprises or away from them according to whether profits or losses are made in them (123, 1877, p. 298; 176, 1889, p. 298; § 258, p. 401).

Walras specified that the capital-goods services are provided exclusively by the capital goods that were in existence at the very beginning of the entire tatonnement process. In some discussions of tatonnement, he stated "that the new capital goods do not function during the period" (249.XIII, p. 265). Moreover, he placed his statement that "production and capitalization will be able to continue, but, of course, with the changes resulting from the existence of the new capital goods" (176, 1889, p. 280) after his assertion that equilibrium has been reached, implying that the new capital goods produced in disequilibrium are not used until equilibrium is found. He postulated arbitrarily that the new capital goods lie idle in disequilibrium to try to insure that there would be no changes in the maximum potential amounts of capital-goods services during the course of the tatonnement, and hence in the supply functions for them. Otherwise his equations, in which those amounts are parameters, and in which the functions are assumed to be unchanging, would have solutions that are not the equilibrium values of the variables of the model.

Contradictions in the model

Despite "accepting [the] necessity" (176, 1889, p. 280) of irrevocable disequilibrium phenomena and specifically of the fact that new capital goods are produced during the phases of the tatonnement, Walras did not accept the necessity that the new capital goods are used during the tatonnement. The structure and functioning of his mature model is thereby rendered less than coherent in regard to the equilibrating process and equilibrium by the logical problems created by his arbitrary postulate.

It cannot be that the new capital goods are held in inventories by their producers, because Walras stated that they are sold to capitalists during each reprise. For the supply functions of capital goods services at the beginning of each reprise to be unchanged, it would have to be the case, therefore, that the buyers of the new capital goods hold them in inventories during the tatonnement and do not try to make money from offering their potential services for sale. That condition is not an outcome of the structure and functioning of the model and cannot be made consistent with it. Walras gave no reason founded in economic behavior, rational or irrational, for supposing that the new capital goods are not used during the tatonnement. His arbitrary postulate contradicts his theory of saving and investment, which is based on the supposition that the reason capital goods are acquired is to maximize utility by renting them out or using them in their own firms. Their owners therefore would not let the new capital goods lie idle. The supply functions for the services of the new capital goods of each type would be added into the total of capital goods services of each type offered for sale. That total would change during the tatonnement and would, specifically, be different at the beginning of each reprise. The "given conditions of the problem" cannot be "invariable during all the time that the tatonnements take."

Moreover, the supply functions for old capital-goods services cannot be the same at the beginning of or during each reprise of tatonnement. Walras assumed, to deal with the most interesting case, that aggregate investment is positive (123, 1877, p. 284; 176, 1889, p. 271; § 242, p. 361), although if it were negative there would still be the following sort of consequences. The flow of new capital goods into the inventories of capitalists is an asset effect that alters their demand and supply functions for all types of commodities. For example, it changes the quantities of old capital-goods services that they want to offer at each price at the beginning of each reprise.

Even if it is arbitrarily assumed that the supply functions for the services of old capital goods do not change and that no services of new capital goods are offered, the extensive disequilibrium behavior that Walras built into the course of the tatonnement of the model would have precisely the consequence that his supposed equilibrium equations do not give the equilibrium values. Disequilibrium transactions alter the distribution of a given amount of a commodity. Disequilibrium production of a commodity alters the total amounts of it and therefore the amounts possessed by particular individuals. The changes in the amounts of goods held by individuals alter their demand functions for goods and services and their supply functions for goods and services, thus altering the equilibrium values of the variables. With respect to new capital goods, for example, during each phase of the tatonnement, in the course of which savings occur and therefore additional new durable capital goods are produced and sold, and consequently at the beginning of each new reprise, capitalists have different amounts of those goods and therefore have different demand functions for additional capital goods. That leads to a set of prices at which their production is stabilized that differs from the set during each reprise. The equilibrium of the system is therefore path dependent for that reason, in addition to others that have been discussed.

Capital use and accumulation give rise to other sources of difficulties in Walras's model. Let it be supposed for a moment as Walras supposed, disregarding the illogical aspects of the model, that only the old capital goods are used during the tatonnement and that the new capital goods are put into use only when the tatonnement is ostensibly finished, that is, as soon as an ostensible static equilibrium obtains. A first problem is that Walras did not take account of the depreciation of old capital goods properly speaking during the tatonnement. Some of them reach the end of their productive life during the tatonnement; others are partially used. There is no flow of maintenance of fixed capital goods properly speaking in use, so there cannot be the same amounts of old capital goods at the beginning of each reprise. There must be less. To insure that there are the same amounts, he should have assumed that investment equals depreciation. Alternatively, he could have assumed, contrary to reason, that the fixed capital goods do not wear out and are indestructible, as he did in part of his treatment of the maximum utility of new capital goods (176, 1889, p. 300). Even those assumptions would not have eliminated, from a purely logical point of view, the difficulty posed by the use of primary materials. The variable capital that is not held in inventories but that is used and therefore used up during the course of a reprise must also be exactly replaced if the services of variable capital goods are to be the same at the beginning of each reprise. That is a necessary condition, but Walras did not provide any market mechanism to ensure that the amounts of newly produced variable capital goods equal the disequilibrium amounts that are bought and used.

Whether or not the fixed capital goods in use depreciate, by assuming that the particular batch of capital goods in use during the tatonnement does not change, Walras created a second problem for his model. Demands and relative prices of inputs and outputs change during the tatonnement. The changing demands for final goods shift derived demands to some capital goods in the existing stock, and away from others. The problem, rightly pointed out by Fabio Petri (2004, Chapter 5), is that the demand for some or many capital goods would decrease, but lowering their prices could not lead to their employment for the production of different commodities because they are technologically incapable of being adapted. Most capital goods have specific uses. If the form of the capital stock in use cannot be changed to respond to changing demands for the services of particular capital goods, the prices of the unused capital goods would fall toward zero, but their owners still could not tempt producers to use them. There would therefore be unemployment to some degree of some or many capital goods. The absurdity of the situation is increased by the fact that the response to the changing pattern of demand for capital goods would be to increase the production of some new capital goods, namely of the kinds of capital goods for which prices have increased. Those new goods, however, according to Walras's assumption, are nevertheless not put on the market during the tatonnement to augment the supply of the old capital goods the prices of which have increased.

Walras's assumption of fixed coefficients of production poses a third problem. The amounts of the inputs released from the production of commodities that are less in demand may not fit the proportions in which they are required in the industries for whose products demand increases. Once again, there would be involuntary unemployment of resources, a condition that Walras did not envisage.

A fourth problem is that Walras was in error to have believed that capital accumulation is compatible with the type of equilibrium that he envisaged in his discussion of tatonnement. The equilibrium to which he referred is "factitious, existing only transitorily while his model is held in a state of arbitrarily suspended animation by the postulate that additions to the capital stock are not used – a *deus ex machina* that interrupts the incomplete working of its endogenous processes. The instant the postulate is removed, the 'equilibrium' is ruptured . . ." (Walker 1987b, pp. 860–61). As soon as the additions to the stock of capital are put into use, which Walras stated occurs at what he supposed is the end of the tatonnement, relative prices, outputs of many different commodities, and seeming parameters continue to change, and it is revealed that a static equilibrium did not exist. Thus the mature comprehensive model is inherently dynamic in two respects. First, the tatonnement is a dynamic, time-consuming process. Second, the model turns into a growth model because the use of the additions to the capital stock propels it beyond a stationary equilibrium and onto a path of economic growth. Indeed, Walras recognized as much when he stated, as noted, that, after the tatonnement is over, "Production and capitalization will be able to continue, but, of course, with the changes resulting from the existence of the new capital goods" (176, 1889, p. 280), and when he analyzed the transition that occurs to what he called "a progressive society" – a dynamic system in the sense of one in which there is capital accumulation and an increase in the labor force, and in which aggregate output grows (123, 1877, pp. 312–23; 176, 1889, pp. 318–29; §§ 323–24, pp. 584–98).[6]

Nevertheless, there is nothing contradictory in the model created by Walras's assertion that the (maximum possible) amounts of the services of *land* and of *workers* are the same at the beginning of each reprise and thus during the entire course of the equilibrating process in the model, as he believed was substantially true in reality. In the model, the amount of land is fixed (123, 1877, pp. 224, 278; 176, 1889, pp. 207, 266; § 236, pp. 277, 352), and so is the technology used on it (123, 1877, p. 310; § 322, p. 580). The size of the work force (123, 1877, pp. 278–79; 176, 1889, p. 266; § 237, pp. 352–53), its efficiency, the workers' preferences, and the work week (205, 1898, p. 275) are fixed. Changes in those conditions do not occur as an endogenous consequence of the tatonnement process in the model, so they are truly parametric constants with respect to that process.[7] Moreover, services cannot be accumulated. The *maximum possible* flow of them that could be provided at any moment by the land and human capital is therefore unchanged during the whole of the tatonnement process, and, in particular, is the same at the beginning

---

[6] William Jaffé believed that Walras's writings on a progressive society constitute merely a "coda," an addendum rather than an integral part of his central body of theorizing (Jaffé 1978). Michio Morishima (1996) and other economists (for example, Currie and Steedman 1990) disagree with that contention. They argue that Walras intended his general equilibrium model to lead to and to be the point of departure for the development of a model of economic growth. In fact, this chapter shows that the implications of Walras's mature comprehensive model, his central body of theorizing, are that it becomes a growth model when the use of new capital goods occurs.

[7] Similarly, there is no contradiction in Walras's model occasioned by his assuming that the preferences of the economic agents for consumer goods and for saving are unchanged by disequilibrium transactions and disequilibrium production (176, 1889, p. 280).

of each reprise of tatonnement. The *supply functions* for the services of land and labor will change, however, even if the amounts of those factors and preferences for work and income do not change, because the functions also have the holdings of consumer durables and capital goods properly speaking as arguments, and those arguments change during the course of the tatonnement.

Uniqueness

Walras's study of uniqueness was limited to the consideration of pure exchange in a model of an isolated market and in a multi-market model. Regarding the former, in which one commodity is exchanged for another, he used graphs and verbal reasoning to arrive at the conclusion that an isolated market may have more than one set of values at which *ex ante* supply and demand are equal (106, 1874, p. 74; § 68, p. 99). Regarding a multi-market system, he concluded on the basis of incomplete verbal reasoning that "generally," in the sense of "ordinarily," multiple equilibria do not occur. That was an opinion, not a proof (106, 1874, p. 156; § 156, pp. 241–42). If he had tried to use his equation system to furnish a proof he would have been unsuccessful, because, as has been explained, it does not describe the model. Furthermore, the proof, if it had been forthcoming, could not have established that there are multiple equilibria. It would have established only that there are, from the mathematical point of view, more than one set of solutions to the equations. If the initial conditions and the dynamics of the model were to be specified in sufficient detail, the solution set to which the model actually converges and that is therefore the unique equilibrium set would be known (see Walker 1997b, pp. 132–141).

IV. Mathematical treatment of phenomena

Mathematical treatment of existence

Walras developed a second analytical approach to the characterization of the economy and of his model in order to supplement and add precision to his verbal reasoning in the demonstration of their outcomes. It consisted of attempts to use equations to represent the phenomena in his model that were amenable to mathematical treatment (for example, 123, 1877, pp. 245–65; §§ 200–220, pp. 301–30). Of course, he had to use verbal reasoning to form the equations. Thus he gave economic meanings to mathematical symbols and reflected his conviction of the equilibrating nature of markets in the real economy and hence in his model by constructing equations that express the condition of economic equilibrium. He claimed to have proved the existence of equilibrium in his model because the number of unknowns in his equations equals the number of independent equations (for example, 123, 1877, pp. 250–51; 176, 1889, pp. 233–34; § 205, pp. 306–7). As is well known, that equality does not establish existence, for three reasons.

A contradiction between the model and the equations

The first reason is that the model to which he had reference – the mature comprehensive model – is path dependent but the equations he used do not take account of that feature. Starting with an assumed state of disequilibrium, Walras tried to use equations in which the initial holdings of consumer goods and capital goods are parametric constants in order to deduce a different set of holdings of commodities – the equilibrium set – reached through a series of changes of the set of holdings. That is illogical. Walras's attempt to establish the existence of equilibrium in the model with the use of the equations was an impossible task. Many of the constants in the equations are actually endogenous variables in the model, changing during the course of the equilibrating process. Thus once the adjustment process has begun, the symbols in the equations no longer have referents in the model; or, to put it the other way around, the changing values of the variables in the model are not symbolized in the equations. The equilibrium values of the model are therefore not the ones indicated by the solutions to his equations.

To determine whether static equilibrium exists in a variation of the mature comprehensive model, Walras would have had to exclude capital accumulation, and, in recognition of the fact that many of the phenomena that he treated as parameters in his equations are really variables in his model, he would have had to use equations that are appropriate for determining whether a path-dependent system has solutions, namely a set of differential or difference equations, or a mixture of the two. Walras's failure in those regards was surely facilitated by his habit of writing the equations for supply and demand quantities with only prices between the parentheses on the right-hand side, never introducing symbols to show what he assumed were the constants in those functions (see Van Daal and Walker 1990). Had he done so, he would probably have recognized much earlier than 1899 that the model did not behave in the manner that the equations supposed. As it was, it took him until that year to recognize the implications of the contradiction between his comprehensive model and the equations.

The second reason is that, even if the model were not path dependent, or even if Walras had correctly described it with a set of dynamic equations, his assertion would have been erroneous because he neglected to consider free goods, which are used in positive amounts but have zero prices.

The third reason is that he did not introduce the requirement that the solutions to his equations all be non-negative, which is necessary inasmuch as negative prices or quantities of commodities are nonsense, except in accounting balances and concepts such as a negative rate of interest, which have no role in the question of existence. Nevertheless, his studies of existence went far beyond those of other nineteenth-century economists, inasmuch as he dealt with the question of the existence of general rather than particular equilibrium and tried to do so with the use of mathematics.

Stability and the equation system

Walras's attempts to treat stability mathematically do not deal with his model but with his equation system. He tried to develop a technique of mathematical iteration whereby he could determine the direction of change of the variables in the equations. That he was conducting an exercise in mathematical iteration is plain from his statements that various conditions are selected and imposed on the equations by the theoretician who is contemplating them. In that capacity, Walras picked a random initial disequilibrium set of prices and determined the associated excess demand quantities. He then selected new prices either greater or smaller than the initial ones in accordance with the Walrasian pricing rule, and evaluated the absolute excess demand quantities to see if they displayed a tendency to decrease; that is, to see if the prices and quantities converged to a solution set (for example, 123, 1877, p. 293–98; §§ 252–54, pp. 387–89).

In one exercise of mathematical iteration, for instance, referring to "the conditions of the tatonnement that we apply at the present," Walras arbitrarily assumed that the quantities produced of the numeraire and of capital goods are constant, changed their prices, and then examined the successive sets of disequilibrium quantities produced (176, 1889, p. 286; § 254, p. 388). He made particularly clear his role as a theoretician who uses arbitrary postulates in the study of equations by commenting that "the assumption of the fixity of the prices of the other commodities is an essentially momentary and provisional assumption which plays a part only in a partial phase of the general tatonnement and takes the place of the assumption of the variation of those prices in the other phases" (239, 1895, 2, p. 631). Again, signaling that he was conducting a mathematical exercise in iteration regarding a hypothetical situation, he noted that "in the conditions of tatonnement that we apply at the present, the prices of services are fixed and do not change" (176, 1889, p. 239; § 212, p. 317). That is a condition he could put into the equations, thereby implicitly changing the structure and manner of functioning of the situation he contemplated, but that cannot be true of the endogenous processes that take place in the model. If the model is allowed to generate its path without the theoretician introducing modifications, those prices will not be constant during the tatonnement. There are many pages in the *Eléments* on which Walras made similar arbitrary assumptions regarding the variables instead of tracing out the endogenously determined variations in the model.

Walras asserted that the mathematical iterations in his equations reveal that the prices in his model converge to an equilibrium (123, 1877, pp. 291, 300; § 252, p. 379; § 258, p. 401). He contended that the direction of change of the variables in the equations induced by his postulated changes of prices are the same as occur in the model, describing the iterative changes as variations of disequilibrium transactions and of disequilibrium production (176, 1889, p. 292):

In these conditions, it can be accepted that the change in the quantity manufactured of each new capital good has brought the price and the average cost of the good closer than the changes in the quantities manufactured of other new capital goods, supposing them all to have changed in the same direction, have caused the price and average cost to differ. The system of new quantities manufactured and of new prices and average costs is thus closer to equilibrium than the previous set, and it is necessary only to continue the tatonnement to approach it more and more closely (176, 1889, p. 293; with a change, § 258, p. 399).

It is clear yet once again that Walras was not discussing a virtual system. In that passage, as throughout his account of the functioning of the mature comprehensive model, the activity has occurred in the recent past; the supplies and demands are *ex post*. The different quantities of goods have been manufactured; they are produced in successively changing disequilibrium amounts and sold at disequilibrium prices during the course of the tatonnement.

In his mature phase of theorizing, Walras believed that the real economy, *ceteris paribus*, was characterized in a general sense by his static system of equations and therefore would end up with the same solutions as those equations if they had the necessary numerical coefficients: "The result of the flow of the interrelated phenomena of reality is truly the empirical solution" of the equations (123, 1877, p. 365; § 370, p. 651). After finishing his iterations with his equations, the "indicated tatonnement," he expressed that opinion first with respect to the market for consumer goods (123, 1877, p. 255; § 212, p. 319) and then with respect to capital goods:

> Now the indicated tatonnement is exactly that which generates itself on the capital market when the new capital goods are sold according to the mechanism of raising and lowering prices . . . (176, 1889, p. 287; with changes, § 254, p. 390).

Walras also evidenced his belief that his mathematical exercises demonstrate the stability of real markets by asserting that the price changes that he discussed in relation to his model occur in a real economic institution, the Paris Bourse (210, 1900, p. 267; § 254, p. 390; and see 176, 1889, p. 289; § 255, p. 391).

Comparative statics

Walras's belief that the real economy and his mature comprehensive model are stable equilibrating systems was his justification for comparative static analysis. He undertook it in order to analyze the impact on equilibrium of changes of parameters, such as preferences, the quantity of money, and the quantity of a commodity held by the participants (for example, 106, 1874, pp. 134–37; 176, 1889, pp. 159–63; §§ 137–38, pp. 209–14. 176, 1889, pp. 127–28; § 103, pp. 149, 151. 106, 1874, p. 104; § 103, p. 151. 123, 1877, p. 294; 176, 1889, p. 309; § 265, p. 430). Walras's verbal analyses of the directions of change of the variables in his model resulting from changes of the parameters were plausible, but the defect of his comparative statics, as well as of his mathematical iterations, was that he undertook his analyses with equations that could be used only to determine the stability of a virtual model without net investment, that is, one unlike his model and, of course, unlike the real economy.

   To have identified the true new equilibrium values resulting from parametric changes in the mature comprehensive model, Walras would have had to take account of the changes generated by the course of the tatonnement itself and deal with the irrevocable movement to the true new equilibrium, which would be a path of growth. The path would be generated, as has been seen, because, "Production and capitalization will be able to continue" (176, 1889, p. 280) after the tatonnement is over. His iterations and his comparative statics do not relate to that model.

V. Other processes in the model

Monetary processes[8]

One of the fundamental aspects of Walras's legacy was ignored by most
economists until attention was drawn to it by Arthur W. Marget (1931,
1935), namely Walras's analysis of the role of monetary behavior in
the real economy and his incorporation of that role into his mature
comprehensive model (see Walker 1996, Chapter 12). Even when that
aspect has not been ignored, it has often been misunderstood.[9] The task
of understanding his views is complicated by the fact that he constructed
or tried to construct more than one model of monetary behavior and, as
a related matter, by his espousal of three different theories of money
during the course of his career.[10] In his mature comprehensive model,
he used a cash-balance approach (168, 1886; 176, 1889),), stating that
money is held because it will be needed as a medium of exchange. Was
that approach integrated into the model Walras associated it with in
such a fashion that the model functions as an equilibrating monetary
economy?

Takashi Negishi (1989) asserted that the integration is not possible
because he believed that there is no uncertainty in Walras's models and
that money has no place in that type of model. Negishi does not make
clear whether he refers to subjective beliefs about the future magnitudes
of variables in states of disequilibrium and equilibrium, or only the
latter. Some economists, like Martin Currie and Ian Steedman (1990),
contend that there is no uncertainty in any state of Walras's mature
comprehensive model. To others, however, it seems clear that uncertainty
in disequilibrium is one of its features. That position – and hence an
implied rejection of Negishi's argument – is taken by, for example, A.
van Witteloostujin and J. A. H. Maks (1990).

---

[8] Walras's treatment of money in the mature comprehensive model has been exhaus-
tively described, explained, and analyzed elsewhere (Walker 1996, Part I, Section II,
and especially Chapter 11 of that book).

[9] H. C. Hilton (1995) has rightly observed that many economists have formed their ideas
about Walras's views on money and credit from reading inaccurate interpretations of
them.

[10] There are differences between the monetary aspects of the model he presented in his
creative phase, in his mature comprehensive model, and in his last comprehensive
model. The latter name is explained in the introduction and in Chapter 6, and the
writings to which that name is given, including the monetary aspects of the model,
are analyzed in Walker 1996, Chapters 17 and 18. In his creative phase, Walras
expounded the idea of a "circulation to be cleared" and used an equation of exchange.
In his final phase of theorizing, he contended that money is held for the purpose of
obtaining its service of availability.

Walras did not state that there is no uncertainty in his mature comprehensive model (as distinct from his written pledges sketch), and he constructed the mature model in such a fashion that there has to be uncertainty in order for it to function. It would be absurd to suggest that the participants in that model are certain at the beginning of a tatonnement or during it about the dates of future transactions and the magnitudes of future prices, offers, demands, money balances, other asset holdings, and other economic variables. If they had certain knowledge of the future equilibrium values of the variables, no tatonnements would be necessary or possible. There would be no series of disequilibrium prices. Everything that Walras wrote about disequilibrium behavior in his mature comprehensive model would have been nonsensical. Furthermore, after the equilibrium configuration of variables is reached, there is no reason in Walras's model why the participants would believe, contrary to all their experience, that there will be no future changes in asset holdings, prices, and dates of transactions. They are uncertain of the duration of the equilibrium variables. As long as that configuration obtains, however, they either would not want to change their behavior or would not be able to change it, so their realization that the situation is not going to remain unchanged forever is not a cause of change. Change would be initiated by an exogenous shock that alters the specific elements entering into the structure of anticipations and the degree of uncertainty of beliefs. Walras did not state that the participants are certain of the future; he stated that they are *clairvoyant* (see Chapter 4). As such they are sagacious and they reason lucidly, but they do not have perfect foresight in the mature model.

Walras analyzed the role of true money and specifically the demand for cash balances in the context of an economy in which there are irrevocable disequilibrium transactions and disequilibrium production; thereby he successfully integrated the use of money into the mature comprehensive model (see Marget 1931, 1935).[11] Due to the manner of functioning of markets in that model, true money is an essential part of the exchange process, and hence it is inextricably linked with and necessary for the attainment of equilibrium. To summarize Walras's contributions in this regard: He defined desired real and nominal cash balances and identified their role; devised a dynamic period analysis and used it in application to a model of the money market; developed metallic-money and fiat-money models; introduced the activities of banks; integrated the rate of interest

---

[11] One scholar argues that money is not compatible with any of Walras's general equilibrium models (Bridel 1997, pp. 141–45). Discussing a virtual Walrasian model, other economists, such as Antoine Rebeyrol (1998), present at length a demonstration that money is fully integrated into it, or rather into their interpretation of it.

into the dynamics of his model, making the demand for cash balances a function of that rate; distinguished circulating and savings balances and identified their role; and analyzed the causes of variations in the velocity of money.

Thus Walras used his perceptions of the behavior of the real economy to develop the most sophisticated and realistic monetary model that had been achieved by any economist by 1889, anticipating central features of the analyses of monetary matters made by J. M. Keynes, D. H. Robertson, and J. R. Hicks during the 1920s and '30s.

Consumer sovereignty and the allocation of resources

Like other neoclassical economists, Walras bequeathed to later economists a concern with the allocation of economic resources among different economic activities. In that regard, he described economic behavior and processes that have come to be known as the action of consumer sovereignty. Explaining the way that it operates in the real economy to determine the set of commodities that are produced, Walras noted that workers are hired to produce the commodities that consumers demand, and are laid off in industries in which consumer demand decreases. Therefore, "the consumer is in the last analysis, the true demander of labor" (97, 1872, booklet, p. 35). Identifying, in an early exposition, the entrepreneur as being "only an intermediary between the worker and the consumer" (ibid., p. 36), Walras explained that the entrepreneur transmits the desires of the latter to the production side of the market, thus allocating resources so that the set of commodities produced is in accordance with the structure of consumer demands and hence reflects consumer preferences and purchasing power (123, 1877, p. 231; 176, 1889, p. 214; § 188, pp. 283–84).

That implies that the structure of economic activities responds to changes in consumer demand. Walras explained that the reason why the price of a consumer commodity becomes greater than its average cost is because consumers shift their demand in favor of it. They bid up its price, thus making its production profitable, and that induces entrepreneurs to produce more of it. The reason the price becomes less than the average cost is because consumers decide that they do not want to consume as much of the commodity as before at each possible price. The suppliers are forced to lower the price, the firms incur losses, and they therefore produce less of the commodity (176, 1889, p. XVIII; pp. 15–16). Changes of consumer demand are also transmitted to the capital goods industries through increasing or decreasing the demand for the goods that they supply to consumption goods industries; and changes of consumer demand influence the markets for the productive services that are used to produce the consumer goods. Walras incorporated all those matters into his model.

Welfare economics

Closely related to the concept of consumer sovereignty, Walras developed a thesis that became a central issue in the study of welfare economics, namely that free competition, "contrary to the denials of the socialists" (176, 1889, p. 306; § 264, p. 425), tends to generate a maximum of well-being for society (123, 1877, pp. 266, 305; 176, 1889, pp. 251, 306; § 221, p. 334; § 264, p. 425). He emphasized that this results from actions by economic agents to maximize their utility, from the existence of a set of prices that would equalize supply and demand, from the sovereignty of the consumer, and from the other features of a competitive economy that constitute his model. Mixing up his equations and his model once more, he declared that the theory makes clear that "the mechanism of free competition leads precisely to the solution by tatonnement of this system of equations; from which it follows that the mechanism creates maximum satisfaction" (239, 1889, 2, pp. 364–65; and see 176, 1889, p. 306; § 264, p. 424).

That implicit confusion can be neglected in the interests of identifying Walras's central point, which is that the maximization of satisfaction tends to occur in markets for both consumer commodities and capital goods:

The mechanism of free competition is, under certain conditions and within certain limits, a self-driving mechanism and automatic regulator of the transformation of savings into capital goods as well as the transformation of services into products. And thus ... free competition in regard to exchange and production procures the maximum utility of services and of products ... , [and] free competition in regard to capital formation and credit procures the maximum utility of new capital goods ... (176, 1889, p. 287; § 264, p. 424).

The maximum is a relative one, because it depends upon the distribution of income and wealth and the dynamic characteristics of a freely competitive economy, features that result in it moving toward a particular set of equilibrium values. As will be seen in Chapters 9 and 10, subsequent economists tried to find the proof of the proposition that eluded Walras.

VI. The legacy of the mature comprehensive model

The chapters in this part of the book have set forth the legacy of Walras's period of maturity as an economic theoretician, a legacy based upon a remarkable grasp of the features of the economic life of his time. By 1889, he had a fully formed conception of the interrelatedness of economic phenomena, incorporated into a model of general equilibration and equilibrium that was almost complete and that was in most respects well constructed. It dealt with the important parts of a freely competitive economic system – exchange, consumption, production, and capital formation, all undertaken with the use of money. His account of non-virtual economic behavior was a laudable effort to provide a model that explained the real economy on an abstract level. He identified the changing phenomena in disequilibrium such as prices, the variations in hiring of services in particular firms, and related variations of sales that occur as entrepreneurs adjust levels of output in order to maximize profits. The phenomena include the participants' holdings of money and the amounts of each type of capital good. The amount and composition of investment vary with changes in the costs and prices of capital goods, in the incomes generated by them, and in the rate of interest on money savings.

A competitive system of production and exchange is vast and complicated in its many details, but Walras divined its underlying order. He found simplicity in the motivation of consumers, namely their desire to maximize utility; simplicity in the driving force that makes the system responsive to changes in tastes and technology, namely the entrepreneurs' desire to maximize profits; and simplicity in the uniformity of the mechanism whereby markets undergo adjustments, namely the functioning of competitive pricing. Walras's ideas on these matters have become standard parts of modern models of competitive market systems.

The written pledges sketch

CHAPTER 6

Rationale for the written pledges sketch and its characteristics

I. The problem and Walras's solution

A review of the problem

It has been seen in Chapter 5 that Walras explained, in reference to reality and to his mature comprehensive model (see, for example, 123, 1877, pp. 253, 255; 176, 1889, pp. 235, 238, 294; § 209, p. 315; § 212, p. 319; § 258, p. 401), that production and exchange occur at disequilibrium prices, varying as prices change during the course of the adjustment of the markets toward their equilibrium set of variables. In the model, holdings of goods and money are parameters for individual static supply and demand functions. Disequilibrium transactions alter the distribution of goods and money, resulting in changes in those functions. Disequilibrium production alters the amounts of goods and hence the holdings of goods, and thus also changes supply and demand functions. Walras came to realize with increasing clarity that those disequilibrium phenomena create a problem for the logical structure of his work, considered in relation to his equation system. Inasmuch as the equations of supply and demand have parameters that are actually endogenous variables in the model, their solutions – prices, rates of employment of resources, incomes, outputs, and quantities traded – are not the values toward which the model actually converges. The mature comprehensive model is therefore non-virtual in disequilibrium as well as in regard to what takes place when the equilibrium prices are quoted. Walras realized that the equations he represented as relating to the mature model of general equilibrium do not in fact describe it. They relate to a different type of model.

The written pledges sketch[1]

Walras did not try to formulate the equations that could be used to find the general equilibrium values of the variables of his mature comprehensive

---

[1] The first part of this chapter summarizes briefly the relevant parts of Walker 1996, Part II, in which the written pledges sketch and Walras's last comprehensive model in general (see below) are examined in detail.

175

model. He decided instead to try to construct a model of which his existing equations would be a description. He therefore had the objective of replacing his mature comprehensive model with a virtual one (see Chapter 5, note 2), intending the latter to be the underpinning of and justification for his virtual system of equations of general equilibrium. In that failed effort, Walras abandoned the philosophical and methodological guidelines of his creative and mature phases. He discarded the procedure of drawing ideal types and general facts from (his perception of) reality. He put fictional elements into that effort, made fundamental assumptions that were not only contradictory to fact but also that resulted in a distortion of reality, sketched a scenario of hypothetical situations that had no relation to the real economy, and presented as conclusions various conditions and outcomes that could not be deduced from his assumptions and that contradicted the conditions and functioning of the real economy.

Walras first presented the idea of written pledges in a note published in 1899 (206, 1899, p. 103). "Written pledges" is the translation of the words *engagements écrits* or *engagements par écrit* that were used in French securities markets at the time Walras was writing (see, for example, Marinitsch 1892, pp. 64, 234) and are used today. To refer to *engagements écrits*, he chose the word *bons*, but because that means "*engagements écrits*" in the use he made of the word in 1899,[2] it is best translated as "written pledges." That describes the item and practice in question and is historically authentic.

---

[2] It is interesting that, in the context of discussing a partially planned economy in 1896, Walras used the word *bons* with a meaning that is totally different from written pledges. In that economy, the *bons* are tokens, denominated as either numeraire-work units or numeraire-silver units, distributed to would-be buyers by the state. Unlike written pledges, they have nothing to do with price formation. They are not used to convey desired supply quantities at different suggested prices prior to production; they are a medium of exchange, used to pay, at prices that are fixed by the state, for goods that have already been produced (194, 1896, pp. 228–30). Some economists contend that Walras's general equilibrium model, by which they mean their conception of his 1899 written pledges sketch, is literally a blueprint for a planned economy or is adaptable for that purpose. One scholar offers the baffling notion that Walras presented a model economy that is simultaneously both planned and unplanned – the "astonishing paradox of a decentralized economy that turns out to be a planned system" (Ménard 1990, p. 109; and see De Vroey 1987). Most economists (see, for example, Morishima 1996), however, indicate that it is clear that Walras's models were intended by him to enable him to understand the capitalist economy of his day, which he regarded on an abstract level as a private enterprise system of decentralized markets. In fact, the mature comprehensive model has nothing to do with a planned economy, and there is nothing in the 1899 written pledges sketch that suggests one. It is true that Walras considered aspects of a partially planned economy, but, as noted at the beginning of this footnote, he did that in an explicit treatment of precisely that topic (194, 1896), not in a development or application of his written pledges sketch.

In that first note and in the sketch that he introduced into the fourth edition of the *Eléments* (1900, 210), Walras asserted that he wanted to achieve the virtual property in all aspects of the model and in all its phases by assuming that suppliers of services and suppliers of products do not produce or sell disequilibrium amounts (210, 1900, p. VIII; pp. 6–7). Instead, they make written pledges to provide the amounts that they write down on slips of paper, provided that the price that is currently quoted is found to be the equilibrium price. Consumers write pledges to supply productive services, and those pledges are supposed to be handed to producers of products; producers write pledges to supply products and those are supposed to be handed to consumers (210, 1900, p. 224; § 214, p. 323). Walras stated that suppliers vary the amounts offered at suggested prices until the desired supply and demand of every commodity become simultaneously equal in every market, and that only when that condition is fulfilled are trade and other economic activities allowed to take place (210, 1900, pp. 215, 224, 260, 298, 302; pp. 5–7; § 207, p. 309; § § 213–14, p. 323; § 251, p. 377; § 273, p. 441; § 274, p. 447).

Walras first assumed that there is a virtual tatonnement, naturally without the equilibrium prices being known in advance; that is, with uncertainty. Then he dealt with a period of time during which transactions and the delivery of commodities go on at the equilibrium prices, with no uncertainty, just as J. R. Hicks (1939, pp. 122–27) subsequently (without acknowledging Walras's construction) did with the days of his "week" following the Monday on which prices are determined. In his discussions of uncertainty, Walras had reference to constancy of asset holdings and to knowledge of prices and the timing of transactions. He modeled behavior regarding given consumer and business inventories and holdings of money and acquisitions of them over a period of time starting at the present in this way: "By assuming [the] given conditions invariable during a certain period of time, and by assuming the prices of products and of services, and the dates at which they are bought and sold known regarding the entire period, we do not leave open the possibility for any uncertainty" (210, p. 300; § 273, pp. 443, 445). He made a parallel construction about given business inventories of primary material and products, and of money, and the acquisition of inputs during the period. Once more he wrote that there could be "uncertainty resulting from the possibility of changes in the given conditions of the problem and the difficulty of foreseeing them. But, here also, by suppressing that possibility for a certain period of time, and by assuming [the economic variables are] known for that entire period, we suppress all causes of uncertainty" (ibid., p. 301; ibid., p. 445). Walras's treatment in that regard is typical of the character of his last comprehensive model.

Those were Walras's assertions, and commentators on the sketch have accepted them at face value. They have persuaded themselves that there is, in the fourth edition, a formulation of a complete tatonnement process conducted by means of written pledges and eventuating in general equilibrium in which actual production and sales of services and products occur. That, however, is not the case. Of course, Walras asserted that there is a tatonnement and that general equilibrium supply and demand quantities exist in the model and are found, but those were just unsupported postulates, not a consequence of his assumptions, not an outcome of the structure of the sketch and the behavior of its participants.

Indeed, Walras was claiming results that, for three reasons, are impossible for the model that he wanted to construct – that is, impossible given his particular formulation of the characteristics of written pledges and given how he imagined they would be used. First, he assumed that would-be demanders do not make written pledges, in the mistaken belief that it is unnecessary for them to do so. Nor did he provide the would-be demanders with any alternative means of expressing their desires. Consequently, no demands are expressed in the markets by either would-be purchasers of services or would-be purchasers of products. Potential suppliers of services and potential suppliers of products therefore have no way of knowing the quantity demanded nor therefore whether demand and supply are equal or not (Walker 1996, pp. 382–83). So strong, however, is the conditioning of the economist's mind in regard to the supposition that markets always have demands as well as supplies, that describers of the sketch, including the present writer on two occasions, have read into it something that is not there, namely buyers who make written pledges, and have furnished their version with that feature (Schumpeter 1954, p. 1008; Patinkin 1965, p. 533; Jaffé 1967, pp. 12, 18; Jaffé 1983, p. 241; Morishima 1977, p. 55; Walker 1987a, p. 859; Walker 1987b, p. 765).[3]

Second, Walras did not finish his written pledges sketch in some other major respects, presenting instead a hodge-podge of situations that, together with the incomplete written pledges markets, have been called his last comprehensive model. That "model" is briefly mentioned in the next section of this chapter. This matter of the incompleteness of the sketch has been discussed elsewhere (Walker 1991; 1996, Part II) so here it is sufficient to mention some examples of its deficiencies. Walras neglected to provide for the equalization of price and average cost in

---

[3] That idea, totally without foundation, has now been disseminated at the level of textbooks on the history of economic thought, as witness the statement: "In the fourth edition he added the notion of *bons* or tickets: when a set of prices is tried, producers *and purchasers* issue tickets showing what they would *buy* and sell at those prices" (Staley 1989, p. 174; emphasis added).

each firm by means of variations in the supplies that producers pledge to produce. Also, although he mentioned old capital goods and land in the fourth edition of the *Eléments*, he did not provide markets for them in the last comprehensive model and therefore, obviously, neglected to assume that written pledges are used in connection with them. He discussed markets for circulating capital and money, but he assumed that written pledges are not used in them. Walras did not assume, regarding the exchange of consumable services among consumers, that consumers write pledges to supply consumable services to consumers who are would-be purchasers of them; nor that the latter write pledges to purchase consumer services (210, 1900, p. 224; § 215, p. 324). Therefore, neither would-be suppliers nor would-be demanders express their trading desires with the use of written pledges. In the written pledges sketch, there is no exchange mechanism on either side of the markets for the consumable services that Walras asserted are sold; or, more accurately, those markets do not exist in that sketch.

Third, Walras gave the written pledges process certain features that would make it impossible to allocate inputs among suppliers, and impossible to allocate outputs among demanders even if demanders were able to make written pledges. The result of the foregoing problems is that the device of written pledges is so deeply flawed that it cannot serve as a tatonnement mechanism (Walker 1996, pp. 393–94).

Nor is Walras's sketch of written pledges markets realistic in any sense of that word or useful as an explanatory device or thought experiment. It cannot be used as the basis of an applied model because of its lack of demand functions and its incompleteness in other major respects. Even if it were to be changed and completed, the amended version would describe behavior that has no counterpart in reality and would fail to make reference to variables that exist in reality. No data could be drawn from the real economy to provide the numerical coefficients of an economic version of it, and no real economic problem could be analyzed with it, because all ex post variables – production, consumption, savings, and so forth – in the real economy are disequilibrium magnitudes from the viewpoint of general equilibrium. Inasmuch as Walras assumed that the written pledges markets are virtual, there is no place for such magnitudes even in an amended version of his sketch.

A surprise discovery

As I wrote to a number of Walrasian scholars on May 15, 2002,[4] during the previous week I had happened upon an article that dealt with the

---

[4] I addressed my letter to professors Richard Arena, Jan van Daal, Jean-Pierre Potier, and Antoine Rebeyrol.

subject of one of my own articles, "Walras's Theories of Tatonnement" (Walker 1987a), and that had almost the same title. My discovery was "La théorie des tâtonnements chez Walras," by Joseph de Zatarin (1972). Just as William Jaffé had done before him (1969) and as I did fifteen years after him, De Zatarin noted the obvious and well-known fact that written pledges are used in the fourth edition of the *Eléments* but not in the first three, identified non-virtual tatonnement*s* without written pledges and virtual tatonnement*s* with them, and presented a view of Walras's treatment of both exchange and production.

De Zatarin's introduction to his article seems like some of the ideas in my article, and his laudable concern was, like mine, the issue of whether or not the solutions to Walras's equations identify the equilibrium values of the variables in his various models. It becomes clear in the body of De Zatarin's text, however, that our views of the characteristics of Walras's writings on the subject are not at all the same. For example, De Zatarin believes that, in the case of production without written pledges, the equations are invalid because of "le résidu," a concept that he did not explain, and "la dynamique." In actuality, it is the changes in the parameters of Walras's equations resulting from disequilibrium trade and production that render their solutions invalid. As an example of indefensible reasoning, De Zatarin contends that because written pledges are not used in Walras's model of pure exchange, the equations do not give the equilibrium magnitudes. Apparently explaining his reference to dynamics, De Zatarin argues that the equations do not do so for the reason that the variations of the prices quoted by the agents during the tatonnement change the values of the commodities possessed by the agents. If that were true, it would also, contrary to De Zatarin, occur if written pledges were used in exchange, and would occur in a complete written-pledges model of production also. In each case, the values would change during the tatonnement. It is not, however, true that the equations are invalidated by changes of the values. Walras's exposition of supply and demand functions indicates that a trader has an *ex ante* demand or supply quantity that is a function of each possible price of the commodity and of other variables, and for which the trader's stock of the commodity, money, and preferences are parameters. Each possible valuation of the trader's stock is therefore uniquely related to and determined by each possible price; the trader takes that valuation into account in determining his supply or demand quantity at any given possible price. Thus each valuation is implied by the possible price and the stock, and is therefore automatically one of the implicit arguments of the Walrasian demand or supply function. Changes of the valuations no more *change* the functions than do changes of the price.

The functions would be changed if the changes of the price directly, or via the change of the valuation, change the traders' preferences. That is a possibility that Walras was entitled to assume did not happen, for otherwise static supply and demand functions would not exist; the quantity would not be a function of an independent variable – the price – along with other independent variables. Preferences would not be a parametric condition but would change with each price. A demand curve could be defined for given preferences, but the trader could not move along it. If the price changed, the curve would shift.

Moreover, De Zatarin bases much of his analysis upon considerations drawn from the modeling of the results of asymmetric information and from game theory, which are both inappropriate for the understanding of the market situation that Walras contemplated.

The foundation, substance, and *raison d'être* of De Zatarin's brief article is his acceptance, without even the most cursory examination of Walras's written pledges sketch, of the notion that it is a complete functioning model. That means that, as is the case with other past writers on the subject, the characteristics that De Zatarin attributes to it, analyzes, and criticizes are in fact his own inventions. Long before writing *Walras's Market Models* (1996), I rejected the idea that Walras had a model of tatonnement with written pledges, for the reasons explained in this chapter; that is, briefly, because his sketch is not only incomplete but also fundamentally flawed as a conception. That is why I did not introduce into my 1996 book the ideas on that subject that I had expressed in my 1987a article. There is therefore no point in my dissecting the many problematic aspects of De Zatarin's brief and cryptic contentions about Walras's model of exchange and his treatment of the production and pricing of consumer commodities without and with written pledges. I am in disagreement not only with the part of my 1987a article that deals with the tatonnement with written pledges, but also with Jaffé, De Zatarin, and other scholars who base their analyses on the supposition that Walras presented a model of such a process.

The last comprehensive model

The collection of various submodels in the fourth edition, dating from different editions and differing in structural and behavioral ways, will be called Walras's last comprehensive model of general economic equilibrium (Walker 1996, Chapters 17, 18) because he presented them as such, and for the sake of brevity of expression, although they do not in fact constitute a coherent model (see ibid.). He featured suppliers' written pledges in what has just been noted are incomplete sketches of some markets, but he did not in any respect carry out his plan (210, 1900, p. VIII; pp. 5, 7) to convert into written-pledges markets all the older submodels – non-virtual components of his mature comprehensive model – that he brought over from the third edition to the fourth. During the course of preparation of the fourth edition, he mentioned written pledges only a few times and with decreasing frequency and finally abandoned the subject before he finished the revision, never to mention it again in any of his writings. Thus he introduced some markets in the fourth edition – such as the markets for long- and short-term loans – in which written pledges are not used. This was the case in his entire exposition of markets for circulating capital and money. In some instances he presented, in a particular place in the *Eléments*, a commodity as being traded in a market in which written pledges are used, and, in another place in the *Eléments*, one and the same commodity as being traded in a market in which they are not. Walras therefore presented disequilibrium production and exchange as occurring in some markets but not in others, a situation contradicted by his (unsupported) assertion in the fourth edition that exchange and production occur only when all equilibrium prices are found, contradicted by his virtual equation system, and exacerbated by the circumstance that there is no pricing process nor exchange or production in the written pledges "markets." Thus the chaotic collection of non-virtual and incomplete written pledges markets do not constitute a functioning general equilibrium model.

Also symptomatic of Walras's increasing difficulty in undertaking theoretical construction is the confused state of his efforts to introduce a revised theory of money in the fourth edition. He incorporated into Leçon 29 on circulating capital and money in that edition approximately twenty-seven lines about phases of tatonnement, at the beginning of which he specified that written pledges are used (210, 1900, p. 302; § 274, p. 447; see Chapter 8, entry 206). He made no reference whatsoever to them, however, in his immediately following discussion of the phases, nor elsewhere in Leçons 29 and 30, thus once more leaving his written pledges sketch incomplete and the functioning of written pledges trading unexplained. The twenty-seven lines were the reset lines of the last two-thirds of the "Note" (206, 1899, p. 103) that he wrote after he finished his article on the "Equations de la circulation" (ibid., pp. 85–102) and that he appended to it without in any way recognizing the content of the note in the article itself; that is, without changing his modeling of markets for circulating capital and money to reflect the use of written pledges. As the "Equations de la circulation" became the almost verbatim exposition of monetary phenomena in the fourth edition, that exposition is therefore substantially devoid of reference to written pledges. Walras did not alter his treatment of these matters in the nearly identical posthumously published fifth edition of the *Eléments* (224, 1926).

Moreover, the models of markets for circulating capital and money in the fourth edition are incomplete and indeed nonsensical for a variety of other reasons (Walker 1996, Chapter 18). As Pascal Bridel rightly indicated, there is in the fourth edition "no genuine monetary theory" (Bridel 1997, p. 133). That was necessarily the case, given the incompatible and dysfunctional mixture of nonvirtual and incomplete written pledges markets in that edition. Money could not be a functioning aspect of markets in such a context. There is an important lesson to be drawn from the analysis of the incompleteness of Walras's sketch, which is why that analysis was worth undertaking (Walker 1996). It is that what are presented as being economic models should not be accepted as being logically complete if the results that they are alleged to have are not generated by institutions, procedures, technologies, rules, and other structural and behavioral underpinnings.

Various scholars have, of course, written articles that purport to establish the existence of equilibrium in one or another of Walras's models, using equations that he set forth in the *Eléments* (for example, Walker 2001, *1*, ch. 22; *2*, chs. 3, 5, 20, 22). In fact, however, the equations do not describe the mature comprehensive model, or the written pledges sketch, or the last comprehensive model, for the reasons just explained. Those articles on existence are therefore instead examples of how elements of Walras's constructions have been used by modern scholars in new fields of study.

II. Accounting for the poor quality of the revisions in the fourth edition

Most of Walras's theorizing after 1895 was of inferior quality. In particular, his revisions in the fourth edition of the *Eléments* reveal his incapacity, in his final phase of theoretical activity, to formulate theoretical constructions that necessitated extended chains of logical reasoning, and to develop a coherent comprehensive model. This judgment that the quality of most of his theorizing after 1895 is poor is independent of whether or not it was worse or better before that date, whether his output increased or not, whether his work was like or unlike that of other economists, whether his health deteriorated or not, and indeed, whether or not any explanation of the defective characteristics of his work is made. In recognition of this, contrary to the allegations of Pascal Bridel (1998, p. 232), Michel De Vroey (1999), and Fabio Petri (2004,

p. 149), in my studies of Walras's last phase of theorizing (Walker 1996, pp. 321–419), I did not mention his health as evidence supporting my contentions about the quality and quantity of his work. His adoption of the device of written pledges, for example, was not an aberration occasioned by the state of his health. Walras had theoretical reasons, however misguided, for wanting to revise the *Eléments* in the way that he attempted, and he was perfectly clear about wanting to change his model of markets to one in which written pledges are used (210, 1900, p. VIII; pp. 6–7). It was by means of detailed economic analysis that I showed that the quality of his work was poor after 1895, and that his execution of his plan for the revision was flawed and incomplete (Walker 1996, pp. 321–419), as regards both the written pledges sketch and the treatment of the markets without written pledges that he introduced in the fourth edition. I also asserted that the quantity of his theoretical output diminished (ibid., p. 322).

As a matter of some interest, however – although of no consequence for my economic analysis – I sought to explain why the quality and quantity of Walras's work diminished. The most probable explanation I could think of was that his health deteriorated. In contrast, Bridel contended that "the apparent worsening of Walras's health between 1890 and 1892 has probably more to do with a teaching load he found unbearable. As a matter of fact, soon after his retirement in 1892, his publishing rate went up quite drastically – hardly a sign of a sudden softening of the brain" (Bridel 1998, p. 232). Bridel thereby imputed to me a diagnosis that I never made and that I explicitly disavowed when I stated that my attribution of Walras's difficulty with theoretical construction late in life to his poor health was "not to suggest that Walras was then or ever became senile" (Walker 1996, p. 322).

Thus Bridel alleged that Walras's health improved after he was free of teaching duties, and that his productivity consequently increased.[5] Those assertions will be examined. It will first be seen whether Walras felt better after he retired, whether he believed that his health affected his analytical abilities, and then whether his publishing rate went up.

The case for believing that Walras's health deteriorated was made by him, not by me; I simply recorded his statements in my book. It was not necessary to quote all his many reiterations of those circumstances; instead, from the mass of evidence, I chose representative and fully descriptive assertions (ibid., pp. 321–22, 400–401), and I repeat them here, with some additional material. Walras indicated that his health became worse shortly after he retired in early July 1892 and that it

---

[5] The same contentions are made in De Vroey 1999.

continued progressively to deteriorate. On August 1, 1892, he wrote that walks were no longer therapeutic and that he had begun to intersperse his studies with manual work to prevent himself from pursuing extended and fatiguing chains of thought (239, 1892, 2, pp. 499–500). In July 1893 he noted that he continued to abstain from all intellectual work and in consequence felt better, leading him to form the intention of abstaining similarly for another year (239, July 1, 1893, 2, p. 563). His "physical forces" and his "intellectual forces" (239, October 10, 1893, 2, p. 594), he reported, became tolerable only if he did not work very much and became intolerable if he did. Nevertheless, he generally did not feel well. A year and four months after retiring he wrote to Wicksell that he had attentively read a book of Wicksell's "despite the state of my brain, which prohibits me from undertaking that sort of work" (239, November 10, 1893, 2, p. 598).

Six and a half months later – about two years after ceasing teaching – Walras stated that he had not been getting better and complained once more that he was physically and intellectually exhausted: "My brain is still in quite a pitiful state; it is not probable that I will be able to undertake new work" (239, May 27, 1894, 2, p. 603). He explained that he had to abandon his plan of writing a book on applied economics and one on normative economics (ibid.). He wanted to write an exposition of doctrine linking those two books but felt he would be unable to do that; the effort to do so, he wrote, "caused me painful cerebral troubles" (ibid.). He abandoned it also in favor of restating some of his ideas in an essay (205, 1898, section VII), the first draft of which took him eighteen months to complete. Walras lamented that he found sustained analytical work involving chains of reasoning particularly difficult. Thinking through the aspects of the equations of marginal productivity is "a point on which I must reflect very calmly, because my head is very tired and refuses all work that is even remotely intense and sustained" (239, October 30, 1895, in 239, 2, p. 651). In February 1896, he was unable to make more than a few minor changes, all of them purely editorial, to produce the third edition of the *Eléments d' économie politique pure* (1896). He explained that it differed from the second (1889) only by the elimination of the lessons on the applied theory of money and by the addition of three appendices of already published material. That procedure, he stated, enabled him to avoid trying to undertake a revision, "a task," he wrote, "which I fear I am no longer capable of doing" (192, 1896, p. X). He wrote to a friend in November 1896: "I am no longer involved with economic theory and normative economics. I am tranquilly going to take two years to have the volume of Applied Economics printed and my work will be finished." During the boring days of winter, he explained, "my head can no longer work and even distractions exhaust me" (239, November 11, 1896, *2*, p. 702).

Walras began to prepare the fourth edition of the *Eléments* in the first part of 1899, and in the course of doing so altered his treatment of money. That task, he reported, "has made me very tired and even quite indisposed" (239, May 6, 1899, *3*, p. 71). He finished it only "with infinite difficulty and fatigue which have made me ill and left me in that condition all summer" (239, November 19, 1899, *3*, p. 93). A few days later, he wrote, initially referring to "1898–99": "In 1899 (after 41 years of work and strife, being 65 years old and completely at the end of my forces), I had to retire definitively from active political economy," although he thought he would be able to finish definitive editions of his works (249.XIII, November 26, 1899, p. 513; and see p. 517). That was his condition during the first few months of 1899 when he wrote the "Equations de circulation," which, as noted above, became the revision of the monetary theory in the *Eléments*, and that was his condition during the ensuing summer when he made most of the rest of the revisions to the *Eléments* to produce the fourth edition.

The revision took him longer than he expected. He was not quite finished with it by October 1899, but he ceased work on it, writing that "I have renounced two things which fatigue and irritate me [overexcite my nerves]: the problems of mathematical economics and attempts to formulate contemporary propaganda"[6] (239, October 6, 1899, *3*, p. 90). He began a period of rest lasting about five weeks that, he reported on November 19, enabled him to recover (239, 1899, *3*, p. 93). He evidently felt that the revision was incomplete because he then began again to try to make some changes, but he found it so difficult to concentrate and construct that his sporadic efforts dragged on for three more months, until the end of March 1900, by which time he was "dead tired" (239, April 7, 1900, *3*, p. 114). It had taken him eleven months, from May 1899 to the end of March 1900, to write some half-lines, lines, and pages that, added together, total a little less than 34.5 pages, and his modifications had dwindled in the course of the revision until finally he abandoned the task and left it unfinished (as shown in Walker 1996, Part II).

A few months later, he wrote that he could not "read or write or talk very long without having a crisis of cerebral congestion during the night. In short, my brain, which for a long time has asked for mercy has openly revolted and refuses me its service" (239, October 27, 1900, *3*, p. 125). He could not follow chains of reasoning, noting in 1901 that "my cerebral and nervous fatigue is extreme and my attention span

---

[6] He meant "persuasive policy proposals."

is very limited" (239, December 21, 1901, *3*, p. 182). His condition continued to worsen, and by 1903 it was very bad: "My nerves and my brain are extremely weakened and fatigued. I can hardly any longer write or converse without having an attack [a nervous crisis] during the night" (239, April 6, 1903, *3*, pp. 223–24). "I am actually suffering very much," he wrote in 1904. "My strength is totally exhausted. I cannot converse, read or write for half an hour without having an attack during the night" (239, February 28, 1904, *3*, p. 246). His daughter read to him and he dictated letters to her, but, he explained, "I do not have her read economics, and I do not dictate to her any letters except those that are as short as possible" (ibid.). In October 1904, he was invited to write a piece on A.-A. Cournot's contributions to economics, but he could not manage to do the work so it was assigned instead to Albert Aupetit (249.VII, p. 444). He explained: "I suffer from a cerebral neurosis which forbids me to do any work at all, even that of writing a letter unaided" (239, November 3, 1904, *3*, p. 256). What he produced after ten months, with Cournot's name in the title as a formality, was six pages that had the objective of referring to some of his own past writings, and that in actuality did little more than list them (213, 1905).

Thus Walras stated that his health continued to deteriorate after his retirement and that it worsened with each passing year. His contention is credible. A condition is properly described as a deterioration of a scholar's mental and physical state if it troubles his waking hours and disturbs his sleep, leads to his incapacity to concentrate for very long, initially limits his efforts to write, then forces him to abandon totally his revisions of his writings and theoretical research in general, and ultimately renders him unable to read or write or talk for more than half an hour.

III. Walras's productivity

The purpose of the following account is to establish the facts and to draw attention to the need for careful investigation before making pronouncements about Walras's productivity. I was in a position to assess it because I spent a great deal of time during six years compiling and annotating the list of his writings (Walker 1987c), and I am in an even more advantageous position to judge his output after having spent a great deal more time refining the bibliography (Appendix, Part 2) during the nineteen years since I prepared the first edition. Inasmuch as I reported that by 1896 Walras "was publishing very little theoretical work, and occupied himself, on a greatly diminished scale, primarily with applied topics and with his old papers" (Walker 1996, p. 322), and inasmuch

Table 1. *Walras's Productivity: Number of Pages Newly Published or Written*

	Economics				
	Theory	Other	Total	Other	Grand Total
1858–1871	260	1,310	1,570	501	2,071
1872–1877	448	218	666	135	801
1878–1895	479	271	750	245	995
1896–1900	59	98	157	0	157
1901–1910	0	50	50	3	53

as he and I both asserted that he became incapable of undertaking new theoretical constructions, it is reasonable to ask whether the objective record supports those contentions. Are those statements true or (as has been alleged) false (Bridel 1998, De Vroey 1999)?

Walras's productivity is measured by the number of pages he wrote, as first shown in Table 1. The details of the calculations are given in the Appendix to this chapter. The periods selected are those to which I referred in *Walras's Market Models* (1996, pp. 7–13) as the phases of his journalistic and experimental period (1858–1871), of great creativity (1872–1877), of intellectual maturity (1878–1895), and of decline. That latter phase is divided into the periods 1896 through 1900, the year of the publication of the fourth edition of the *Eléments*, and 1901 thorough 1910, the year of Walras's death. The data are used to calculate Table 2, which shows the average number of pages per year. The results are robust. Changes in the years included within each period and even changes in the dating or classification of one or another publication do not affect the general picture.

The results are also quite clear. It is strikingly evident that Walras's average annual theoretical output was much greater in his creative phase, 1872–1877, than in any other. The "economics-other" column

Table 2. *Walras's Productivity: Average Number of Pages Per Year*

	Number of Years	Economics				
		Theory	Other	Total	Other	Grand Total
1858–1871	14	18.57	93.57	112.14	35.78	147.93
1872–1877	6	74.67	36.33	111.0	22.5	133.5
1878–1895	18	26.61	15.06	41.67	13.61	52.28
1896–1900	5	11.8	19.6	31.4	0	31.4
1901–1910	10	0	5.0	5.0	0.3	5.3

for the years 1858–1871 records the pages in his three early economics books and his voluminous output as a young journalist during the years 1858–1871. Despite that output, which was on a level of economic sophistication lower than the applied studies of his creative phase, his total economics average productivity was as great during the latter phase and his total productivity did not decrease greatly. His average output in every category was much less in every phase after 1877. It is also evident that after 1895 his average annual output of economic theory, total economics, and other writings (and therefore his total output) *declined*, and that his output in every category was small in absolute terms.

Let us examine even more closely Bridel's contention that it is "*a matter of fact*" – as distinct, he meant, from what he wished to portray as mistruths that I concocted – that Walras's productivity *increased "quite drastically*" shortly after his retirement in 1892 (Bridel 1998, p. 232, emphasis added). Counting new writings, as is done throughout this examination, the facts are that in 1888–1892, the five years prior to 1893, Walras published a total of 147 pages of economics (and zero of other) writings, or 29.4 pages per year, and that in the next five years, 1893–1897, he published 126 pages of economics (and zero of other) writings, or 25.2 per year – that is, not a drastic increase, not a medium-sized or even a small increase, but in fact a *decrease*.

What about Walras's contention that he was running out of mental energy in regard to his economic theorizing after 1893? Walras's output of theoretical writing was an average of 28.4 pages per year during 1888–1892. Then, after his retirement, reflecting his admitted decline in mental powers in constructing chains of abstract reasoning, his theoretical writings fell to an average of 1.2 pages per year in the period 1893–1897 – a *drastic decrease*. Let 1890 be selected as an initial year so as to exclude Walras's revision of the *Eléments* published in 1889. That will eliminate the *Eléments'* augmentation of his pre-retirement average output and will thus present the most favorable possible setting for Bridel's contention that Walras became very much more productive after he retired in 1892. Walras's total number of pages of new theoretical writings was four in 1890, eight in 1891, and eight in 1892. The average for those three years was 6.7 pages. The average then fell to *zero* for the next three-year period. Specifically, the facts are that shortly after his retirement, the number of pages of new theory that he published was zero in 1893, zero in 1894, and zero in 1895. By the way, it is not that Walras was writing theoretical material that would later be published. He was not revising the *Eléments* during those three years: he was not writing any new theory at all.

Walras's theoretical productivity, total and per year, continued to diminish after 1895, and it was virtually exhausted during the summer of 1899, when he was trying to revise the *Eléments*. Moreover, if theoretical creativity were the criterion by which his output was judged, it would have to be recognized that there was little of that after 1889. The tables show this clearly, but it is evident even by taking averages of long periods. During the fifteen-year period 1874 through 1889, he wrote 708 pages of theory, an average of 44.25 pages per year. In contrast, during the eleven-year period 1890 through 1900, he wrote 79.5 pages of theory, 53.5 of which were the defective material that he put into the fourth edition of his *Eléments* (19 pages of the "Equations de circulation" including the "Note" (206) plus 34.5 additional lines). That is an average of only 7.2 pages per year. The facts of the matter are the contrary of what Bridel and De Vroey asserted.

Apart from those theoretical writings, what Walras did after 1895 was to work with old papers and reflect on the past, as shown by the publications listed in Chapter 8. He assembled collections of his old essays. He developed plans for the publication of the collected economic writings of his father and himself. He compiled an autobibliography and wrote a brief autobiographical note. He wrote a few pages of applied economics that were elaborations of ideas that he had conceived many years previously – restatements of methodological and philosophical views, and of his favorite economic policy schemes.

What about Walras's contention that his health in the period 1900 to 1907 was continuing to deteriorate so that he found theoretical construction impossible? What about his assertions that he became virtually incapable of writing anything unaided, even a letter? Bridel and De Vroey have inexplicably pointed to my quotations of Walras's letters as evidence of what the two scolars represent is my inability to recognize truth, and evidence of the ridiculousness of the notion that Walras had a phase of intellectual decline manifested in decreased productivity. It has just been shown that their contentions are contrary to the facts regarding years prior to 1900. Is their view supported by the data for subsequent years? Was Walras's last decade fruitful? If he was accurately representing his mental and physical condition, the record should show that he became unproductive. Table 3 presents the evidence. Virtually all the revisions to the 1900 edition of the *Eléments* were made in 1899, so a row could be added for 1900 showing little or no theoretical writing in that year also. That row would also show only three pages of "economics-other" writing and zero other writings, for a grand total of about three pages.

Table 3. *Pages Newly Published or Written,*
1901–1910

| | Economics | | Other |
	Theory	Other	Other
1901	0	0	0
1902	0	0	3
1903	0	0	0
1904	0	0	0
1905	0	6	0
1906	0	0	0
1907	0	0	0
1908	0	14	0
1909	0	28	0
1910	0	2	0

The data speak for themselves regarding the quantitative facts. They reveal clearly the continuing and intensified cruel effects of Walras's ill health on his productivity. As he indicated in his letters and as the record shows, he made no more attempts at writing economic theory after about the end of 1899, and he wrote a total of only nine pages of new economics ("economics-other") and other professional writing ("other") during the seven-year period 1901 through 1907. The six pages he published in 1905 (213) have not a single novel idea in them; they concern brief descriptions of his major publications, as explained earlier. In 1906 he assembled "La paix par la justice sociale et le libre échange" (215), published in 1907. It was excluded from the count of his pages because it consists of summaries of and extracts from his earlier publications, *Recherche de l'idéal social* (90, 1868), the "Esquisse d'une doctrine économique et sociale" (205, 1898 Part VII), and a verbatim reproduction of almost all of the "Théorie du libre échange" (197, 1895). The fourteen pages recorded in the table for 1908 constitute an article (216) on his father's economics. That is a descriptive piece that made no demands upon Walras and that contains no new ideas. Similarly, the twenty-eight pages he wrote in 1909 are not really new research. They consist of two articles. One is an undemanding descriptive article (218) that contains not a single new idea. In it he quoted Louis Ruchonnet, the Swiss statesman, at considerable length, summarized very briefly some of his own publications using phrases that he had often used before, advocated yet again his proposal that the government purchase all land, praised Switzerland for providing him with intellectual freedom, and that is all. The other article (219) is one in which he sketchily repeated economic formulas and discussions found in the Eléments, and restated briefly his decade-old notions about the parallels between economics and mechanics.[7] Walras did not accomplish any original research after March 1900.

APPENDIX

The source for the data in the tables is the definitive bibliography of Walras's writings (Chapter 8). The numbers in parentheses are those assigned to the entries in the bibliography. The following procedures were followed.

The items that appear in the "economics-theory" column are those that Walras classified as theory, or that are economic models or theoretical constructions. If Walras classified a text as applied economics, then the relevant pages were put into the "economics-other" column, except for some items that were, nevertheless, credited to him as economic theory. This was true in the case of entries 148, 153, 154, 158 and 169. His article on H.-H. Gossen (163) is history of economic thought, but its analytical and critical approach merits it being counted as theory. A dubious classification was the placement of one of his early treatments of taxation, *Théorie critique de l'impôt* (27) in the theory column. Walras classified a note on the quantity theory of money (199) as applied economics but it is here classified as theory. A small part of the material in some of the entries classified as "economics-other" is theoretical in nature, but in most cases they are truly applied economics and not works of theory, much less of original theorizing. Moreover, there are many pages in the "economics-other" column that could be put into the "other" (non-economics) column because they deal with philosophy or methodology or thoughts about human nature or the desirable way of organizing society or other such topics. This is true of entry 189, "Théorie de la propriété," which has some unoriginal theoretical statements but deals principally with social questions in a normative way. The "other" column records Walras's output of literary productions such as his novel, short story, literary criticism, and reviews of paintings.

Excluded from the statistics were republications of Walras's writings. Also excluded, because they were not research or were not his own writings, were his personal note (183); his assembly of his father's

---

[7] Jean-Pierre Potier describes the article well by saying that "it does not constitute new research," but is instead a summary of Walras's past contributions (Potier 1994, p. 277).

bibliography (187), his lecture notes (252, 253) – which did not do more than present the ideas and frequently very nearly the same language as are found in his publications; his mainly undated "Notes d'humeur" (251); his translation of W. S. Jevons's treatise (144); his contribution to a translation of H.-H. Gossen's treatise (260); his abridgement (230) of the *Eléments*; his autobiographical note (212); and his autobibliographies (214, 240, 262). The few pages of his undated and unpublished essays (250, 254–59, 261), all empirical in content, were not counted precisely because it is not known in what year they were written, although Walras evidently wrote them all during his early years. He prepared the lecture notes mainly during the 1870s. Adding the undated essays and the lecture notes among Walras's new writings would therefore have the effect of augmenting the contrast between his earlier and his later productivity, thereby increasing the imbalance pointed out in this study.

The "Recherche de l'idéal social" was published as a series in columnar form in *Le Travail* in 1867 and 1868. Three of the parts were published in 1867 and three in 1868. The series was republished in book form in 1868 (90), so instead of using the number of newspaper columns, the 226 book pages that they required are credited partially to 1867 and partially to 1868. The lengthy introduction to the book is credited to 1868.

Unless there were exceptional circumstances, as was the case regarding the mémoires discussed below, if it is known that Walras wrote an entry in a year earlier than the date of its publication, the entry is credited to the earlier year. For example, he wrote entry 51, published in December 1866, in January 1863, so it credited to that year; he wrote entry 197, published in July 1897, in March 1895, so it is added into the total for 1895. This procedure was not applied to Walras's four theoretical mémoires (103, 118, 119, 122). They were not counted inasmuch as all the ideas and much of the identical language in those mémoires are in the first edition of the *Eléments*, which was counted. It would have been too complicated to do otherwise, and then to try to pick out the parts of the *Eléments* that do not duplicate the mémoires. Walras read one of them (103) in Paris in August 1873, before the publication of the first part of the *Eléments* (106), and read another (118) in Lausanne in December 1875 after the publication of that part, but both mémoires were included in it. He wrote much of Part 2 of the *Eléments d'économie politique pure* (123) before 1875, but not all, because he continually revised the text during the period 1875 to September 1877, even altering the proofs. Part 2 of the *Eléments* includes the ideas and most of the language of the two mémoires (119 and 122) that were read to the Société vaudoise des Sciences naturelles in 1876, one of which was published in that year and the other in March 1877. It is not possible, however, to determine specifically the date on which Walras wrote many of the words of Part 2, so all of it is credited to 1877, the year of its publication. This treatment does not influence the outcome shown in the tables because the four memoires and the first edition of the *Eléments* were all published in the range of years of Walras's creative period.

Walras wrote the manuscript entry 95 in 1871. It comprises 37 autograph pages. As published in entry 249.XI, pp. 385–409, it takes a little more than 24 pages, which have been duly added into the count of theoretical writings.

Walras's essays on economics education are a mixture of normative, philosophical, and methodological analyses of economics studies, discussions of free competition as a policy, other economic policies, other applied economic topics, and non-analytical references to the views of other economists on such topics, so they have been classified under "economics-other." This is true of entries 97, 141, and 152. Walras wrote entry 141, published in 1879, partly during 1878 and partly during 1879, so it is divided between those two years. Walras's publications in 1891 (179) and 1892 (180) were credited to those respective years and not to the third edition of the *Eléments* (192, 1896), in which they were republished as Appendixes I and II, respectively. Entry 181 was not counted because it is a translation into English of entry 180. For the second edition of the *Eléments* (176), the number of newly written pages was calculated as the length of the second edition minus the length of the first edition, namely 116 pages. They were attributed to 1889. No pages were counted from the third edition (192) because it is simply a reprint of the second edition minus the lessons on applied monetary topics plus the addition of the appendixes. The 1894–1895 "Note sur la Refutation de la Théorie anglaise de Fermage de M. Wicksteed" (entry 191, with lines that add up to 8 pages of print), became Appendix III. In the presentation in entry 249.VIII, pp. 715, 717–22, that appendix has lines that add up to 6.25 pages. Entry 191 was not counted, however, because it does not contain new research. As noted in the Appendix, Part 2, Walras simply patched it together by using passages and equations from the second edition of the *Eléments*, by reproducing Wicksteed's equations and quoting or paraphrasing his work, and by presenting an analysis authored by Enrico Barone.

The fourth edition of the *Eléments* (210) contains only 34.5 pages of newly published writing, calculated by counting precisely the lines and pages that Walras added to that edition, but excluding his partial rewording of the short subtitle indexes preceding each lesson and excluding lessons 29 and 30 on the theory of money except as indicated below, because those lessons are a republication of entry 206, the "Equations de la circulation," with a few slight changes. The 19 pages of entry 206 are credited to 1899, the year Walras wrote it. When he put it into the *Eléments*, he eliminated some lines in the two Leçons, and added 29 lines of new writing (see entry 206), which equal about 0.8 of a page in the fourth edition. Those lines are duly added into the total of new writings for 1900.

Walras wrote a version of many or all of the 34.5 net new pages in the fourth edition during 1899, so many of them should be credited to that year, but he continued to make small changes until the end of March 1900, so some of the words could be credited to 1900. All the pages are, in any case, allotted to the period 1896–1900, and the grouping of years makes the allocation as between 1899 and 1900 unimportant.

Entry 188 was published in 1896, but its twenty-two pages are not credited to that year but to 1868, when Walras wrote them. The expansion of the ideas in entry 188 to ninety pages (entry 99), although dated 1872–1873 by Walras, appeared in 1872, and is credited to that year.

Walras's publications in newspapers were quantitatively of importance in some of the years during the 1860s. Where possible, newspaper columns were counted as equaling the number of pages that were required to reprint them in book form, and where possible the pagination of the republication of the article in entry 249 was used. A newspaper column was otherwise counted as being equal to two pages.

The *Etudes d' économie sociale* (193) is excluded, except for the material not previously published, namely a "Note" of two pages in length (see 193). The *Etudes d' économie politique appliquée* (205), is excluded, with two exceptions. The first is the "Note sur la 'théorie de la quantité'," which was not previously published. The second relates to group VII of the collection, titled "Esquisse d'une doctrine économique et sociale." Part of the "Esquisse" had been published, namely "Politique française. La prière du libre penseur" (202, 203); those two essays were originally published in the same year as the *Etudes* were published. Most of the substance of the previously unpublished parts of the "Esquisse" had already been published. Walras wrote several drafts of them during the period September 1893 to February 1895, one of which amounted to twenty-five pages. He continued to add to the text, finishing a revision shortly before March 1897. He then kept working on the text, not completing the last version, thirty-one manuscript pages in length, until April 1898 (see 249.X, pp. XIX–XX). Walras's increasing difficulty of composition is well illustrated by his taking four years and four months to write those thirty-one pages. The article also reveals two characteristics of most of his work after 1895: the repetition of ideas that he had expressed long before the 1890s and the treatment of themes that were not on the same level of difficulty as economic theory. Nevertheless, the 28 previously unpublished pages of the last version of the "Esquisse," plus the 9 pages of the "Politique française" and the "Prière," as published in entry 249.X, pp. 405–32, are credited to him as "new writings." In an effort to reflect the dates when he wrote them, they have been divided into six parts. Seventeen pages are attributed to 1893 and the remaining twenty pages are divided up by allotting four pages to each year during the period 1894 through 1898. Only two other entries for the year 1898 were new writings, namely numbers 200 and 201, totaling thirty-five pages.

Walras's writings

CHAPTER 7

Some bibliographical remarks

I. Description of the definitive bibliography

I finished the preparation of the first edition of the bibliography of Léon Walras's writings in 1986 (Walker 1987c). These remarks and the bibliography that follows are revised versions, made necessary by new information and publication events during subsequent years. I compiled the first edition of the bibliography in the conviction that it would be a valuable research aid to scholars who are interested in his work, and that has proved to be the case. Articles are written on Walras's ideas each year and many other papers refer to his ideas and cite his publications, and the authors are no longer at the disadvantage of not knowing of the existence of many of his writings. Formerly, scholars were familiar only with the part of his writings that appears in his *Eléments d'économie politique pure* and in the two volumes of his collected papers (194 and 205), although that is a very important part. Especially in need of the information provided in this bibliography is the historian of thought who wishes to explore the development of Walras's ideas.

Since the time that I prepared the first edition, the Centre Auguste et Léon Walras (recently renamed TRIANGLE, Unité Mixte de Recherche 5206 du Centre National de la Recherche Scientifique) at the Université de Lyon 2 began the project of publishing Auguste and Léon Walras's *Œuvres économiques complètes* (*OEC*, entry 249), and all the volumes in that series that are devoted to Léon's writings have now appeared. This bibliography and those volumes are complementary. Chronological and annotated, this bibliography will be useful to the Walrasian scholar not only because of whatever it possesses in the way of comprehensiveness, precision, and wealth of detail, but also because it draws to the researcher's attention economic entries that can be readily located in the *OEC*. It also lists and annotates many items that are not in the *OEC*. In the following remarks, the publication of Walras's writings in the *OEC* is excluded from consideration unless specifically indicated to the contrary.

Walras published an autobibliography in 1897 (see entry 196) that is incomplete in many respects other than the obvious one of not including writings that date from years after its composition. The other bibliography that has thus far been published, presented by Georges-Henri Bousquet in 1964 (238), is Walras's manuscript autobibliography of economic writings compiled by him in 1906 (214), with some additions. It contains the following entries listed by Walras: 125 numbered items, ten unnumbered items that were unpublished at the time that Walras compiled the list, and one unnumbered item (199 in the present bibliography) that was published for the first time in 1898 (see 205). It also contains three entries published after 1906 that were added by Bousquet (see 238). Thus it has a total of 139 entries. That autobibliography is unsatisfactory. It is seriously incomplete regarding both published and unpublished items. Some entries are assigned to the wrong year. Some of the titles are erroneous and many of them are incomplete. The citations are all incomplete because Walras neglected to give the numbers of the journal issues and the pagination of his articles, the journal volume for most of his articles, and the place of publication and publisher of his books. He briefly annotated some of the entries, as the complete transcript of his autobibliography in my possession shows, but none of his annotations was included by Bousquet. In his autobibliography Walras classified the entries into six subject-matter categories such as economic policy, applied economics, and economic policy and justice. His categorization has not been copied in the present bibliography because its taxonomic accuracy and value is debatable with respect to some of the items, and because he did not list and hence did not categorize many of the entries that appear in the present bibliography.

Every effort has been made to make the bibliography a useful research tool. It corrects all the deficiencies of Bousquet's presentation of Walras's autobibliography and contains a great deal more information. It provides a much more complete listing than has been given before. With respect to the initial publications of Walras's writings, it is probably complete, with the exception that references have not been included to publications in journals of Walras's letters if they also appear in *Correspondence of Léon Walras and Related Papers*, edited by William Jaffé (239). There are a few exceptions to this rule. For example, entry 101 appears in the bibliography because it was an open letter, published in a journal before it was mailed; entry 164 appears because it is a letter addressed to the editor of the journal in which it was published; and entry 211 was similarly an open letter published in the month that it was written. I use the term "probably complete" because I have inferred from my experiences during the years in which I compiled the bibliography and revised it that no amount of diligence can exclude the possibility that minor items have escaped my search. Be that as it may, this bibliography includes all the entries that appear in Walras's autobibliography, and gives many additional economic entries plus the bibliographies themselves (214 and 238). In contrast to Bousquet's presentation, the economic entries that date from before Walras's death in 1910 total 191, not counting his autobibliography or his autobiography in French (212) and in Italian (217), or his bibliography of his father's writings (187), although he so included it. These figures include reprints and translations. Microforms are not included.

With respect to unpublished economic manuscripts, the present bibliography lists 36. In this discussion, an "unpublished manuscript" means one that was unpublished during Walras's lifetime. Some of them are difficult to classify as such, however, because, like entry 151, they were used as the basis of a text that was published during Walras's lifetime. The 36 entries probably include every manuscript that Walras intended to be a research paper or extended statement, as distinct from jottings and brief notes. Despite the publication of the *OEC* volumes since the preparation of the first edition of this bibliography, in the present edition the entries for economic manuscripts have been presented as they originally appeared, so that the reader can learn their titles and the fact that they were unpublished during Walras's lifetime, and can then turn to the *OEC* for the texts. The bibliography indicates if they were published prior to their appearance in the *OEC*, and gives the entry number of the published version.

The bibliography includes the compilations of Walras's jottings and brief notes that have been published (242; 249.XIII, pp. 509–622). The compilations are unclassifiable entries that are counted only in the grand total. Furthermore, the bibliography is complete in the respect that it includes Walras's 26 literary (non-economic) writings, some of which have relevance for his economic ideas, and his "Bibliographie littéraire" (263), of which I possess a complete transcript, whereas his autobibliography lists only his economic writings. Thus the total number of entries is 263. Of course, that is not an indication of the amount of original material in his texts. His practice of republishing his articles and memoires, and of including verbatim copies or the substance of already published material in texts with a new or similar title, greatly increases the number of entries in the bibliography, as do reprints, translations, and the separate listing of both unpublished and published forms of texts.

The present bibliography establishes the correct title of each entry and presents the titles that Walras, in his autobibliography and "Bibliographie littéraire," gave to items published without a title. Unlike the lists of Walras's writings prepared by other scholars, the present one indicates the dimensions and location of unpublished manuscripts. It provides the date of composition of 53 of the unpublished manuscripts. It describes the contents and pagination of the contents of volumes of collected papers. It gives complete bibliographical information on republications, indicating whether changes were made in the entry when it was republished. With respect to articles, it specifies whether they were reprinted as offprints and whether they were republished in a collection. It gives the location in the *Correspondence* of the many summaries of entries provided in that source. It includes Walras's annotations, indicated by the phrase, "Walras explained that..." or by a similar phrase, if they add information about the entries.

Regarding published materials, which constitute the vast majority of Walras's writings and are by far the most important part, I have been able to establish almost all the bibliographical information by using my collection of originals or copies of Walras's publications. I supplemented the information in my collection by using the papers and other materials in the William Jaffé collection that is now in the York University library in Canada, by trips and telephone calls to libraries, and by communicating with Ms. Marlyse Vernez and Mr. Christian Graf, reference librarians at the Bibliothèque Cantonale et Universitaire in Lausanne, to whom I am very grateful for clear, detailed, and accurate information. I wish to thank Ms. Carol E. Connell and Mr. Blaine Knupp, bibliographer and reference librarian, respectively, at the University Libraries, Indiana University of Pennsylvania, for their skilled assistance in tracking down obscure texts in a variety of languages. I also wish to thank Kunio Nakakubo of Himeji Dokkyo University, Japan, for supplying some of the information that appears under entry 234 and all of the information for entries 225, 246, and 247. For information that appears under entry 226 and especially under entry 234, I am indebted to the editorial section of Iwanami Bunko. I am grateful for financial support from Indiana University of Pennsylvania for my preparation of the first edition of the bibliography. Since preparing it, I resigned my positions at IUP in order to devote myself to research, and the definitive edition is one of the fruits of my current independent way of life.

Regarding Walras's unpublished economic and non-economic manuscripts, I have used a variety of sources to identify them. Those materials were either listed by Walras in his autobibliography of economic writings or in his "Bibliographie littéraire," listed by William Jaffé, together with their archival location and classification number, in the notes to the letters in his edition of Walras's correspondence, identified through my examination of microfilms and transcripts collected by Jaffé, or noted by him in his papers, together with their archival location and classification number. With respect to the unpublished manuscripts, I am therefore greatly indebted to Jaffé.

It should be noted that, with a few exceptions, Walras's unpublished professional papers constitute part of the Fonds Walras, the archival materials deposited in the Département des manuscrits of the Bibliothèque Cantonale et Universitaire de Dorigny, on the university campus near Lausanne, Switzerland. The materials in the Fonds Walras have been reclassified, but the old classification numbers, referring to folders (in roman numerals) and items within those folders (in arabic numerals) in the archives, are still valid and are given in the present bibliography. The Lyons Collection, to which reference is made in entry 8, was called the "Collection Walras de la Faculté de Droit de Lyon." That collection, which had not been classified at the time that I listed that entry, is now under the care of the research unit 5206.

II. Jaffé's plans

Jaffé's work on Walras's writings leads one to wonder why he did not publish a bibliography of them. The answer is an interesting story that deserves to be told in this context. Jaffé did not prepare and publish Walras's bibliography for the same reasons that he did not write Walras's biography, because the bibliography was to be part of that biography. Specifically, it was to be the last part, in the manner, he told me, of the bibliography at the end of Lionel Robbins's book on Robert Torrens. The reasons are made evident in the following excerpts from our correspondence. I first quote from a letter to Jaffé that I sent him on January 7, 1980, in response to a letter in which he had referred to the project that he titled the *Life and Writings of Léon Walras* as "the other thing."

I think that you may be incorrigible in your tendency to stray from the straight and narrow path. . . . I'm forced to conclude that you have tended to avoid THE OTHER THING for the last 25 years . . . because you really don't want to work on it. You don't want to go through the effort of immersing yourself in all the source material so as to recapture the perfect intimacy and fluency with the source material that would facilitate the documentation of the account of LW's life. I think other subjects interest you more than what you have come to regard as a chore. I will therefore conclude this topic by exhorting you to take up the task once more, although I must admit, in compassion, that I'm reminded of the lines by Ogden Nash in his "Ode to Duty." They go something like this: "Oh Duty, why doest thou not have the visage of a sweetie or a cutie!" We must embrace Duty despite her austere countenance!

Jaffé's response, in a letter to me dated January 28, 1980, was as follows:

What you say about my notorious delay in getting out the *Life and Writings* book may be true. May I be pardoned for seeing the matter differently? I do not think I really did not want to work on it, as you suppose. From the very start I did not want to do anything else; but I was inhibited. I doubted whether I could do justice to the materials I was quarrying, not only because of their mass and complexity, but also because I was afraid I lacked the literary capacity to turn these materials to readable account, to penetrate their psychological and historical import, and to reveal their analytical significance, at least in a manner acceptable to modern economists. If it was principally for economists that I was writing, I felt technically inadequate. I tried then to make up for these inadequacies by turning my attention to recent developments in theoretical economics, but found I had neither the training nor the ability to keep up with it. Moreover, biographical writing as such did not appear to me to have any standing in the guild of which I wanted desperately to be a member in good repute.

How could I hope for the professional recognition I craved from economists, as I spent year after year in archival research, learning to decipher diabolically obscure manuscripts...? Surely cost-benefit analysis would have demonstrated that if the same time and effort were spent on mastering matrix algebra, topology, set theory, etc., I should have fared better in the eyes of my colleagues. And yet I stubbornly, if not wisely, persisted in my thankless grubbing.

Jaffé should have added that he directed his attention for many years to his translation of Walras's *Eléments*, and of course, his archival research resulted in his superb edition of Walras's correspondence and related papers.

Jaffé went on to explain that "despite the inhibitions and gnawing self-doubt, I never abandoned the idea of writing a properly documented *Life and Writings*," but that, nevertheless, his efforts to begin the project

... were interrupted by the shock of retirement and nearly a decade was lost in pursuit of a stable post sufficiently remunerative to afford the peace and quiet for the accomplishment of my task. ... [Then] the upheaval of the move to York was shattering. And here at York, in order to consolidate as well as I could a non-tenured position, I felt it would be too much of a risk to retire to the biography without turning out small publication after small publication for whatever they might be worth. And so progress with the biography suffered. That, in brief, is my side of the story. Perhaps I protest too much and perhaps you are right in your surmise, that *au fond*, I "really don't want to work on it." How can I say? Only time will tell, if enough is allotted to me.

Unfortunately, that was not to be. He was already terminally ill when he wrote those words, and had become incapable of sustained detailed work. For the last fifteen years of his life he had devoted himself to writing articles, and then his intellectual mission was over. Nevertheless, he left a legacy of work on the *Life and Writings* project, namely notes and preparatory writings dealing with Walras's antecedents and early life, and bibliographical notes. I used the biographical material and wove it in with long extracts from French sources to prepare an article (Jaffé 1984), and I have incorporated his bibliographical notes into the following bibliography, so that what he accomplished has not been lost.

III. Comparison with the first edition

The compilation of the first edition of the bibliography absorbed many hours of my time for six years, so many that I sometimes felt that it had taken on an evolving and demanding life of its own. In November 1986, I wrote in the introduction to that edition that,

... it is so long and the history of many of the entries is so complex that the probability of new pieces of information about them turning up is very high. I could therefore probably spend several more years refining it. Moreover, as time passes, additional items are published or republished, thus requiring that the bibliography be extended. At last, however, I have called a halt to my efforts. Believing that the bibliography is complete in all important and most minor respects as of the present date, I have decided it is time to give the results as they now stand to those who need them.

In fact, the first edition has thus far proved to be almost complete regarding the listings of Walras's writings. In the present edition, there are only five new entries regarding original writings, as distinct from new entries regarding reprints and translations of publications that were listed in the first edition of the bibliography. The five entries are: an early article (40); a short note (81) that was implicitly included in the first edition's entry 75; an early economic manuscript (95); some early philosophical notes (251); and a more complete presentation of jottings (252) than was given in the first edition's entry 226. Normally, it would not be expected that a scholar's scribblings would be included in his bibliography, but I have judged that entries 251 and 252 are of sufficient interest to merit it.

The present edition has nevertheless required a great deal of time and effort, again, because of the complexity of the subject. I never halted my efforts to improve the bibliography, carefully accumulating a plethora of additional information. For example, the lessons that were assembled to constitute entry 90 have been noted in a total of 6 entries (*Le Travail* in 1867 and 1868), and the annotations now indicate whether a lesson in that series or part of the lesson appeared in an earlier publication (see 34 and 51). Other annotations have been added and many of the annotations have been clarified or augmented. The reprints indicated in entries 221, 222, and 232 have been added. Bibliographical information has been added to many of the entries. Typographical errors, such as errors of pagination, have been corrected.

The bibliography has also been brought up to date by presenting important reprints up to the present, and translations of exceptional interest up to the present. The publication of Walras's complete economic writings in nine volumes of the *OEC* renders superfluous any additional reprints of those writings and any additional listings of reprints in this bibliography. Each volume of the *OEC* has, of course, a table of contents, and now that the index (249.XIV) has been published, researchers will be able readily to find Walras's economic writings in that definition collection.

The form used for the bibliographical entries differs from that of the entries in the general list of references. This is because the entries of Walras's writings are in many cases quite complex, partially resulting from their intrinsic character and partially because more information is required about them than for general references. For Walras's handwritten manuscripts, for example, the size of the pages in centimeters is given. For books, the number of pages is given. In order to make a long and complex entry clear, therefore, the information is broken up into short parts by full colons and periods, unlike the general references for which there are no periods in the listing. The short references in the bibliography do not need the indicated measures, but it would be inconsistent to adopt one form for the long entries and another for the short ones. Readers of the bibliography will have no difficulty understanding the meaning of the numerical parts of the entries.

CHAPTER 8

The definitive bibliography of the writings of Léon Walras

1858

1 "Notes de voyage." Unpublished.

This title is a penciled addition by Walras to his "Bibliographie littéraire" (entry 260). The entry was assigned by him to 1858.

2 *Francis Sauveur*. Paris, E. Dentu, 1858. xxxv, 260.

This is a novel.

3 "Préface sur L'Art et la littérature dans la démocratie." Unpublished.

This title is a pencilled addition by Walras to his "Bibliographie littéraire" (entry 260). The entry was assigned by him to 1858. On the cover of the copy of *Francis Sauveur* (entry 2) in D. A. Walker's possession, Walras wrote and initialed the words "Avertissement et corrections pour une 2ème édition." Among the corrections, Walras wrote a superscript "(1)" before the word "PREFACE" (page VII), and at the top of the page he wrote "L'art et la démocratie.[1]" It is probable, therefore, that entry 3 is actually his renamed preface to *Francis Sauveur* and has therefore been published.

1859

4 "Philosophie de l'art. 1ère partie: Ontologie." Autograph manuscript, Fonds Walras V 6, unpublished (1859), 39 leaves, 25 cm. by 19 cm.

Walras added the title in pencil to his "Bibliographie littéraire" (entry 260). The entry was assigned by him to 1859. Some of the sentences in entry 4 appear word for word in entry 9.

5 "Salon de 1859." *Le Bonhomme*, May 29, 1859.

The periodical was published in Bordeaux. The entry is in the form of a letter dated May 24, 1859. Its length is 116 cm. on 5 columns of print.

6 "De la propriété intellectuelle. Position de la question économique." *Journal des Economistes, Revue de la Science Economique et de la Statistique*, 2nd series, *24*, no. 12 (December 15, 1859): 392–407.

This is a review of *De la propriété intellectuelle, études par MM. Frédéric Passy, Victor Modeste et P. Paillottet, avec une préface par M. Jules Simon.* Paris, E. Dentu, 1859.

The *Journal* was then in its 6th year, it having been founded in 1853.

7 "La Lettre." *Revue Française, 16*, no. 4 (1859): 193–206; no. 5 (1859): 275–85.

This is a short story.

8 "Du sens esthétique; de l'art; et des opinions en matière d'art." Autograph manuscript, Fonds Walras, unpublished (1859): 48 p., 22.3 cm. by 16.8 cm.

For a summary, see entry 239, letter 9, n. 4, where the title is given the variation "les opinions," instead of "des opinions," and where a version of the manuscript is described as preserved "in the Lyons Collection, 35 foolscap pages in length, signed and dated 'Paris, 1859, 3 rue de l'Abbaye.'"

1860

9 "Philosophie des sciences économiques." *Journal des Economistes, Revue de la Science Economique et de la Statistique*, 2nd series, *25*, no. 2 (February 15, 1860): 196–206.

This is an advance publication of the material appearing on pages 4–15 and 29–38 of entry 15.

The *Journal* was in its 20th year, it having been founded in 1841.

10 "Des octrois, à propos de la loi belge." *La Presse*, 25th year, July 12, 22, and August 3, 1860.

11 "De la mise en valeur des biens communaux." *La Presse*, 25th year, September 20, 21, and 23, 1860.

For a summary, see entry 239, letter 41, n. 2.

12 "De la cherté des loyers à Paris." *La Presse*, 25th year, October 19, 26, 29, and November 6, 1860.

For a summary, see entry 239, letter 51, n. 2.

13 "La Bourse et le développement du capital." *La Presse*, 25th year, December 25 and 26, 1860.

For a summary, see entry 239, letter 55, n. 2.

14 "Paradoxes économiques. I – Que le sens commun n'est point le critérium de la science en général, ni en particulier celui de l'économie politique." *Journal des Economistes, Revue de la Science Economique et de la Statistique*, 2nd series, *28*, no. 12 (December 15, 1860): 373–91.

For a brief summary, see entry 239, letter 34, n. 7.

15 *L'économie politique et la justice. Examen critique et réfutation des doctrines économiques de M. P.-J. Proudhon, précédés d'une Introduction à l'étude de la question sociale.* Paris, Librairie de Guillaumin & Cⁱᵉ, 1860. LXIV, 255, plus an unnumbered "Table des Matières."

This was reprinted, New York, Burt Franklin, 1970.

16 "Application des mathématiques à l'économie politique (1ᵉʳᵉ Tentative, 1860)." Autograph manuscript, Fonds Walras V, unpublished (1860): 8 p., 26.5 cm. by 19.6 cm.; 3 leaves, on one of which there is a graph.

For a summary, see entry 239, letter 148, n. 33.

1861

17 "De l'élévation du taux de l'escompte." *La Presse*, 26th year, January 23 and 26, 1861.

For a summary, see entry 239, letter 61, n. 4.

18 "A M. Félix Solar, rédacteur en chef de la Presse." *La Presse*, 26th year, February 15, 1861.

19 "L'avenir économique de l'Italie (1861)." Autograph manuscript, Fonds Walras V 1, unpublished (1861): 5 p., 26.4 cm. by 19.5 cm.

A notation in Walras's hand reads: "Utilisé pour la bibliographie Errera."

20 "L'exposé de la situation de l'Empire. (1861)." Corrected draft manuscript, Fonds Walras V 6, unpublished (1861): 2 leaves, 26.3 cm. by 19.6 cm.

21 "L'industrie moderne et l'économie politique." Autograph manuscript, Fonds Walras VII X, unpublished (1861): 15 p., 26.1 cm. by 20.1 cm.

22 "Mémoire de M. Fould. (novembre 1861)." Autograph manuscript, Fonds Walras V 6, unpublished (November 1861): 5 p., 26.3 cm. by 19.9 cm.

23 "Paradoxes économiques. II. De la richesse naturelle ou gratuite. – De la richesse sociale ou économique. – De la richesse intellectuelle." Rough draft manuscript, partly in pencil and partly in ink, Fonds Walras V 1, unpublished (1861): 5 leaves, 25.9 cm. by 19.7 cm.

This manuscript appears to be the second installment of the "Paradoxes économiques" (entry 14). It is related to the first installment (entry 14) in style and subject matter. Two manuscripts in folders labeled "Paradoxes économiques" are in the Fonds Walras at Lausanne under the classification mark F. W. V 1. A pencilled note included with those folders lists the following as the third and fourth items among seventeen "inédits utilisés": "3. 2e paradox[e] économique (1861)" and "4. 3e id." It is probable that those descriptions refer to the manuscripts, though neither of them is numbered. See entry 24.

24 "Paradoxes économiques. (1861) II. Que le point de vue économique est le point de vue social par excellence." Autograph manuscript, Fonds Walras V 1, unpublished (1861): 20 p., 26.2 cm. by 19.6 cm.

Walras numbered this II although he gave the same number to entry 23.

The text was used for *Recherche de l'idéal social* (entry 90).

25 "Des réformes économiques." Autograph manuscript, Fonds Walras V 1, unpublished (1861): 12 p., 26 cm. by 20 cm.

This appeared in substance as entry 46.

For a summary, see entry 239, letter 59, n. 3.

26 "Le nouveau régime commercial." Autograph manuscript, Fonds Walras VII X, unpublished (1861): 5 p., 26.3 cm. by 19.6 cm.

For a summary, see entry 239, letter 70, n. 3.

27 *Théorie critique de l'impôt, précédée de Souvenirs du Congrès de Lausanne.* Paris, Guillaumin et Cie, 1861. 8°, XXXVI, 119.

This is the basis of a paper delivered at the International Congress on Taxation, July 1860. See entry 194, section IV of the contents, where pages 95–111 were republished. Walras put the substance of part of entry 27 into the *Eléments d'économie politique pure*, and reprinted large parts of it in entry 28.

28 *De l'impôt dans le canton de Vaud. Mémoire auquel un quatrième accessit a été décerné ensuite du concours ouvert par le Conseil d'Etat du canton de Vaud sur les questions relatives à l'impôt.* Lausanne, Imprimerie de Louis Vincent, 1861. 8°, 100.

This was submitted by Walras to the committee of the canton in 1860. The Vaud council paid for the publication of 500 copies. See entry 194, section IV of the contents, for Walras's later use of the text.

For a summary, see entry 239, letter 64, n. 1.

1862

29 "Note sur la suppression des octrois en Belgique et la réforme de l'impôt dans le canton de Vaud." Corrected draft manuscript, Fonds Walras V 6, unpublished (1862): 8 leaves, 20.7 cm. by 13.5 cm.

1863

30 "*Principes de la théorie des richesses*, par M. Cournot."
L'Indépendant de la Moselle, July 13, 1863.
This review was republished in *Augustin Cournot, Recherches sur les principes mathématiques de la théorie des richesses. Nouvelle édition avec des compléments de Léon Walras, Joseph Bertrand et Vilfredo Pareto, publiée avec une introduction et des notes par Georges Lutfalla*. Paris, Marcel Rivière & Cie, 1938, 225–32.
For a summary, see entry 239, letter 86, n. 4, part 1.

31 "*La crise cotonnière et les textiles indigènes*, par J. E. Horn."
L'Indépendant de la Moselle, July 27, 1863.
For a summary, see entry 239, letter 86, n. 4, part 2.

32 "*De l'esprit-communal et de la routine administrative*, par M. de Labry." *L'Indépendant de la Moselle*, August 19, 1863.
For a summary, see entry 239, letter 86, n. 4, part 3.

33 "De la constitution de la propriété en Algérie." *L'Indépendant de la Moselle*, September 2 and 21, and October 12, 1863.
For a summary, see entry 239, letter 86, n. 4, part 4.

34 "Du matérialisme et du spiritualisme en économie politique et sociale." Autograph manuscript, Fonds Walras V 1, unpublished (1863): 32 p., 28.3 cm. by 22.9 cm.
This was used for entries 74, 76, and 79, which are the first three lessons of entry 90.
For a summary, see entry 239, letter 90, n. 1.

1864

35 "*L'atmosphère est un engrais complet*, par M. le Dr. Schneider."
L'Indépendant de la Moselle, January 13 and 16, 1864.
For a summary, see entry 239, letter 86, n. 4, part 5.

36 "De l'enseignement de l'économie politique dans les Facultés de Droit." Jellygraphed copy of autograph manuscript, Fonds Walras V 1, unpublished, undated (probably October 1864): 13 p., numbered 64–77, 28.5 cm. by 23.7 cm.
For a summary, see entry 239, letter 93, n. 2.

37 "Recherche de l'Idéal Social en matière de propriété et d'impôt." Autograph manuscript, Fonds Walras V 1, unpublished (1864): 17 p. plus 10 p., 26.5 cm. by 19.5 cm.
Walras envisioned the imminent publication of this entry, writing on the title page: – "Paris, Librairie de Guillaumin et Cie Editeurs,

1863." He wrote "1864" at the top of the title page, but at least some
of the text was written in 1863.

38 "Le Sénatus-consulte du 2 décembre 1861 et les crédits supplé-
mentaires des exercices 1862 et 1863." Autograph manuscript,
Fonds Walras V 6, unpublished (1864): 18 p., 22.7 cm. by 17.4 cm.
For a summary, see entry 239, letter 86, n. 2.

1865

39 "De l'organisation financière et de la constitution légale des associations populaires." *Journal des Economistes, Revue de la Science
Economique et de la Statistique,* 2nd series, *45,* no. 135 (March,
1865): 361–81.
This was republished in entry 43.
For summaries, see entry 239, letter 96 and the enclosure to
letter 99.

40 "Projet de loi sur les sociétés à responsabilité proportionelle."
Moniteur Financier, March 5, 1865, 9–16.
An offprint of this was published in Paris, Imprimerie de Dubuis-
son et Cie.

41 "Les sociétés coopératives et la législation. Lettre au Rédacteur de
la Presse." *La Presse,* 30th year, April 20, 1865.
The editor's name was Rouy.

42 "*Le crédit et les finances,* par Victor Bonnet." *Journal des
Economistes, Revue de la Science Economique et de la Statistique,*
2nd series, *48,* no. 144 (December 1865): 480–83.

43 *Les associations populaires de consommation, de production et de
crédit. Leçons publiques faites à Paris en janvier et février 1865.*
Paris, E. Dentu, 1865. xxiii, 222.
This was reprinted under the editorship of Oscar Nuccio,
Rome, Edizioni Bizzari (R. Pioda), Ristampe Anastatiche de Opere
Antiche e Rare, 1969.

1866

44 "Le mouvement d'association et la politique libérale." *La Presse,*
31st year, April 2, 1866.

45 "L'Association à la française." *La Presse,* 31st year, April 20, 1866.

46 "Programme économique et politique." *Le Travail, 1,* no. 1 (July
31, 1866), cols. 1–7. Unsigned.
This is, in substance, entry 25.
For a summary, see entry 239, letter 59, n. 3.

The complete reference to the journal is: *Le Travail. Organe international des intérêts de la classe laborieuse. Revue du mouvement coopératif. Publié par MM. Léon Say et Léon Walras.* Bruxelles, Ve Parent et Fils; Paris, Librairie des Auteurs et Compositeurs, 1867–1868, 2 vols. In the first volume, labeled "*Première Année,*" are bound no. 1 (July 31, 1866) through no. 12 (June 30, 1867). In the second volume, labeled "*Deuxième Année,*" are bound no. 1 (July 31, 1867) through no. 12 (June 30, 1868).

47 "Société coopérative immobilière. [1] Type d'habitation à bon marché. [2] Combinaison financière." *Le Travail*, [1] *1*, no. 2 (August 31, 1866), cols. 44–46; [2] *1*, no. 3 (September 30, 1866), cols. 76–78. Unsigned.

48 "A propos d'un article de M. Horn." *Le Travail*, *1*, no. 4 (October 31, 1866), cols. 121–22. Unsigned and without title.

The above title was given to the article by Walras in his autobibliography (entries 216 and 239).

49 "De la cherté du pain et de l'établissement de boulangeries coopératives." *Le Travail*, *1*, no. 4 (October 31, 1866), cols. 100–103. Unsigned.

For a summary, see entry 239, letter 148, n. 19.

50 "Discussion sur les associations coopératives à la Société d'économie politique de Paris." *Le Travail*, *1*, no. 5 (November 31 [sic], 1866), cols. 132–38. Unsigned.

51 "Socialisme et libéralisme. Lettres à M. Ed. Scherer." *Le Travail*, *1*, no. 4 (October 31, 1866), cols. 116–19; no. 6 (December 31, 1866), cols. 180–83; no. 8 (February 28, 1867), cols. 244–47. Unsigned.

This was written in January 1863. It was republished in entries 90 and 93.

52 "Des doctrines en matière d'association coopérative." *Le Travail*, *1*, no. 6 (December 31, 1866), cols. 164–66. Unsigned.

For a summary, see entry 239, letter 148, n. 20.

53 *Les obligations populaires, leçons publiques faites à Paris en février et mars 1866 par MM. Léon Say et Léon Walras, Administrateurs de la Caisse d'Escompte des Associations Populaires.* Paris, Guillaumin et Cie, Editeurs, 14 rue Richelieu et E. Dentu, Editeur, 17 et 19, Galerie d'Orléans (Palais Royal), 1866. 8°, 59.

From the Table of Contents:

Des Opérations de la Caisse d'escompte des Associations populaires, par
   M. Léon Walras 35
Les obligations populaires 57

The latter brief note was presumably authored by both Walras and Say.

For a summary, see entry 239, letter 148, n. 11.

The Caisse d'Escompte failed. The accountant A. Rousseau gave what he believed to be the reasons for that failure in a lengthy report to the Governor of the Bank of France and a liquidator. Walras defended the administrators of the Caisse in a *"Contre-mémoire"* completed October 1870, for a summary of which see entry 239, letter 143, n. 2.

54 *Des opérations de la caisse d'escompte des associations populaires. Leçon publique faite à Paris en mars 1866.* Paris, Guillaumin et Dentu, 1866, 33–48.

This is an offprint of pages 35–56 of entry 53, with original pagination.

1867

55 "Enoncé de principes relatifs aux associations populaires coopératives pour servir d'exposé des motifs d'un Projet de loi sur les Sociétés à responsabilité proportionnelle." *Le Travail, 1,* no. 7 (January 31, 1867), cols. 200–194. Unsigned.

56 "Le crédit gratuit réciproque." *Le Travail, 1,* no. 7 (January 31, 1867), cols. 216–17. Unsigned and without title.

The above title was given to the article by Walras in his autobibliography (entries 214 and 238).

57 "La liberté des sociétés." *Le Travail, 1,* no. 8 (February 28, 1867), cols. 227–28.

58 "Le futur parti." *Le Travail, 1,* no. 8 (February 28, 1867), cols. 229–31.

59 "De la gratuité par la réciprocité dans les banques d'échanges." *Le Travail, 1,* no. 9 (March 31, 1867), cols. 259–61. Unsigned.

For a summary, see entry 239, letter 148, n. 22.

60 "Entrave au libre exercice du travail. – Quatre prévenus, imprimeurs sur étoffes." *Le Travail, 1,* no. 9 (March 31, 1867), cols. 264–65.

This appears under the title TRIBUNAUX – Tribunal de 1re Instance de la Seine (6e Chambre).

The title given to this entry by Walras in his autobibliography (entries 214 and 238) is "Les sociétés de résistance."

61 *"Les Idées de Mme Aubray, comédie en 4 actes,* par M. Alexandre Dumas fils." *Le Travail, 1,* no. 10 (April 30, 1867), cols. 311–14. Unsigned.

The book that was the subject of this review was published in Paris, Michel Lévy, 1867. 8°, 119.

62 "Discussion sur les coalitions et les grèves à la Société d'économie politique de Paris." *Le Travail*, *1*, no. 10 (April 30, 1867), cols. 291–97.

For a summary, see entry 239, letter 148, n. 23.

63 "Le projet de loi sur les sociétés à capital variable." *Le Travail*, *1*, no. 11 (May 31, 1867), cols. 324–25. Unsigned.

64 "Les erreurs du système monétaire français." *Le Travail*, *1*, no. 11 (May 31, 1867), cols. 325–29. Unsigned.

For a summary, see entry 239, letter 148, n. 24.

65 "La Bourse." *Le Travail*, *1*, no. 11 (May 31, 1867), cols. 338–41

This appeared as part I of entry 70, pp. 1731–35.

66 "Les Sociétés Coopératives." *Le Travail*, *1*, no. 11 (May 31, 1867), cols. 341–45.

This appeared as part III of entry 70, pp. 1748–51.

67 "Sur les sociétés à capital variable." *Le Travail*, *1*, no. 12 (June 30, 1867), cols. 355–63.

This appeared in a section titled "La discussion du corps législatif."

For a summary, see entry 239, letter 109, n. 3.

68 "Syndicat du crédit à Paris." *Le Travail*, *1*, no. 12 (June 30, 1867), cols. 363–67.

69 "Conférence faite par M. Horn sur le Crédit, la Mutualité Syndicale, L'Assurance et la Contre-Assurance." *Le Travail*, *2*, no. 1 (July 31, 1867), cols. 20–24.

70 "La Bourse et le crédit." In *Paris Guide, par les principaux écrivains et artistes de la France*. Paris, Librairie internationale; Bruxelles, Leipzig, and Livourne, A. Lacroix, Verboeckhoven et Cie, 1867; vol. 2, pp. 1731–51.

The *Paris Guide* was published in two volumes, called "parties," but the covers, title pages, and tables of content were put on the wrong set of contributions for some or perhaps all of the copies. Thus, for at least some copies, Walras's article appears in the volume incorrectly stated to be *"PREMIÈRE PARTIE. LA SCIENCE–L'ART,"* instead of *"DEUXIÈME PARTIE. LA VIE."*

For a summary, see entry 239, letter 148, n. 29.

71 "Congrès international coopératif." *Le Travail*, *2*, no. 2 (August 31, 1867), cols. 35–36.

72 "Société d'économie politique de Paris." *Le Travail*, *2*, no. 3 (September 30, 1867), cols. 70–85.

73 "Les syndicats de garantie mutuelle." *Le Travail*, *2*, no. 3 (September 30, 1867), cols. 85–87.

74 "Recherche de l'idéal social. Leçons publiques faites à Paris en 1867 et 1868. Première Leçon. – Concurrence du principe de l'Intérêt et du principe de la Justice dans les questions économico-sociales." *Le Travail*, *2*, no. 4 (October 31, 1867), cols. 111–22.
 The source of the substance of this entry is entry 34.

75 "De l'éducation des filles." *Le Travail*, *2*, no. 5 (November 30, 1867), cols. 133–35.

76 "Recherche de l'idéal social. Leçons publiques faites à Paris en 1867 et 1868. 2ᵉ Leçon. – Intervention des doctrines philosophiques. Lutte actuelle du matérialisme et du spiritualisme sur le terrain de l'économie politique et de la science sociale." *Le Travail*, *2*, no. 5 (November 30, 1867), cols. 141–51.
 The source of the substance of this entry is entry 34.

77 "La science et le socialisme." *Le Travail*, *2*, no. 6 (December 31, 1867), cols. 164–65.
 This was reprinted in 1918 with the title "Le Socialisme Scientifique" (entry 222).

78 "La sécurité générale." *Le Travail*, *2*, no. 6 (December 31, 1867), cols. 166–68.

79 "Recherche de l'idéal social. Leçons publiques faites à Paris en 1867 et 1868. 3ᵉ Leçon. – Critique du matérialisme. Critique du spiritualisme. Nouveau point de vue de la morale sociale." *Le Travail*, *2*, no. 6 (December 31, 1867), cols. 177–87.
 The source of the substance of this entry is entry 34.

1868

80 "Le socialisme scientifique." *Le Travail*, *2*, no. 7 (January 31, 1868), cols. 198–205.

81 "Observations." *Le Travail*, *2*, no. 7 (January 31, 1868), cols. 203–4.
 This is a reply to Jean Macé, Charles Küss, Boulogne, and Léon Say, whose remarks were published in the same issue of *Le Travail*.
 For excerpts from entry 81, see entry 239, letter 124, n. 2.

82 "Recherche de l'idéal social. Leçons publiques faites à Paris en 1867 et 1868. 4ᵉ Leçon. – De l'homme et de la destinée humaine au double point de vue physiologico-économique et psychologico-moral." *Le Travail*, *2*, no. 7 (January 31, 1868), cols. 206–16.

83 "Recherche de l'idéal social. Leçons publiques faites à Paris en 1867 et 1868. 5ᵉ Leçon. – De la concordance de l'intérêt et de la justice." *Le Travail*, *2*, no. 8 (February 29, 1868), cols. 240–50.

84 "Le mouvement d'instruction populaire." *Le Travail*, *2*, no. 9 (March 31, 1868), cols. 259–60.

85 "Recherche de l'idéal social. Leçons publiques faites à Paris en 1867 et 1868. 6ᵉ Leçon. – De l'individu et de l'État. Formule générale de constitution de la science sociale." *Le Travail*, 2, no. 9 (March 31, 1868), cols. 273–84.

86 "De la spéculation, étude d'économie financière." *Le Travail*, 2, no. 10 (April 30, 1868), cols. 292–95; 2, no. 12 (June 30, 1868), cols. 357–61. Unsigned.

For a summary, see entry 239, letter 148, n. 28.

87 "Les réunions publiques." *Le Travail*, 2, no. 12 (June 30, 1868), cols. 373–74. Unsigned.

This was published without a title in the section titled "Nouvelles." The above title was given to the article by Walras in his autobibliography (entries 214 and 238).

88 "*Histoire de Napoléon Iᵉʳ*, par P. Lanfrey, tomes I et II. Paris. Charpentier … 1867." *Le Travail*, 2, no. 12 (June 30, 1868), cols. 378–80. Unsigned.

For a summary, see entry 239, letter 131, n. 2.

89 "Méthode de conciliation ou de synthèse." Manuscript.

This was first published in 1896 (entries 188 and 194). Walras used entry 89 as the basis of entry 99.

90 *Recherche de l'idéal social. Leçons publiques faites à Paris. Première série (1867–68) Théorie générale de la société*. Paris, Guillaumin & Cⁱᵉ et Agᶜᵉ Génˡᵉ des Auteurs et Compositeurs, 1868. XXXII, 194.

This included entries 74, 76, 79, 82, 83, and 85, entries that, in turn, used entries 24 and 34. It was republished in entry 194.

1869

90 "Application des mathématiques à l'économie politique (2ᵉᵐᵉ Tentative 1869–70)." Autograph manuscript, Fonds Walras V 5, unpublished (1869–70): 47 p., 27 cm. by 21.6 cm., plus 2 smaller unnumbered sheets, plus 4 sheets of formulas and graphs.

For a summary, see entry 239, letter 148, n. 33, where the three major parts of the manuscript are described.

1870

92 "Intérêts des comptes courants." Manuscript, jellygraphed copy, Fonds Walras V 6, unpublished (1870): 5 leaves, 26.9 cm. by 21 cm.

1871

93 "Correspondance sur l'entrée à Lausanne des troupes de l'armée de l'Est." *Journal des Débats*, 8 (February 1871).

This title and the publication information were added in pencil by Walras to his "Bibliographie littéraire" (entry 260), and the title is the one he gave to the manuscript of the text in the Lyons Collection. See entry 239, letter 177, n. 4.

94 "Economie domestique. Conférences faites à Lausanne (aux internes français, février-mars 1871)." Manuscript, jellygraphed copy, Fonds Walras V 6, unpublished (1871): 36 p., 23.2 cm. by 15.4 cm.

The Lausanne copy is faded and completely illegible.

For a summary, see entry 239, letter 180, n. 4.

95 "Application des mathématiques à l'économie politique – 3e tentative – 1871 – la bonne (v. p. 15)." Autograph manuscript, 37 p.

96 "Des billets de banque en Suisse." *Bibliothèque Universelle et Revue Suisse*, 76th year, new period, *41*, no. 163 (July 1871): 321–42.

For a summary, see entry 239, letter 188, n. 4.

1872

97 "Discours d'installation en qualité de Professeur ordinaire d'économie politique à l'Académie de Lausanne prononcé dans la séance académique du 20 octobre 1871." *Séances académiques du 23 octobre 1869, du 31 octobre 1870 et du 20 octobre 1871, Discours d'installation.* Lausanne, Imprimerie Siméon Genton, 1872: 69–93.

This was also published in a booklet, *Séance académique du 20 octobre 1871, Discours d'installation*, Académie de Lausanne, no date: 18–42.

For a summary, see entry 239, letter 187, n. 2.

98 "Système des phénomènes économiques. 10 Leçons publiques faites à l'Hotel de Ville de Genève (1872)." Autograph manuscript, Fonds Walras V 1, unpublished (1872): 24 leaves, 28.9 cm. by 21.7 cm.

This was described by Walras as "10 Leçons publiques faites à Genève 1871–72," and placed by him under 1871 in his autobibliography (entries 214 and 238).

For a summary, see entry 239, letter 198, n. 2.

99 "Exposition et conciliation des doctrines sociales." Corrected draft manuscript, Fonds Walras V 1, unpublished (1872): 90 p., 28.8 cm. by 21.8 cm.

This was described by Walras as "6 Leçons publiques faites à Genève 1872–73 (inédit)." Walras stated (entry 194, p. 175) that he wrote the text (entry 89) on which this entry is based in 1868. Much of the substance of entry 99 appears in entry 194.

For a summary, see entry 239, letter 214, n. 3.

100 "Cours elémentaire à l'Ecole Industrielle." Autograph manuscript, Fonds Walras V 6, unpublished course (1872–1873): 21 leaves, 22.4 cm. by 17.7 cm.

1873

101 "Sur la théorie mathématique de l'échange." *Bulletin de la Société Vaudoise des Sciences Naturelles*, *12*, no. 70 (September 1, 1873): 317–21.

This is an open letter to Paul Piccard, dated October 25, 1873, and read to the Société vaudoise des sciences naturelles on November 5, 1873.

102 "Le cadastre et l'impôt foncier." *Bibliothèque Universelle et Revue Suisse*, 78th year, new period, *48* (November 1873): 470–90; (December 1873): 610–29.

This was republished, with very minor changes and with section titles added, in entry 194, 387–421, and in entry 228, 410–44. A long footnote on pages 477–478 of the original article was omitted from those entries. See entry 239, letter 236, n. 4, for the text of that footnote.

1874

103 "Principe d'une théorie mathématique de l'échange." *Séances et Travaux de l'Académie des Sciences Morales et Politiques (Institut de France), Extrait du Compte-rendu rédigé par M. Ch. Vergé. Collection*, new series, 33rd year, *101*, tome I, Paris, Alphonse Picard (January 1874): 97–116, 1 plate.

Walras read this paper to the Académie des sciences morales et politiques in Paris on August 16 and 23, 1873. The paper is listed in the table of contents on page 848 under "Communications des savants étrangers." It is followed by a summary of observations on it by Pierre-Emile Levasseur, Valette, and Louis Wolowski (117–20). The paper was republished in the *Journal des Economistes, Revue de la Science Economique et de la Statistique*, 3rd series, *34*, no. 100 (April 1874): 5–21, 1 plate, without the observations; republished as an offprint with new pagination, Orléans, Imprimerie

Ernest Colas, 1874, pp. 24, 1 plate; bound in entry 124; republished in entry 160; and republished in entry 244. It was translated into Italian by Gerolamo Boccardo as "Principio d'una teoria matematica dello scambio" in entry 137, and translated into German by Ludwig von Winterfeld as "Prinzip einer mathematischen Theorie des Tausches" in entry 157.

104 "De l'influence de la communication des marchés sur la situation des populations agricoles. Mémoire lu à la Société Vaudoise d'utilité publique dans la séance du 29 avril 1874." *Journal de la Société Vaudoise d'Utilité Publique*, no. 5 (May 1874): 103–16; no. 6 (June 1874): 121–35.

This was republished in entry 205, pp. 239–64.

105 "Correspondance entre M. Jevons, Professeur à Manchester et M. Walras, Professeur à Lausanne." *Journal des Economistes, Revue de la Science Economique et de la Statistique*, 3rd series, *34*, no. 102 (June 15, 1874): 417–22.

This consists of a letter from W. S. Jevons to Walras, May 12, 1874, in French translation, and a letter from Walras to Jevons, May 23, 1874, in French. The entry was republished as an offprint, Paris, Guillaumin. 8°, 8; bound in entry 124; published in Italian translation in entry 137; published in German translation in *Mathematische Theorie der Preisbestimmung* (entry 157) with Jevons's letter in bad English; and republished in entry 160 with Jevons's letter in French translation.

106 *Eléments d'économie politique pure ou Théorie de la richesse sociale*. 1st edition, 1st part. Lausanne, Imprimerie L. Corbaz & Cie; Paris, Guillaumin & Cie; Bâle, H. Georg, 1874. 8°, VIII, 208, 2 plates.

This includes lessons 1–34; §§ 1–207. The title on the paper cover reads: *ÉLÉMENTS D'ÉCONOMIE POLITIQUE PURE*, and bears as subtitles in roman font the titles of sections I, II, and III: Objet et divisions de l'économie politique et sociale. Théorie mathématique de l'échange. Du numéraire et de la monnaie.

The words *"OU THÉORIE DE LA RICHESSE SOCIALE"* appear on the title page, but not on the cover.

107 *"Eléments d'économie politique pure*, par Léon Walras." *Revue de Théologie et de Philosophie et Compte Rendu des Principales Publications Scientifiques*, Lausanne, Georges Bridel Editeur (October 1874): 628–32.

This is an unsigned account of the *Eléments* that appeared under the title "Philosophie." It refers in a footnote on page 628 to entry

106. It was listed by Walras as number 61 under 1874 in his auto-bibliography (entry 214), and was erroneously listed under 1873 in Bousquet's presentation of the autobibliography (entry 238).

108 *"L'Italia industriale, stud. j. del Prof. Alberto Errera, con parti-colare riguardo all'Adriatico superiore (regno d'Italia ed impe-rio Austro-Ungarico).* Roma-Torino-Firenze. Ermanno Loescher libraio-editore, 1873. *Le nuove istituzioni economiche nel secolo XIX,* di Alberto Errera, professore titolare di economia politica. Milano. Fratelli Trèves editori, 1874." *Journal des Economistes, Revue de la Science Economique et de la Statistique,* 3rd series, *36,* no. 107 (November 1874): 329–34.

The meaning of "stud. j." is "juridical studies."

For a summary of this review, see entry 239, letter 318, n. 2.

1875

109 "Economie politique." *La Revue, Journal Politique, Agricole, Industrial et Commercial, Paraissant le Mercredi et le Samedi, 7,* no. 2 (January 9, 1875). Unsigned.

The journal was published in Lausanne.

110 *"Résumé des principaux faits statistiques du Danemark.* Publié par le Bureau royal de statistique. Copenhague, imprimerie de Bianco Luno, 1874." *Journal des Economistes, Revue de la Sci-ence Economique et de la Statistique,* 3rd series, 37, no. 111 (March 1875): 492. This review is signed J. C.

111 "La loi fédérale sur l'émission et le remboursement des billets de banque." *Gazette des Tribunaux Suisses, Journal Hebdomadaire de Jurisprudence et de Législation, 11,* no. 32 (August 12, 1875): 241–43.

112 *"Biblioteca dell'Economista. Raccolta delle più pregiate opere moderne italiane e straniere di economia politica,* diretta dal profes-sore Gerolamo Boccardo. Terzia serie. Torino, Unione tipografico-editrice, 1875." *Journal des Economistes, Revue de la Science Economique et de la Statistique,* 3rd series, *40,* no. 118 (October 1875): 157–59.

For a summary of this review, see entry 239, letter 324, n. 5.

113 "Rapport sur le calcul des réserves de la Cie La Suisse au 31 décembre 1874." Autograph manuscript, Fonds Walras V II, unpub-lished (April 14, 1875): 62 p., 25.3 cm. by 20 cm.

For a brief description of the contents, see entry 239, letter 393, n. 3.

114 "Une branche nouvelle de la mathématique. De l'application des mathématiques à l'économie politique." Corrected draft manuscript, Fonds Walras V 1, unpublished in French (1875): 37 p., 29.2 cm. by 21.7 cm.

This was published in Italian translation (entry 117).

For a summary, see entry 239, letter 344, n. 2.

115 "L'Etat et les chemins de fer." Manuscript, 1875.

This was first published in 1897 (entry 196), and appears in English translation in entry 245.

1876

116 "La loi fédérale sur le travail dans les fabriques." *Gazette des Tribunaux Suisses, Journal Hebdomadaire de Jurisprudence et de Législation*, 11, no. 5, February 10, 1876.

117 "Un nuovo ramo della matematica. Dell'applicazione delle matematiche all'economia politica." *Giornale degli Economisti*, *3*, no. 1 (April 1876): 1–40.

This is a translation by Gerolamo Boccardo of entry 114. It was republished as an offprint, Padua, Premiata tipografia alla Minerva, 1876. 8°, 40.

118 "Equations de l'échange." *Bulletin de la Société Vaudoise des Sciences Naturelles*, *14*, no. 76 (October 1876): 367–94.

Walras read this paper to the Société vaudoise des sciences naturelles on December 1 and December 15, 1875. It is preceded by the general title, *Théorie mathématique de la richesse sociale*, and a prefatory note (365–66) signed "L. W., Chateau de Glérolles, par St-Saphorin, Vaud (Suisse). 8 août 1876." The note discusses the four "mémoires": "Principe d'une théorie mathématique de l'échange" (entry 103), "Equations de l'échange" (entry 118), "Equations de la production" (entry 119), and "Equations de la capitalisation" (entry 122). Walras explained that entries 118 and 119 were to be published "in the present number" of the *Bulletin*, that is, in "BULL. SOC. VAUD. SC. NAT. XIV. 76.," as printed at the top of the page on which the prefatory note begins. The offprint was bound together with an offprint of the "Equations de la production," Lausanne, Imprimerie Ed. Allenspach Fils, 1876, 3–30. The title page of the pamphlet offprint erroneously ascribes the paper to volume XV, for it reads: "Extrait du *Bulletin de la Société vaudoise des sciences naturelles.* – 2ᵉ S. Vol. XV. Nᵒ 76," the "2ᵉ S" referring to the second series of the journal. Entry 118 was bound in entry 124; and republished in entry 160, 33–53. In the latter, the prefatory note became the "Preface des quatre premiers mémoires," 5–6. Entry 118 was translated into Italian by Gerolamo Boccardo as "Equazioni dello scambio" in entry 137, with the prefatory note as a "Prefazione," and translated into German by Ludwig von Winterfeld as "Gleichungen des Tausches" in entry 157, with the prefatory note as a "Vorwort."

The substance of this entry appears in entry 123 and subsequent editions.

119 "Equations de la production." *Bulletin de la Société Vaudoise des Sciences Naturelles, 14*, no. 76 (October 1876): 395–430.

Walras read this paper to the Société vaudoise des sciences naturelles on January 19 and February 16, 1876. Entry 119 was republished as an offprint and bound together with an offprint of the "Equations de l'échange" (entry 118), Lausanne, Imprimerie Ed. Allenspach Fils, 1876, pp. 31–66. Although the offprint indicates that it was published in "BULL. SOC. VAUD. SC. NAT. XIV. 76." the title page of the pamphlet offprint reads as in the case of entry 118, because the two entries shared the same title page. The remark regarding the erroneous volume printed on the title page of the offprint of entry 118 therefore applies also to entry 119. Entry 119 was bound in entry 124; and republished in entry 160, 55–82. It was translated into Italian by Gerolamo Boccardo as "Equazioni della produzione" in entry 137, and translated into German by Ludwig von Winterfeld as "Gleichungen der Produktion" in entry 157.

The substance of this entry, including most of the equations, appears in entry 123 and subsequent editions of the *Eléments d'économie politique pure.*

120 "Note sur l'impôt progressif." Rough draft manuscript, Fonds Walras V 1, unpublished (November 1876): 4 p., 25.1 cm. by 19 cm.

Walras indicated on the title page that it was "Utilisée pour le 'Problème fiscal' (Et. Ec. soc.)" (see entry 194, 431–41; entry 228, 454–64). The first two pages of this paper are virtually the same as the beginning of the second part of "Le problème fiscal" (entry 190), entitled "Critique de l'impôt comme fait normal et définitif," page 454 to the end of the top paragraph on page 458: "..., la science pour l'empirisme." Some of the other sentences in entries 120 and 190 are identical.

121 "Note sur le 15 1/2 légal." *Journal des Economistes, Revue de la Science Economique et de la Statistique*, 3rd series, *44*, no. 132 (December, 1876): 454–57.

This was followed by "Réponse de M. Cernuschi," 457–58. Entry 121 was republished as part of a pamphlet entitled *Théorie mathématique du bimétallisme*, Paris, Guillaumin, 1881, 3–6 (see entry 153); and in entry 160, 119–23.

1877

122 "Equations de la capitalisation." *Bulletin de la Société Vaudoise des Sciences Naturelles*, *14*, no. 77 (March 1877): 525–61.

This was preceded by the title: "Théorie mathématique de la richesse sociale" (525). It was followed by an "Observation" (562–64) that dealt with the four mémoires listed under entry 124. Walras read entry 122 to the Société vaudoise des sciences naturelles. In the *Bulletin* the date of delivery was given as July 6, 1876, but Walras represented it as July 5 in three places: on the title page of the offprint mentioned below, in the first footnote (page 82) of the version published in entry 160, and in his autobibliography (entries 214 and 238). Walras's explanatory note described under entry 118 continues by indicating that entry 122 was to be published "in the following number of the *Bulletin*," namely in number 77, the one that was to follow the number in which entries 118 and 119 appeared. Nevertheless, the title page composed for the offprint reads "Extrait du Bulletin de la Soc. Vaud. des Sciences Naturelles. 2^e S. Vol. XV. N° 77". That is erroneous because entry 122 appeared in volume XIV, which comprises numbers 75, 76, and 77 published in February 1876, October 1876, and March 1877, respectively. Walras correctly listed entry 122 in his autobibliography (entries 214 and 238) as appearing in volume XIV. The top of the first page (525) of the offprint of entry 122 states that the entry is part of "BULL. SOC. VAUD. SC. NAT. XIV. 76," the same volume and number as in the case of entries 118 and 119, but the "*76*" is an error. Moreover, the offprint of entry 122 produced by L. Corbaz is dated 1876, regarding which Mr. Christian Graf (see Chapter 7) has informed D. A. Walker that "it is quite possible that the *tiré à part* [separate printing or offprint] was published before the appearance of the article in the *Bulletin*." A further complication is that in Bousquet's presentation of Walras's autobibliography (entry 238), entry 122 appears as item 71 under 1876, whereas in D. A. Walker's transcript of Walras's autobibliography, the paper appears as item 71 under 1877. As Bousquet's presentation also wrongly puts the second part of the first edition of the *Eléments d' économie politique pure* (entry 123) under 1876, and lists no items as appearing in 1877, it is clear that Bousquet or the printer neglected to insert the date 1877 before the items that Walras listed under that year.

In his autobibliography, Walras listed entry 122 with the title "Equations de la capitalisation et du crédit," but the last three words were not added to the title until 1883 (entry 160). Entry 122 was, as indicated, republished as an offprint, Lausanne, L. Corbaz et Comp., 1876, 67–103, followed by the "Observation," 104–6; and bound in entry 124. It was republished in entry 160, with a number of changes, as "Equations de la capitalisation et du crédit," 83–112, followed by the "Observation," 113–15. The revised version, as presented in entry 160, was translated into Italian by Gerolamo Boccardo as "Equazioni della capitalizzazione e del credito" in entry 137, followed by the "Osservazione," and translated into German by Ludwig von Winterfeld as "Gleichungen der Kapitalisirung und des Kredites" in entry 157, followed by the "Schloss" that is, "Observation"). The "Observation" appears with some changes in the second part of the first edition of *Eléments d'économie politique pure* (entry 123), 364–66, and in subsequent editions.

The substance of entry 122 appears in entry 123 and subsequent editions.

123 *Eléments d'économie politique pure.* 1st edition, 2nd part. Lausanne, Imprimerie L. Corbaz & Cie; Paris, Guillaumin & Cie; Bâle, H. Georg, 1877. 8°, 209–407, 1 plate.

This includes lessons 35–64, §§ 208–385. The paper cover bears as subtitles in roman font the titles of sections IV, V, and VI: Théorie naturelle de la production et de la consommation de la richesse. Conditions et conséquences du progrès économique. Effets naturels et nécessaires des divers modes d'organisation économique de la société.

The words "*ou Théorie de la richesse sociale*" (see entry 106) do not appear on the cover.

There is no title page, for the reason that entry 123 is the continuation of entry 106.

124 *Théorie mathématique de la richesse sociale. Quatre mémoires lus à l'Académie des sciences morales et politiques, à Paris, et à la Société Vaudoise des Sciences Naturelles, à Lausanne,* Paris, Guillaumin & Cie, 1877. 8°, 145, 1 plate.

In this entry are bound offprints of the following papers in their original published versions: (1) "Principe d'une théorie mathématique de l'échange" (entry 103); (2) "Correspondance entre M. Jevons ... et M. Walras ..." (entry 105); (3) "Equations de l'échange," preceded by a prefatory note (entry 118), 365–66; (4) "Equations de la production" (entry 119); (5) "Equations de la capitalisation" (entry 122), followed by the "Observation" (see entry 122).

125 "Analyse de la Théorie mathématique de la richesse sociale." Manuscript, Fonds Walras V b 21, unpublished (March 1877).

1878

126 "Exposition de tableaux et d'études de M. Bocion." *Gazette de Lausanne*, no. 1 (January 2, 1878). Unsigned.

This is a commentary on the work of François Bocion.

The full name of the newspaper was *Gazette de Lausanne et Journal Suisse*. Its issues were numbered sequentially within each calendar year. 1878 was the 79th year of that journal, it having been founded in 1799.

127 "Chronique de la quinzaine," under the title "Feuilleton." *Gazette de Lausanne*, no. 10 (January 12, 1878). Signed "Paul."

Walras listed this entry in his "Bibliographie littéraire" (entry 260) as "Gleyre et Courbet. Réalisme." Walras probably wrote the entry on January 10, the day in the calendar of saints of the little-known hermit Paul, whose name Walras assumed.

128 "Chronique de la quinzaine," under the title "Feuilleton." *Gazette de Lausanne*, no. 22, (January 26, 1878). Signed "Paul."

Walras listed this entry in his "Bibliographie littéraire" (entry 260) as "Victor-Emmnanuel. Le général Cousin-Montauban. F.-V. Raspail. Le théâtre de campagne."

129 "Chronique de la quinzaine," under the title "Feuilleton." *Gazette de Lausanne*, no. 34 (February 9, 1878). Signed "Paul."

Walras listed this entry in his "Bibliographie littéraire" (entry 260) as "La Correspondance de Sainte-Beuve."

130 "Chronique de la quinzaine" under the title "Feuilleton." *Gazette de Lausanne*, no. 46 (February 23, 1878). Signed "Paul."

Walras listed this entry in his "Bibliographie littéraire" (entry 260) as "Discours de M. Du Bois-Raymond sur l'Histoire de la civilisation et la Science de la nature. L'américanisme."

For a summary, see entry 239, letter 401, n. 5.

131 "Chronique de la quinzaine," under the title "Feuilleton." *Gazette de Lausanne*, no. 58 (March 9, 1878). Signed "Paul."

Walras listed this entry in his "Bibliographie littéraire" (entry 260) as "Rodogune. La tragédie. Les Femmes Savantes."

132 "Chronique de la quinzaine," under the title "Feuilleton." *Gazette de Lausanne*, no. 70 (March 23, 1878). Signed "Paul."

Walras listed this entry in his "Bibliographie littéraire" (entry 260) as "M. Victor Hugo: Histoire d'un Crime; La Légende des Siècles, nouvelle Série, T. II."

133 "Chronique de la quinzaine" under the title "Feuilleton." *Gazette de Lausanne*, no. 82 (April 6, 1878). Signed "Paul."

Walras listed this entry in his "Bibliographie littéraire" (entry 260) as "Le tour du monde en 80 jours. Le Théatre de Marionnettes de M. Marc-Monnier."

134 "Chronique de la quinzaine," under the title "Feuilleton." *Gazette de Lausanne*, no. 93 (April 20, 1878). Signed "Paul."

Walras listed this entry in his "Bibliographie littéraire" (entry 260) as "Le Dictionnaire de l'Académie française."

135 "Chronique de la quinzaine," under the title "Feuilleton." *Gazette de Lausanne*, no. 105 (May 4, 1878). Signed "Paul."

Walras listed this entry in his "Bibliographie littéraire" (entry 260) as "Charlotte Corday et Vera Zassoulitch."

136 "Chronique de la quinzaine," under the title "Feuilleton." *Gazette de Lausanne*, no. 117 (May 18, 1878). Signed "Paul."

Walras listed this entry in his "Bibliographie littéraire" (entry 260) as "Exposition des Beaux-Arts à Lausanne. Exposition des Amis des Arts à Neuchâtel."

137 *Teoria Matematica della Ricchezza Sociale. Quattro Memorie lette all'Accademia delle scienze morali e politiche a Parige ed alla Società delle scienze naturali a Losanna, da Leone Walras, Professore di economia politica nell'academia di Losanna.* Translated by Gerolamo Boccardo, Bibliotheca dell'economista, 3rd series, *2* (1878).

These are translations into Italian (1) of the prefatory note described in entry 118: "Prefazione," 1291–92; (2) of entry 103: "Principio d'una teoria matematica della scambio," 1293–1310, 1 plate; (3) of entry 105: Corrispondenza tra il Signor Jevons professore a Manchester ed il Sig. Walras Prof. a Losanna, 1311–13; (4) of entry 118: "Equazioni della scambio," 1314–32; (5) of entry 119: "Equazioni della produzione," 1333–56; (6) of entry 122: "Equazioni della capitalizzazione e del credito," 1357–83; and (7) of the "Osservazione" in entry 122, 1384–85.

138 "Bibliographie des ouvrages relatifs à l'application des mathématiques à l'économie politique, en collaboration avec le Professeur Jevons." *Journal des Economistes, Revue de la Science Economique et de la Statistique*, 4th series, *4*, no. 12 (December 1878): 470–77.

139 "De l'assurance sur la vie." *La Suisse, Société d'Assurances sur la Vie à Lausanne, Almanach pour 1879*, Lausanne, Imprimerie L. Corbaz & Comp., 1878. 8°, 5–12.

The title on the front cover of this booklet is *Almanach de La Suisse 1879*.

For a summary, see entry 239, letter 414, n. 3.

140 "Rapport sur la réserve correspondant à une fraction d'année dans le cas de l'assurance au décès." Autograph manuscript, Fonds Walras V II, unpublished (1878): 6 leaves, 25.8 cm. by 20.5 cm.

The title was recorded by Walras in his autobibliography (entry 214) with the following difference: "là fraction," instead of "à une fraction," and the entry was marked: "Lausanne, 2 décembre 1878." The manuscript was also described by Walras as having 8 pages. It is a sequel to entry 113.

1879

141 "De la culture et de l'enseignement des sciences morales et politiques." Bibliothèque Universelle et Revue Suisse, 84th year, 3rd period, 3, no. 7 (July 1879): 5–32; no. 8 (August 1879): 223–51.

For a summary, see entry 239, letter 418, n. 2.

142 "De l'émission des billets de banque." Gazette de Lausanne, no. 285 (December 2, 1879) and no. 286 (December 3, 1879).

This is a summary of "Théorie mathématique du billet de banque" (entry 148), which Walras read to the Société vaudoise des sciences naturelles on November 19, 1879.

143 "Amélie Lasaulx en religion Sœur Augustine. Traduction autorisée des souvenirs d'Amélie de Lasaulx. Lausanne. Imer, éditeurs. 1880." Gazette de Lausanne, December 29, 1879. Unsigned.

This is a review of a biography, 369 pages in length, that was written anonymously and translated anonymously from German into French. In fact, the translator was Walras's friend, Charles Secrétan. Walras evidently had an advance copy of the book.

144 *Théorie de l'Economie politique, par W. Stanley Jevons, L.L.D. (Ed.) M.A. (L.), F.R.S., Professeur d'économie politique au Collège de l'Université, à Londres, Examinateur de Sciences philosophiques et morales à l'Université à Londres. 2ᵉ Edition revue et augmentée avec une préface nouvelle et des appendices.* Autograph manuscript, Fonds Walras 1966, unpublished (Autumn 1879): 79 leaves, 25.1 cm. by 19 cm., and one large sheet of unfinished copied graphs, 43 cm. by 29.5 cm.

This is a translation of W. Stanley Jevons's *Theory of Political Economy*, 2nd ed., London, Macmillan, 1879.

See entry 239, letter 465, second paragraph, for Walras's plan, never carried out, to publish his translation together with entries 124 and 250 and an introduction.

145 "Note sur l'organisation de l'enseignement de l'économie politique à l'Ecole pratique des Hautes Etudes." Autograph manuscript, Fonds Walras V 1, unpublished (1879): 2 leaves, 26.4 cm. by 20.9 cm.

Walras added to the title: "remise à M. Albert Dumont."

A copy of the manuscript given to William Jaffé by Etienne Antonelli is reproduced in entry 239, letter 455, n. 6. That copy is not complete. The transcript in the possession of D. A. Walker of the manuscript in the Fonds Walras contains in addition three introductory paragraphs on the organization of instruction in "économique et politique."

1880

146 "*Deux Méprises. Nouvelles*, par Mme Bonzon de Gardonne, Paris, Sandoz et Fischbacher; Neuchatel, Jules Sandoz; Genève, Desroges: 1880." *Gazette de Lausanne*, January 30, 1880. Unsigned.

147 "La Bourse, la spéculation et l'agiotage." *Bibliothèque Universelle et Revue Suisse*, 85th year, 3rd period, *5* (March 1880): 452–76; *6* (April 1880): 66–107.

This was republished in entry 205, 401–45, with section titles added.

148 "Théorie mathématique du billet de banque." *Bulletin de la Société Vaudoise des Sciences Naturelles*, 2nd series, *16*, no. 83 (May 1880): 553–92, 1 plate.

Walras read this paper to the Société vaudoise des sciences naturelles on November 19, 1879. It was republished, with some minor changes, in entry 160, 145–75, 1 plate; and, with some additional changes, in entry 205, 339–75, 1 plate.

149 "De la propriété intellectuelle." *Gazette de Lausanne*, no. 136 (June 10, 1880), no. 137 (June 11, 1880), and no. 138 (June 12, 1880).

150 "*Opuscules et pensées*, par Giacomo Leopardi. Traduit de l'italien et précédé d'une préface par Auguste Dapples. Paris, Germer-Baillière, 1880." *Gazette de Lausanne*, September 24 and 25, 1880. Unsigned.

The book (in 8°, XVI, 198) was published in the series *Bibliothèque de philosophie contemporaine*.

151 "Défense des salaires." Unpublished, manuscript, 1880.

A note by Walras reads: "Conférences faites à Lausanne (inédit) utilisées pour l'Economie politique appliquée [entry 205] et la défense des Salaires en 1897" (entry 198).

152 "De l'Enseignement de l'économie politique en France." Autograph manuscript, Fonds Walras V 1, unpublished (1880): 16 p., 27.8 cm. by 21.5 cm.

1881

153 "Théorie mathématique du bimétallisme." *Journal des Economistes, Revue de la Science Economique et de la Statistique*, 4th series, *14*, no. 41 (May 1881): 189–99, 1 plate.

This was republished as part of a pamphlet entitled *Théorie mathématique du bimétallisme*, Paris, Guillaumin, 1881, 6–16, 1 plate. In the pamphlet, it followed a reprinting of Walras's "Note sur le 15 1/2 légal" (entry 121). Entry 153 was republished, with minor changes, in entry 160, 123–34.

154 "Théorie mathématique du prix des terres et de leur rachat par l'Etat. Mémoire lu à la Société vaudoise des sciences naturelles à Lausanne, dans la séance du 17 novembre 1880." *Bulletin de la Société Vaudoise des Sciences Naturelles*, 2nd series, *17*, no. 85 (June 1881): 189–284.

This was republished in entry 160, 177–253; in entry 194, 267–350; and in entry 244.

155 "Lettera del prof. Léone Walras al presidente del Circolo Universitario prof. Alberto Errera." Letter dated January 26, 1881 published as a preface (1–2) to *Teoria matematica della Moneta, Conferenza fatta al Circolo Universitario A°, Genovesi in Napoli del Marchese Pasquale del Pezzo, dottore in legge, studente del 4° anno di matematiche. Estratto dagli Atti al Circolo universitario napolitano Antonio Genovesi*. Napoli, Tipografia A. Trani, 1881. 23 p.

156 "Exposition de tableaux et d'études de M. Bocion." *Gazette de Lausanne*, December 3, 1881. Unsigned.

This is a commentary on the work of François Bocion (see entry 126).

157 *Mathematische Theorie der Preisbestimmung der wirthschaftlichen Güter, Vier Denkschriften gelesen vor der Akademie der moralischen und politischen Wissenschaften zu Paris und vor der*

naturwissenschaftlichen Gesellschaft des Waadt-Landes zu Lausanne. Von Léon Walras, Professor der Wirtschaft an der Akademie zu Lausanne. Vorwort, signed by Léon Walras, Schloss Glerolles bei St-Saphorin, Waadt (Schweiz), August 1876. Translated by Ludwig von Winterfeld. Stuttgart, Verlag von Ferdinand Enke, 1881. 8°, VII, 96, 1 plate.

This is a translation of entry 124. Entry 157 was reprinted, Glashütten im Taunus, D. Auvermann, 1972.

Table of contents: "Vorbemerkung des Uebersetzers," dated February 1881, V–VI, signed: Lausanne im Februar 1881, Ludwig von Winterfeld; Walras's "Vorwort", dated August 1996, VII–VIII; "I. Prinzip einer mathematischen Theorie des Tausches," 1–17, 1 plate at end of book; Correspondenz zwischen Herrn Jevons und Herrn Walras, with Jevons's letter of May 12, 1994 in English and Walras's letter of May 23, 1994 in French, 13–22. "II. Gleichungen des Tausches," 23–40; "III. Gleichungen der Produktion," 41–65; "IV. Gleichungen der Kapitalisirung und des Kredites" (the version that appears in entry 160), 66–91; "Schluss" ("Observation"), 92–107.

1882

158 "De la fixité de valeur de l'étalon monétaire." *Journal des Economistes, Revue de la Science Economique et de la Statistique*, 4th series, *20*, no. 10 (October 1882): 5–13, 1 plate.

This was reprinted separately, no date, 8 pp., 1 plate; and republished in entry 160, 135–44, as part III of "Théorie mathématique du bimétallisme." The article was reprinted with only one substantial change as Leçon 35 of the second edition of the *Eléments d'économie politique pure* (entry 176), numbered Leçon 32 in the 4th edition (entry 210).

In the second edition, the passage from line 11 of p. 408 to line 31 of p. 409 was substituted in place of the following passage in the article: "La fixité remarquable de valeur de l'étalon bimétallique dans notre example tient toutefois à ce que, dans cet exemple, les variations dans la quantité d'or et de l'argent, qui sont les seules dont nous ayons tenu compte, se contrarient le plus souvent. Quand ces variations sont dans le même sens, ainsi que cela arrive au commencement et à la fin de la période considerée, les variations de la courbe de prix de l'étalon bimétallique sont sensiblement égales aux variations des courbes de prix de l'un ou l'autre des deux étalons monométalliques."

1883

159 "A M. le Rédacteur du Figaro." *Figaro*, June 17, 1883.
     This was described by Walras as "Entrevue L. Say (a été reproduit par le Journal des Débats du 18 Juin ou 19 Juin)."
160 *Théorie mathématique de la richesse sociale*. Lausanne, Corbaz & Cie; Paris, Guillaumin & Cie; Rome, Ermanno Loescher e Co.; Leipzig, Verlag von Duncker & Humblot, 1883. 4°, 256, 6 plates.
     This was reprinted, Osnabrück, O. Zeller, 1964.
     This is a collection of the following previously published papers: (1) "Principe d'une théorie mathématique de l'échange" (entry 103), 7–25, 1 plate, and the "Correspondance entre M. Jevons, Professeur à Manchester et M. Walras, Professeur à Lausanne" (entry 105), 26–31; (2) "Equations de l'échange" (entry 118), 33–53; (3) "Equations de la production" (entry 119), 55–82; (4) "Equations de la capitalisation et du crédit" (entry 122), 83–123. Those four papers were preceded by a "Préface des quatre premiers mémoires," dated August 1876, 5–6, that is identical, except for the opening words and the addition in 1883 of two footnotes, to the prefatory note to entry 118. The papers were followed by an "Observation" (see entry 122), 113–15; (5) "Théorie mathématique du bimétallisme" (entry 153), 119–44, 3 plates; (6) "Théorie mathématique du billet de banque" (entry 148), 145–75, 1 plate; (7) "Théorie mathématique du prix des terres et de leur rachat par l'Etat" (entry 154), 177–253, 1 plate. The last three papers were preceded by a "Préface des trois derniers mémoires," dated November 1882, 117–18. In one of the above-mentioned footnotes, Walras pointed out that the first four papers had been translated into Italian (entry 137) and German (entry 157).

1884

161 "Monnaie d'or avec billon d'argent régulateur. Principes proposés à la conférence monétaire pour la prorogation de l'Union latine." *Revue de Droit International et de Législation Comparée*, *16*, no. 6 (December 1, 1884): 575–88.
     This was republished as a pamphlet, Bruxelles et Leipzig, Librairie Européenne C. Muquardt; La Haye, Belinfante Frères; Paris, Durand et Pedone-Lauriel, 1884. 16; and in entry 205, 3–19.

1885

162 "Un système rationnel de monnaie." *Gazette de Lausanne*, no. 9 (January 12, 1885).

163 "Un économiste inconnu, Hermann-Henri Gossen." *Journal des Economistes, Revue de la Science Economique et de la Statistique*, 4th series, *30*, no. 4 (April 1885): 68–90.

This was republished in *Etudes d'économie sociale* (entry 194), 351–74. A very slightly abridged translation into English is presented in Henry William Spiegel, *The Development of Economic Thought, Great Economists in Perspective*, New York, Wiley and London, Chapman, 1952, 471–88.

164 "Rectification de M. Léon Walras à propos d'un article sur H. H. Gossen." *Journal des Economistes, Revue de la Science Economique et de la Statistique*, 4th series, *30*, no. 5 (May 1885): 260–61.

This is a letter, dated April 29, 1885, addressed to the editor of the *Journal*. It was republished in entry 239, letter 647.

165 "*Primi Elementi di Economia Politica,* di Luigi Cossa, professore nella R. Università di Pavia. Sesta edizione. – Milano, Hoepli, 1883. *Primi Elementi di Scienza della Finanze,* del dottor Luigi Cossa. Terza edizione. – Milano, Hoepli, 1882." *Bibliothèque Universelle et Revue Suisse*, 90th year, 3rd period, *27*, no. 8 (August 1885): 445–47.

For a brief summary, see entry 239, letter 656, n. 2.

166 "D'une méthode de régularisation de la variation de la valeur de la monnaie." *Bulletin de la Société Vaudoise des Sciences Naturelles*, 2nd series, *21*, no. 92 (August 1885): 71–92.

Walras read this paper to the Société vaudoise des sciences naturelles on May 6, 1885, and it was reported in the *Bulletin*, no. 93, p. XXV. It was republished as is indicated in entry 167; and in entry 205, 26–49.

167 "Contribution à l'étude des variations des prix depuis la suspension de la frappe des écus d'argent." *Bulletin de la Société Vaudoise des Sciences Naturelles*, 2nd series, *21*, no. 92 (August 1885): 93–103, 1 plate.

This paper was written in collaboration with Alfred Simon. It was read to the Société vaudoise des sciences naturelles on June 3, 1885, and reported in the *Bulletin*, no. 93, pp. XXVII–XXVIII. It was republished together with entry 166 in a pamphlet with the title of entry 166 plus the words "par M. Léon Walras," and the title of entry 167 plus the words "par MM. Alfred Simon et Léon Walras," Lausanne, Corbaz et Comp., 1885. 8°, 22, 11; and in the X, 49–59, 1 plate.

1886

168 "Théorie de la monnaie." *Revue Scientifique (Revue Rose)*, 3rd series, *11*, no. 15 (April 10, 1886): 449–57; no. 16 (April 17, 1886): 493–500. *Collection, 37*.

This paper was reprinted as an offprint, Paris, Bureau des Revues, 1886. 4°, 24; and republished in entry 205 as part of entry 169. The article is constituted of the "Introduction"; Part I, "Exposition des Principes," §§ 1–13; and Part II, "Critique des systèmes," §§ 14–26 of Walras's complete *Théorie de la monnaie* (entry 169).

169 *Théorie de la monnaie*. Lausanne, Imprimerie Corbaz & Cie; Paris, L. Larose & Forcel; Rome, Loescher & Cie; Leipzig, Verlag von Duncker & Humblot, 1886. 8°, XII, 123, 4 plates.

This was republished, with changes, in entry 205, 63–152, and Plates II–III and IV–V. The "Introduction," 3–22, Part I, "Exposition des Principes," 25–55, and Part II, "Critique des systèmes," 57–85, were part of entry 168. A preface and Part III, "Desiderata statistiques," §§ 27–40, were added to them to form entry 169.

170 "*La question sociale*, par Ch. Secrétan." *Gazette de Lausanne*, no. 171 (July 22, 1886).

1887

171 "Léon Walras, *Théorie de la Monnaie*, Lausanne et Paris, 1887." *Revue d'Economie Politique*, *1*, no. 1 (January–February 1887): 91–101.

This is a synopsis by Walras of his *Théorie de la Monnaie* (entry 169), so the date in the title is incorrect. The synopsis was unsigned. It was published in the section titled "Bulletin Bibliographique."

See entry 239, letter 762, n. 3 for an editorial footnote to the review.

172 "La livre étalon et la livre Sterling, projet pour rendre la mesure de la valeur indépendante du prix de l'or et pour asseoir le système monétaire sur une base solide par W. Cross. 4 lettres de l'Aberdeen Herald du 29 décembre 1855 et des 5, 12 et 19 janvier 1856." Autograph manuscript, Fonds Walras V III, unpublished (March 1887): 16 leaves, 22.5 cm. by 18.1 cm.

This is a translation by Walras of William Cross's "A Standard Pound versus the Pound Sterling, A Project for Rendering the Measure of Value Independent of the Price of Gold, and Establishing the Monetary System on a Secure Foundation, in Four Letters Reprinted from the Aberdeen Herald of 29th December 1855 and 5th, 12th and 19th January, 1856, Edinburgh, Sutherland and Knox; Glasgow, Griffin; Aberdeen, L. and J. Smith, 1856, 32 pp."

See entry 239, letter 793, second paragraph, for Walras's evaluation of Cross's proposal.

173 "Note sur la solution du problème monétaire anglo-indien communiquée à la Section économique de l'Association britannique pour l'avancement des Sciences, réunie à Manchester." *Revue d'Economie Politique*, *1*, no. 6 (November–December 1887): 633–36.

This was published in English translation (entry 174); and republished in entry 205, with an additional note, 159–61.

1888

174 "On the Solution of the Anglo-Indian Monetary Problem." *Report of the Fifty-seventh Meeting of the British Association for the Advancement of Science held at Manchester in August and in September 1887*, London, John Murray, 1888.

This is a translation of entry 173.

1889

175 "Théorème de l'utilité maxima des capitaux neufs." *Revue d'Economie Politique*, *3*, no. 4 (May–June 1889): 310–15.

This was republished as §§ 257 and 258 of the *Eléments d'économie politique pure*, 2nd edition (entry 176).

For unpublished additional ideas of Walras's on the subject, see entry 239, letter 851, n. 5.

176 *Eléments d'économie politique pure ou Théorie de la richesse sociale*. 2nd edition. Revue, corrigée et augmentée. Lausanne, F. Rouge; Paris, Guillaumin & Cie; Leipzig, Verlag von Duncker & Humblot, 1889. 8°, XXIV, 524, 6 plates.

This edition contains an introductory chapter, "Des fonctions et de leur représentation géométrique. Théorie mathématique de la chute des corps," 3–21, which does not appear in subsequent editions.

177 "Opinions émises à la commission d'experts touchant la révision de la loi fédérale sur l'émission et le remboursement des billets de banque." Unpublished manuscript (1889).

This is item 97 in Bousquet's presentation (entry 238) of Walras's autobibliography of 1906 (entry 214), but is unnumbered in Walras's original manuscript, in which he gave the number 97 to his preceding entry (176 in the present bibliography). The manuscript, communicated to William Jaffé by Etienne Antonelli, was published by Jaffé in entry 239, letter 925, n. 12.

1890

178 "Observations sur le principe de la théorie du prix *de MM. AUSPITZ et LIEBEN." Revue d'Economie Politique, 4,* no. 3 (May–June 1890): 320–23.

This article appeared as Appendix II in the third and subsequent editions of *Eléments d'économie politique pure,* and was translated into English in entry 235, 483–88.

1891

179 "De l'échange de plusieurs marchandises entre elles." *Mémoires et Compte Rendu des Travaux de la Société des Ingénieurs Civils,* 5th series, *44,* no. 1 (January 1891): 42–49.

Walras read this paper to the *Sociéte des ingénieurs civils,* October 17, 1890. It was reprinted as an offprint, Paris, Cité Rougemont, 1891. 8°, 9 including the cover and a following blank page, plus a page with 4 diagrams. It appeared, after revision, as Part I of Appendix I to *Eléments d'économie politique pure* in the third and subsequent editions. A translated version of entry 179 appeared in entry 181. A résumé in 21 lines of print, erroneously reporting that Walras explained how buyers and sellers act to minimize (sic) their utility, appeared in *Résumé paraissant les premier et troisième vendredis de chaque mois,* Séance du 17 octobre 1890, Société des Ingénieurs civils, 314–15.

1892

180 "Théorie géométrique de la détermination des prix. De l'échange de produits et services entre eux. De l'échange d'épargnes contre capitaux neufs." *Recueil Inaugural de l'Université de Lausanne,*

Travaux des Facultés. Lausanne, Imprimerie Ch. Viret-Genton, 1892. 169–76, 1 plate.

In slightly revised form this entry became Parts II and III of Appendix I to the *Eléments d' économie politique pure* in the third and subsequent editions. A translated version of entry 180 appeared in entry 181. See entry 192 for an offprint of the appendix.

181 "Geometrical Theory of the Determination of Prices." *Annals of the American Academy of Political and Social Science*, *3*, no. 63 (July 1892): 45–64.

This is a translation of a version of entries 179 and 180. It was translated under the supervision of Irving Fisher and contains a "Translator's Note" by him, 45–47.

1893

182 "Le probléme monétaire anglo-indien." *Gazette de Lausanne*, no. 172 (July 24, 1893).

This was reprinted in entry 205 in section II of "Le Problème Monétaire," 162–67.

1894

183 "Personal Note." *Annals of the American Academy of Political and Social Science*, *4*, no. 5 (January 1894): 165–68 [657–60].

This is a biographical and bibliographical note.

184 "Le problème monétaire." *Gazette de Lausanne*, no. 49 (February 27, 1894).

This was reprinted in entry 205 in section III of "Le Problème Monétaire," 168–74, with the words "en Europe et aux Etats-Unis" added to the title.

185 "La monnaie de papier." *Gazette de Lausanne*, no. 286 (December 3, 1894).

This was incorrectly listed under 1893 by Walras in his autobibliography (entry 214).

For a summary, see entry 239, letter 1202, n. 2.

1895

186 "Le péril bimétalliste." *Revue Socialiste*, *22*, no. 127 (July 15, 1895): 14–25.

This was republished, with corrections, in entry 205, 175–190.

187 "Bibliographie de [mon] père." Unpublished, manuscript, 1895.

This was listed by Walras as an unnumbered item under 1895 in his autobibliography (entry 214). In entry 238, Bousquet added to it a note referring the reader to the entry numbered 216 in this bibliography.

1896

188 "Méthode de conciliation ou de synthèse." *Revue Socialiste, 23,* no. 136 (April 15, 1896): 385–406.

This is the publication of entry 89. Entry 188 was republished in entry 194, 175–202, where Walras stated (p. 175) that he wrote entry 89 and therefore entry 188 in 1868, and used it in the writing of entry 99.

189 "Théorie de la propriété." *Revue Socialiste, 23,* no. 138 (June 15, 1896): 668–81, 1 plate; *24,* no. 139 (July 15, 1896): 23–35, 1 plate (plate II).

This was republished with minor alterations in entry 194, 205–39. The principal modification is that the mathematics in the footnotes in the version in the *Revue Socialiste* were placed in the body of the article.

190 "Le problème fiscal." *Revue Socialiste, 24,* no. 142 (October 15, 1896); 386–400; *24,* no. 154 (November 15, 1896): 537–51.

This was republished, with minor changes, in *Etudes d' économie sociale,* 1896 edition (entry 194), 422–62; 1936 edition (entry 228), 455–85. Entry 120 is the source of much of the substance of entry 190 and of many of its sentences.

191 "Note sur la réfutation de la théorie anglaise du fermage de M. Wicksteed." *Recueil publié par la Faculté de Droit de l' Université de Lausanne à l' occasion de l' Exposition nationale suisse.* Geneva, Imprimerie Ch. Viret-Genton, 1896, 3–11.

Walras dated the "Note" proper (pp. 3–8) "Septembre 1894." The galleys are stamped "16 Jan. 96" and the page proofs are stamped "21 Jan. 95," which misstates the year. In each case, the stamp is of the "Imprimerie Typographique Ch. Viret-Genton, Lausanne." Before the *Recueil* version appeared, Walras added a postscript (pp. 9–11) and dated it "Octobre 1895." Walras pencilled "1895" on the cover of an offprint of the *Recueil* version. The title of the note appears on the front cover of the offprint; the inside of that cover is blank; and the title is repeated and the text begins on the following page. The offprint has the same pagination as the *Receuil*.

The entry was republished in 1896 with some alterations as Appendix III to the third edition of *Eléments d' économie politique pure* (entry 192), 485–92, and was translated into English in entry 235, 489–95. Walras drew the substance and most of its details of the "Note" proper from the 31st Leçon of the second edition of the *Eléments* (entry 176), the first seven pages of which were, with a few changes on the seventh page, the 55th Leçon of the first edition. He simply quoted or paraphrased passages and copied equations from the 31st Leçon, quoted passages from the 22nd (p. 254) and 32nd (pp. 367, 369), reproduced equations from other lessons in the second edition (§§ 199, 274), quoted or paraphrased passages written by Philip Wicksteed and reproduced his equations, and, in the postscript, presented an analysis authored by Enrico Barone.

The entry does not appear as such in the 1900 and 1926 editions of *Eléments d'économie politique pure*, but Walras incorporated the part of it that was directly concerned with marginal productivity into Leçon 36 of those editions.

For probable additions that Walras intended to make to entry 191, see entry 239, letter 1223, n. 6.

192 *Eléments d'économie politique pure ou Théorie de la richesse sociale*. 3rd edition. Lausanne, F. Rouge; Paris, F. Pichon; Leipzig, Verlag von Duncker & Humblot, 1896. 8°, XXIV, 496, 6 plates.

The introduction and the lessons that this edition shares with the second edition differ in only very minor respects from those in the latter, and have the same pagination. To create the third edition, Walras eliminated the introductory chapter (see entry 176) and four lessons on the applied theory of money that were in the second edition, and added three brief appendixes consisting of material written during 1890 through 1895, as explained under entries 179, 180, and 191.

193 *Appendice aux Eléments d'économie politique pure (Théorie géométrique de la détermination des prix)*. Lausanne, F. Rouge; Paris, F. Pichon; Leipzig, Verlag von Duncker & Humblot, 1896. 20, 1 plate.

See entries 179 and 180.

194 *Etudes d'économie sociale (Théorie de la répartition de la richesse sociale)*. Lausanne, F. Rouge; Paris, F. Pichon, 1896. 8°, VIII, 464, 3 plates.

This edition was reprinted under the editorship of Oscar Nuccio, Rome, Edizioni Bizzari (R. Pioda), Ristampe Anastatiche de Opere Antiche e Rare, CLVII, 1969, and a new edition was published in 1936 (entry 228).

Entry 194 is a collection of the following materials, of which all but two pages were already published. In section "I. RECHERCHE

DE L'IDEAL SOCIAL": "Socialisme et libéralisme. Lettres à
M. Ed. Schérer"; "Théorie générale de la société "; "Note"
(not previously published); "Méthode de conciliation ou de
synthèse." In section "II. PROPRIETE": "Théorie de la propriété"; "La question sociale"; "De la propriété intellectuelle." In
section "III. REALISATION DE L'IDEAL SOCIAL": "Théorie
mathématique du prix des terres et de leur rachat par l'état";
"Un économiste inconnu: Hermann-Henri Gossen". In section "IV.
L'IMPOT"": "De l'impôt sur le revenu et de l'impôt sur le capital,"
constructed from § 4 of Théorie critique de l'impôt (entry 27) and
from De l'impôt dans le Canton de Vaud (entry 28); "Le cadastre
et l'impôt foncier"; "Le problème fiscal."

195 "Prospectus."

This was undated but assigned by Walras to 1896 in his autobibliography (entries 214 and 238). The prospectus, distributed by
the Paris publisher, F. Pichon, announces the publication of the
third edition of *Eléments d' économie politique pure* and outlines its
contents.

For a long extract from this entry and a summary, see entry 239,
letter 1237, n. 7.

1897

196 "L'Etat et les chemins de fer." *Revue du droit public et de la science
politique en France et à l' etranger*, 7, no. 3 (May-June 1897): 417–
36; 8, no. 1 (July-August 1897): 42–58.

This article is the publication of entry 115. It was republished in
entry 205, 193–236 and translated into English in entry 245. In the
first installment, a footnote to the title translates as follows: "This
memoir was written during 1875 at the request of two members
of the Council of State of Vaud, at a time when the question of
the purchase of the railroads [by the state], being considered again
in Switzerland at the present time, had been raised in the canton
of Vaud. . . . I have used it myself since then as assigned reading
in my course in applied economics, adding to it the advances of
thought provided to me by various publications that have successively appeared in which the authors have been more or less in
agreement with my point of view. I leave this piece just as it was
originally written, confining myself to analyzing the works with
which it deals in a final Note." The first installment was followed by
five lines listing Walras's professional positions and a short bibliography of "principales publications" and "mémoires scientifiques"
(436–38) signed, "The Editorial Staff," but evidently written by

Walras (see entry 238). The second installment was followed by a "Note" (58–61) that cited and summarized books that confirmed or completed Walras's views on the subject.

197 "Théorie du libre échange." *Revue d'Economie Politique*, *11*, no. 7 (July 1897): 649–64.

This was written in March 1895. It was republished in entry 205, 286–304.

198 "L'économique appliquée et la défense des salaires." *Revue d'Economie Politique*, *11*, no. 12 (December 1897): 1018–36.

This was republished in entry 205, 265–85.

199 "Note sur la «théorie de la quantité»." Manuscript (1897).

This was published in entry 205, 153–58.

1898

200 "Théorie du crédit." *Revue d'Economie Politique*, *12*, no. 2 (February 1898): 128–43.

This corresponds to sections I, II, and V of "Théorie du crédit" in entry 205, 307–18 (sections I and II), and 329–36 (section V). Section III in entry 200 corresponds to section V in entry 205.

201 "La caisse d'épargne postale de Vienne et le comptabilisme social." *Revue d'Economie Politique*, *12*, no. 3 (March 1898): 202–20.

This appears in form and substance in entry 205, 376–98.

202 "Politique française." *Gazette de Lausanne*, no. 162 (July 14, 1898).

This was reprinted in entry 204 with the indicated new title; and in entry 205, 485–90, with small and unimportant changes in wording.

203 "La prière du libre penseur." *Gazette de Lausanne*, no. 165 (July 18, 1898).

This was reprinted in entry 205, 491–95, with small and unimportant changes in wording.

204 "Esquisse d'une doctrine économique et social." *L'Association Catholique – Revue des questions sociales et ouvrières*, 23rd year, *46* (December 15, 1898): 571–76.

This was published in the section entitled "Documents et Faits sociaux." It is a retitled reprint of entry 202. It was reprinted in entry 205, 485–90, as the first part of the last section of group VII.

205 *Etudes d'économie politique appliquée (Théorie de la production de la richesse sociale)*. Lausanne, F. Rouge; Paris, F. Pichon, 1898. 8°, 499, 4 plates (I, II–III, IV–V, and VI).

This edition was reprinted under the editorship of Oscar Nuccio, Rome, Edizioni Bizzarri (R. Pioda), Ristampe Anastatiche de Opere

Antiche e Rare, CLVIII, 1969; and a new edition was published in 1936 (entry 229). The edition indicated by entry 249.X has been translated into English (entry 250).

Entry 205 is a collection of the following materials, most of them already published. In section "I. MONNAIE": "Monnaie d'or avec billion d'argent régulateur"; "Mesure et régularisation des variations de la monnaie"; "Théorie de la monnaie," reproducing the entire Théorie de la monnaie (entry 169) with changes that took this route: Parts of entry 169 were introduced, with alterations, into entry 176, and those changes were then introduced into "Théorie de la monnaie" in entry 205. The other articles in section I are: "Note sur la 'théorie de la quantité' " (not previously published); "Le problème monétaire," which contains "Note sur la solution du problème monétaire anglo-indien"; "Le problème monétaire anglo-indien"; "Le problème monétaire en Europe et aux Etats-Unis"; "Le péril bimétalliste." In section "II. MONOPOLES": "L'Etat et les chemins de fer." In section "III. AGRICULTURE, INDUSTRIE, COMMERCE ": "L'influence de la communication des marchés sur la situation des populations agricoles"; "L'économie politique et la défense des salaires"; "Théorie du libre échange." In section "IV. CREDIT ": Théorie du crédit." In section "V. BANQUE ": "Théorie mathématique du billet de banque"; "Caisse d'épargne postale de Vienne et le comptabilisme social." In section "VI. BOURSE": "La Bourse, la spéculation et l'agiotage." In section "VII. ESQUISSE D'UNE DOCTRINE ECONOMIQUE ET SOCIALE ": "Distinction entre la science pure, la science morale, la science appliquée et la pratique"; "Science pure de l'homme et de la société"; "Science pure de la richesse sociale"; "Théorie morale de la répartition de la richesse sociale. Rachat des terres par l'Etat"; "Théorie appliquée de la production de la richesse sociale. Régularisation des variations de valeur de la monnaie"; "Politique française. La prière du libre penseur." In group VII, all the parts except the one between the last set of quotation marks (see entries 202 and 203) were previously unpublished, although Walras had already published most of their substance. He put together the first drafts of the first five parts of group VII during the period September 1893 to February 1895.

1899

206 "Equations de la circulation." *Bulletin de la Société Vaudoise des Sciences Naturelles* 35, no. 132 (June 1899): 85–103.

This paper was read to the Société vaudoise des sciences naturelles on May 3, 1899, and incorporated, with changes, into the fourth edition of the *Eléments d' économie politique pure* (entry 210). It was translated into Italian by Vilfredo Pareto (entry 207). In a "Note" appended to the article (p. 103), Walras introduced the device of "bons" with the objective of constructing a virtual model.Walras reproduced pages 85 to half-way down page 94 as Leçon 29 of the fourth edition of the *Eléments* (210) except that he omitted about 7 lines from p. 91, and incorporated the last 26 lines of the "Note" as § 274 of the Leçon. He inserted the first 11 lines of the "Note" into § 207 of that edition. He reproduced the remaining pages of entry 206 as Leçon 30 of the fourth edition, with the following changes: He eliminated 13 lines from p. 98, and added 17 lines of new writing into §§ 279 and 280. To finish Leçon 30, he then added 12 lines of new writing at the end of the "Equations de circulation" material, and then about three pages that he took from the second (entry 176) and third (entry 192) editions.

See entry 239, letter 1401, n. 3, and letter 1407, n. 3 for additional bibliographical information.

207 "Sulle equazioni della circolazione (Comunicazione a la Società di Scienze naturale di Vaud, Seduta del 3 maggio 1899)." *Giornale degli economisti*, 2nd series, *19*, no. 2 (August 1899): 110–16.

This is a translation by Vilfredo Pareto of an abridged version of entry 206.

See entry 239, letter 1407, n. 3 for additional bibliographical information.

208 "Sur les équations de la circulation." Unpublished manuscript (1899).

This entry is the same in substance as entry 206.

1900

209 "Note sur l'équation du taux du revenu net." *Bulletin Trimestriel de l'Institut des Actuaires Français*, *11*, no. 43 (December 1900): 162–64.

See entry 239, letter 1454, n. 8, where it is explained that this entry is in substance the same as § 242 of entry 210 with the exception of a difference in the last equation of entry 210.

210 *Eléments d' économie politique pure ou Théorie de la richesse sociale*. 4th edition. Lausanne, F. Rouge; Paris, F. Pichon, 1900. 8°, XX, 491, 5 plates.

This was reprinted, Paris, Librairie Générale de Droit et de Jurisprudence, 1976.

1902

211 "Lettre à M. P. Pic. Lettre de M. L. Walras en réponse à l'étude bibliographique de M. P. Pic." *Questions Pratiques de Législation Ouvrière et d'Economie Sociale*, *3*, no. 4 (April 1902): 105–7.

212 "Autobiographie." Originally unpublished until 1908 (entry 240).
This was published in an Italian translation in 1908 (entry 217). The French original was first published in 1965 (entry 240). A corrected version of entry 212 appears in entry 249. V, pp. 11–27. For a definitive account of Walras's autobiographical efforts see entry 239, *1*, p. 1, n. 1.

1905

213 "Cournot et l'économique mathématique." *Gazette de Lausanne*, no. 163 (July 13, 1905).
This was republished almost in its entirety in entry 237.
For a summary, see entry 239, letter 1593, n. 2.

1906

214 "Bibliographie économique." Autograph manuscript, Fonds Walras IV a 7 (1906).
This was unpublished until presented by G.-H. Bousquet in entry 238. Entry 214 is described in Chapter 7 of the present book.

1907

215 "La paix par la justice sociale et le libre échange." *Questions Pratiques de Législation Ouvrière et d'Economie Sociale*, *8*, no. 6 (June 1907): 169–78; nos. 7–8 (July–August 1907): 221–32; nos. 9–10 (September–October 1907): 279–86.
In this article, Walras summarized and copied passages from a number of his previous writings, in particular from entries 82, 154, 189, 197, and part VII of entry 205.
Entry 215 was republished, with an introduction (pp. I–II) in which Walras noted contributions by his father and himself, in Lyon, A. Storck & Cie, Paris, F. Pichon & Durand-Auzias, 1907. II, 30.
For a brief description of the contents of entry 215, see entry 239, letter 1623, n. 4.

1908

216 "Un initiateur en économie politique, A.-A. Walras." *Revue du Mois*, *6*, no. 32 (August 10, 1908): 170–83.

This was republished as an offprint, Paris, Editions de la *Revue du Mois*, 1908. 14.

217 "Leone Walras–Autobiografia." *Giornale degli Economisti*, 2nd series, *37*, no. 6 (December 1908): 603–10.

This is a translation by Maffeo Pantaleoni of entry 212. See entry 239, *1*, p. 1, n. 1, for information about the translation, and see entry 240 for the original French autobiography.

1909

218 "Ruchonnet et la socialisme scientifique." *Gazette de Lausanne*, supplement, April 13, 1909.

Walras read this paper on the occasion of his jubilee on July 10, 1909. The paper was republished in *Revue Socialiste*, *50*, no. 295 (July 1909): 577–89; and as an offprint with a cover differing from the journal's cover by giving the date of publication as "Juillet-Décembre 1909", and by stating "Paris, Rédaction et Administration" instead of "Paris, Marcel Rivière & Cie."

For a summary, see entry 239, letter 1696, n. 7.

219 "Economique et mécanique." *Bulletin de la Société Vaudoise des Sciences Naturelles*, 5th series, *45*, no. 166 (June 1909): 313–27.

This paper was republished as an offprint, Lausanne, Imprimeries Réunies, S. A., 1909, 15 p. The article and its accompanying letter to Walras from Henri Poincaré were republished in entry 236.

1910

220 *"Histoire des doctrines économiques depuis les physiocrates jusqu'à nos jours*, par Charles Gide et Charles Rist, Paris, Larose et Tenin, 1909." *Gazette de Lausanne*, January 6, 1910.

For a summary of this review, see entry 239, letter 1782, n. 2.

1918

221 "De la mise en valeur des biens communaux." *La Clairière, Revue Syndicaliste Bi-Mensuelle*, 1st year, no. 14 (February 15, 1918): 663–75.

This is a reprint of entry 11. An introductory note was authored by A. Daudé-Bancel.

222 "Le Socialisme Scientifique." *La Clairière, Revue Syndicaliste Bi-Mensuelle*, 1st year, no. 18 (April 15, 1918): 883–91.
This is a reprint of entry 80.

1922

223 *Théorie des Geldes. Die Stabilisierung des Geldwertes als das Problem von heute und vor fünfzig Jahren.* Translated by Richard Kerschagl and Stephan Raditz. Jena, Verlag von Gustav Fischer, 1922. 8°, 115, 4 plates.
This entry is preceded by a "Vorwort" by the editors (5–6), and an "Einleitung/Das Problem der besten Geldschopfung; theoretische Problemstellung und historische Entwicklung" (7–26), primarily by Kerschagl. The translation of *Théorie de la Monnaie* (entry 169), primarily by Raditz, is on pages 27–115.

1926

224 *Eléments d'économie politique pure ou Théorie de la richesse sociale. Edition définitive revue et augmentée par l'auteur.* Paris, R. Pichon et R. Durand-Auzias; Lausanne, F. Rouge, 1926. 8°, XX, 491, 5 plates.
This is the fifth edition of the *Eléments*, differing from the fourth in only a very few minor respects. It has been reprinted (entry 233) and translated into Japanese, English, Chinese, Italian, and Spanish. Section I has been translated into Portuguese.

1931

225 *Reon Warurahsu Junsui-Keizaigaku Nyumon.* Translated by Miyoji Hayakawa. Tokyo, Nihon-Hyoron-sha, 1931. 204, 15 cm., table.
This is a translation into Japanese of entry 124, in part via entry 157. Its title translates as *Introduction to Walras's Pure Economics.* As Hayakawa indicated in his preface, he used both the original French text and the German translation, abridged the text, modified some parts, and omitted the correspondence between Walras and Jevons and the mathematical appendix.

1933

226 *Junsui keizaigaku yôron.* Volume 1. Translated by Sumio Tezuka. Tokyo, Moriyama shoten, 1933.

This is a translation into Japanese of entry 224. Tezuka divided the text into two volumes. The first volume was published with a foreword dated March 1933. It includes the first four sections of entry 224 (Leçons 1–22). The second volume was not published in the form in which Tezuka left it (see entry 234). When he used the Roman alphabet, as in his letters to Europeans, the translator represented his given name as "Juro" and spelled his last name "Tedzuka."

1934

227 "De l'unité de la valeur (Correspondance entre Léon Walras et Henri Laurent)." *Revue d'Economie Politique*, 48 (July–August 1934): 1255–78.

This correspondence between Walras and Hermann (not Henri) Laurent was presented by Etienne Antonelli. Two letters of dubious relevance are missing, for which see entry 239, letters 1410 and 1529. See entry 239, letter 1374, n. 2 for a brief discussion of the entry and of the missing letters.

1936

228 *Etudes d'économie sociale (Théorie de la répartition de la richesse sociale). Edition définitive par les soins de Gaston Leduc.* 2nd edition. Lausanne, F. Rouge et Cie; Paris, R. Pichon et R. Durand-Auzias, 1936. 8°, VIII, 488, portrait.

This is an edition of entry 194. The content differs from that of entry 194 in that Leduc, following Walras's wishes, inserted "Souvenirs du Congrès de Lausanne" on pages 379–400, preceded by a preface by Walras dated June 1899 (377–78). After page 400, the content is the same as appears on pages 377–462 of entry 194.

229 *Etudes d'économie politique appliquée (Théorie de la production de la richesse sociale). Edition définitive par les soins de Gaston Leduc.* 2nd edition. Lausanne, F. Rouge et Cie; Paris, R. Pichon et R. Durand-Auzias, 1936. 8°, 499, portrait, 6 plates.

This is an edition of entry 205. The content and pagination of entries 205 and 229 are the same.

1938

230 *Abrégé des éléments d'économie politique pure par Léon Walras. Précédé d'un avertissement et révisé par les soins de Gaston Leduc.*

Paris, R. Pichon et R. Durand-Auzias; Lausanne, F. Rouge et Cie, 1938. 8°, 399, 4 plates.

Walras prepared this abridged version of entry 210 for use in a course on mathematical economics to be taught by Albert Aupetit. Walras's daughter, Aline, gave the abridgement to Etienne Antonelli, who, in 1911, became the first person to use it in a classroom in France.

This was reprinted in 1953.

1940

231 *Objecto e divisões da economia política e social.* Translated by Eduardo Salgueiro. Lisbon, Editorial "Inquerito," no date. 75, 19 cm.

This is a translation into Portugese of Section I of entry 224. The date of publication is indicated in the introductory text.

1950

232 Oulès, Firmin, editor. *L'Ecole de Lausanne. Textes choisis de L. Walras et V. Pareto*, Paris, Librairie Dalloz, 1950.

This entry includes excerpts from a variety of Walras's published writings. The excerpts are too fragmentary to list separately.

1952

233 *Eléments d'économie politique pure ou Théorie de la richesse sociale. Edition définitive revue et augmentée par l'auteur.* Paris, Librairie Générale de Droit et de Jurisprudence, R. Pichon et R. Durand-Auzias, 1952. 8°, XX, 491, 5 plates.

This is a reprint of entry 224, differing from it in only the following respect, apart from corrections – sometimes defectively executed – of typographical errors. On page IX of the fourth edition of the *Eléments* (entry 210), the first line of the second paragraph reads: "Mais c'est surtout la théorie de la monnaie qui a été sensible-" and the second line reads in part: "ment modifiée par suite des études que j'ai poursuivies." On page IX of entry 224 a defect of printing left a blank at the end of the first line, so that it reads: "Mais c'est surtout la théorie de la monnaie qui." The word "qui" is mainly obliterated and the remaining 2 cm of the line are blank. The second line reads as in entry 233. D. A. Walker's copies of the corrections that Walras made to the fourth edition that were incorporated into the 1926 edition, and of the corrections that Walras wanted to be made but that were not carried out in print, reveal that he did not change anything on page IX, so he evidently wanted it to continue to appear as it had in the fourth edition. Nevertheless, when the 1952 reprint was prepared, the typesetter or an editor filled in the blank in the 1926 edition so as to make it read: "Mais c'est surtout la théorie de la monnaie qui a été entiére-". Walras was therefore mistakenly represented as writing "entièrement modifiée" instead of "sensiblement modifiée."

Entry 233 was reprinted in 1976 by the same publisher.

1953

234 *Junsui keizaigaku yôron*. Revised by Masao Hisatake. Tokyo, Iwanami-Shoten, 1953–1954. 2 vols. Vol. 1, 357; vol. 2, 344.

This is a revision of entry 226 and of the unpublished (second) volume of Tezuka's 1933 translation. The volumes are in "Bunko" style, namely pocketsize. The first volume was published in 1953 and the second in 1954. In volume 1, Tezuka's given name is printed "Sumio." In volume 2, it is printed "Juro." Volume 1 is introduced by Ichiro Nakayama. Hisatake wrote in his postscript that he respected Tezuka's translation insofar as possible; that he corrected the mistranslations, of which there were not many; and that his major contribution was to update the terminology and expressions. Hisatake placed the diagrams in the text instead of at the end, and translated Walras's lesson summaries and inserted them at the beginning of each lesson. Five thousand copies of volume 1 were printed and 4,000 of volume 2, all of which were sold by 1963.

1954

235 *Elements of Pure Economics or The Theory of Social Wealth*. Translated by William Jaffé. Published for the American Economic Association and the Royal Economic Society. Homewood, IL., Richard D. Irwin; London, George Allen and Unwin Ltd, 1954. 620.

This is a translation into English of entry 224. It is annotated by Jaffé with "Translator's Notes," 497–558, and collated with previous editions by him in "Table," 559–63, and in "Collation of Editions," 565–610. It was reprinted, New York, Augustus M. Kelley, 1969; Fairfield, NJ, Augustus M. Kelley, 1977; Philadelphia, Orion Editions, 1984; and London and New York, Routledge, 2003.

1960

236 "Economique et mécanique." *Metroeconomica*, *12*, fasc. 1 (April 1960): 3–13.
      This is a republication of entry 219.

1962

237 "Cournot et l'économique mathématique." *Revue d'Economie Politique*, *72*, no. 1 (January–February 1962): 61–64.
      This is a republication, almost in its entirety, of entry 213.

1964

238 "L'Autobibliographie inédite de Léon Walras (1906) (Les Deux Autobibliographies de Léon Walras)." Presented by G.-H. Bousquet. *Revue Economique*, no. 2 (March 1964): 295–304.
      This entry is described in the Introduction to the present bibliography. Bousquet added the items that appear as entries 216, 218, and 219 in the present bibliography. The parenthetical title given by Bousquet was in recognition of the bibliography of Walras's works published in 1897 (see entry 196), the entries in which are included within the 1906 autobibliography (entry 214). Bousquet noted that the 1897 bibliography was signed, "The Editorial Staff," but explained that it was obviously written by Walras.

1965

239 *Correspondence of Léon Walras and Related Papers.* Edited and annotated by William Jaffé. Published for the Royal Netherlands Academy of Sciences and Letters. Amsterdam, North-Holland Publishing Company, 1965. 3 vols. Vol. 1: XLIII, 799; vol. 2: XXVII, 763; vol. 3: XXIII, 538.
      Each volume has a portrait of Walras.
240 "Notice autobiographique." In entry 239, *1*, 1–15.
      William Jaffé wrote: "The text of this Autobiographical Note was established by collating a manuscript copy presented to me in [the] 1930s by Léon Walras's daughter, Aline Walras, and written in her hand, with another manuscript copy written in the same hand and preserved among the late professor Henry Ludwell Moore's papers at Columbia University" (239, *1*, p. 1, n. 1). Jaffé then summarized the history of Walras's writing of the autobiography. A version that

takes account of variations in other drafts of the autobiography appears in 249.V, pp. 11–27.

1966

241 *Li lun ching chi hsüeh yao i.* Translated by Wang tso-ts'ê. T'ai-pei, T'ai-wan, yin hang. Publisher: ching hsiao che Chung hua shu chü, no date. 574, 2 vols.

This is a translation into Chinese of entry 224. The date of publication, assumed from internal evidence, is almost certainly 1966.

1967

242 "Pensées et réflexions." *Cahiers Vilfredo Pareto, 11* (1967): 104–40.

This entry consists of previously unpublished short notes written by Walras to express his opinions privately on a variety of personal, social, political, and institutional matters. The notes were preserved in manuscript form by having been copied by Aline, his daughter. The manuscript was found by G. H. Bousquet in the Lyons Collection and presented by him with an introduction (103–4) and annotations.

1974

243 *Elementi di economia politica pura.* Translated by Anna Bagiotti. Torino, Unione TipograficoEditrice Torinese, 1974. 656, 5 plates.

This is a translation into Italian of entry 224. The introduction is by Giuseppe Palomba.

Biographical and bibliographical notes were authored by Giovanni Busino.

244 *L'Application des mathématiques à l'économie politique et sociale.* New York, Burt Franklin Reprints, [1974].

This is a reprint of "Principe d'une théorie mathématique de l'échange" (entry 103), and of "Théorie mathématique du prix des terres et de leur rachat par l'Etat" (entry 154).

1980

245 "The State and the Railways." *Journal of Public Economics, 13,* no. 1 (February 1980), 81–100.

This is a translation of entry 115, which was published in entry 196.

1983

246 Junsui keizaigaku yôron. Translated by Masao Hisatake. Tokyo,
Iwanami-Shoten, 1983. XXVII, 531.

This is a translation of entry 224.

Because of the extensive changes in the style of written Japanese
since the publication of entries 226 and 234, Iwanami Publishing
asked Hisatake to make this new translation. He also provided a
27-page introduction and a 3-page postscript.

1984

247 *Warurasu, Shakaiteki Tomi no Sugakuteki Riron.* Translated by
Toshinosuke Kashiwazaki. Tokyo, Nihon-Keizai-Hyron-Sha, 1984.
130.

This is a translation into Japanese of the texts listed before part
(5) under entry 160; that is of entry 124. The title of entry 247
translates as *Walras, The Mathematical Theories of Social Wealth*.

1987

248 *Elementos de economía política pura (o Teoría de la riquesa social).*
Edited and translated by Julio Segura. Madrid, Alianza Editorial,
1987. 818.

This is a translation into Spanish of entry 224, with an introduction and commentary by Segura.

249 Auguste and Léon Walras, *Œuvres économiques complètes.* Edited
by Pierre Dockès, Pierre-Henri Goutte, Claude Hébert, Claude
Mouchot, Jean-Pierre Potier, and Jean-Michel Servet, under the
auspices of the Centre Auguste et Léon Walras. Paris, Economica,
1987–2005.

The volumes of the writings of Léon Walras are:

V. *L'économie politique et la justice.* Edited by Pierre-Henri
Goutte with the collaboration of Jean-Michel Servet, 2001.

VI. *Les associations populaires coopératives.* Edited by Claude
Hébert and Jean-Pierre Potier, 1990.

VII. *Mélanges d'économie politique et sociale.* Edited by Claude
Hébert and Jean-Pierre Potier, 1987.

VIII. *Éléments d'économie politique pure ou Théorie de la richesse
sociale,* comparative edition. Edited by Claude Mouchot,
1988.

IX. *Éléments d'économie sociale (Théorie de la répartition de la
richesse sociale).* Edited by Pierre Dockès, 1990.

X. *Études d'économie politique appliquée (Théorie de la production de la richesse sociale).* Edited by Jean-Pierre Potier,
1992. Translated into English (entry 250).

XI. *Théorie mathématique de la richesse sociale et autres écrits
d'économie pure.* Edited by Claude Mouchot, 1993.

XII. *Cours. Cours d'économie sociale. Cours d'économie politique appliquée.* Matériaux du *Cours d'économie politique
pure.* The first of these texts was edited by Pierre Dockès,
and the second by Jean-Pierre Potier; they edited the third in
collaboration with Pascal Bridel, 1996.

XIII. *Œuvres diverses.* Edited by Pierre Dockès, Claude Mouchot,
and Jean-Pierre Potier, 2000.

XIV. *Tables et index.* Prepared by Roberto Baranzini, Claude Mouchot, and Jean-Pierre Potier, 2005.

250 *Studies in Applied Economics   Theory of the production of social
wealth.* Translated and introduced by Jan van Daal. 2 vols. Vol. 1,
lxviv,193, 1 photograph; vol. II, xii, 223. London and New York,
Routledge, Taylor & Francis Group, 2005.

This is a translation into English of entry 205. It was prepared
under the auspices of the Centre Auguste et Léon Walras, Université Lyon-2. There is an extensive introduction by Jan van Daal
(volume 1, xv–lxvii). Most of the annotations are translations of
those made by Jean-Pierre Potier in entry 249.X. In volume 1, the
main text, including Potier's notes and notes added by the translator, is on pages 1–193. In volume 2, the main text, including
Potier's notes and notes added by the translator, is on pages 195–
394; the index of persons for both volumes, with biographical notes,
is on pages 395–407; and the subject index for both volumes is on
pages 408–17.

UNDATED OR WITH SEVERAL DATES

251 "Notes sur la Métaphysique et la science d'Etienne Vacherot,
notamment sur les chapitres relatifs à l'analyse et à la critique
de l'intelligence." Two autograph manuscripts, 1859–1861, unpublished, Fonds Walras IS 1927, V/16/20.

These are notes on a work of Vacherot's (see 249.X, p. 503). The
first is a summary of Vacherot's ideas; the second is constituted of
quotations culled from his book.

252 "Notes d'humeur," in the "Collection Walras de la Faculté de Droit
de Lyon," "Fonds Leduc," and "Collection Antonelli." Autograph
jottings and copies by Aline Walras, various dates and undated.

The collections are described in 239, *1*, p. XII and in 249. XIII,
pp. 503–8. Many of the jottings are presented in entry 242, and

a complete presentation of the jottings that are in the collections listed above is given in 249.XIII, pp. 509–62.

253 "Cours d'Economie Sociale professé à l'Université de Lausanne. (Théorie de la répartition de la richesse sociale). " Autograph manuscript, Fonds Walras V 6, unpublished course, pages 1–240, 253–76, 301–6, 313–36; 28.7 cm. by 21.7 cm.

254 "Cours d'Economie Politique Appliquée professé à l'Université de Lausanne (Théorie de la production de la richesse social)." Autograph manuscript, Fonds Walras V 6, unpublished course, 167 leaves, 29.3 cm. by 21.7 cm.

255 "Sur les décrets du 19 janvier 1867." Autograph manuscript, Fonds Walras V 6, unpublished, 5 p. and 3 leaves, 20.2 cm. by 15.3 cm.

256 "Les pétitions au Sénat." Autograph manuscript, Fonds Walras V 1, unpublished, 4 p., 26.4 cm. by 19.7 cm.

257 "De la viande à bon marché." Autograph manuscript, Fonds Walras V 6, unpublished, 2 leaves, 21.2 cm. by 16 cm.

258 "La situation politique en 1868." Autograph manuscript, Fonds Walras V 6, unpublished, 5 p., 20.3 cm. by 15.8 cm.

259 "Voies et moyens pour la suppression de l'octroi à Paris." Autograph manuscript, Fonds Walras V 6, unpublished, 10 leaves, 26.3 cm. by 19.6 cm.

260 "*Etudes sur la monnaie*, par Victor Bonnet, 1 vol. in 8°, Paris, Guillaumin, 1870." Autograph manuscript, Fonds Walras V 1, unpublished, 6 p., 27 cm. by 21.7 cm. 27 cm. by 21.7 cm.

261 Hermann Heinrich Gossen, *Expositions des lois de l'échange et des règles de l'industrie qui s'en déduisent.* Translated by Léon Walras and Charles Secrétan. Manuscript, unpublished.

This is a translation into French of Hermann Heinrich Gossen, *Entwicklung der Gesetze des menschlichen Verkehrs.* It was edited by Jan van Daal, Albert Jolink, Jean-Pierre Potier, and Jean-Michel Servet and published in Paris, Economica, 1995. 346.

In a letter to W. S. Jevons, Walras indicated that the translation was made during January and February 1879 (239, 1879, *1*, p. 597). It is included in this bibliography because Walras may have made some contribution to it. Not all the information about who did the work of translation is in agreement. The editors state without qualification, regarding Walras and Secrétan, that the translation "was the fruit of their collaboration" (259, 1995, p. 19), and indeed in 1879 Walras referred to "the translation that I made with the aid of one of my colleagues and that will soon be finished" (239, 1879, *1*, p. 597). The decision to put Walras's name first on the title page of entry 259 is nevertheless more than questionable, for Walras also wrote that, in Secrétan's office, "we read and put into French entire books in German and English, him dictating, me writing, interrupting each other to reach agreement on an idea or an expression of which I needed to have an exact and complete translation" (242, 1967, p. 128). In 1885, he wrote that Secrétan offered to translate a book in German "for me, like he translated Gossen's" (239, 1885, 2, p. 49). In yet another place, Walras indicated clearly that Secrétan "wished to take the trouble to read that work with me and to dictate to me, during the reading, a complete translation, which was made extremely valuable by his admirable knowledge of the two languages French and German" (194, 1896, p. VII).

262 "Etude de deux courbes réelies de variation de prix moyen d'un certain nombre de marchandises." Autograph manuscript, Fonds Walras V, circa 1887, unpublished: 6 p., 22.2 cm. by 17.3 cm.

263 "Bibliographie littéraire." Autograph manuscript, Fonds Walras 1966, unpublished.

This consists of 25 entries, all included in the present bibliography.

PART II

Walras's influence

CHAPTER 9

Models constructed by Walras's contemporaries and immediate successors

I. Vilfredo Pareto

Background

In 1848, Europe was ablaze with revolutionary activity fueled by opposition to monarchy and by enthusiasm for democracy, socialism, and liberal reform. In Italy, the authorities retained their positions and punished the dissidents. One of the persons whose life was disrupted by the situation was the Marquis Raphael Pareto, the head of an old Genoese family. His republican sentiments put him into opposition with the policies of the government so he took refuge in France, where he married a French woman. Thus it was that their son, the second most important economist in the early development of the theory of general equilibrium, was born in Paris on July 15, 1848, and christened Federico-Vilfredo-Damaso. From 1852 to 1858 the family lived in Genoa, Liguria; then an amnesty in 1858 made it possible for the marquis to move to Casale Monferrato, Piedmont. The Paretos spoke French at home, and Vilfredo spent thirty years of his life in the French-speaking part of Switzerland. His second companion, with whom he lived for the last twenty years of his life and whom he married shortly before his death, was French. Pareto therefore drew upon both French and Italian cultures. It has been said that three-quarters of his heart was Italian and one-quarter French (see Walker 2003).

Pareto learned as a youth to love the Greek and Latin classics, and began the studies that were to make him profoundly erudite as a classicist. He also loved mathematics. During his high school years he first attended the Istituto Tecnico Leardi and then the Règio Istituto Tecnico in Turin, concentrating on physics and mathematics and graduating from the latter in 1864 at the age of 16. He entered the University of Turin in that same year, graduating with a degree in mathematics and physical sciences in 1867. He then entered the Scuola di Applicazione per Ingegneri and obtained a Dr. Ingegneria diploma in January 1870. Another influence upon Pareto was the work of H. T. Buckle (1872), a historian whose work he read when he was twenty years of age, and who impressed upon him the idea that social sciences could be developed on the same level of rigor as the physical sciences (Pareto to Antonio Antonucci, December 7, 1907, in Antonucci 1938, p. 17; and in Busino 1973, p. 613). Many passages in his writings also reveal the influence of mathematics, his studies of physical science, and his classical studies, which he used to support his views on modern problems.

In 1870, Pareto began work as a railway engineer in Tuscany, headquartered in Florence. In 1873 he became deputy head of an iron and steel foundry, then technical director in 1875, and director general in 1880. Frequently he dressed in workman's clothing, but his casual appearance did not imply that he was not a perfectionist. He demanded excellence from himself and from the engineers he supervised. In 1886 he began to give occasional lectures on economics at the University of Florence. He gave up engineering in 1890 – actually he was fired for losing large sums of money in iron commerce speculation – and began to concentrate on publicizing his public policy views and on his academic studies.

Although Pareto succeeded to his father's title and was proud of "the ancient origins of his family, as noble and venerable as those of Savoy" (Einaudi 1935, p. 338), he never used his title. He accepted being addressed as "professor," but thought it was even preferable to be called "mister" (ibid.); a person who knew him well said that he sometimes made gentle fun of his nobility. Nevertheless, there was more than a hint of an aristocratic manner in his scathing denunciations of his adversaries. He married the Countess Allesandrina Bakounine in 1889, which has led to the notion that he was linked by marriage to the Russian anarchist Mikhail Bakunin. In fact, Bakunin belonged to a totally different family. Neither party entered into the marriage for material considerations. Pareto declared that he was never interested in money in his entire life, not any more on the occasion of his marriage than on any other, and it is true that Allesandrina was impoverished. Nevertheless, his declaration was contradicted by the vigor of his efforts to protect his considerable inheritance from the depredations of socialists, and by his moving to Céligny to avoid the taxes of the Canton of Lausanne (ibid., p. 342). The Paretos did not have any children, which pleased Pareto. He believed that "the divine Malthus," as he referred to the Englishman, had correctly identified problems created by overpopulation. Preferring cats to children, Pareto exhorted his friends to make science rather than babies.

During the years that he lived in Florence and Fiesole, Pareto read voraciously, gathering together an abundance of information on a wide variety of topics, information that he was to use in his subsequent creative endeavors. Because he had to spend ten hours a day working for a living, much of his reading had to be done at night, and as he was afflicted with insomnia, he would study far into the early hours of the morning. It was at this time that he was influenced by the French sociologist Auguste Comte, by Charles Darwin, and by Herbert Spencer, the English philosopher who applied Darwinist ideas to an explanation of the development of civilizations even before Darwin had published his treatise on the origin of species.

In the 1870s and 1880s, Pareto was much occupied with practical economic policies. During those years, he was a very active pacifist and humanitarian, opposing the oppression of the weak by the strong. His characteristic reaction upon detecting such oppression was to launch a verbal attack on the oppressors. He believed passionately in individual freedom, a sentiment that differed from his family's on that topic. "From this I can say ... that my feelings were not acquired, but were the effect of a character that I had from the time of my birth" (Pareto to Antonio Antonucci, December 7, 1907, in Antonucci 1938, p. 18; and in Busino 1973, p. 613). The convictions that animated him, he wrote, were that the "sovereignty of the people was an axiom. Liberty was the universal panacea. ... Militarism and religion were the major scourges of humanity" (ibid., p. 19). His studies of the economic thought of the period 1776 to 1870 led him to become ardently in favor of laissez-faire economic liberalism. Classical economics, he declared, "was a perfect or almost perfect science" (ibid.). "Even for those people who are most firmly attached to an ideal of economic liberty ..., it is almost impossible to understand exactly the mentality of the extreme liberals, such as Pareto was in this epoch. Liberalism was for them an ideal, almost a sort of religion ... " (Bousquet 1960, pp. 39–40; and see Bousquet 1928b). Pareto thought that a purely competitive private enterprise economy, free of government intervention and regulation, was the best possible system, on both the domestic and the international levels. He believed strongly in the free-trade movement, and, during his career in business, published many articles and pamphlets in both Italian and French, protesting bitterly that the tariffs and other foreign trade restrictions of the Italian government constituted, in effect, a tax on consumers (Pareto 1898a). Eager to have an impact on government policy, he stood for a position on the town council of San Giovanni in 1877 and was elected. He ran for public office again in 1880 and 1882, but without success.

Pareto felt deceived when a left-wing government came into power in 1876, because it did not support the principles of liberalism that he espoused, and particularly because it continued protectionist policies. The intervention of the state into the economic life of a country, he argued, gives rise to much corruption. He confided to Walras that he was thinking of leaving Italy in order to devote himself exclusively to pure science. He felt that he had achieved nothing in Italy. He wanted, for example, to lecture on economics, but, he complained to Walras:

Here I am prohibited from doing that. I wanted to teach a course in mathematical economics, without pay, you understand. The government opposed it. Any citizen is permitted to give as many lectures as he wants, but they must not be in a series so as to constitute a course! It doesn't suit me to buy the good will of the Italian government by prostituting science in its service. Thus, I cannot hope to express my ideas except in a foreign county (239, 1893, 2, p. 546).

His bitterness became extreme. "To live well in this country, one has to be a thief, or a friend of thieves. Therefore, I very much want to leave it" (ibid., p. 547).

Obviously, Pareto disagreed very strongly with socialist reasoning, and especially with the idea of state intervention or control of the economy, and with Karl Marx's ideas about surplus value and wages funds (Pareto 1902–1903). Nevertheless, Pareto accepted the concept of the class struggle. He believed that socialism could enable the underprivileged to have a voice in social decisions, and he supported the rights of socialists to freedom of speech and political action. In the spring of 1898 there were violent riots in Italy, resulting from increases in the price of bread. Almost 90 people died and nearly 800 republicans and socialists were arrested. Pareto was angered by the government's policy and welcomed into his home in Switzerland a number of socialists who had to flee from Italy. In recognition of that and of his eminent stature as a scientist, the socialists called him "the Karl Marx of the bourgeoisie," a label that Pareto did not appreciate.

Although he had displayed great energy in pursuing liberal causes, as late as his fortieth year Pareto had shown no evidence of being capable of contributing to economic science. He was enormously learned, but he had not used that knowledge to fashion new ideas. "If he had died at forty-two years of age, nobody would have suspected that he would someday be a thinker, and I suspect that, even in the most detailed Italian works on the history of economic or political thought, his name would have appeared solely as part of a footnote, at the bottom of a page. That silence would have been justified" (Bousquet 1960, p. 46).

Walras's influence

During the 1880s, Pareto began to become interested in pure economic theory. A chance meeting in a train with the well-known Italian economist Maffeo Pantaleoni was a decisive event. It led Pareto to read Pantaleoni's book on the principles of economics, which showed Pareto the importance of economic theory. In particular, it pointed the way to mathematical economics, and therefore to the economics of Léon Walras and the concept of general economic equilibrium. He was also urged to study Walras's positive economics by Georges de Molinari, a prominent Italian economist. Toward the end of the 1880s, Pareto studied Walras's mature comprehensive model appreciatively, and he started to apply mathematics to economic theory and to economic policy formulation. Pareto noted that,

Pantaleoni has worked steadily to make the scientific study of economics familiar in Italy. I can deny this less than any other person, since it is to his influence that I owe my studying of mathematical economics. I had read Walras, but had neglected the gold in his work in favor of seeing nothing but the sterile vein-stone of metaphysical reasonings. I was disgusted by them. Since they seemed absurd to me then and have continued to seem to me to be absurd, I had no confidence that such theories could have a place in an experimental science. But after having read the *Principles* of Pantaleoni, I modified my opinion of Walras. I started again to study him, and this time I could find the gold in his work, that is to say, the concept of economic equilibrium (Pareto quoted in Bousquet 1928, p. 18, and Ricci 1924, p. 10).

Walras's conception of the interconnections, equilibrating processes, and general equilibrium of a multi-market competitive economy, and his use of mathematics, were central to Pareto's economic reasoning. "The study of his works," Pareto wrote, "initiated me into the theories of mathematical economics and was at the origin of my own research" (Pareto to Maffeo Pantaleoni, June 16, 1909, in Pareto 1960, *3*, appendix 38, p. 429):

It is no exaggeration to say that the idea of general equilibrium formed the scientific thought of Pareto, and that all his work . . . is founded on that idea. . . . The influence of the ideas of Walras in regard to economic equilibrium was . . . decisive on the mind of Pareto. . . . Moreover, his work in economic theory was founded directly on Walras's system, and would be inconceivable without its existence. The linkage of the thought of the two great scientists is total (Bousquet 1960, pp. 48–49).

Pareto emphasized the importance of the legacy of Walras's equation system, declaring that economists are indebted to him "for the general representation of economic equilibrium in equations," and asserted that "the discovery of this highly generalized formulation marks the beginning of a very important epoch for the development of new theories" (Pareto 1898b, p. 320, translated in Jaffé 1977, p. 199; Jaffé 1983, p. 79). He assured Walras "that no person who studies mathematical economics should forget to accord you the very great honor of having been the first to establish the system of equations that governs economic equilibrium" (239, Pareto to Walras, 1901, *3*, p. 154). Applying himself to the subjects of Walras's mature comprehensive model, Pareto made it more general in some important respects, replaced some of its questionable assumptions, refined some of its parts, and made original contributions in the course of improving it.

Many of Walras's contemporaries and successors found his *Eléments* difficult to read, even when he confined himself strictly to verbal reasoning. Georges-Henri Bousquet noted regarding himself that he certainly belonged to the group of economists who regarded Walras's *Eléments* as a great treatise, but he also thought that the exposition in it is "detestable: off-putting, dull, prolix," of such a character as to discourage even readers who would be predisposed to appreciate it (Bousquet 1964, p. XI). One of Pareto's achievements was to set forth the Walrasian theory of general equilibrium in ways that were comprehensible to those who could read Italian and French, and he presented some of his ideas in articles in English. Displaying the gift of felicitous expression, his exposition was very effective in the seventy-five pages of his *Cours d'économie politique* (1896/1897) that were specifically devoted to economic theory, and in his *Manuale d'economia politica* (1906), subsequently translated into French (1909). His definitions and explanations of economic phenomena were necessarily verbal, and his analyses of complex economic processes in the body of the text in those treatises were also carried out by means of verbal reasoning in the manner of Walras. He therefore made it much easier for the theory of general equilibrium to be understood by those who were not mathematically well equipped. Another effective aspect of Pareto's presentation was his abundant use of statistical data, rendering it crystal clear that he conceived of economic theory as properly dealing directly with the real world. The profusion of facts that he was able to present and to organize in order to illustrate and substantiate his theoretical positions, and the soundness and clarity of his statistical reasoning, reveal that he would have been a great statistician if he had chosen that specialty. Nevertheless, Pareto's economic theories did not become widely influential outside of Italy and France until the 1930s, when there was a "Pareto revival," centered primarily on his contributions to welfare economics.

Unlike Walras, who put equation systems into his texts and often interspersed them with symbols and equations, Pareto confined his mathematics to footnotes in the *Cours*, and to an appendix in the *Manuale*. He remarked that "many people think that the advantage arising from the use of mathematics consists in making demonstrations more rigorous. This is an error. A demonstration well constructed by the method of ordinary logic is just as rigorous as one made by the application of that other kind of logic which bears the name of mathematics" (Pareto 1897, pp. 490–91). He pointed out that he employed mathematics to deal with a certain type of problem: "The advantage of mathematics lies chiefly in this, that it permits us to treat problems far more complicated than those generally solved by ordinary logic," especially to demonstrate the conditions of general equilibrium in detail regarding the different components of the economy (ibid., p. 491).

Pareto met Walras in Clarens in 1891 and they entered into an extensive correspondence with each other. In the early 1890s, Pareto published a series of articles on economic theory and the use of mathematics in the formulation of economic policies, convincing Walras that he would develop the Walrasian line of general equilibrium analysis. Thus it was that, because of his approach to economics, Pareto was offered (after Walras's retirement, and recommended by Walras and Pantaleoni) the position that Walras had held at the University of Lausanne (239, 1893, 2, note 4, pp. 553–54). He began his duties there in 1893 and, unlike Walras, he was a popular teacher. The students applauded when he entered the classroom and when he left it. Eventually he decided to retire to devote himself exclusively to research. His request to do so was refused twice by the Canton of Vaud, and then accepted in 1911, when the onset of heart disease lent urgency to his request.

Pareto distinguished pure economic theory and applied economics, and he agreed with Walras that the scope of pure economic theory is limited to economic facts and relationships regarding which free will does not play a part. Like Walras, he believed that there are economic laws, similar in their validity to the laws discovered by natural science. An anecdote illustrates how that opinion was an integral part of his thinking. His remarks at a conference prompted Gustav Schmoller, the German economist of the historical school, to contradict him by declaring that there are no economic laws. At the close of the meeting Pareto asked him, seemingly in need of advice, whether he knew of a restaurant where a free meal could be had that evening. Schmoller replied that of course there was no such place. Pareto allowed a significant pause to occur and then remarked: "There you see the action of the natural laws of economics," thereby, he believed, effectively answering Schmoller's comment. Pareto's irony and propensity to engage in biting repartee, often ferocious, did not diminish even in his last years.

Empiricism

In his exposition of the components that he featured in his economic model, Pareto was, like Walras, writing about his understanding of the behavior of the real economy of his day. It is patently obvious that he was analyzing real firms, consumers, entrepreneurs, workers, capitalists, and landlords, and real technology and institutions. His identification of their nature and his explanations of their behavior was his model. Like Walras, he discussed that matter explicitly, stating that he was analyzing the real economy and asserting that assumptions and hypotheses should be realistic (Pareto 1916/1963, pp. 28–30). He likewise argued that inferences from them should be evaluated by empirical studies. "Theories, their principles, their implications, are altogether subordinate to facts and possess no other criterion of truth than their capacity for picturing them" (ibid., p. 30). "I am a believer in the efficiency of experimental methods to the exclusion of all others. For me there are no valuable demonstrations except those that are based on facts" (Pareto 1897, p. 491). Regarding economics specifically, "political economy is conceived as a natural science. Therefore it must be studied only in the light of the experimental method . . ." (Pareto 1912, pp. 467–68). The equations of general equilibrium can be evaluated only by reference to "concrete facts" (ibid., p. 493):

All the conclusions to which deductive studies founded on the general equations of the economic equilibrium can lead us must finally be verified by a careful scrutiny of facts, both present and past – that is to say, by statistics, by close observation, and by the evidence of history. This is the method of all the material sciences. Deductive studies in political economy must not be opposed to the inductive; these two lines of work should, on the contrary, supplement each other, and neither should be neglected (ibid., p. 500).

Pareto also espoused the method of successive approximations of theory to the real economy, by which he meant the progressive introduction into economic theories of empirically derived considerations so as to achieve progressively detailed degrees of realism (Pareto 1896/1897, *1*, pp. 16–17; *2*, pp. 15, 78). The situation in economic theorizing is of the same nature as in physical science:

If we simplify our problem by supposing a heavy body to be falling in a vacuum and attracted by the earth alone, we may infer the well-known theory of falling bodies. We thereupon complicate the problem by introducing the fact of the air's resistance, and in this way arrive at theories approaching more and more closely to reality.
    Such are the considerations which lead to the method of successive approximations in political economy (Pareto 1897, p. 490).

In other respects, there were contrasts between Walras and Pareto. Walras never gave up his interest in practical economic problems, whereas Pareto eventually turned his back upon them. Walras advocated the intervention of the state in certain respects, whereas Pareto rejected such intervention. Pareto did not agree with Walras on all theoretical matters. "If there are some points on which I think you are wrong, I have told you that frankly" he wrote to Walras (239, 1901, *3*, p. 154). Unlike Walras, Pareto believed that the methods of positive science should not be confined to the realm of pure economic theory (where free will is absent) but should be used in the study of all aspects of economics and of human behavior generally, including therefore those in which free will does play a part. Unlike Walras, as has been seen, Pareto did not think that moral philosophy was part of economics, and he detested the specific content – "the stupidity" (Pareto 1909, in Pareto 1960, *3*, letter 596) – of Walras's social economics, which he considered to be "metaphysical" (Pareto 1897, p. 491). "I do not accept in the slightest," he wrote, "his metaphysical way of treating science" (Pareto 1908, in Pareto 1960, *3*, letter 590). He lamented: Although, "I have always freely acknowledged my obligation to . . . Walras . . . , Walras nevertheless became my enemy, because I would not lend myself to his metaphysical notions" (Pareto 1911, in Pareto 1948, p. 62).

II. Pareto's contributions to economics

Theory of demand

Pareto's theory of consumer demand is a central pillar of his model of general equilibrium. He used Walras's mathematical form of expression of supply and demand, and was similarly contemptuous of literary discussions of those functions. The terms supply and demand, he exclaimed, "like all the terms of non-mathematical economics, have been employed in an unrigorous, equivocal, ambiguous manner, and the considerable number of purposeless, vain, and disorganized discussions of which they have been the subject is truly unbelievable" (Pareto 1909, p. 220). He adopted some of the features of Walras's theory, but reformulated it in two major ways.

First, he replaced Walras's assumption that it is possible to specify the number of units of satisfaction obtained from an amount of a commodity with the assumption of ordinal utility. Pareto thought that it is not impossible in principle to measure utility objectively (see Kirman 1987, p. 805), but he observed that no one has "been able to discover how one could go about measuring it" (Pareto 1909, p. 664). He therefore dropped the assumption that the levels of utility can be measured cardinally. Pareto then modified the indifference analysis of preferences (Pareto 1896/1897, *1*, p. 35; 1909, pp. 168–70, 183–84) that had been initiated by Francis Y. Edgeworth (1881), retaining indifference curves but assuming that utility is ordinally measurable. The consumer, he asserted, is able to specify that he prefers one batch of commodities to another – without being able to state by how much it is preferred – or to specify that he is indifferent to them (Pareto 1909, p. 540). Because utility is not in fact objectively cardinally measurable, this desirable theoretical advance replaced a restrictive assumption with one that is less restrictive but that nevertheless facilitates the derivation of demand functions.

Second, Pareto replaced Walras's assumption that the utility obtained from a commodity depends only on the amount of that commodity consumed. Edgeworth had recognized that the utilities of different commodities are not independent, and by putting that consideration into an ordinal utility framework, Pareto made his second major contribution to consumer demand theory. He argued that the marginal utility of a commodity depends not only on the amount of it consumed but also on the amounts consumed of other commodities (Pareto 1893b, pp. 299, 306–7), and that some commodities are substitutes for each other and others are complements. He explored these matters verbally and mathematically, showed the related forms of indifference maps, and deduced some of the consequences for demand functions (ibid.; Pareto 1896/1897, *1*, pp. 10–11; 1909, pp. 249–59).

Pareto then formulated a theory of consumer demand based on the further assumptions, made by Walras, that the consumer wants to maximize his utility and knows how to do so (see Marchionatti and Mornati 2003), and that the quantity he demands of a commodity is a function, in principle, of the prices of all consumer commodities, given his income and preferences (Pareto 1896/1897, *1*, p. 35). Through the use of calculus, in the manner of Walras, Pareto repeated Walras's demonstration that changes in quantities supplied and demanded can be shown to be determinate functions of changes in prices. Pareto also affirmed Walras's conclusion that the consumer achieves maximum utility by purchasing the amounts of any two commodities for which the ratio of their marginal utilities is equal to the ratio of their prices, although Pareto expressed that condition in the way appropriate for an ordinal indifference analysis (Pareto 1909, p. 559). He thereby derived a consumer demand function for commodities that was more general than Walras's. Pareto then followed Walras in demonstrating how changes in the quantity demanded of one commodity are determinate functions of changes in the price of that commodity and of other commodities, and how the responsiveness of consumer demand to a change in any price can be measured as a function of that change. Pareto's reformulation of Walras's account of consumer behavior was adopted by many Continental economists shortly after his *Cours* appeared, and, together with the work of Irving Fisher (1892) and Eugen Slutsky (1915), was developed into the modern theory of consumer demand.

Existence, uniqueness, and stability of equilibrium

Like Walras, Pareto used a set of simultaneous equations in an effort to describe the characteristics of his model of general equilibration and equilibrium of a competitive economy, with the difference that he constructed a completely disaggregated version (Pareto 1896/1897, *1*, pp. 44–61). That is, instead of using market supply and demand functions in the manner of Walras, Pareto used the individual supply and/or demand functions of each economic agent – of each consumer, of each resource supplier, and of each firm – a completely microeconomic approach. Pareto's Walrasian model gave rise to the disaggregative approach used by many economists.

Adopting the same procedure Walras did, and thus committing the same error, Pareto asserted that equilibrium exists in his model because the number of independent equations equals the number of unknowns, namely the number of prices and quantities of commodities (ibid., pp. 26, 44–46, 61; 1909, p. 658). Moreover, he was oblivious to the fact that his virtual equations, like Walras's, could not provide the equilibrium values of the variable in his non-virtual model. As for uniqueness, adding his authority to the error that persists to this very day, Pareto asserted that multiple equilibria exist (Pareto 1909, p. 197).

Stability

Walras's attempts to show that his mature comprehensive model is stable were studied by his contemporaries and immediate successors. The starting point of their work was naturally that particular model, with all of its irrevocable disequilibrium processes and phenomena – naturally, because that is the one presented in the editions of the *Eléments* they studied, Walras having not yet devised the written pledges sketch when they began to learn his theories.[1] Furthermore, the influence of Walras's elaboration of non-virtual disequilibrium behavior continued to be manifested in certain academic quarters – by H. L. Moore, J. A. Schumpeter, and Henry Schultz, for example – long after the publication of the written pledges sketch in 1899 and 1900.

Pareto, in particular, studied the mature comprehensive model in the years that preceded his writing of the *Cours*. Like Walras, he treated stability by giving a verbal analysis of how a freely competitive economy moves toward equilibrium. In his studies of economic adjustments, he

---

[1] See Pareto's acknowledgement of receipt of the second edition of the *Eléments* that Walras sent him in 1891 (239, 1891, *2*, p. 465) and Fisher's acknowledgement of receipt of the almost identical third edition (239, 1896, *2*, p. 676).

simply assumed that a freely competitive economy is stable. With respect to exchange, Pareto declared that the tatonnement process featured in Walras's mature comprehensive model accurately described the disequilibrium behavior of the real market system: "Walras has shown that the bargaining that takes place in free competition is the means of solving the equations of exchange by repeated attempts" (ibid., pp. 24–25). "Mr Edgeworth has objected that that is only *one* means" by which markets move toward equilibrium. "He is right," Pareto declared, "but the way indicated by Mr Walras is truly the one that describes the largest proportion" of markets (ibid., p. 25) – exactly what Walras had contended. With respect to production, Pareto argued that Walras's idea of tatonnement in that aspect of economic activity should also be adopted and for the same reason that Walras had espoused it, namely that it was an accurate description of what happened in the real economy: "Mr Walras has shown that the competition of entrepreneurs and traders is a means of solving the equations of the equilibrium of production through successive attempts. This idea, in general, seems very fruitful for economic science" (ibid., pp. 45–46). Pareto therefore used Walras's mature concept of tatonnement in all his formulations of competitive economic adjustments in the 1890s and subsequently, not paying any attention to the written pledges sketch that Walras devised in 1899.[2]

Thus in Pareto's model of competitive general equilibrium, as in Walras's, prices, transactions, and production undergo successive irrevocable changes until equilibrium of the entire market system is reached. Pareto and all subsequent modelers of competitive general equilibrating processes assumed that prices are changed iteratively in the same direction as the sign of the market excess demand, which was described above as the essence of Walras's idea of tatonnement in exchange; and

---

[2] Expressing an opinion contrasting with these pronouncements of Pareto's, and with Chapter 5 of this book, Emeric Lendjel contends that Walras arranged an account of the disequilibrium behavior of freely competitive markets in such a fashion that it was in accordance with his scheme of mathematical iteration and that Pareto dissented from that view. Walras wanted "to arrange matters so that the behavior of competitive markets corresponds to a mathematical method of numerical solution of equations. The second approach [Pareto's] emphasizes the organizational coherence of the pricing process. That approach tends to neglect the mathematical dimension of the tatonnement, thus attaining a greater descriptive richness" (Lendjel 1999, p. 312). It is certainly true that Pareto did not want mathematical techniques to be used to determine how markets are represented, but neither did Walras. If Lendjel was contending that Walras constructed his mature comprehensive model so as make it justify his equations, that is not an accurate opinion. Lendjel probably meant that Walras decided to construct the written pledges model to achieve that purpose. Lendjel represents Pareto as arguing against that model but in fact, as noted, he did not discuss it, and his work was squarely based on the mature model.

Pareto and all others who constructed competitive models with disequilibrium production assumed that output is changed iteratively in each firm in the same direction as the sign of price minus average cost, which was described above as the essence of Walras's idea of tatonnement in production.

Pareto also claimed to have treated stability mathematically, believing that he used his equations to study dynamics in a way similar to the one Walras had tried to develop in his mathematical iterations. Pareto believed that his own treatment of dynamics resulted in a highly realistic model:

I have endeavored to extend to dynamic questions the use of the equations given for the static equilibrium. The most accurate description possible of the economic phenomenon is to be reached in this way. Is it not a most remarkable fact that a system of equations should thus be able to express not only the general character of economic phenomena, but every single detail as far as we may have any knowledge of them (Pareto 1897, p. 492).

Reminiscent of passages in Walras's writings (205, 1898, p. 467), Pareto declared that "the entire body of economic theory is henceforth bound together in this way and knitted into an integral whole" (ibid.).

The entrepreneur

Walras's contemporaries and successors praised his concept of the entrepreneur and were influenced by it. Francis Y. Edgeworth, who disagreed with the idea that the entrepreneur makes zero profits in equilibrium, nevertheless wrote in recognition of the importance of Walras's theory that "Professor Walras is one of the first who correctly conceived the *entrepreneur* as buying agencies of production . . . and selling finished products in [different] markets, which thus become interdependent" (Edgeworth 1889, p. 435). Enrico Barone based his work on the entrepreneur entirely upon it, affirming "how profound and correct is Walras's conception of an entrepreneur who, under the conditions postulated, makes neither gain nor loss. . . . It is absolutely astounding that the conception should have been made the subject of criticism. . . . I frankly must confess myself absolutely incapable of understanding how any difficulty whatever can arise as to the validity of this conception, which is indeed most simple" (Barone 1896, p. 145).

Pareto likewise adopted Walras's theory of the entrepreneur and extended it. For the case of free competition, he treated the cases of speculation and production. Accepting Walras's analysis of the activity of speculators (Walras 1880, pp. 370, 379), Pareto explained that, by responding to price changes by buying or selling, speculators transmit information about the state of demand and supply to the production side of the economy, and they facilitate the process of transforming savings into new capital goods (Pareto 1896/1897, 2, pp. 242–45). "The social function of speculators, insofar as they do not act directly on prices, is to solve the equations of economic equilibrium in the best and promptest manner possible" (ibid., p. 245).

Regarding entrepreneurs in firms that produce commodities, Pareto followed Walras's account to the effect that, by buying and selling, entrepreneurs also cause the economy to move toward an equilibrium in which their profits are zero (Pareto 1909. p. 197). He extended the analysis of how entrepreneurs behave in the phase of disequilibrium, however, in two major ways. First, he recognized that they make errors in their production decisions:

It is necessary to produce commodities a certain time and sometimes a very long time before they are consumed. In order for there to be a perfect adaptation of production to consumption it would be necessary: 1° that consumer demand be predicted; 2° that the results of the process of production be accurately predicted. It is impossible to do these two things with precision.

In the present state of economic organization, it is the producers and the merchants who try to make those predictions. If they guess correctly, they make money; if they are mistaken, they ruin themselves (Pareto 1909, p. 530).

Second, Pareto realized that entrepreneurs keep changing their profit goals and thereby repeatedly modify the path taken to equilibrium, and that as a result the equilibrium values of the variables change. Thus disequilibrium transactions and disequilibrium production in the real economy not only change the total amount of commodities in the system and their distribution, and therefore the supply and demand functions (the causes of path dependency in Walras's and Pareto's model), they are also associated with errors of expectations and consequent revisions of plans on the part of real entrepreneurs, which also cause path dependency in Pareto's model (Pareto 1896/1897, 1, pp. 18–19; Steiner 1999).

Pareto also examined the case of a monopolistic entrepreneur (Pareto 1896/1897, 1, pp. 62–69, passim). The profits he makes, Pareto observed, are not reduced to zero by the force of competition. He is able to restrict output and thereby to charge indefinitely a price for his product that is greater than its average cost, which he would not be able to do if he were in a freely competitive industry. Like Walras, Pareto argued that private monopolies are obstacles to an optimum allocation of resources and to efficient rates of their use. "It is easy to see that in all cases the monopolist's profit is obtained only by harming others" (ibid., p. 69). Pareto wanted to integrate monopoly into a general equilibrium setting, but, like Walras, had to content himself with a model containing a system of freely competitive markets and unrelated instances of monopoly.

Economics of the firm

Pareto took Walras's theory of production in the firm as the point of departure for his own treatment of that subject. As was the case in Walras's analysis, entrepreneurs are the central agents in Pareto's theory of production in the firm. They choose the technology that is used and hence select either fixed or variable coefficients. It will be remembered that, in the terminology used by Walras, the "coefficients of production" are the quantities of each of the kinds of productive services that are used in the production of one unit of the output of a firm. Pareto introduced the consideration that in some firms the proportions in which economic resources are combined are fixed, and that in other firms they can be varied. Drawing the consequences of those phenomena, Pareto formulated a version of the theory of marginal productivity that was a significant extension of Walras's work (Pareto 1896/1897, 2, pp. 84–90). An implication that Pareto drew from his own account is that, in some firms, the proportion of capital goods services to labor services can be altered in accordance with changes in the relative prices of capital and labor, while in others it cannot be (Pareto 1909, pp. 327–28). He analyzed the combination and amounts of inputs hired by a firm and explained the distribution of its revenue among the owners of the economic resources that contribute to producing it.

In all of those reasonings, Pareto was setting forth his perception of what happened in reality. Thus his line of argument when he considered variable coefficients was not that their variability was a purely logical possibility, but that they are actually variable in many real firms. Failure to recognize that situation is to misrepresent the facts:

We have already noted the error that consists in believing that the coefficients of production depend only on the technical conditions of production.

Another completely erroneous theory is the theory of *fixed proportions*....

Now, the majority of economists who use the theory of *fixed proportions* seem to believe that there exist certain proportions in which the factors of production are combined, independently of the prices of those factors. That is false (ibid., pp. 326–27).

Pareto strengthened his exposition by providing examples of how the proportions are varied (ibid.).

Cecil G. Phipps (1954), in a neglected but brilliant contribution, evaluated the controversy between Walras and Pareto over the respective merits of their treatment of minimization of costs of a given output and maximization of profit. Phipps remarked that both authors used so much verbiage that it is "difficult, if not impossible, to determine precisely what they wished to say," that some of their notation was incomplete, and that they unnecessarily restricted themselves to a linear homogeneous production function. He showed that the notion that they reached different solutions is incorrect, that "while their *approaches* to the problem were different, their solutions are equivalent" (ibid., p. 31). Phipps concluded that:

> In sum, the assumptions of Pareto appear to be more complicated, more limited and incomplete, and therefore less useful than those of Walras as emended here. However, since the two approaches lead to equivalent results, it is a matter of personal choice which method is to be followed in the solution of the problem of production (ibid., p. 38).

Welfare economics

Pareto studied Walras's thesis that free competition generates a relative maximum of welfare for a society, and based his analysis on Walras's work. Walras's assertions of that condition do not mean that he had a sound proof of it. Pareto explained the shortcomings of Walras's analysis, and refined the analysis of the conditions for maximum efficiency in exchange, in production, and in the capital goods market (Pareto 1896/1897, 2, 90–104). "The members of a group," Pareto contended, "enjoy, in a certain state of the economy, a maximum of well-being when it is impossible to find a means of altering that state a little in such a way that the well-being of every one of the members increases or that the well-being of every one of the members decreases. That is to say, a small change . . . is agreeable to some but disagreeable to others" (Pareto 1909, p. 354). In other words, in an optimum situation it is impossible to make anyone better off without making someone worse off. In recognition of his contribution, the condition that he identified is known as a Pareto optimum.

Pareto also developed an analysis of the welfare aspects of production and consumption of consumer commodities that was patterned on Walras's theorem on the maximum utility of new capital goods (176, 1889, pp. 301–7; §§ 263–64, pp. 417–25). One of Pareto's notable contributions in this regard was to distinguish between the conditions for maximizing individual welfare, and the conditions for maximizing the welfare of society as a whole. He showed that earlier writers had committed a fallacy of composition, assuming that because one individual may improve his welfare if he acts alone, all individuals can necessarily do so if they act simultaneously to try to achieve that goal. For example, if national income is constant, one individual may be able to acquire more income, but all individuals cannot do so.

Neither Walras nor Pareto, nor anyone else, has proved that pure competition necessarily achieves a social welfare maximum, but Pareto showed that pure competition provides part of the situation that would be necessary to achieve such a maximum. He became the first theorist to demonstrate with a high degree of rigor that, subject to various conditions, a state of maximum efficiency can be achieved by an economy of the type that Walras described in his model. Pareto's formulation and his disaggregative approach became the foundation of the "new welfare economics," the study of maximum efficiency and well-being developed during the 1930s and '40s. Thus Walras's legacy in this regard was, via Pareto's work, to stimulate the development of twentieth-century welfare economics.

Another interesting feature of Pareto's welfare economics is his demonstration that "pure economic theory does not give us a truly decisive criterion for choosing between an organization of society based on private property and one based on socialism" (Pareto 1909, p. 364). He believed that, in principle, socialism can achieve a maximum of well-being if it follows policies that have the same results as pure competition (Pareto 1896/1897, 2, 92–93). Evidently, however, he thought that, in practice, socialism would not follow those policies. He did not, of course, have the benefit of the analysis by the Austrian school of economic thought of the inherent flaws and inevitable failure of central planning, but he seems to have come to the same conclusion: "The abuse and the scandals of the system of protection . . . are well made for giving us an idea of what awaits us when socialism will reign in all its glory. Then many people will recognize, a little late, how poorly advised they have been to abandon the defense of economic liberty" (Pareto 1893a, p. 36). "We will be with the socialists when they aid us in resisting the present oppression; we will say goodbye to them when they decide to substitute another for it" (Pareto 1899, p. 216).

Pareto's law

The personal distribution of income in many different economies and at many different times appeared to Pareto to have a general form in common, an idea that he did not owe to Walras. He devised an equation to describe that form and analyzed its goodness of fit to statistical data drawn from a number of countries and relating to different eras. Believing that the results validated his hypothesis, Pareto concluded that "the distribution of income is not the effect of chance" (Pareto 1896/1897, 2,

p. 315). He contended that there are underlying laws of production and of the use of economic resources that cause the income distribution to be of that general form. Pareto's law was therefore interpreted as casting doubt upon the possibility of altering the distribution of income by government policies. That implication was not palatable to many social reformers, and, undeterred by their lack of scientific method or evidence, they harshly criticized his conclusions. Pareto was not perturbed by that. He was concerned with discovering the realities of the matter: "The investigator who is in search of the law of the distribution of wealth does not aim to encourage or dissuade anyone; he is simply intent on discovering the truth" (Pareto 1897, p. 487).

It should be noted that even if Pareto's law were true, that would not imply that the personal distribution of income cannot be affected, for example by a socialist government, by taxes, and by transfer payments, as Pareto was well aware (ibid., p. 500). In any case, the law is an interesting hypothesis: "Few if any economists seemed to have realized the possibilities that such invariants hold out for the future of our science. ... Invariants of this type might lay the foundations of an entire novel type of theory" (Schumpeter 1949, in 1951, p. 121 and note).

General socioeconomic equilibrium

Pareto came to believe, like most economists, that an understanding of economic behavior necessitates an understanding of the functioning of society in general, so after 1905 he concentrated on the latter. He contended that "political economy is but a part – and a small part – of the more general science of sociology. It considers only one aspect of the things we see around us. To complete our knowledge we must also consult other branches of social science" (Pareto 1912b, p. 468). Just as there are interconnections between economic variables, he argued, so also are there interconnections between non-economic variables, and between them and the economic ones.

The economic aspects of Pareto's sociological studies dealt with what he called subjective behavior, particularly the behavior considered in applied economic studies and normative principles and judgments. Whereas Walras's social economics was the expression of his own value judgments about how society and the economy should be organized and conducted, the value judgments that Pareto was interested in studying, whatever their character and consequences, are those made by the members of a society. He believed that many aspects of life must be taken into consideration in the formulation of economic policies and normative economics, and therefore doing so requires bringing to bear information and laws developed in many branches of knowledge. That idea had been espoused in a more limited form by Walras in regard to the use of economic theory in the formulation of policies to solve practical problems (Chapter 4).

Pareto's sociology was not an abandonment of economic analysis. It was an attempt to achieve a theory of the general equilibrium of society as a whole (Pareto 1916).[3] Two thinkers that influenced his adoption of that goal were Auguste Comte, who wanted to see the development of a unified social science, and Herbert Spencer. Pareto was not able to achieve a satisfactory synthesis of the diverse materials that enter into the problem, not only because the task is too great for one individual to accomplish, but also because it is probably impossible, for it amounts to a theory of the equilibrium of every aspect of human life. Moreover, it is by no means clear, and certainly has never been demonstrated, that society as a whole is an equilibrating system. It is indeed highly unlikely that many of its parts, such as criminal activity, sports, and artistic, theatrical, and musical life, are equilibrating phenomena, or even what equilibrium could possibly mean in those aspects of behavior. In any event, Pareto was unable to show that a society tends to move toward a certain equilibrium configuration in its class relations, its judicial system, its political system, and so forth, as well as toward an equilibrium of the economic variables in the manner described by Walras. This should not diminish our appreciation of the magnitude of Pareto's achievement in pointing out the many respects in which economic activities and the other aspects of private and social life are interrelated.

Pareto's conservativism

There was a difference between Pareto's attitude in his last years toward intellectual system building and politics on the one hand and toward his economic theory on the other. He never abandoned the latter. He never, for example, declared himself against his theory of demand or against general equilibrium analysis in economics. As he grew older, however, he became critical of the ideas of Comte and Spencer, declaring that they were pseudoscientists; he continued to affirm a variation on the idea of the class struggle while continuing his vehement opposition to socialist doctrines; and he rejected the political beliefs of his youth. Concluding that foolish leaders were elected and that elected governments obeyed the will of the majority no matter how ignorant it was, he questioned the

---

[3] See Busino 1987, pp. 801–3 for an instructive brief discussion and appreciation of Pareto's sociological ideas.

results of democracy. By the time of his death on August 19, 1923, he had become an embittered conservative. "When I was young," he wrote,

I made light of, or at least excused, the evils of democracy. The French Terror [I believed] was nothing more than a slight stain on the luminous picture of the French Revolution. ... I did not realize that my reasoning was only an attempt to give a logical appearance to what my emotions led me, in every respect, to want to believe (Pareto 1907, in Bousquet 1960, p. 26; Pareto to Antonucci, December 7, 1907, in Antonucci 1938).

The attacks that Pareto made in his old age on reformers, democracy, and humanitarianism, and his approval of Mussolini's early reforms – views that are painfully embarrassing to those who recognize his genius and have learned from his works – cannot obscure the greatness of his contribution as an economist and social scientist. It should also be remembered that he refused many of the honors that the fascists heaped upon him, and wrote that they should not continue on the course of restricting freedom of academic expression, nor seek to erect a corporate state.

Pareto was an exceptional thinker, a highly creative scholar, able to discern what was sound in previous science and to find new truths. The range of his intellectual vision was enormous. He was uniquely endowed with the ability to deal with theoretical and empirical aspects of science, to analyze and to synthesize. His economic theorizing was unobstructed by metaphysics, sophistical epistemology, or the haze of error that normative convictions can interpose between reality and the apprehension of it. He had a clear, direct, and sensible understanding that the relation that should exist between theory and its subject matter is that the former should describe, explain, and predict reality. His powers of reasoning, and the crystalline clarity of his methodological views on how hypotheses should be obtained, verified, and used, greatly contributed to the solidity of his achievements. His was a truly seminal intellect, blazing paths that have been fruitfully followed by generations of subsequent scholars. Social scientists will always be indebted to him.[4]

III. The second generation

Some economists of the school of Lausanne

Walras's methods and theories influenced a number of members of the generation of economists that succeeded him. In France, Walras did not have many followers during his lifetime, with the notable

---

[4] For an expression of that indebtedness, see Allais 1968, p. 408.

exceptions of Albert Aupetit, who attempted to elaborate the theory of money in a general equilibrium setting (1901) and made other contributions to Walrasian economics (1914), and Etienne Antonelli (1939), who delivered lectures on Walras's theories at the University of Lyons (1914) and contributed in other ways to the dissemination of Walras's ideas (for example, Antonelli 1939; and see Potier and Walker 2004). Hermann Laurent (1902), Władyslaw Zawadzki (1914), and Jacques Moret (1915) gave expositions of mathematical economics and general equilibrium theory. There were a few non-Continental adherents of Walras's approach and theories. With respect to much of his work, Irving Fisher (1892, 1896) adopted a Walrasian outlook and methods (see Introduction, note 10). Arthur Bowley (1924) was the first important English academic who supported Walrasian tenets. Henry Ludwell Moore's (1929) ideas will be discussed below.

Many of those who expounded and elaborated upon the ideas of Walras and Pareto were Italian. Among them was Enrico Barone (1896), who developed fundamental aspects of the theory of marginal productivity that was begun by Walras and improved by Pareto. Barone also contributed to the theory of public finance, and used general equilibrium theory in a model of a socialist economy (1908). Maffeo Pantaleoni should also be mentioned, not so much for contributions to general equilibrium theory, although he certainly adhered to Walrasian tenets, but because, as has been seen, his 1889 book on economics persuaded Pareto that Walras's work was worthy of being studied. Another economist who certainly benefited from Walras's legacy was Pasquale Boninsegni. He taught at the University of Lausanne after Pareto's departure, making contributions to the theory of general equilibrium until the 1930s. He wrote to Walras, whom he called "cher Maître": "I know you through your contributions, of which I am a modest popularizer, and through the devotion of your former direct students" (239, 1908, *3*, pp. 364, 368–69).

A complication in the history of Walrasian ideas is that Pareto was thought by a number of economists to have founded a school of his own (Schumpeter 1954, pp. 829, 855, 858; Walker 1997a). They were inspired directly by him, so to them the school of Lausanne meant the "Paretian school" rather than the Walras-Pareto school. Scholars of that persuasion included the civil engineer Giovanni Battista Antonelli; Antonio Osorio, whose book (1913) was introduced by Pareto; Luigi Amoroso (1909, 1921); Alfonso de Pietri-Tonelli (1924, 1927); Umberto Ricci (1924); and economists of the generation after Pareto, such as Constantino Bresciani-Turroni, Gustavo Del Vecchio, Luigi Einaudi, and Marco Fanno.

Arthur W. Marget observed that "extravagant praise has been bestowed on the monetary theory of Pareto by members of the Lausanne school who have had no such words of praise for the monetary theory of Walras's" (Marget 1935, p. 152), in no small measure because Pareto wrote as though no such theory existed. Guido Sensini (1929, p. 215), for example, stated that everything that is true regarding the theory of money is found in Pareto's work. These are strange notions, considering that Pareto can hardly be said to have had a monetary theory and did not even regard the question of money as being on a theoretical level (Bridel 1997, pp. 154–58), whereas Walras had brilliant insights on the role of money. Among the French, Roberto A. Murray (1920) ignored some of Walras's main contributions to economic theory and praised Pareto's, and François Divisia (1928) believed that Pareto was the formulator of the true theory of price determination. One of Pareto's obituarists, his former student Pierre Boven, wrote that:

> In economic theory, he has not only continued Léon Walras's work; he has profoundly modified the theories of his predecessor, and has greatly advanced the "School of Lausanne," not only by new discoveries, but also and above all by the direction he gave to that school, by extracting it little by little from extra-scientific preoccupations (Boven 1923).[5]

The view that Pareto was not greatly indebted to Walras has its modern exponents. Roberto Marchionatti and Enrico Gambino (1997, p. 1322), for example, contend that "Joseph Schumpeter's widely accepted judgment that Pareto's work is 'completely rooted in Walras's system' constitutes a misreading of Pareto. In fact, already during the period 1892–1900, Pareto traces the methodological outlines of an economic science profoundly different from that of Walras" (see also Bruni 2002).

Nevertheless, the underappreciation, depreciation, or disregard of Walras's writings by those scholars does not obviate the facts that in following Pareto they were benefiting from Walras's legacy, that in praising Pareto they were praising the Walrasian heritage upon which he admittedly based his economics, and that their research solidified the position of Walras's work as the basis of Continental neoclassical economics.[6]

---

[5] While Bousquet agreed with that opinion in a general sense, he confessed that he found certain shortcomings in Pareto's work (Bousquet 1971).

[6] Here is an interesting assessment: "The stock of Marshall declined on the market of reputations relative to those of Léon Walras, Stanley Jevons, Knut Wicksell, and Francis Edgeworth. After being underestimated as an eclectic, John Stuart Mill's terms of trade steadily appreciated vis-à-vis David Ricardo's. After Vilfredo Pareto succeeded to Walras's Chair at Lausanne, Pareto's reputation at first tended to eclipse that of his master; but Schumpeter's championship of the unique and stellar worth of the system of general equilibrium helped engineer a Kondratieff wave that brought Walras to the top of the microeconomics pole" (Samuelson 1998, p. 329).

B. Johan Gustav Knut Wicksell

Walras's legacy

A major economist of the second generation that developed Walras's theory of general equilibrium was Knut Wicksell, a Swede who was born in 1851. Like Pareto, he did not begin his contributions to economics until middle age. Like the young Pareto, he was deeply committed to liberal causes, writing and lecturing with a reformist attitude about topics like prostitution, birth control, and prison reform. His interest in the latter was stimulated by his imprisonment, at the age of 57, for being excessively outspoken against organized religion. It was concern over such issues that began his interest in economics, and led to his seeking and obtaining a position at the University of Lund in 1900. He retired in 1916 and died in 1926.

Wicksell gladly admitted his indebtedness to Walras. On the occasion of sending him a copy of one of his books (1893), he began by mentioning that he had a rather complete collection of Walras's writings, and that their used covers showed how intensively he had studied them. He had tried in his book to "emphasize on all the topics your manner of reasoning and to set forth the price equations, much superior to those of Jevons (239, 1893, 2, p. 596)." He had, he continued, defended Walras's doctrine against the objections of critics, one of whom had accused Walras of an error that he had not committed, and another of whom had evidently only superficially read his work. He finished by writing:

> I have not been able to follow you completely on the subject of production, of capitalization, and of credit, but that does not prevent the fact that, fundamentally, it is always your general method of treating the problem in question that I employ, with the sole modification of having introduced the new conception of capital and interest. ...
>
> My debt of gratitude to you is therefore very great, and I hope that I have not failed to mention it in the course of my book (ibid.).[7]

Contributions

Wicksell was concerned with the real economy and hence with non-virtual behavior, just as Walras had been in developing his mature

---

[7] Schumpeter justly observed of Wicksell that "no finer intellect and no higher character have ever graced our field. If the depth and originality of his thought do not stand out more clearly than they do, this is only owing to his lovable modesty, which lead him to present novelty semi-hesitatingly, as little suggestions for the improvement of existing pieces of apparatus, and to his admirable honesty, which pointed incessantly to his predecessors, Walras, Menger and Böhm-Bawerk" (Schumpeter 1954, p. 862).

comprehensive model. Most of Wicksell's expositions consist of verbal accounts of economic behavior and verbal reasoning to analyze it and deduce its consequences, but he also, as has just been intimated, used Walras's mathematical method of symbolizing some of the features that he identified, representing their interrelationships, and discovering some of their consequences. Wicksell's greatest contribution to general equilibrium theory is his analysis of many of the features of the economy that result from the use of money (Wicksell 1898).[8] Disagreeing with the quantity theorists' idea of the neutrality of money, he described how it affects the real parts of the system – the processes of production, consumption, saving, and investment. Drawing upon Walras's intellectual legacy (123, 1877, pp. 278–311; 176, 1889, pp. 261–312; §§ 231–71, pp. 345–436), Wicksell followed Walras in constructing a model of the determination of the rate of net income from the use of capital goods, and of the determination of the market and equilibrium rates of interest (Wicksell 1898/1936). Exploring the interrelationships between the quantity of money, the interest rate, and the level of prices, he introduced his well-known distinction between the market and the natural rates of interest, the origins of which can be found in Walras's writings. According to Wicksell, "This natural rate is roughly the same thing as the real interest of actual business. A more accurate, though rather abstract, criterion is obtained by thinking of it as the rate which would be determined by supply and demand if real capital were lent in kind without the intervention of money" (ibid., p. xxv). The market rate of interest, on the other hand, is the rate of interest charged by banks to lend money. In equilibrium, he explained, the natural rate of interest equates the supply and demand for savings. Wicksell's distinction enabled him to see that it "is not a high or low rate of interest in the absolute sense which must be regarded as influencing the demand for raw materials, labor, and land or other productive resources, and so indirectly as determining the movement of prices. The causative factor is the current rate of interest on loans as compared with . . . the natural rate of interest on capital" (ibid., pp. xxiv–xxv). It was, in fact, Walras who had explored some of these matters in his mature comprehensive model.

---

[8] An opinion shared by many economists of Wicksell's *Interest and Prices* is that "few books can have contained such a wealth of fundamental ideas calling for further elucidation and development, and though probably even now there would be no complete or even close agreement as to which were the best of Wicksell's ideas, or the line of development to which they pointed, it is safe to write down *Interest and Prices* as one of the two or three outstanding theoretical works of our period" (Hutchison 1953, p. 245).

Examination of the relation between those two rates also enabled Wicksell to identify some important aspects of changes in the price level and business fluctuations. For example, if the natural rate is above the market rate of interest, the returns to physical capital exceed the cost of borrowing, and an expansion of investment occurs, financed through an expansion of bank credit. Prices rise, reducing the purchasing power of consumers. Because they are forced to buy less, the amount of economic resources used to make consumer goods is reduced, thus making available a greater amount of economic resources for the production of capital goods. The price level will be stable if the market rate equals the natural rate of interest.

Wicksell's contribution to the theory of capital drew upon Walras's theory of capital, but supplemented and extended it by introducing Eugen von Böhm-Bawerk's ideas about time and capital. Wicksell analyzed how the structure of capital goods depends not only on the number of units of investment, but also upon the length of time during which the inputs are invested. He asserted that "the importance of the time-element in production was never properly appreciated by Walras and his school. The idea of a *period* of production or of capital-investment does not, as we have said, exist in the Walras-Pareto theory; in it capital and interest rank equally with land and rent; in other words, it remains a theory of production under essentially non-capitalistic conditions, even though the existence of durable, but apparently indestructible instruments, is taken into account" (Wicksell 1901/1934, *1*, p. 171). Wicksell's analysis made it possible for him to explore such concepts as the investment of capital for longer periods of time as distinct from larger amounts of investment, and to examine the effect of technological change on the distribution of income.

Wicksell combined the marginal productivity theory of distribution with Walras's marginal utility theory of value. He showed that in a state of competitive equilibrium, each unit of each type of economic resource employed in a firm would be paid the value of the amount of output that a unit of the resource contributes to production. He proved that, if the firm's production function is homogeneous of the first degree, the sum of the payments to the owners of the economic resources determined in that way would equal the total value of the output (ibid., pp. 124–33).

Wicksell, like Walras, viewed the market economy and free competition favorably, but believed that social welfare and the desire to maximize profits are not necessarily compatible. He therefore disagreed with Walras's and Pareto's contention that a competitive economy generates a maximum of utility in a society. That proposition, he declared, was the Lausanne school version of harmony economics. A strong argument can be made that Wicksell and that school disagreed because they held different views of the possibility of making interpersonal comparisons of utility and had different social and political philosophies (Syll 1993). It should be added, however, that Wicksell did not sufficiently recognize the qualifications (noted in Potier 1998) that Walras made to the doctrine that pure competition results in maximum satisfaction (see Chapter 5).

C. Joseph A. Schumpeter

Schumpeter made substantial contributions to the analysis of disequilibrium exchange and disequilibrium production. Indeed, his life work can be seen to be an investigation of non-virtual economic disequilibrium: of what causes it, of what happens during its phases, of how it follows what he believed to be cycles. His early theorizing on this matter (1911/1926) manifested the influence of Walras's theory of the entrepreneur, and toward the end of his life he emphasized that Walras's idea that the entrepreneur earns profits only in disequilibrium is essential for "clear thinking on profits" (Schumpeter 1954, p. 893). Schumpeter identified the "innovating entrepreneur." That economic agent introduces new commodities and business methods, including production processes, capital goods that incorporate new technology, and the exploitation of newly discovered natural resources. Businesses that use outmoded methods and technologies and the products associated with them are displaced by the enterprises that the innovators establish – "new combinations mean the competitive elimination of the old" (Schumpeter 1911/1926, p. 67). The process of innovation therefore creates disequilibrium and leads either to monopoly or to an adjustment process involving prices, disequilibrium transactions, and disequilibrium production and consumption.

To explain the latter, Schumpeter adopted the adjustment mechanism that Walras had identified whereby entrepreneurs channel resources into the production of profitable commodities. That enabled Schumpeter to explain the movement toward a competitive equilibrium that ensues after a secondary wave of investment by imitative entrepreneurs ends the monopoly created by the innovating entrepreneur. If that investment is not prevented by laws, regulations, and patents that maintain the monopoly, or by the economic power of the monopolist, as new firms are created the output of the industry will increase until profit becomes zero, thus eliminating the incentive for further investment. Thus, through the work of Schumpeter, Walras's model of the entrepreneur became a fundamental strand of Continental thought on that subject.

D. Henry Moore and Henry Schultz

Moore was another important economist of the generation immediately following Walras's who benefited from Walras's legacy. He closely studied and built upon Walras's general equilibrium model, even insisting upon using Walras's nomenclature and notation (Moore 1929). Moore was convinced that Walras had correctly delineated the interconnectedness of a market economy and the method necessary for studying that feature. Moore affirmed that "the central problem to the solution of which Walras gave his life was the interdependence of all economic quantities..." (Moore 1929, p. 2). Moore also asserted that Walras's legacy in that regard was seminal, that his "solution of the problem of the mathematical conditions of equilibrium in a static state inspired an ideal conception of the goal toward which future investigators must work" (ibid.). "A comprehensive treatment of economic questions in a changing society must take cognizance of the interdependence of all types of economic change, and the only kind of treatment that will lead to rational forecasting and control is mathematical in character" (ibid.). Regarding economic variables, it was Walras, he wrote, who had seen "the necessity of expressing in simultaneous mathematical equations the conditions of their common determination. To facilitate his inquiry he created a hypothetical static state having the properties that are familiar to all students of economic theory" (ibid.).

Moore tried to develop a dynamized version of Walras's model and to test it empirically. He believed that the assumption of pure competition and the static features of the model, which resulted in "an hypothetical static state in a stable equilibrium," should be replaced (ibid., p. 111). In this connection, it should be recognized that one type of dynamic system is a model that moves from a disequilibrium state to a static equilibrium in which aggregate output and its composition are constant. That would be a model without capital accumulation in which the dynamics are a tatonnement process such as the one Walras had in mind. Another type of dynamic motion is that of a model that not only has an equilibrating process like the tatonnement but also has a positively (or conceivably negatively) sloped path of change of aggregate output over time. In that case the tatonnement leads the economy to that path and the economy then expands (or contracts) along it. Of course, there are a variety of other possibilities, such as fluctuations around the path, displacements of the path, and so forth.

Moore wanted, first of all, to develop a growth-path model of the type just described. He argued that Walras's model "cannot be made to resemble a real, moving equilibrium because the approach to reality would destroy the network of implications by means of which it exists" (ibid., p. 110). Publishing his work in 1929, he justly claimed priority for this undertaking: "No mathematical economist, as far as I am aware, has ever attempted to pass from [my] or any similar presentation of a statical, hypothetical equilibrium to a realistic treatment of an actual, moving general equilibrium" (ibid., p. 106), applicable to the real economy (ibid., pp. 110–11).

Moore's way of trying to accomplish that task was to construct a system of dynamic general equilibrium equations that determine the equilibrium trend values of the variables, and to use statistically derived functions. General equilibrium theorists should take "partial elasticities of demand, partial elasticities of supply, and partial relative efficiencies of organization," and weave "these concrete functions into a network of continuous relations describing the solidarity of exchange, production, capitalization, and distribution as a moving general equilibrium" (ibid., p. 92). The next part of Moore's plan was to use his modified version of Walras's model to study business cycles. The economy, he contended, follows an oscillatory path about a moving position of normal equilibrium, and an explanation of that feature requires an investigation of the way that recurrent and non-recurrent exogenous shocks are translated into economic oscillations (ibid., pp. 146–74). Moore also undertook empirical tests of general equilibrium models, and he tried to add to general equilibrium theory by introducing imperfectly competitive market structures into a model of a dynamically growing economy. Although he did not finish any of the tasks he had set for himself, Moore was able to add constructively to the general equilibration and equilibrium approach employed by Walras in his mature comprehensive model, and he had a clear vision of some of the directions that economic theory and statistical implementation needed to take.

As has been mentioned, Henry Schultz (1893–1938) was also a careful and enthusiastic student of Walras's theories and, through his publications and teaching, was important in the transmission of Walras's legacy to other economists. His writings express his interest in the theory and methods of Walras's mature comprehensive model, and have nothing to do with virtual general equilibrium modeling. He also developed mathematical economic methods and applied them in econometric studies (Schultz 1938), furthering the type of empirical statistical studies advocated by Moore, who was his teacher at Columbia University (Mosak 1987, pp. 261–62). Schultz stimulated William Jaffé to read Walras's *Eléments*, and influenced his decision to translate that work (Jaffé in 235, 1954, p. 8; Walker 1983, p. 29) and thereby to make Walras's ideas accessible to Anglophone economists. Schultz wrote two articles (1929,

1932) on marginal productivity in relation to general equilibrium, and two articles on the interrelations of demand, price, and income (1933, 1935). As it happened, the type of work that Moore and Schultz hoped would be done was for many years largely displaced by concern with other issues relating to virtual general equilibrium models, as will be seen in Chapter 10.

Models drawing upon the heritage of the written pledges sketch, 1930 to 1971

I. Introduction

The previous chapter has explored the first phase of the realization of Walras's prediction that subsequent economists would draw upon his mature comprehensive model, the second phase being considered in Chapter 11. The present chapter examines the aspects of his written pledges sketch accepted by general equilibrium theorists after 1929, and that, in accordance with their interpretations of that sketch, formed the starting point of their own contributions and influenced their ongoing research.

There is a need for the clarification undertaken in this chapter of aspects of the history of general equilibrium theorizing, as a brief preview of some of those aspects demonstrates. Mark Blaug remarked that, "It was (Henry) Schultz, Hicks, Hotelling, Lange and Samuelson who were responsible in the golden decade of the 1930s in bringing about this revival of GE theory" (Blaug 1997, p. 253; and see Arrow 1968, p. 380). That statement should be qualified. In the first place, it does not take account of most of the major developments in general equilibrium theorizing in the 1930s, namely of those that took place outside of the United States and England, a matter that will be discussed shortly. Second, a number of qualifications can be made about the precise contributions and dates of the work of the scholars Blaug mentioned. It was in the 1920s that Henry Schultz sustained the vitality of the Walrasian non-virtual tradition and was joined by others. It may be that Oskar Lange (1904–1965), in his "little book On the Economic Theory of Socialism (Lange 1936–37)[1] taught an entire generation to appreciate the supposed practical relevance of Walrasian GE theory" (Blaug 1997, p. 253). Lange made

---

[1] This is the publication in book form of two articles (Lange 1936, 1937). For biographical information about Lange, see Kowalik 1987. Abba Lerner's work on the same type of topic will not be considered here because it concerns the application of general equilibrium principles to socialism and the control of economies, rather than adding to economic knowledge on such questions as price formation, the existence of equilibrium, and stability.

his major contributions, however, in the 1940s, and they were mainly inspired by questions posed by John Maynard Keynes. The Lange did draw on Walras's legacy, albeit indirectly, especially in one research program in which he relied on "mathematical tools of general economic equilibrium as developed and modified by Henry Schultz, R. G. D. Allen and Paul Samuelson, but especially by J. R. Hicks" (Kowalik 1987, p. 124). Harold Hotelling (1895–1973), a mathematical statistician, did not contribute anything to the analysis of purely competitive general equilibrium. It is true that one of his very few papers on economics bore the words "stability" and "competition" in the title (Hotelling 1929). Nevertheless, that paper was concerned, not with general equilibrium nor even with purely competitive markets, but with insights given by game theory to the understanding of spatial competition in oligopolistic market structures. Paul Samuelson (1915–), who had just begun his career toward the end of the 1930s, wrote nothing on the subject of general equilibrium theory during that decade. His first analysis of stability, made in 1941 (see below), was noted by J. R. Hicks (1946, pp. 336–37), but Hicks did not do more than make the brief suggestion that it would open "a most promising line of investigation" (ibid., p. 336). "In spite of its importance, Samuelson's work remained isolated and gave rise to no significant developments" (Ingrao and Israel 1990, p. 335) until 1958 (Arrow and Hurwicz 1958).

Claude Ménard, disagreeing with Blaug, states that a revival of interest in Walrasian general equilibrium did not start until after 1940. He writes that there was not much more than "the germ of a school" of Lausanne before that date and it "was to bloom only after 1940. ... If there is such a thing as a Lausanne school, its expansion is mostly a contemporary phenomenon" (Ménard 1990, pp. 99, 104). Ménard's view is as difficult to appreciate as is Blaug's. The historical record shows that neither the 1930s nor the 1940s can properly be described as a period of revival of general equilibrium theory, because there was no period in which it was not studied. After Walras, to mention only the major figures in the history, the theme was first carried forward by a number of French theoreticians during Walras's life and subsequently (see Zylberberg 1988, 1990), in numerous publications by Enrico Barone until 1924 and Vilfredo Pareto until 1927, by many Italian followers of Pareto during his lifetime, and by Knut Wicksell until 1926. Gustav Cassel was productive on the topic of general equilibrium during the period 1918 to the early 1930s. Henry Schultz wrote influential articles on marginal productivity and the Lausanne school in 1928. H. L. Moore was studying general equilibrium in the two decades after 1910, publishing his major contribution in 1929, and the Ukrainian-born Jacob

Marschak and the Danish Frederik L. B. Zeuthen were examining Walrasian systems in 1928. There was intense interest in general equilibrium theory during the 1930s on the part of some economists in Austria, as is well-known (see, for example, Weintraub 1983; Brems 1986) and as this chapter fully recognizes. The Germans Hans Neisser (1932) and Heinrich von Stackelberg (1933), and Zeuthen (1933) examined the existence of equilibrium in Walrasian systems in additional writings that predated and therefore obviously owed nothing to the economists mentioned by Blaug. Thus it was always true, during and since the time of Walras, that leading theoreticians cultivated general equilibrium theory with unabated enthusiasm and in an unbroken chain (see also Walker 1990, pp. 137–38; 1997a).

To limit the scope of this chapter in a reasonable way, only the general equilibrium theorists who made significant original contributions will be considered. The discussion does not deal with the theorists' philosophies and methodological views. Nor does it present a comprehensive history of modern general equilibrium modeling, because much of that work has no real connection with Walras's ideas. Modern theory has gone far beyond his constructions, incorporating concepts and developing in directions of which he had not the slightest idea. Nor would there be in any event a useful purpose served by repeating the details of the contents of the theorists' relevant papers and books, for they are well presented in the primary sources and explained and analyzed many times in secondary sources. The purpose of the remainder of this book is to point out whatever specific links to Walras's economic ideas there are in economic models developed by his contemporaries and successors. The models are therefore classified and briefly examined strictly from the special points of view and interests of this study. A few facts about the careers of some of the economists involved before 1936 are given, if the information is useful to establish the importance of the person, the lines of transmission, and the geographical reach of Walras's influence.[2]

II. Karl Gustav Cassel

Background

Gustav Cassel's work on general equilibrium theory is a direct descendant of Walras's written pledges sketch. Cassel was born in Sweden

---

[2] Biographical information about all the economists that are mentioned is available in a variety of publications, notably Eatwell et al. 1987.

on October 20, 1866, attended Uppsala University and the University of Stockholm, and was appointed professor of economics and financial science at the latter institution in 1904. He had a wide variety of interests. His career began with the publication of a long article in 1899 in which he expressed almost all the ideas about price formation that he was to espouse in later years (Cassel 1899). Shortly thereafter, he argued innovatively in favor of marginal cost pricing for railways and other enterprises for which rates are regulated (Cassel 1900). In *Nature and Necessity of Interest* (Cassel 1903), he repeated and extended in some respects Walras's theory of capital. He published the first edition of *The Theory of Social Economy*, his major economic treatise, in 1918. He rejected Eugen von Böhm-Bawerk's ideas about time-preference and capital, and pointed out that Böhm-Bawerk did not grasp the fact that the prices of factors of production and of commodities are mutually determined, so that it is pointless to suggest that the prices of the former are determined by those of the latter or vice versa (Cassel 1932, p. 195). In his own theory of capital, Cassel resurrected Nassau Senior's notions about abstinence, to which he added his original idea of the importance of life-cycle motivations in saving behavior (Cassel 1903, 1932).

Cassel became an authority on international monetary affairs. He was an important analyst of the German reparations question after World War I. He advised the League of Nations and many governments on monetary matters, expressing his ideas in, notably, *The World's Monetary Problems* (Cassel 1921). In that work, on the basis of his reasoning that the ratio of the rates of exchange of the currencies of two countries should be the same as the ratio of their general price levels, he developed an influential purchasing-power parity theory of exchange rates. He adhered to the quantity theory of money and to an overconsumption theory of business fluctuations (Cassel 1918, 1932). Unlike those of his contemporaries who wanted the gold standard to be an automatic regulator of the money supply and prices, Cassel contended that the monetary authority could and should regulate the bank rate of interest, thus obtaining the beneficial consequence that "the conditions for the development of trade cycles would be radically altered, and that indeed our familiar trade cycles would be a thing of the past" (Cassel 1928, p. 529). Highly critical (Cassel 1937) of J. M. Keynes's *General Theory of Employment, Interest and Money* (1936), he opposed efforts to stimulate the economy by means that would directly increase income, such as public works. Among his achievements was the book *On Quantitative Thinking in Economics* (Cassel 1935), which, together with his many empirical studies and keen insight into statistical economic questions, established his position as an exceptionally capable early econometrician. He died on January 15, 1945.

Approach and theoretical foundations

In his first important essay (1899), Cassel had the sole purpose of giving a clear exposition of Walras's ideas; he consistently used Walras's general equilibrium approach as a basis for his work during his entire career; and he carried a number of the specific constructions of Walras and Pareto forward in the stream of economic studies. Nevertheless, he did not acknowledge the extent of his debts to those economists. One of Walras's correspondents wrote to him about that essay as follows:

> With respect to Mr. Cassel, I would say . . . he wishes to contribute something new and independent in the domain of [pure economic theory] and that he is unable to. Basically he accepts, with some paraphrases, all of your theory of exchange, but to differentiate his work, however, he rejects average marginal utility which is in a manner common to several persons, but retains subjective marginal utility, measuring it by the price of the commodities. . . . He obtains the equations of exchange which basically result from your fundamental equations. With respect to the theory of production, he accepts all of your theory almost without alteration, but without admitting it, proclaiming you to be his "predecessor." The Gentleman has very great pretensions, but very little original force (239, 1899, *3*, pp. 90–91).

Cassel did not even mention Walras or Pareto in the later editions of his *Theory of Social Economy* (for example, Cassel 1932).

Cassel disagreed with a number of the components of the models that those two economists had developed. He rejected the marginal utility theory of value, whether based on cardinally or ordinally measurable utility:

> This purely formal [utility] theory, which in no way extends our knowledge of actual processes, is in any case superfluous for the theory of prices. . . . This deduction of the nature of demand from a single principle, in which so much childish pleasure has been taken, was only made possible by artificial constructions and a considerable distortion of reality (Cassel 1918, p. 81).

Cassel argued that because the amount of commodities consumed could not be known until the set of equilibrium prices and quantities is determined with the use of a general equilibrium system of equations, the marginal need that is satisfied and therefore the marginal utility to each consumer could not be known until that set is determined. He concluded that, "What we call 'marginal utility' – if we now wish to introduce this conception – thus occupies exactly the same place as an unknown in the problem as does price, and it is therefore obviously absurd to cite 'marginal utility' as a factor explaining price" (1932, p. 147).

In place of that concept, Cassel wanted to substitute the principle of scarcity, in response to which Knut Wicksell commented that something is scarce

... only in relation to wants, or to the extent it becomes an object of demand. And the degree of scarcity is measured in exactly the same way as marginal utility, by the strength of the next unsatisfied need, which first causes the commodity to be recognized as "scarce". In other words, scarcity and marginal utility are fundamentally one and the same thing (Wicksell 1919, in 1934, p. 221).

Instead of using utility theory explicitly, Cassel assumed in his model of general equilibrium that demand functions are primitive constructions, which has led many commentators to declare that he anticipated revealed preference theory. Paul Samuelson (1993, pp. 515, 517) has firmly rejected that view, arguing that Cassel instead had a "revealed demand" approach, which seems a reasonable assertion inasmuch as Cassel denied the value of regarding demand functions as being expressive of underlying preference functions.

Cassel did not accept the Walras-Pareto doctrine that maximum satisfaction is obtained by a perfectly competitive economy, arguing that large-scale enterprises are much more efficient than small-scale ones, but are "absolutely incompatible" with free competition (Cassel 1932, p. 129). Moreover, competition generates monopoly; it brings "into being its own antithesis," so "to take free competition as the starting-point for a general theory of prices is of very little use" (ibid., p. 129). That was an implicit criticism of the procedure adopted by Walras and Pareto.

Cassel thought that in most production processes the factors of production are indivisible, or that it is very often impossible to use less of one factor without throwing the others out of work (ibid., p. 179). In his equation system, he consequently adopted the assumption of technologically fixed coefficients of production, as Walras had done in much of his work. It has been seen, however, that Walras also treated the case of variable coefficients, which is a necessary assumption for the Walras-Pareto theory of marginal productivity. Perhaps in order to avoid completely rejecting that theory, Cassel suggested in his literary account that substitution among factors is possible (ibid., pp. 179–81).

Cassel's three models

Cassel's general equilibrium models were inferior to those of Walras and Pareto, for reasons that will be made clear, but he nevertheless made an original contribution to the subject. He presented three models based upon Walras's general equilibrium equations and his virtual approach that consequently have become known as Walras-Cassel models. The use of that name is understandable, but unless it is interpreted with a full recognition of the facts of the matter, it is, strictly speaking, misleading. Walras's major contribution, his mature comprehensive model, is incompatible with Cassel's models, and the construction of Walras's to which the name refers is just an incomplete sketch, not a proper model.

Cassel first constructed a virtual model of pure exchange with fixed available amounts of the commodities (ibid., pp. 138–40). He defined a demand function aggregated over all demanders for each commodity, the quantity demanded being a function of all prices. For each commodity, he set the demand function equal to the fixed supply and declared that there is an equilibrium set of prices because there are as many equations as unknowns. Inasmuch as the money expenditures of the consumers are given, absolute prices are determined.

In the second model, which he called a model of the stationary state because the quantities of the commodities produced are constant, Cassel assumed once more that the amounts of money to be spent by consumers are given. The quantities of the factors of production are given constants, their supply functions are perfectly price-inelastic, and the factors are always fully employed. In accordance with Walras's assumption, the technical coefficients are given. With great clarity and simplicity, Cassel then constructed a system in which the demand and supply for each commodity produced and for each factor of production are equal, and in which the output and the input sides of markets are linked. He then dropped the assumption that the incomes and expenditures of the consumers are given, and introduced equations that result from his identification of them as the owners of the factors of production. Their prices and quantities, and hence the incomes of their owners, are determined as part of the general equilibrium of an expanded system.

In the third model, Cassel presented a dynamized virtual Walrasian general equilibrium system.[3] He was concerned not with a position of equilibrium but with a path of growth. His interest in the theory of

---

[3] Claude Ménard (1990), evidently referring to Walras's static equation system, contends that the structure of his model makes its dynamization inherently impossible. The discussion of this matter by Ménard and others, like that of so many issues, is difficult to follow because the participants mix together Walras's equations and his models, and mix together the mature comprehensive model and their interpretation and elaboration of the written pledges sketch. In fact, Ménard's opinion is unconvincing because Cassel did what Ménard states is impossible and because John von Neumann and other theoreticians similarly constructed models that dynamized Walrasian-type general equilibrium equation systems.

economic growth was probably inspired by Walras's investigation of some of the properties of a growing economy (123, 1877, lessons 51–52; 176, 1889, lesson 28; 249.VIII, lessons 35–36). Cassel's reasoning and his exposition of the model were verbal. Continuing to use Walras's general equilibrium approach, and continuing to build on a restatement of Walras's equations, he discussed the modifications that were necessary to the equations of his second model and briefly outlined a model that is always in equilibrium. He called it a model of the uniformly progressing state. He assumed that the amounts of the reproducible factors of production increase at a fixed rate (Cassel 1918; 1932, pp. 152–55), amounts that Walras had treated as parameters, and verbally deduced the consequences. As in Cassel's second model, the factors are always fully employed and the technical coefficients of production are fixed. Cassel showed that the economy expands uniformly at a fixed rate. The prices of the factors and of consumer commodities remain unchanged as the economy grows. The production of each commodity increases at that fixed rate, as do money incomes, demands, supplies, savings, investment, and consumption (ibid., p. 153). The model thus introduced the concept of steady-state growth. Anticipating the Harrod-Domar model, it is an original early formulation of a multiplier-accelerator process.

Character and limitations of the models

A serious limitation of Cassel's general equilibrium models is that they are devoid of behavioral content, and are therefore devoid of features, plausible or otherwise, to which his equations could have reference. Walras's and Pareto's models are vastly richer. They took pains to draw from the real economy the institutions, procedures, technology, rules, and pricing processes in their models, and only then tried to describe many of those characteristics or their outcomes with equations. Walras, for example, used 116 pages for his theory of exchange alone. In contrast, Cassel used only 16 pages to present all three of his models. He made no mention of the characteristics of markets or the behavior of suppliers and demanders, offering no explanation of how prices are formed. His models are even more highly idealized systems than Walras's written pledges sketch. That was a sketch of a virtual model, but Walras described it as having a disequilibrium state and, indeed, he introduced the device of written pledges with the intention that the model would be virtual but would also have a process of adjustments in disequilibrium that would lead it to general equilibrium. Cassel, on the other hand, constructed models that he simply assumed are always in equilibrium; they have no tatonnement process. That greatly simplified them, and therefore Cassel's theoretical task, because he had no reason to examine the questions of the existence of equilibrium or of stability or whether or not there are multiple solution sets of the variables. It also means, however, that he did not provide any explanation of why his models should be considered theoretically interesting or empirically applicable.

Nevertheless, Cassel's models were very influential. He widely disseminated knowledge of a type of formalistic general equilibrium system. One reason for his success was that his exposition was readily comprehensible, a feature that it owed to its simplistic character. Another reason was the languages in which his book appeared. He originally published it in German (Cassel 1918), which was the language spoken and written by the important Continental general equilibrium theorists in the 1930s. Through the English versions of his books, he was instrumental in communicating some of Walras's economic ideas to Anglophone economists. The work of Walras, in French, and of Pareto, principally in Italian and French, had a relatively limited readership, whereas Cassel's text, in German or English (Cassel 1932), was used in many European universities and was considered to be the definitive statement of general equilibrium theory. It was the standard theoretical textbook for students and for the mathematicians and economists who were members of the Vienna Colloquium in the 1930s (Weintraub 1983, pp. 4–5, 7). It thus became the starting point of the investigations of the existence of equilibrium undertaken by Karl Schlesinger and Abraham Wald. It was a stimulus to the work of John von Neumann on general equilibrium, and, although of far less importance than the ideas of Walras and Pareto to J. R. Hicks, it probably had a role in the development of Hicks' views on static and dynamic models (Hicks 1965, pp. 13, 39).[4]

III. Virtual Walrasian modeling

Modeling in the 1930s

During the 1930s, in addition to Cassel, the economists who were most important in the study of virtual Walrasian general equilibrium systems were Karl Schlesinger (1889–1939), Hans Philipp Neisser (1895–1975), Abraham Wald (1902–1950), John von Neumann (1903–1957), and John R. Hicks (1904–1989). Paying no attention to the first, second, or third editions of the *Eléments* and without examining the fourth (or fifth)

---

[4] Unlike his monoglot Anglophone contemporaries, Hicks had the advantage of being able to read Italian, French, and German.

edition with sufficient attention to discern its problems, those economists followed Walras's 1899 suggestion that a virtual general equilibrium model be devised and analyzed. They interpreted that to mean a suggestion "to construct an equation system alongside terminology indicating that it relates to a virtual purely competitive model." To those economists, that (together with some of Walras's particular assumptions) was Walras's legacy regarding the study of general equilibrium. They were concerned with the existence, uniqueness, and, to a lesser extent, stability of equilibrium – matters they conceived of as being properties of their equation systems.

Neisser's contribution to the question of interest here was a trenchant critique of Cassel's models (Neisser 1932), a critique that undoubtedly stimulated the Viennese circle of economists to reexamine them. One member of that circle was Schlesinger, a Hungarian who had settled in Vienna. In the late 1920s and in the 1930s, that city was a center of intellectual developments in many fields, a stimulating environment for the development of scientific thought that attracted scholars from all over Europe. Schlesinger wrote a dissertation (Schlesinger 1914) that extended Walras's theory of money in a general equilibrium setting, and later took up the theory of general equilibrium proper. He has a place in this history primarily because of his influence on Wald and because he publicized an idea of Zeuthen's (1888–1959). The latter considered problems first detected by William Lexis in 1881, namely that Walras did not introduce conditions into his equation system that would ensure that their solutions are real and non-negative (Lexis 1881; see Jaffe 1971, p. 105, n. 58). Zeuthen realized that the total amount of a commodity used in all economic processes must be smaller than or equal to the total amount produced. If there is a positive excess supply, the price of the commodity must be zero (Zeuthen 1928, p. 27; Zeuthen 1933, pp. 2–3; Brems 1986, p. 250; Brems 1987, 4, p. 944). Apparently independently conceiving of those conditions, but crediting Zeuthen for having done so, Schlesinger noted that Walras and Cassel had dealt only with scarce economic resources and therefore assumed that all commodity prices are positive (Schlesinger 1933–1934). He recognized, in contrast, that there are free inputs, like air, sunshine, and sometimes water, and accordingly modified the equations that Cassel had based on Walras's work. Schlesinger did that by recognizing zero prices and by introducing complementary slack conditions via the use of inequalities. His procedure made it clear that it is impossible to say that equilibrium exists in a model simply because there are as many equations as there are unknowns. In reality, prices are positive or zero, none of a commodity may be produced in a particular period, and quantities produced are obviously positive, so equations with any pretense to realism must reflect those conditions by having solutions that are equal to or greater than zero. Recognizing that necessity did not, however, constitute a proof of existence.

The research of Zeuthen and Schlesinger drew attention to the fact that no one had rigorously established whether or not an equilibrium for a perfectly competitive virtual economy exists. If not, a virtual competitive model would not behave in the way that general equilibrium theorists, such as Walras in his last phase and Cassel, had asserted. It would not be an equilibrating system. Its variables – suggested prices and desired demands and supplies – would not tend, in disequilibrium, to move in the direction of equilibrium values, because such values would not exist. The entire system of equations would have to be rejected. In the subsequent study of this matter, the techniques used for examining existence, and, to some extent, stability became very sophisticated, and the "models" – actually equation systems – became not only far removed from the behavior of any past or present real economy. but also unattached to an underlying hypothetical structure of institutions and behavior.

Abraham Wald (1902–1950) was a Rumanian mathematician and statistician. He visited the Mathematical Institute of the University of Vienna in 1927, where he met Karl Menger, who was professor of mathematics at the University and – a circumstance that contributed greatly to his interest in economics – the son of the Austrian economist Carl Menger. Karl Menger referred Wald to Schlesinger, who persuaded Wald to consider the question of existence. The model that Wald chose and modified to do that was Walrasian, in the form presented by Cassel and altered by Zeuthen and Schlesinger (Wald 1934–1935, 1936; see Menger 1973, p. 51). Like those economists, therefore, Wald followed the tradition of Walras's 1899 sketch by constructing a virtual model. Walras, however, had perceived very clearly the necessity of postulating some hypothetical market characteristics – the written pledges procedure – that he hoped would justify his virtual equation system. Wald, in contrast, simply made the postulate that transactions, production, and consumption occur only at a set of prices at which the entire system is in equilibrium. He made no attempt to explain by means of a hypothetical market model how that could possibly happen. Consequently, he did not give his readers any reason to believe that his equation system was linked to anything in the sense of having referents, either real or imaginary.

Wald adopted Walras's assumption that markets are purely competitive, and that utilities are regarded by consumers as independent of each other. He departed from Walras's procedures by assuming that prices are functions of quantities, rather than the other way around,[5] and that individual and market desired consumption, which he did not clearly distinguish, do not depend on the distribution of income. He also made the assumption that the quantities demanded of all commodities are positive, not recognizing that some bundles of commodities are not demanded at any positive price (Dorfman, Samuelson, and Solow 1958, p. 367). Wald was able to provide a proof that a set of solutions that satisfied his criteria for economic acceptability exists for the equation system that he constructed. The result of those special restrictions on the equations, however, naturally had the consequence that his proof of the existence of general equilibrium applies to a highly special case. It was, moreover, an unrealistic case, precisely because Wald was not dealing with a conception of the real economy but responding to the exigencies of building a virtual equation system, just as Walras had tried to do in 1899. He did not actually prove existence in an economic model because he did not construct one that had behavior in it that would result in the properties that he postulated for his equations.

The issue of uniqueness of the solutions to a system of general equilibrium equations relating to exchange had been touched on by Walras (Chapter 5), and Wald followed his example by studying that question in reference to his own system of equations. He assumed that either all commodities are gross substitutes, or that the weak axiom of revealed preference with reference to market demand functions is true. The first of these assumptions is that, for any two commodities, a rise in the price of one of them increases the quantity demanded of the other one; the second is that if at a first set of prices a bundle of commodities x^2 costs no more than the bundle x^1 associated with the first set of prices, and the consumers as a whole choose x^1, then it has been revealed to be superior to x^2. Therefore at a second set of prices at which x^2 is actually bought, that bundle must cost less than the first bundle because otherwise the preferences revealed by the purchase of the first bundle would be contradicted (see Dorfman, Samuelson, and Solow 1958, p. 368). Wald determined that, with either of those assumptions, the system has only one set of prices at which supply and demand quantities would be simultaneously equal in all markets.

Thus Wald initiated the era of proofs of existence and uniqueness of solutions in virtual general equilibrium theory, and if the scope of his work was limited by his extremely restrictive assumptions, it was nevertheless an ingenious achievement and it drew attention to the question

---

[5] He assumed a strictly pseudomonotone inverse demand function.

of those proofs. Karl Menger accurately predicted the kind of research agenda that general equilibrium mathematicians would be influenced to follow:

> I wish to remark in conclusion that with Wald's work we bring to a close the period in which economists simply *formulated* equations, without concern for the existence or uniqueness of their solutions, or at best made sure that the number of equations and unknowns be equal (something that is neither necessary nor sufficient for solvability and uniqueness). In the future as the economists formulate equations and concern themselves with their solution (as the physicists have long done) they will have to deal explicitly with the deep mathematical questions of existence and uniqueness (Menger in Baumol and Goldfeld 1968, p. 288).

It has been pointed out elsewhere that the deep questions of general equilibrium theorizing are not those that Menger identified and that Wald explored, but are instead the construction of models that are genuine functioning systems – that is, with institutions, rules, technology, participants, and market pricing procedures (Walker 1997b, p. 142 and passim). Applying Menger's advice to incomplete virtual models – incomplete because they are actually equation systems substantially without economic referents – has led to research that has no economic interpretations.

John von Neumann (1903–1957) was the next person to develop a virtual general equilibrium construction. He was a Hungarian, schooled in Budapest and Zurich, who very early showed an exceptional aptitude for mathematics. In 1927, when he was twenty-four, he accepted a position on the faculty at the University of Berlin and two years later at the University of Hamburg. During the next three years he became well-known for his contributions to algebra, set theory, and quantum mechanics. In 1930 he began teaching at Princeton, where he remained for the rest of his academic career. Probably stimulated by his visits to Vienna, where he met Karl Menger in 1932, von Neumann presented his general equilibrium model at Menger's mathematical seminar in that city in 1936 and published it in 1937.

Von Neumann wanted to go beyond the study of the stationary equilibrium of a Walrasian system without capital accumulation, a system in which production and consumption proceed at constant rates in equilibrium. He therefore attempted to dynamize virtual general equilibrium modeling, which Walras had contended was a desirable goal, which Moore had set out to do, and which Cassel had succeeded in doing. Von Neumann's point of departure was the Walrasian equation system as it had been modified and extended by Cassel, Zeuthen, and Schlesinger. Having assimilated the Walrasian legacy of 1899, he assumed pure competition and that the economy he invented has no disequilibrium transactions or disequilibrium production, and he proceeded to construct a microeconomic model of moving equilibrium.

Von Neumann's model had a variety of aspects that made it a special and very peculiar case, such as the assumption that there are unlimited amounts of natural resources so that primary factors of production other than labor are free, that every firm hires some of every input or produces some of every output, that overproduced goods are always totally free, that entrepreneurs and capitalists do not consume anything, that there are no consumer preferences, that there are no demand functions, and that consumption per worker is always at the subsistence level. Von Neumann followed the example of Cassel and Wald in neglecting to provide structural features, technology, institutions, and market processes that would result in a virtual system, thus solidifying that neglect into a tradition that has lasted to this day in the construction of virtual models. Like Cassel, he simply assumed that his model is always in equilibrium, without explaining how that could be possible, and therefore did not consider the stability or uniqueness of equilibrium.[6] There is a major difference, however, between Cassel's and von Neumann's models, namely that whereas the rate of growth of the economy is exogenously determined in the former, it is endogenously determined in von Neumann's. He assumed there is positive net investment equal to the excess of income over the amount of consumption that is a necessary subsistence minimum. The result is that the stock of capital goods, the total output of the economy, and the income of its members grow continuously through time. He proved that, in his model, equilibrium exists, and that the equilibrium rate of interest equals the equilibrium rate of growth.

Von Neumann has been extravagantly praised for constructing his model, but a historical perspective makes it clear that the major durable contributions of his paper were his development in it of activity analysis, and, for some economists, his use of the fixed-point theorem technique of determining the existence of equilibrium.[7] The sheer unreasonableness of his assumptions and the absence of content in his model regarding the functioning of markets, economic institutions, characteristics of firms,

---

[6] See La Volpe 1936 for a general equilibrium model that is also dynamic and always in equilibrium.

[7] Tjalling Koopmans observed that "the paper contains the first explicit statement ... of what has been subsequently called the activity analysis model of production. ... [It displays] a model of competitive equilibrium. ... [T]he paper contains the first rigorous, formal, and fully explicit model in non-aggregative capital theory ..." (Koopmans 1964, p. 356).

consumers, workers, and entrepreneurs, soon led to another attempt to develop a dynamic model.[8]

J. R. Hicks's model

That attempt was made by John R. Hicks (1939, 1946; see Bliss 1987, p. 641). His purpose was to extend the Continental tradition on general equilibrium theory and to convey his ideas to those who read English. He drew upon Walras's ideas in several major respects.

First, he recognized the crucial importance of the interrelatedness of economic variables. "It turns out, on investigation," Hicks wrote, "that most of the problems of several variables, with which economic theory has to concern itself, are problems of the interrelation of markets. ... What we mainly need is a technique for studying the interrelations of markets" (Hicks 1939, p. 2). The technique that he used was, of course, in a general sense the one that Walras had initiated, namely general equilibrium analysis. Hicks acknowledged the value of Walras's legacy and its development by his immediate successors in this way:

> When looking for such a technique we are naturally impelled to turn to the works of those writers who have specially studied such interrelations – that is to say, the economists of the Lausanne school, Walras and Pareto, to whom, I think, Wicksell should be added. The method of General Equilibrium, which these writers elaborated, was specially designed to exhibit the economic system as a whole, in the form of a complex pattern of interrelations of markets. Our own work is bound to be in that tradition, and to be a continuation of theirs (ibid.).

Second, Hicks followed Walras in assuming that all markets are purely competitive (ibid.). He arrived at that decision in the belief that his only choices in the selection of market structures for his model were either ubiquitous perfect competition or ubiquitous monopoly:[9] "a general abandonment of the assumption of perfect competition, a universal adoption of the assumption of monopoly, must have very destructive consequences for economic theory ..." (ibid., p. 83). "Let us, then, return to the case of perfect competition" (ibid., p. 85).

Third, like Walras, Hicks counted equations and unknowns to try to establish the existence of equilibrium, although he wanted to do more than that. He used

---

[8] It has been contended (Kurz and Salvador 2004) that "all the salient features of the von Neumann model are classical in spirit," but surely the classicals' assumptions had closer connections to the economic realities of their time than von Neumann's did to those of any time in world history.

[9] See the variety of models with mixed market structures listed in the bibliography for Chapter 11.

...the results of our revised theory of Subjective Value to rework the General Equilibrium analysis of Walras and Pareto. Most important here is the opportunity thrown open to us to transcend the mere counting of equations and unknowns, and to lay down general laws for the working of a price-system with many markets. This is the main thing which needed to be done in order to free the Lausanne theory from the reproach of sterility brought against it by Marshallians (ibid.).

Fourth, in his effort to transcend the counting procedure, an effort that took the form of developing what he believed are "the Foundations of Dynamic Economics," Hicks noted yet again Walras's heritage. The study of those foundations, he wrote, "is concerned particularly with that setting-out of problems which, as we saw, was the main concern of General Equilibrium analysis in its Walrasian stage. I shall go into the matter in much greater detail than Walras did in his sketch of a theory of capital" (ibid., p. 6).

Fifth, Hicks drew upon Walras's legacy of 1899 by constructing a model that is so close to being virtual as to be in effect that type of system. He used the technique devised by Walras in 1899, without mentioning Walras in that connection, whereby all the equilibrating activity takes place in an initial stage, followed by equilibrium behavior during the subsequent stage (206, 1899, p. 103; 210, 1900, p. 302; § 274, p. 447). Hicks featured disequilibrium trading as occurring in his model on the first day of each analytical week, and then assumed that during the ensuing days of the week all economic activity takes place at the equilibrium prices established on the first day. For simplicity, this will be discussed with reference to a market for a single commodity, but the process occurs in all the markets of his model.

During the first day, transactions occur at a series of disequilibrium prices. After trade takes place at such a price, the participants have different holdings of money and the commodity, and that results in a new set of individual and hence of market supply and demand curves. Unless a special assumption is made, Hicks noted, such as Alfred Marshall's assumption that the marginal utility of money is constant, the new curves intersect at a price different from the solution price of the preceding pair. The path of the unrealized solution price traced out by the series of market curves falls or rises. When the current actual price reaches the value at which the current pair of market curves intersect, that price is the equilibrium value. The remaining trade on Monday takes place at that price as does all trade during the rest of the week. The price at which the initial pair on Monday intersect is not the same as the price at which the last pair of curves intersect. The static equations describe only the former because they contain the initial distribution of the assets as a parameter, and they therefore do not furnish the equilibrium price. To discover its value, it is necessary to have a dynamic model that traces the path of the actual price and transactions, reveals how the changing holdings of assets alter supply and demand, and determines the equilibrium price.

Walras, as has been seen, chose to try to deal with this problem by eliminating disequilibrium transactions in his written pledges sketch. Hicks, to his credit, was not prepared to construct a model that would have such an extreme result, nor to adopt Marshall's assumption. He followed a different line of reasoning and procedure to accomplish, as he thought, the same objective. He stated, on two grounds, that the equilibrium price in a non-virtual market is not appreciably different from what it would be if the market were virtual.

The first is that disequilibrium prices are, to use his word, "likely" to be close to the equilibrium price. He asserted that, "If any intelligence is shown in price-fixing, they will be" (ibid., 129). He thus introduced an implication about the knowledge of the market supply and demand functions by someone or other, and an implication about the institutions and procedures of price formation (perhaps that there is a market authority that suggests and sets prices?) that are alien to the impersonal, purely competitive markets that were the avowed subject of his model. Hicks meant that "not much" trading would occur at prices far from the one that turns out to be the equilibrium value: "If very extensive transactions take place at prices vastly different from equilibrium prices, the disturbance will be serious. But I think we may reasonably suppose that the transactions which take place at 'very false' prices are limited in volume" (ibid.). That reasoning is mistaken regarding the normal case in which the demand quantity is an inverse function of the price, and the supply quantity is a direct function of it. In that case, the volume of trade would be greater at a price close to the current solution price than if the price were further away from that value.

The second grounds for Hicks's contention is that the "gains to the buyers mean losses to the sellers, and vice versa. Thus, whenever the two sides are at all similar in their distribution of increments of expenditure among different goods, a shift in demand will be partially offset by corresponding shift in supply" (ibid.). That does not make sense. Trading a commodity is not a game in which buyers or sellers gain or lose money or commodity. Both buyers and sellers gain utility from trade. Buyers obtain amounts of the commodity and sellers obtain money. The amounts that buyers obtain are not "losses" borne by the sellers, nor is the money they receive a "loss" to the buyers. Furthermore, the situation to consider is not the distribution of increments of expenditure among different goods. The situation to consider is what happens within each given market to buyers' demand functions as they give up money and acquire the commodity at differing prices, and to sellers' supply functions as they acquire money and give up the commodity at different prices. On a market day, after trade at any price, the market demand curve always shifts to the left, and the market supply curve also always shifts to the left, but it is not meaningful to say that the shifts partially or wholly offset each other. The question is: How far to the left do each of the market curves shift, and what happens to their slopes. The well-known answer is that what happens to the individual and hence the market functions depends on the form of the preference functions. Given the initial stocks of money and commodity and the sequence of prices, it is ultimately the latter functions that determine by how much the equilibrium price in each market differs from the price at which the initial market desired supply and demand would be equal (Walker 1971a, 1971b).

Thus, on the basis of what Hicks presented as reasoning but is really a number of arbitrary postulates imposed upon his model and unfounded in economic behavior, he asserted that the equilibrium price in any market in which irrevocable disequilibrium transactions occur is not different or not appreciably different from the equilibrium price that would result if there were no such transactions (Hicks 1939, pp. 128–29).[10] In other words, he believed there is no appreciable difference between his model and a purely virtual model in regard to the determination of equilibrium prices. Hicks then postulated that the equilibrium prices found on the first day rule during the subsequent days of the week. In other words, there is no disequilibrium activity on those days. Thus he did not employ Walras's device of pledges to trade but only at equilibrium prices, believing that he achieved the virtual effect without it.

It has just been indicated that Hicks did not establish that disequilibrium transactions are unimportant, and he could not have done so without making very special assumptions about the forms of the preference functions. In actuality, the equilibrium price in any market will in most cases be affected significantly by disequilibrium transactions. In addition to that matter, there are a variety of relevant phenomena other than the type of effects that Hicks had in mind that result from changes in the amounts of money and consumer and capital goods held by individuals. Economic activity at disequilibrium prices includes the hiring of factors of production at disequilibrium prices and the payment of disequilibrium incomes. The amounts hired and the incomes paid differ

---

[10] It is also to Hicks's credit that he avowed, in the second edition of *Value and Capital*, about his assertion: "I endeavored, in the note on pp. 127–9 to provide that justification, but I did not pretend to be very satisfied with the results. However this was all I could do with the technique which was at my disposal" (Hicks 1946, p. 336).

from and may well be quantitatively much larger than the amounts hired and incomes paid at equilibrium prices. Likewise, the occurrence of dis-equilibrium rates of saving and investment affects many variables. Those phenomena have significant impacts upon desired and actual supply and demand quantities and hence upon the path to equilibrium and the set of equilibrium values.

The fact is that Hicks did not expend much effort on the matter in question because he was not really concerned with the equilibrating process: "Since we shall not pay much attention to the process of equi-libration which must precede the formation of the equilibrium price, our method seems to imply that we conceive of the economic system as being always in equilibrium" (ibid., p. 131). Today it would be thought strange to presume to treat the "Foundations of Dynamic Economics" (Hicks 1939, Part III) and the stability of equilibrium (ibid., pp. 245–72, 315–25) without considering very extensively the question of what hap-pens in disequilibrium.

Post-Hicksian virtual Walrasian modeling

In the thirty years after Hicks's work, the constructors of virtual models wove new themes and techniques together with those that had had their origins in Walras's ideas. Hicks's work stimulated Paul A. Samuelson to make important contributions to the understanding of the different types of stability in the early 1940s. In that period, Samuelson did not, however, even mention the behavior of economic agents that could cause the variables in a model to move toward or away from equilibrium. He did not construct a model with participants, commodities such as consumer goods, services and capital goods, and pricing institutions and procedures, and then examine it to determine if equilibrium exists in it or if it is stable. Rather, he constructed various equation systems to illustrate different types of adjustment processes, some of them physical, that are stable or unstable (Samuelson 1941a; 1941b; 1947, pp. 257–355).

In the 1950s and '60s, Kenneth Arrow, Gérard Debreu,[11] and Frank Hahn, among others, developed aspects of virtual general equilibrium theory. Maurice Allais constructed both virtual and non-virtual mod-els "in the line of descent from Walras, Fisher and Pareto" (Belloc and Moreaux 1987, p. 78)." Arrow wrote that, "Of course Hicks' Value and Capital made the biggest impression on me . . ." (Arrow to E. Roy Weintraub, November 19, 1981, quoted in Weintraub 1983, p. 29), thus

---

[11] Autobiographical information provided by Debreu is published in Bini and Bruni 1998.

indicating the most important conduit by which he was indirectly influenced by Walras's legacy. Arrow's attention was thereby drawn to the issue of competitive equilibrium. Believing that Wald had dealt with an unsatisfactorily special case, and that Hicks had not pronounced the last word on the matter, Arrow declared that the existence of a solution to the equations of general equilibrium was "an open question" (ibid.). In tackling that question, both Arrow and Debreu independently turned away from the specific type of mathematics that had been used by Walras, Pareto, Cassel, and Wald. Arrow and Debreu used set theory instead of calculus. This enabled them to deal with the complexities of the problem, and to ensure that the conditions they deemed necessary prevailed in the equilibriums of their models.

They also used game theory, developed by von Neumann and his collaborator, Oskar Morgenstern, an Austrian who had also joined the faculty at Princeton (von Neumann and Morgenstern 1944). It cannot be said that they owed any of their ideas on that topic to Walras. Rather, their dealing with the strategies of economic competitors and the results of their interactions enlarged the scope of theorizing about competition. John Nash (1950, 1951), showed that game theory is applicable to the study of the existence of a competitive equilibrium in a virtual type of game played by many persons. He defined the conditions of equilibrium that exist in games in which the participants cooperate and in those in which they do not.

The non-cooperative equilibrium that Nash presented was developed and generalized to some extent by Arrow and Debreu in their exploration of a model with more general properties than Wald's (Debreu 1952; Arrow and Debreu 1954). Following in the tradition of the model Walras had envisioned in 1899, it was perfectly competitive and also virtual, and was therefore similarly a special case. They demonstrated that the equilibria generated by a virtual competitive economy are Pareto optimums, giving maximum efficiency and well-being. Optimum distributions of income and resources, they showed, are characterized by sets of prices that equate supply and demand quantities, and are therefore competitive equilibria. "The existence theorem presented here gives general conditions under which there is, for [a certain type of] social system, an equilibrium, i.e. a situation where the action of every agent [is constrained by choices made by other agents] and no agent has incentive to choose another action" (Debreu 1952, p. 887). Arrow and Debreu explained the conditions that must prevail if equilibrium exists, such as the necessity that prices be non-negative, and they proved that equilibrium exists in their model. They also established, with reference to their own model, the accuracy of Walras's conjecture that the participants in a competitive model attain a constrained and non-unique maximum of well-being in equilibrium.

Subsequently, Arrow and Frank H. Hahn, delving selectively back into the history of the virtual Walrasian tradition, constructed a purely competitive model of that type. To do so, they employed the device of – to use their term – a "super-auctioneer" (1971, pp. 264, 266, 325), one that, as has been seen, has subsequently unjustly been attributed to Walras by other economists and become a firmly established mythic aspect of the Walrasian tradition. That fictional personage, who does not conduct any auctions and does not in any respect represent exclusively sellers, controls an undescribed and unimaginable information-collection system. He also controls an undescribed and unimaginable information-dissemination technology that he uses to quote prices in all markets and to which participants have access to learn those prices in at least related markets. Arrow and Hahn indicate no more about these matters than that he "calls a given set of prices **p** and receives transaction offers from the agents in the economy. If these do not match, he calls another set of prices," following the Walrasian pricing rule, "but no transactions are allowed to take place" (ibid., p. 264). Arrow and Hahn should have explicitly assumed that Walras's device of written pledges is used by the participants to register their desired supply and demand quantities. Without such pledges, it is impossible to see how the auctioneer could be informed of market conditions. Like Walras's sketch, Arrow's and Hahn's model is lacking a means by which the individual supply and demand quantities are totalized in each market. Their model also needs some means by which that information is transmitted to the auctioneer. In any event, he somehow learns the market supply and demand quantities for every commodity, and he changes the prices, somehow transmitting them to each market, until he finds the set that would put them all simultaneously into equilibrium, whereupon he allows economic activities to take place at that set. Arrow and Hahn proved the existence of equilibrium with reference to the equation system ostensibly relating to their principal model and to a variety of other equation sets, none of them justified by an account of market features (ibid., pp. 107–28).

The relative simplicity of virtual Walrasian models – relative to the non-virtual variety and ones with imperfect competition – has occasionally attracted the interest of other scholars. They have devised proofs of existence in models of that type with minor variations in their characteristics, or novel proofs regarding the standard Arrow-Debreu model. Christian Bidard and Reiner Franke (1987), for example, furnished it with a simpler proof. Yvan Lengwiler (1998) dealt with atomless exchange economies that do not fulfill the usual autarky assumption, meaning that the endowments may lie outside the consumption set. He established the existence of a Walrasian equilibrium, namely one in which, briefly, the supply and demand quantities of each commodity are equal, provided the economy is "heterogeneous." Antonio D'Agata (2001) provided a new proof of the existence of a Walrasian equilibrium in virtual pure exchange economies under standard and general assumptions. The proof, which employs a fixed-point theorem, is shorter and simpler than previous ones. Nils Hauenschild and Peter Stahlecker (2002) assumed that individual preferences are strictly monotone. In this case, the continuity of the excess demand functions that is usually assumed to show the existence of a Walrasian equilibrium does not hold for price vectors in which at least one component is equal to zero. Equilibrium prices will not be equal to zero, however, if preferences are strictly monotone. A simple proof of existence in the latter case, very similar to the non-monotone case, is provided by those theorists. A final example is the virtual general equilibrium model with indivisible commodities examined by Takuya Iimura (2003). He proved a fixed-point theorem on a discrete set; using the property of contiguous convexity of the set and the direction-preserving character of Walrasian correspondence. He gave a set of sufficient conditions, in terms of the characteristics of excess demand functions, for the existence of Walrasian equilibrium prices.[12]

The present state of virtual Walrasian modeling

For many years, most theorists chose to elaborate upon the concept of a virtual purely competitive model that had been introduced by Walras. Cassel followed that approach, added the assumption that the system is always in equilibrium, reverted to Walras's use of supply and demand functions aggregated at the market level, and developed a model of steady-state growth. Subsequently, John von Neumann followed Cassel's lead by assuming that his model is always in equilibrium and by developing a virtual purely competitive steady-state growth model. General equilibrium modelers in the years following 1930, like Wald, von Neumann, and Hicks, wanted to determine whether equilibrium exists in a virtual purely competitive model and whether there is a unique solution set of prices.

Kenneth Arrow, Gérard Debreu, Frank Hahn, and other mathematical economists used Walras's ideas about a virtual purely competitive model, Pareto's ideas about efficiency, concepts taken from game

---

[12] The work of other modelers of virtual Walrasian systems is collected in Debreu 1996, Walker 2000a, 2, and Arrow and Debreu 2001.

theory, and the notion of a central price setter to develop further the virtual Walrasian strand of theorizing. Because Walras's notion of the use
of written pledges is manifestly flawed and unworkable, general equilibrium theorists did not mention it, even though their models cannot
function without written pledges.

The scholars who developed and analyzed virtual Walrasian models
have proved the existence of equilibrium in the equation system relating
to them and its uniqueness if one or the other of Wald's assumptions
about demand is made. They have established that very little else can be
said about uniqueness and, regarding Wald's assumptions, "it is quite
clear that uniqueness theorems can only be obtained on assumptions so
restrictive as to appear unacceptable" (Ingrao and Israel 1990, p. 360).
They have also established that very little can be said about the models'
stability. Hugo Sonnenschein and others showed that the characterization
of preferences functions, the assumption of utility maximization, and the
resulting demand functions at the microeconomic level do not result in
any meaningful necessary features of aggregate demand functions. An
aggregate excess demand function can be specified completely arbitrarily and it can nevertheless "be an excess demand function for some
commodity in a general equilibrium economy" (Sonnenschein 1972,
p. 549). An arbitrary function can be constructed that has second partial
derivatives that indicate the local instability of a solution position of the
market and hence the impossibility of global stability. The consequence
is that, "Sonnenschein's theorem (together with its developments and
implications) seems to be an increasingly bulky obstacle blocking all
developments of the theory of general equilibrium in the critical sectors
of uniqueness and stability" (Ingrao and Israel 1990, p. 319).

"Suffice it to say, general equilibrium theory . . . had a very large bur-
den to bear. It proved unequal to this task. Such became clear in a spec-
tacular series of impossibility results that might be called Sonnenschein-
Mantel-Debreu theory after its main promulgators" (Rizvi 2003, p. 384).
Their work "showed that formalist general equilibrium theory had
reached a dead end: no general results beyond existence of equilibrium
were possible" (ibid.). "Strictly, the arbitrariness results put an end to
neoclassical general equilibrium theory of the Arrow-Debreu-McKenzie
variety" (ibid., p. 385), that is to say, the virtual line of purely competitive general equilibrium models that were the descendents of Walras's
written pledges sketch.

In addition to the internal difficulties of that type of model, there
was also the problem of its lack of realism. Walras would have said,
in his mature phase of theorizing, that the virtual model was a triumph
of pure reasoning without recourse to experience, or, more accurately, a

triumph of pure reasoning over experience. It "became increasingly clear to many economists that general equilibrium theory could not fulfill a promise of over 30 years. ... The results had an epoch-ending impact. Erstwhile champions of general equilibrium theory have had to abandon the field. Christopher Bliss thus wrote, 'The near emptiness of general equilibrium theory is a theorem of the theory'" (ibid., p. 384–85). One of the principal participants in the virtual Walrasian research agenda describes matters in this way:

I have always regarded Competitive General Equilibrium analysis as akin to the mock-up an aircraft engineer might build. ...Theorists all over the world have become aware that anything based on this mock-up is unlikely to fly, since it neglects some crucial aspects of the world, the recognition of which will force some drastic re-designing. Moreover, at no stage was the mock-up complete; in particular, it provided no account of the actual working of the invisible hand (Hahn 1981, p. 1036).

The line of research was unrealistic in a number of important respects, the most important of which was its virtual character. This means that the principal achievement of the research – the proof of the existence of equilibrium in the model – was one of logical deduction, not one that is applicable to real purely or approximately purely competitive economic processes, because they are characterized by irrevocable disequilibrium behavior. If those processes have an equilibrium, it is path dependent, and hence its existence is not proven by the virtual approach. Thus, "We are at a turning point in economic theory. Much of the elegant theoretical structure that has been constructed over the last one hundred years in economics will be seen over the next decade to have provided a wrong focus and misleading and ephemeral idea of what constitutes an equilibrium" (Kirman 1999, p. 8).[13] Alan Kirman was referring to the idea of equilibrium in the virtual purely competitive model; that is, equilibrium based on the constancy of the initial conditions during the process of finding it.

The many contributions of virtual purely competitive general equilibrium theorists resulted in a largely completed research agenda. Their extremely clever work has shown what can be achieved in that framework, and what cannot be achieved. The consequence of the latter revelations (that is, the negative results of the Sonnenschein-Mantel-Debreu analyses for the virtual purely competitive models) has divided "those who had worked in the field into two groups: those concerned only to

---

[13] This quotation and the one from Hahn's work are also to be found in Fabio Petri's fine analysis (2004) of the problems of the virtual line of purely competitive modeling (see pp. 1–2 for his use of the quotations).

mourn the loss of global stability and those who see that no progress is possible in that direction and so a change is called for" (Ingrao and Israel 1990, p. 347).[14] The outlook of the latter group has been reinforced by criticisms such as those of Hahn and Kirman. Their contention is that whatever results the virtual line of research may have been able to achieve, they are not relevant for understanding or influencing the real economy. General equilibrium theorists have therefore chosen to heed the counsel calling for a change and have moved on to the consideration of other types of models.

---

[14] There are some questionable aspects (Walker 1991) of Ingrao's and Israel's book (1990). Nevertheless, they provide an excellent survey (ibid., pp. 316–62) of the paucity of the results of purely competitive modeling of the virtual type, and of the impossibility of making further progress in that field of research.

CHAPTER 11

Concluding comments: Walras's ideas in modern economics

This book has told the story thus far of the past influence of Walras's mature comprehensive model and his written pledges sketch. The latter gave rise to the virtual line of general equilibrium research that dominated the agenda of economists working in that field for more than forty years in the twentieth century, and aspects of that line of research continue to be pursued in some modern theorizing. The constructions and functioning of the mature comprehensive model have a secure place in the history of general equilibrium modeling as providing its beginning and as furnishing ideas that have been used throughout its history.[1] In that model, Walras developed a non-virtual model in which economic decisions are made in private markets by entrepreneurs, suppliers of economic resources, consumers, and savers, and in which the markets are purely competitive. It has four major characteristics. First, the markets in it are interrelated, so the values of the economic variables are mutually determined and the impact of a change in a parameter is manifested throughout the economic system. Second, irrevocable transactions, production, consumption, savings, and investment occur in disequilibrium. Third, when the economy is in disequilibrium it moves toward an equilibrium position. Fourth, that position is on a path of growth. The position changes as the economy grows, or possibly contracts, tracing out a path through time. Of course, Walras recognized that in the real economy the movement to equilibrium under a given set of basic conditions is frequently interrupted because changes in those conditions occur frequently. The conditions include the development of new technologies, changes of tastes, changes in the size of the labor force, and changes of government policies. He also recognized, although he expressed the

---

[1] In the light of the vast body and continuing vitality of non-virtual Walrasian modern research it is inexplicable why one author advanced the idea that "the Non-Tâtonnement Line of Research Died Out" (Busetto 1995). A research project with a valid relation to the historical record would be: "Why the non-virtual line of research continues, and why the line of research into virtual purely competitive general equilibrium models has reached some dead ends," the latter being a matter addressed at the end of Chapter 10.

matter in different words, that the position and slope of the growth path are affected by those changes.

Historians of economic thought sometimes exhort modern theorists to study Walras's work, because they would find ideas in it that could be used to advantage in modern theoretical constructions. That exhortation is unnecessary. His legacy is a vital part of modern theorizing and of modern empirical applications of it. Indeed, an exposition of all of modern scholarship that benefits from his work would be impossible, as it would encompass much of modern microeconomic theory – not just general equilibrium models – and some macroeconomics. Economic theorists use every day, as a matter of course, many of Walras's special constructions as modified by his successors. These include the reciprocal nature of demand and supply, general equilibrium demand and supply functions, the rigorously expressed idea of optimization and constrained maxima in economic connections, the individual's budget equation, Walras's law, the Walrasian equilibrium conditions, the Walras correspondence relationships, Walras optimum allocations, the concept of the production function, Walras's contribution to the theory of marginal productivity, the concept of a numeraire, the price-dependent and production-dependent analyses of stability in particular markets, the theorem of equivalent distributions, what is called the Fisher equation, and a cash balances theory of money – not just a cash balances equation. The constructors of many recent models explicitly acknowledge Walras's influence[2] as enriching fields of economic research in addition to the purely competitive situation that he envisaged. There are adaptations and extentions of his ideas in game theory, Cournot-Walras models and other models combining Walrasian features and imperfect competition, Nash-Walras models, bargaining models, fix-price models, Walras-Keynes models (such as ones that blend failures of coordination with multi-market general equilibrium features), and matching and search models.

As has been noted in Chapter 9, the empirical testing of aspects of Walras's mature comprehensive model was initiated during his life by H. L. Moore and continued shortly after Walras's life by Moore and Henry Schultz. Another early development of importance for applied general equilibrium studies of non-virtual economic phenomena, inasmuch as it encouraged the development of econometric research of that nature, was the formation of the Econometric Society in the United States in 1930. At that time, the businessman Alfred Cowles decided to try to improve the dismal state of business forecasting, and saw in

---

[2] A bibliography of recent writings that reflect the influence of Walras's legacies, along with the references for Chapter 11, is placed in a separate section after the references to writings mentioned before this chapter.

the Econometric Society a means of achieving his end. He began to subsidize it and *Econometrica*, in which econometric research on general equilibrium has been published. Likewise, primarily for the purpose of developing general equilibrium economic theory in relation to statistical empirical research, Cowles obtained a charter for the Cowles' Commission for Research in Economics. After the 1930s, "There was clear recognition of the centrality of general equilibrium analysis in the development of economic theory sufficiently rich to provide a basis for empirical work" (Weintraub 1983, p. 19). A notable example is Wassily Leontief's input-output model dealing, for practical purposes, with the interrelations of industries (Leontief 1941).

The continued empirical usefulness of Walrasian models was foreseen by Herbert Scarf, writing about "a renewed interest in policy questions at a microeconomic level":

> The Walrasian model of competition, even though it is sufficiently flexible to incorporate a number of formal modifications, is far from being the exclusive analytical framework for the study of microeconomic problems. But it is an important method of analysis and one whose usefulness, we hope, will be enhanced by the ability to obtain specific numerical solutions (Scarf 1973, p. 17).

Precisely that has happened, as, for example, in the applications of general equilibrium models to the analysis of real problems with the aid of modern computers (see, for example, Scarf and Shoven 1984, Piggott and Whalley 1985, Chang 1997, Gottinger 1998). One such study deserves special mention in a survey of Walras's legacy because of its name as well as its content. It is the multi-country applied econometric general equilibrium model, appropriately called WALRAS, used to quantify and evaluate the effects of agricultural policies (Delormé and Van der Mensbrugghe 1989, Lienert 1989, Martin 1989–1990, Burniaux 1990). The empirical applications of modern general equilibrium show the continuing vitality of Walras's ideas in yet another domain.[3]

Walras's legacy in special respects and in general has therefore been to contribute many important strands of the mainstream of modern economic research and knowledge. Indeed, his legacy is inseparable from that mainstream.

---

[3] One writer has referred to "the paucity of the interpretative results produced by Walras's equilibrium theory" and contended that it "is at best a formal synthesis which is not adequate for stimulating empirical research" (Ménard 1990, p. 119). Adherents of those views also describe his theory as a "thought experiment" (ibid., p. 118), a label chosen to indicate the belief that the proposition that the economy is an equilibrating system cannot be tested and that general equilibrium theory is useless for applications. Evidently those views conflict with the history of empirical research in the general equilibrium field.

References

Allais, Maurice (1968), "Vilfredo Pareto, Contributions to Economics," in *International Encyclopedia of the Social Sciences*, New York: Macmillan Co. and the Free Press, 2, 399–411.

Amoroso, Luigi (1909), "La teoria dell'equilibrio economico secondo il Prof. Vilfredo Pareto," *Giornale degli Economisti*, series 2, *39*, October, 353–67.

Amoroso, Luigi (1921), *Lezioni di economia mathematica*, Bologna: N. Zanichelli.

Antonelli, Etienne (1914), *Principes d'économie pure*, Paris: Librairie des sciences politiques et sociales.

Antonelli, Etienne (1939), *L'Economie pure du capitalisme*, Paris: Guillaumin et Cie.

Antonucci, Antonio (ed.) (1938), *Alcune lettere di Vilfredo Pareto pubblicate e commentate da A. Antonucci*, Rome: Prof. P. Maglione-Editore; Socc. di Loescher & C.; reprinted in Busino 1973 without Antonucci's comments.

Arena, Richard and Ludovic Ragni (1994), "Libre concurrence et méthodologie walrasienne: une tentative de mise en relation," *Economies et Sociétés*, Série Œconomia, Histoire de la Pensée économique, P. E. no. 20–21, *10–11*, 161–82.

Arrow, Kenneth (1959), "Towards a Theory of Price Adjustment," in Moses Abramovitz et al. (eds.), *The Allocation of Economic Resources: Essays in Honor of Bernard Francis Haley*, Stanford: Stanford University Press, 41–51.

Arrow, Kenneth (1968), "Economic Equilibrium," in David L. Sills (ed.), *International Encyclopedia of the Social Sciences*, *4*, no place: Macmillan Company and the Free Press, 376–86.

Arrow, Kenneth J. and Gérard Debreu (1954), "Existence of an Equilibrium for a Competitive Economy," *Econometrica, 22*, July, 265–90.

Arrow, Kenneth J. and Gérard Debreu (eds.) (2001), *Landmark Papers in General Equilibrium Theory, Social Choice and Welfare*, in *Foundations of Twentieth Century Economics*, *3*, Cheltenham, U.K. and Northampton, MA.: Elgar Publishing Limited.

Arrow, Kenneth J. and F. H. Hahn (1971), *General Competitive Analysis*, San Francisco: Holden-Day; Edinburgh: Oliver and Boyd.

Arrow, Kenneth J. and Leonid Hurwicz (1958), "On the Stability of Competitive Equilibrium I," *Econometrica, 26*, 522–52.

Aupetit, Albert (1901), *Essai sur la théorie générale de la monnaie*, Paris: Guillaumin et Cie.

Aupetit, Albert (1914), *Principes d'économie pure*, Paris: Guillaumin et Cie.

Barone, Enrico (1895), "Sopra un recente libro del Wicksteed," unpublished lost mss.; translated into French by Léon Walras as "Sur un livre récent de Wicksteed," in 239, 1895, *2*, 644–48; translated into English by Donald A. Walker, in Jaffé 1983, 182–86.

Barone, Enrico (1896), "Studi sulla distribuzione," *Giornale degli Economisti*, series 2, *12*, February, 107–152.

Barone, Enrico (1908), "Il Ministro della produzione nello stato collettivista," *Giornale degli Economisti*, series 2, *37*, September, 267–93; October, 391–414.

Baumol, William J. and Stephen M. Goldfeld (eds.) (1968), *Precursors in Mathematical Economics*, LSE Series of reprints of scarce works on political economy, no. 19, London: London School of Economics.

Belloc, Bernard and Michel Moreaux (1987), "Allais, Maurice," in Eatwell et al. 1987, *1*, 78–80.

Bidard, Christian and Reiner Franke (1987), "On Walras' Model of General Equilibrium: A Simpler Way to Demonstrate Existence," *Zeitschrift für Nationalökonomie, 47* (3), 315–19.

Bini, Piero and Luigino Bruni (1998), "Intervista a Gérard Debreu," *Storia del pensiero economico, 35*, 3–29.

Blaug, Mark (ed.) (1992a), *Leon Walras (1834–1910)*, an Elgar Reference Collection, in *Pioneers in Economics, 25, Aldershot*, UK and Brookfield, VT: Edward Elgar Publishing.

Blaug, Mark (1992b), *The Methodology of Economics or How Economists Explain*, 2nd ed., Cambridge: Cambridge University Press.

Blaug, Mark (1997), "Competition as an End-State and Competition as a Process," in B. Curtis Eaton and Richard G. Harris (eds.), *Trade, Technology and Economics: Essays in Honour of Richard G. Lipsey*, Cheltenham, UK and Brookfield, VT: Edward Elgar Publishing, 241–62; and in *Not Only an Economist, Recent Essays*, Cheltenham, UK: Edward Elgar Publishing, 66–86; and in Walker 2000a, *1*, 272–93.

Bliss, Christopher (1987), "Hicks, John Richard (born 1904)," in Eatwell et al., *2*, 641–46.

Bompaire, François (1931), *Du principe de liberté économique dans l'œuvre de Cournot et dans celle de l'école de Lausanne (Walras, Pareto)*, Paris: Recueil Sirey.

Bousquet, Georges-Henri (1927), *Essai sur l'évolution de la pensée économique*, Paris: M. Giard.

Bousquet, Georges-Henri (1928a), *Cours d'économie pure*, Paris: Librairie des sciences politiques et sociales.

Bousquet, Georges-Henri (1928b), *Vilfredo Pareto. Sa vie et son œuvre*, Paris: Payot.

Bousquet, Georges-Henri (1960), *Pareto (1848–1923). Le savant et l'homme*, Lausanne: Payot.

Bousquet, Georges-Henri (1964), "Introduction" to Pareto 1896/1897, new edition, Geneva: Librarie Droz, IX–XVII.

Bousquet, Georges-Henri (1971), "Quelques remarques sur Pareto et certains défauts de son œuvre," *Revue Européenne des Sciences Sociales et Cahiers Vilfredo Pareto, 9* (25), 11–27.

Bouvier, Emile (1901), "L'économie politique mathématique, quelques mots à propos du traité de M. Léon Walras," *Revue Critique de Législation et de Jurisprudence, 30* (12), December, 623–29.

Boven, Pierre (1923), "Vilfredo Pareto II. L'œuvre et les théories," *Journal de Genève*, 94th year, no. 229, August 22, 1–2.

Bowley, Arthur L. (1924), *The Mathematical Groundwork of Economics: An Introductory Treatise*, Oxford: The Clarendon Press.

Brems, Hans (1986), *Pioneering Economic Theory, 1630–1980. A Mathematical Restatement*, Baltimore and London: The Johns Hopkins University Press.

Brems, Hans (1987), "Zeuthen, Frederik Ludvig Bang (1888–1959)," in Eatwell et al. 1987, *4*, pp. 944–45.

Bridel, Pascal (1990), "Equilibre, statique comparée et analyse dynamique chez Vilfredo Pareto: remarques sur la contribution de Siro Lombardini," *Revue européenne des sciences sociales, 27* (88), 183–191.

Bridel, Pascal (1997), *Money and General Equilibrium Theory; From Walras to Pareto (1870–1923)*, Cheltenham, UK and Lyme, CT: Edward Elgar Publishing Limited.

Bridel, Pascal (1998), Review of "*Walras's market models*. By Donald A. Walker. Cambridge; New York and Melbourne: Cambridge University Press, 1996," *Journal of Economic Literature, 36* (1), 231–33.

Bridel, Pascal and Elisabeth Huck (2002), "Yet another look at Walras's theory of *tâtonnement*," *European Journal of the History of Economic Thought, 9*, Winter, 513–40.

Bruni, Luigino (2002), *Vilfredo Pareto and the birth of modern microeconomics*, Cheltenham, U.K. and Northampton, MA: Elgar Publishing Limited.

Buckle, Henry Thomas (1872), *The miscellaneous and posthumous works of Henry Thomas Buckle*, edited by Helen Taylor, London: Longmans, Green and Co.

Burgenmeier, B. (1994), "The Misperception of Walras," *American Economic Review, 84* (1), March, 342–52.

Busetto, Francesca (1995), "Why the Non-*Tâtonnement* Line of Reasearch Died Out," *Economic Notes, 24* (1), 89–113.

Busino, Giovanni (ed.) (1973), *Vilfredo Pareto: Epistolario, 1890–1923*, 2 vols., Rome: Accademia Nazionale dei Lincei.

Busino, Giovanni (1987), "Pareto, Vilfredo," in Eatwell et. al. 1987, *3*, 799–804.

Cassel, Karl Gustav (1899), "Grundriss einer elementaren Preislehre," *Zeitschrift für die gesamte Staatswissenschaf, 55* (3), 395–458.

Cassel, Karl Gustav (1900), "Grundsätze für die Bildung der Personentarife auf den Eisenbahnen," *Archiv für Eisenbahnwesen, 23*, 116–46; translated as "The Principles of Railway Rates for Passengers," *International Economic Papers, 6*, 1956.

Cassel, Karl Gustav (1903), *The Nature and Necessity of Interest*, London and New York: Macmillan.

Cassel, Karl Gustav (1918), *Theoretische Sozialökonomie*, Leipzig: C. F. Winter; 4th ed., revised, Leipzig: A. Deichertsche Verlasbuchhandlung Dr. Werner Scholl, 1927.

Cassel, Karl Gustav (1921), *The World's Monetary Problems, Two memoranda presented to the International Financial Conference of the League of Nations in Brussels in 1920 and to the Financial Committee of the League of Nations in September 1921*, London: Constable.

Cassel, Karl Gustav (1923), *The Theory of Social Economy*, translated by Joseph McCabe from the enlarged German 2nd ed., London: T. F. Unwin.

Cassel, Karl Gustav (1928), "The Rate of Interest, the Bank Rate, and the Stabilization of Prices," *Quarterly Journal of Economics, 42* (August), 511–29.

Cassel, Karl Gustav (1932), *The Theory of Social Economy*, translated by Samuel L. Barron from the 5th German edition, London: E. Benn; reprint, New York: Augustus M. Kelley, 1967.

Cassel, Karl Gustav (1935), *On Quantitative Thinking in Economics*, Oxford: Clarendon Press.

Cassel, Karl Gustav (1937), "Keynes' *General Theory*," *International Labour Review, 36*, 437–45.

Clarke, Desmond M. (1991), "Descartes's Use of 'Demonstration' and 'Deduction,'" in Georges J. D. Moyal, (ed.), (1991), *René Descartes: Critical Assessments*, 4 vols., London: Routledge.

Clower, Robert W. (1965), "The Keynesian Counter-Revolution: A Theoretical Appraisal," in F. H. Hahn and F. P. R. Brechling, (eds.), *The Theory of Interest Rates*, London: Macmillan, 103–25.

Collins Robert Unabridged French-English, English-French Dictionary (2002), 6th ed., Glasgow: HarperCollins Publishers.

Cournot, Antoine-Auguste (1838), *Recherches sur les principes mathématiques de la théorie des richesses*, Paris: Hachette.

Cournot, Antoine-Auguste (1863), *Principes de la théorie des richesses*, Paris: Hachette.

Creedy, John (1999), "The Rise and Fall of Walras's Demand and Supply Curves," *Manchester School, 67* (2), March, 192–202.

Currie, Martin and Ian Steedman (1990), *Wrestling with Time: Problems in Economic Theory*, Manchester: Manchester University Press.

D'Agata, Antonio (2001), "Yet Another Proof of the Existence of a Competitive Equilibrium," *Revista de Analisis Economico, 16* (2), December, 155–58.

Davis, John B., D. Wade Hands, and Uskali Mäki (1998), *The Handbook of Economic Methodology*, Cheltenham, UK and Northampton, MA: Edward Elgar Publishing Limited.

Debreu, Gérard (1952), "A Social Equilibrium Existence Theorem," *Proceedings of the National Academy of Sciences, 38*, 886–93.

Debreu, Gérard (1959), *Theory of Value; An Axiomatic Analysis of Economic Equilibrium*, New York: John Wiley and Sons.

Debreu, Gérard (ed.) (1996), *General Equilibrium Theory*, 2 vols., an Elgar Reference Collection, in *The International Library of Critical Writings in Economics*, general editor Mark Blaug, Cheltenham, UK and Brookfield, VT: Edward Elgar Publishing Limited.

Debs, Alexandre (2004), "'To Be' or 'Ought To Be': The Questions of Empirical Content and Normative Bias in Léon Walras's Methodology," *Journal of the History of Economic Thought, 26*, December, 479–92.

De Vroey, Michel (1987), "La possibilité d'une économie décentralisée," *Revue Economique, 38* (4), 773–805.

De Vroey, Michel (1999), "Transforming Walras into a Marshallian Economist: A Critical Review of Donald Walker's *Walras's Market Models*," *Journal of the History of Economic Thought, 21* (4), December, 413–35.

Diemer, Arnaud (2002), "Economie Pure, Economie Appliquée, Economie Sociale, Un point de vue critique sur l'œuvre de Léon Walras?," IIIᵉ Colloque de l'Association Internationale Walras, Lyon, September 20, in *Les Cahiers du CERAS*, hors série no. 3, May, 2004, 235–53, with the title "Economie Pure et Economie Appliquée. Retour sur les origines de l'œuvre de Léon Walras."

Diemer, Arnaud and Jérôme Lallement (2004), "De Auguste à Léon Walras: retour sur les origines du marché et de la concurrence walrassiennes," preliminary version, IVᵉColloque de l'Association Internationale Walras, Nice, September 23–24.

Divisia, François (1928), *Economique rationelle*, Paris: G. Doin.

Dockès, Pierre (1994), "«La société n'est pas un pique-nique»: le socialisme appliqué de Léon Walras," *Economies et Sociétés*, Série Œconomia, Histoire de la Pensée économique, P. E. no. 20–21, *10–11*, 270–325.

Dockès, Pierre (1996), *La société n'est pas un pique-nique: Léon Walras et l'économie sociale*, Paris: Economica.

Dockès, Pierre (1999), "Ce qui est, ce qui devrait être, ce qui sera: Walras's economics as he saw it," *Revue Européenne des Sciences Sociales, 37* (116), 13–36.

Dockès, Pierre, Ludovic Frobert, Gérard Klotz, Jean-Pierre Potier, and André Tiran, (eds.), (2000), *Les traditions économiques françaises 1848–1939*, Paris: CNRS ÉDITIONS.

Dockès, Pierre and Jean-Pierre Potier (2001), *La Vie et l'œuvre économique de Léon Walras*, Paris: Economica; an extract from 249.V, IX–LXXVIII.

Dorfman, Robert, Paul A. Samuelson, and Robert M. Solow (1958), *Linear Programming and Economic Analysis*, New York, Toronto, London: McGraw-Hill Book Company.

Eatwell, John, Murray Milgate, and Peter Newman (eds.), *The New Palgrave: A Dictionary of Economics*, 4 vols., London: Macmillan Press; New York: Stockton Press; Tokyo: Maruzen Company.

Edgeworth, Francis Y. (1881), *Mathematical Psychics: An Essay on the Application of Mathematics to the Moral Sciences*, London: C. Kegan Paul; reprint, New York: Augustus M. Kelley, 1961.

Edgeworth, Francis Y. (1889), "The Mathematical Theory of Political Economy. *Eléments d'économie politique pure*. By Léon Walras," *Nature, 40*, September, 434–36.

Einaudi, Manon Michels (1935), "Pareto as I Knew Him," *Atlantic Monthly, 156*, September, 336–46.

Fisher, Irving (1892), "Mathematical Investigations in the Theory of Value and Prices," in *Transactions of the Connecticut Academy, 9*, July, 3–126; reprint, New York: Augustus M. Kelley, 1965.

Fisher, Irving (1896), *Appreciation and Interest*, publications of the American Economic Association, 3rd series, *11* (4), August, New York: Macmillan Company.

Fisher, Irving (1892), *Mathematical Investigations in the Theory of Value and Prices*, in *Transactions of the Connecticut Academy, 9*, July, 3–126; reprint, New York: Augustus M. Kelley, 1965.

Fontaine, Phillippe (1998), "Menger, Jevons, and Walras Un-homogenized, De-homogenized, and Homogenized: A Comment on Peart," *American Journal of Economics and Sociology, 57* (3), July, 333–40.

Gewirtz, Alan (1941), "Experience and the Non-Mathematical in the Cartesian Method," *Journal of the History of Ideas, 2* (2), April, 183–210.

Giddings, Franklin H. (1896), *The Principles of Sociology*, New York: Macmillan Company.

Gijsel, Peter de (1989), "On the Role of General Equilibrium Theory in Walras's Theory of a Just Society," in Donald A. Walker (ed.), *Classical and Neoclassical Economic Thought: Selected Papers from the History of Economics Society Conference 1987*, Perspectives on the History of Economic Thought, *1*, Aldershot, UK: Edward Elgar for the History of Economics Society, 133–44.

Gustafsson, Bo (1987), "Cassel, Gustav," in Eatwell et al. 1987, *1*, 375–77.

Hahn, Frank (1981), review: "M. Beenstock, *A Neoclassical Analysis of Macroeconomic Policy*, Cambridge Universtiy Press, 1980," *Economic Journal, 91* (364), December, 1036–39.

Hands, D. Wade (1998), "Positivism," in Davis et al. 1998, 374–78.

Hauenschild, Nils and Peter Stahlecker (2002), "A Simple Proof for the Existence of Walrasian Equilibrium under Monotone Preferences," *Economics Bulletin, 4* (4), 1–8.

Hayek, Friedrich August von (1934), "Carl Menger," *Economica*, n.s., *1*, November, 393–420.

Herland, Michel (1996), "Three French Socialist Economists: Leroux, Proudhon, Walras," *Journal of the History of Economic Thought, 18* (1), Spring, 133–53.

Herschel, John F. W. (1831 [1830]), *A Preliminary Discourse on the Study of Natural Philosophy*, London: Longman, Rees, Orme, Browne and Greene.

Hicks, J. R. (1934), "Léon Walras," *Econometrica, 2*, October, 338–48.

Hicks, J. R. (1939), *Value and Capital*; 2nd ed., 1946, Oxford: Clarendon Press.

Hicks, J. R. (1965), *Capital and Growth*, New York and Oxford: Oxford University Press.

Hildenbrand, W. and A. P. Kirman (1988), *Equilibrium analysis: Variations on Themes by Edgeworth and Walras*, in *Advanced Textbooks in Economics, 28*, Amsterdam, New York, Oxford, Tokyo: North-Holland.

Hilton, H. C. (1995), "Léon Walras on Money and Banking," *History of Economics Review, 24*, Summer, 72–78.

Hollander, Samuel and Sandra Peart (1999), "John Stuart Mill's Method in Principle and Practice: A Review of the Evidence," *Journal of the History of Economic Thought, 21* (4), December, 369–97.

Hotelling, Harold (1929), "Stability in Competition," *Economic Journal, 39*, March, 41–57.

Howitt, P. W. (1973), "Walras and Monetary Theory," *Western Economic Journal, 11* (4), December, 487–99.

Huck, Elizabeth (2001), "La neutralité du tâtonnement au regard de la répartition des richesses dans la théorie de la production de Léon Walras. Le cas du tâtonnement sans bons des trois premières éditions des *Eléments d'économie politique pure*," *Revue économique, 52* (3), May, 729–38.

Hume, David (1777), *Enquiries concerning Human Understanding and concerning the Principles of Morals*, 3rd edition; reprint, edited by L. A. Selby Bigge, Oxford: Clarendon Press, 1975.

Hutchison, T. W. (1953), *A Review of Economic Doctrines 1870–1929*, London: Oxford University Press.

Iimura, Takuya (2003), "A Discrete Fixed Point Theorem and Its Applications," *Journal of Mathematical Economics, 39* (7), September, 725–42.

Ingrao, Bruna and Giorgio Israel (1990), *The Invisible Hand: Economic Equilibrium in the History of Science*, translated by Ian McGilvray, Cambridge, MA: MIT Press.

Jaffé, William (1935), "Unpublished Papers and Letters of Léon Walras," *Journal of Political Economy, 43*, April, 187–207. All articles of Jaffé's that are listed in these references are reprinted in Jaffé 1983, except Jaffé 1978 and 1984.

Jaffé, William (1967), "Walras's Theory of *Tâtonnement*: A Critique of Recent Interpretations," *Journal of Political Economy, 75*, February, 1–19.

Jaffé, William (1969), "A. N. Isnard, Progenitor of the Walrasian General Equilibrium Model," *History of Political Economy, 1*, Spring, 19–43.

Jaffé, William (1971), "Reflections on the Importance of Léon Walras," in *Schaarste en Welvaart*, P. Hennipman Festschrift, edited by Arnold Heertje et al., Amsterdam: Stenfert Kroese, 87–107.

Jaffé, William (1976), "Menger, Jevons and Walras De-homogenized," *Economic Inquiry, 14*, December, 511–24.

Jaffé, William (1977), "The Normative Bias of the Walrasian Model: Walras versus Gossen," *Quarterly Journal of Economics, 91*, August, 371–87.

Jaffé, William (1978), Review of *"Walras' Economics: A Pure Theory of Capital and Money*, by Michio Morishima," *Economic Journal, 88*, September, 574–617

Jaffé, William (1980), "Walras's Economics as Others See It," *Journal of Economic Literature, 18*, June, 528–49.

Jaffé, William (1981), "Another Look at Léon Walras's Theory of *Tâtonnement*," *History of Political Economy, 13*, Summer, 313–36.

Jaffé, William (1983), *William Jaffé's Essays on Walras*, edited by Donald A. Walker, Cambridge, New York, Melbourne: Cambridge University Press.

Jaffé, William (1984), "The Antecedents and Early Life of Léon Walras," edited by Donald A. Walker, *History of Political Economy, 16* (1), Spring, 1–57.

Jolink, Albert (1993), "'Procrustean Beds and All That': The Irrelevance of Walras for a Mirowski Thesis," *History of Political Economy, 25*, Supplement, 159–74.

Keynes, John Maynard (1925/1930), "F. P. Ramsey 1903–1930," in *Essays and Sketches in Biography*, New York: Median Books, 1956. 114–24.

Keynes, John Maynard (1936), "William Stanley Jevons 1835–1882," in *Essays and Sketches in Biography*, New York: Median Books, 1956, 125–60.

Keynes, John Maynard (1936), *The General Theory of Employment, Interest and Money*, New York: Harcourt, Brace and Company.

Kirman, Alan P. (1987), "Pareto as an Economist," in Eatwell et al. 1987, *3*, 804–9.

Kirman, Alan P. (1999), "The Future of Economic Theory," in Alan P. Kirman and L.-A. Gérard-Varet (eds.), *Economics Beyond the Millenium*, Oxford: Oxford University Press, 8–22.

Klotz, Gérard (1994), "Achylle Nicolas Isnard, précurseur de Léon Walras ?," *Economies et Sociétés*, Série Œconomia, Histoire de la Pensée économique, P.E. nos. 20–21, *28* (10–11), 29–52.

Koopmans, Tjalling (1964), "Economic Growth at a Maximal Rate," *Quarterly Journal of Economics, 78*, August, 355–94.

Koppl, Roger (1992), "Price Theory as Physics: The Cartesian Influence in Walras," *Methodus, 4* (2), December, 17–28; and in Walker 2001, *1*, 199–210.

Koppl, Roger (1995), "The Walras Paradox," *Eastern Economic Journal, 21* (1), 43–55; and in Walker 2001a, *2*, 268–80.

Kowalik, Tadeusz (1987), "Lange, Oskar Ryszard (1904–1965)," in Eatwell et al. 1987, *3*, 123–29.

Kuenne, Robert E. (1961), "The Walrasian Theory of Money: An Interpretation and a Reconstruction," *Metroeconomica, 13*, August, 94–105.

Kurz, Heinz and Neri Salvadori (2000), "Walras and Ricardo," in Dockès et al. 2000, 967–85.

Kurz, Heinz and Neri Salvadori (2004), "Von Neumann, the Classical Economists and Arrow-Debreu: Some Notes," *Acta Œconomica, 54* (1), 39–62.

La Volpe, Giulio (1936), *Studi Sulla Teoria Dell' Equilibrio Economico Dinamico Generale*, Naples: Jovene; translated by Helen Ampt as *Studies on* the Theory of General Dynamic Economic Equilibrium, Basingstoke and London: Macmillan, 1993.

Lange, Oskar R. (1936), "On the Economic Theory of Socialism, Part I," *Review of Economic Studies, 4* (1), October, 53–71.

Lange, Oskar R. (1937), "On the Economic Theory of Socialism, Part II," *Review of Economic Studies, 4* (2), February, 123–42.

Lange, Oskar R. (1944), *Price Flexibility and Employment*, Bloomington: Principia Press.

Laurent, Hermann (1902), *Petit traité d'économie politique mathématique, rédigé conformément aux préceptes de l' école de Lausanne*, Paris: C. Schmid.

Lendjel, Emeric (1997), "Le «biais empiriste» dans l'interprétation de Walker du tâtonnement walrassien," *Economies et Sociétés*, Œconomia, Histoire de la pensée économique, Série P.E., no. 26, *31* (10), 47–84.

Lendjel, Emeric (1999), "Tâtonnement walrassien et marchandage parétien: Une approche comparative," *Revue européenne des sciences sociales, 37* (116), 295–314.

Lengwiler, Yvan (1998), "Endogenous Endowments and Equilibrium Starvation in a Walrasian Economy," *Journal of Mathematical Economics, 30* (1), August, 37–58.

Lexis, William (1881), "Zur mathematisch-ökonomischen Literatur," *Jahrbücher für Nationalökonomie und Statistik*, new series, *3*, 427–34.

Locke, John (1954), *Essays on the Law of Nature*, edited by W. von Leyden, Oxford: Oxford University Press.

Mantel, R. (1974), "On the Characterisation of Aggregate Excess Demand," *Journal of Economic Theory, 7*, 348–53.

Marchionatti, Roberto and Enrico Gambino (1997), "Pareto and Political Economy as a Science: Methodological Revolution and Analytical Advances in Economic Theory in the 1890s," *Journal of Political Economy, 105* (6), December, 1322–48.

Marchionatti, Roberto and Fiorenzo Mornati (2003), "Pareto et l'économie Mathématique au Début des Années 1890. Quelques Réflexions à Propos des «Considerazioni sui Principii Fondamentali Dell'economia Politica Pura»," in *Histoire et Théorie des Sciences Sociales. Mélanges en l' honneur de Giovanni Busino*, Geneva: Droz, *3*, 51–84.

Marget, Arthur W. (1931), "Léon Walras and the 'Cash-Balance Approach' to the Problem of the Value of Money," *Journal of Political Economy, 39* (5), October, 569–600.

Marget, Arthur W. (1935), "The Monetary Aspects of the Walrasian System," *Journal of Political Economy, 43*, April, 145–86.

Marinitsch, O. (1892), *La Bourse, théorique et pratique*, Paris: Paul Ollendorff.

Marx, Karl (1858), "Introduction" to *Contribution to the Critique of Political Economy*, reprinted in David Horowitz, *Marx and Modern Economics*, New York: Monthly Review Press, 1968.

Marx, Karl (1867), *Capital, 1*, Harmondsworth: Penguins Books, 1976.

McKenzie, Lionel W. (1954), "On Equilibrium in Graham's Model of World Trade and Other Competitive Systems," *Econometrica, 22*, April, 147–61.

Ménard, Claude (1990), "The Lausanne Tradition: Walras and Pareto," and "Commentary" by Donald A. Walker, in Klaus Hennings and Warren J. Samuels (eds), *Neoclassical Economic Theory: 1870 to 1930*, Dordrecht: Kluwer Academici Publishers, 95–136, 137–50.

Menger, Karl (1973), "Austrian Marginalism and Mathematical Economics," in *Carl Menger and the Austrian school of economics*, edited by John R. Hicks and W. Weber, Oxford: Oxford University Press, 38–60.

Mill, John Stuart (1836), "On the definition of Political Economy; and on the Method of Philosophical Investigation Proper to It," *London and Westminster Review*, October; in *Essays on Some Unsettled Questions of Political Economy*, London: John W. Parker, 1844, 120–64; and in *Collected Works of John Stuart Mill, 22*, Toronto: University of Toronto Press, 1967, 309–39.

Mill, John Stuart (1981–1991), *Collected Works of John Stuart Mill*, 33 vols., Toronto: Toronto University Press.

Mirowski, Philip (1989), *More heat than light. Economics as social physics: Physics as nature's economics*, Cambridge: Cambridge University Press.

Moore, Henry Ludwell (1929), *Synthetic Economics*, New York: Macmillan.

Moret, Jacques (1915), *L'Emploi des mathématiques en économie poltitque*, Paris: M. Giard et E. Brière.

Morishima, Michio (1977), *Walras' Economics; A Pure Theory of Capital and Money*, Cambridge: Cambridge University Press.

Morishima, Michio (1996), "Morishima on Ricardo: Two Replies," *Cambridge Journal of Economics, 20* (1), January, 91–109; in Walker 2001, *1*, 278–96.

Mosak, Jacob L. (1987), "Schultz, Henry (1893–1938)," in Eatwell et al. 1987, *4*, 261–62.

Mouchot, Claude (2000), "De quelques problèmes relatifs à l'entrepreneur walrassien," *Les Cahiers du CERAS, Actes du Colloque de l'Association Internationale Walras*, hors série n°1, juin, 49–57.

Murray, Roberto A. (1920), *Leçons d'économie politique suivant la doctrine de l'école de Lausanne*, Paris: Payot et Cie.

Myrdal, Gunnar (1945), "Gustav Cassel in Memoriam," *Ekonomisk revy, 2*, 3–13.

Nash, John F. (1950), "The Bargaining Problem," *Econometrica, 18*, 155–62.

Nash, John F. (1951), "Non-cooperative Games," *Annals of Mathematics, 54*, 286–95.

Negishi, Takashi (1989), *History of Economic Theory*, Amsterdam: North-Holland.

Neisser, Hans Philipp (1932), "Lohnhöhe und Beschäftigungsgrad im Marktgleichgewicht," *Weltwirtschaftliches Archiv, 36* (2), October, 415–55.

Neumann, John von (1937), "Über ein Ökonomisches Gleichungssystem und eine Verallgemeinerung des Brouwerschen Fixpunktsatzes," *Ergebnisse eines Mathematischen Kolloquiums*, Heft 8, 1935–1936 [sic]; edited by Karl Menger, Leipzig and Wien: Franz Deuticke, 1938, 73–83; translated by George Morgenstern as "A Model of General Economic Equilibrium," *Review of Economic Studies, 13*, 1945–1946, 1–9.

Neumann, John von and Oskar Morgenstern (1944), *Theory of Games and Economic Behavior*, Princeton: Princeton University Press.

Niiniluoto, Ilkka (1998), "Induction," in Davis et al. 1998, 246–49.

Osorio, Antonio (1913), *Théorie mathématique de l'échange*, Paris: M. Giard et E. Brière.

Pantaleoni, Maffeo (1889), *Principii di economia pura*, Florence: Barbera.

Pareto, Vilfredo (1893a), "Lettre d'Italie," *Le Monde Economique*, July 8, 35–36.

Pareto, Vilfredo (1893b), "Considerazioni sui principii fondamentali dell'-economia politica pura," *Giornale degli Economisti*, series 2, 7, October, 279–321.

Pareto, Vilfredo (1896/1897), *Cours d'économie politique*, 2 vols., Lausanne: F. Rouge; reprint, edited by G.-H. Bousquet and G. Busino, Geneva: Librairie Droz, 1964.

Pareto, Vilfredo (1897), "The New Theories of Economics," *Journal of Political Economy, 5* (4), 485–502.

Pareto, Vilfredo (1898a), "Protezionismo italiano," *Critica Sociale, Rivista Quindicinale de Socialismo, 7*, February 16, 49–50.

Pareto, Vilfredo (1898b), "De l'économie mathématique," *Zeitschrift für Sozialwissenschaft, 1*, 320–21.

Pareto, Vilfredo (1899), "Liberali e Socialisti," *Critica Sociale, Rivista quindicinale de Socialismo, 8*, September 1, 215–16.

Pareto, Vilfredo (1902–1903), *Les systèmes socialistes*, 2 vols., Paris: V. Giard & E. Brière.

Pareto, Vilfredo (1909), *Manuel d'économie politique*; translated by Alfred Bonnet from the Italian *Manuale d'economia politica*, Milan: Società Editrice Libraria, 1906; translation reviewed and corrected by the author, Paris: V. Giard & E. Brière. The Italian version translated by Ann S. Schwier as *Manual of Political Economy*, New York: Augustus M. Kelley, 1971.

Pareto, Vilfredo (1911b), "Economie Mathématique," in *Encyclopédie des sciences mathématiques, 1*, Paris: Teubner, Gauthier, Villars.

Pareto, Vilfredo (1912a), "Economia Dimessa," *La Libertà Economica, Rassegna settimanale, 10* (17–18), 285–90.

Pareto, Vilfredo (1912b), Review of "*La Teoria della Rendita. By Prof. Guido Sensini. (Rome: Loescher. 1912.)*," *Economic Journal, 22* (3), September, 467–69.

Pareto, Vilfredo (1916), *Trattato di sociologia generale*, 4 vols., Florence: Barbera; translated by Andrew Bongiorno and Arthur Livingston as *The Mind and Society; A Treatise on General Sociology*, New York: Dover Publications, 1963.

Pareto, Vilfredo (1948), *Corrispondenza di V. Pareto*, edited by Guido Sensini, Padua: Cedam (Casa editrice Dr. Antonio Milani).

Pareto, Vilfredo (1960), *Lettere a Maffeo Pantaleoni, 1890–1923*, edited by Guido Sensini, 3 vols., Rome: Banca Nazionale del Lavoro.

Pareto, Vilfredo (1963–2001), *Œuvres complètes de Vilfredo Pareto*, 31 vols., prepared under the direction of Giovanni Busino, Geneva: Droz.

Patinkin, Don (1956), *Money, Interest, and Prices: An Integration of Monetary and Value Theory*, Evanston, IL: Row, Peterson; 2nd ed., New York: Harper and Row, 1965.

Patinkin, Don (1987), "Walras's Law," in Eatwell et al. 1987, *3*, 863–68.

Petri, Fabio (2004), *General Equilibrium, Capital and Macroeconomics; A Key to Recent Controversies in Equilibrium Theory*, Cheltenham, UK, and Northhampton, MA: Edward Elgar Publishing.

Pietri-Tonelli, Alfonso de (1924), "Le equazioni generali dell'equilibrio economico di Vilfredo Pareto," *Giornale degli Economisti*, series 4, *65*, 55–61.

Pietri-Tonelli, Alfonso de (1927), *Traité d'économie rationnelle*, 3rd ed, Paris: M. Giard.

Pirou, Gaëtan (1925), *Les doctrines economiques en France depuis 1870*, Paris: A. Colin.

Pirou, Gaëtan (1934), *Les théories de l'équilibre économique: L. Walras et V. Pareto*, Paris: Les Editions Domat-Montchrestien.

Poinsoit, Louis (1803), *Elements de statique*; 8th edition, Paris: Bachelier, 1842.

Pokorny, D. (1978), "Smith and Walras: Two theories of science," *Canadian Journal of Economics and Political Science, 11* (3), 387–403.

Potier, Jean-Pierre (1994), "Classification des sciences et divisions de l'«économie politique et sociale» dans l'œuvre de Léon Walras: une tentative de reconstruction," *Economies et Sociétés*, Série Œconomia, Histoire de la Pensée économique, P.E. no. 20–21, *28* (10–11), 223–77.

Potier, Jean-Pierre (1998), "Léon Walras and Applied Science: The Significance of the Free Competition Principle," in Gilbert Faccarello (ed.), *Studies in the History of French Political Economy: From Bodin to Walras*, London and New York: Routledge, 369–403.

Potier, Jean-Pierre and Donald Walker (eds.) (2004), *La correspondance entre Aline Walras et William Jaffé et autres documents*, Paris: Economica.

Rebeyrol, Antoine (1998), "The Development of Walras' Monetary Theory," in Gilbert Faccarello (ed.), *Studies in the History of French Political Economy: From Bodin to Walras*, London and New York: Routledge, 319–68.

Rebeyrol, Antoine (1999), *La pensée économique de Walras*, Paris: Dunod.

Rebeyrol, Antoine (2002), "'Yet Another Look'? A Comment," *European Journal of the History of Economic Thought, 9* (4), winter, 541–49.

Redman, Deborah (1997), *The Rise of Political Economy as a Science; Methodology and the Classical Economists*, Cambridge, MA, and London: MIT Press.

Ricci, Umberto (1924), "Pareto e l'economia pura," *Giornale degli Economisti,* series 4, *65*, 27–44; translated as "Pareto and Pure Economics," *Review of Economic Studies, 1* (1–3), 1933–1934, 3–21.

Rizvi, S. Abu Turab (2003), "Postwar Neoclassical Microeconomics," in *A Companion to the History of Economic Thought*, edited by Warren J. Samuels, Jeff E. Biddle, and John B. Davis, Malden, MA, Oxford, UK, Melbourne, Berlin: Blackwell Publishing Ltd., 377–94.

Robert, Paul et al. (eds.) (2002), "Expérimental," *Le nouveau petit Robert*, Paris: Dictionnaires Le Robert, 1001.

Samuelson, Paul A. (1941a), "The Stability of Equilibrium: Comparative Statics and Dynamics," *Econometrica, 9* (2), April, 97–120.

Samuelson, Paul A. (1941b), "The Stability of Equilibrium: Linear and Non-linear Systems," *Econometrica, 9*, April, 97–120.

Samuelson, Paul A. (1947), *Foundations of Economic Analysis*, Cambridge: Harvard University Press.

Samuelson, Paul A. (1993), "Gustav Cassel's Scientific Innovations: Claims and Realities," *History of Political Economy, 25* (3), 515–27.

Samuelson, Paul A. (1998), "Samuelson, Paul Anthony, as an Interpreter of the Classical Economists," in Heinz D. Kurz and Neri Salvadori, eds., *The Elgar Companion to Classical Economics, 2*, Cheltenham, U.K.: Edward Elgar Publishing Limited, 329–333.

Schlesinger, Karl (1914), *Theorie der Geld-und Kreditwirtschaft*, Munich/ Leipzig: Dunker und Humblot.

Schlesinger, Karl (1933–1934), "Über die produktionsgleichungen der ökonomischen Wertlehre," *Ergebnisse eines mathematischen Kolloquiums*, Heft 6, edited by Karl Menger, Leipzig and Wien: Franz Deuticke, 1935, 10–11; translated by William J. Baumol as "On the Production Equations of Economic Value Theory," in Baumol and Goldfeld 1968, 278–80.

Schultz, Henry (1929), "Marginal Productivity and the General Pricing Process," *Journal of Political Economy, 37*, October, 505–51.

Schultz, Henry (1932), "Marginal Productivity and the Lausanne School," *Economica, 12*, August, 285–96.

Schultz, Henry (1933), "Interrelations of Demand," *Journal of Political Economy, 41*, August, 468–512.

Schultz, Henry (1935), "Interrelations of Demand, Price, and Income," *Journal of Political Economy, 43*, August, 433–81.

Schultz, Henry (1938), *The Theory and Measurement of Demand*, Chicago: University of Chicago Press.

Schumpeter, Joseph A. (1910), "Marie Esprit Léon Walras," *Zeitschrift für Volksvirtschaft, 19*, 397–402; English translation in Schumpeter 1951, 74–79.

Schumpeter, Joseph A. (1911/1926), *The Theory of Economic Development; An Inquiry into Profits, Capital, Credit, Interest, and the Business Cycle*; translated by Redvers Opie, New York: Oxford University Press, 1961.

Schumpeter, Joseph A. (1925), "Schumpeter on Böhm-Bawerk," in Henry W. Spiegel (ed.), *The Development of Economic Thought; Great Economists in Perspective*, abridged edition, New York, Science Editions, John Wiley & Sons, 1964, 370–80.

Schumpeter, Joseph A. (1949), "Vilfredo Pareto," *Quarterly Journal of Economics, 63*, May, 345–59; and in Schumpeter 1951.

Schumpeter, Joseph A. (1951), *Ten Great Economists from Marx to Keynes*, New York: Oxford University Press.

Schumpeter, Joseph A. (1954), *History of Economic Analysis*, New York: Oxford University Press.

Schwartz, P. (1972), *The New Political Economy of J. S. Mill*, London: London School of Economics.

Sensini, Guido (1929), "Vilfredo Pareto e la teoria della moneta," *Il Giornale Economico*, September–October; reprinted in Guido Sensini, *Studi di scienze sociali, 1*, Rome: Casa Libraria Editrice Italiana, 1932.

Sonnenschein, Hugo. F. (1972), "Market Excess Demand Functions," *Econometrica, 40*, 549–63.

Sonnenschein, Hugo. F. (1973), "Utility Hypothesis and Market Demand Theory," *Western Economic Journal, 11*, 404–10.

Slutsky, Eugen (1915), "Sulla teoria del bilancio del consomatore," *Giornale degli Economisti e Rivista di Statistica, 51*, July, 1–26.

Stackelberg, Heinrich von (1933), "Zwei Kritische Bemerkungen zur Preistheorie Gustav Cassels," *Zeitschrift für Nationalökonomie, 4*, June, 456–72.

Staley, Charles E. (1989), *A History of Economic Thought. From Aristotle to Arrow*, Cambridge, MA: Basil Blackwell.

Steiner, Philippe (1999), "L'entrepreneur parétien et la théorie de l'action," *Revue européenne des sciences sociales, 37* (116), 103–118.

Stigler, George (1941), *Production and Distribution Theories; The Formative Period*, New York: Macmillan Company.

Syll, Lars Pålsson (1993), "Wicksell on Harmony Economics: The Lausanne School vs. Wicksell," *Scandinavian Economic History Review, 41* (2), Winter, 172–88.

Tatti, Elena (2000), "Être et devoir être chez Léon Walras," in Dockès et al. 2000, 417–28.

Vacherot, Etienne (1858), *La métaphysique et la science ou principes de métaphysique positive*; 2nd ed., 1863, 3 vols., Paris: Librairie de F. Chamerot.

van Daal, Jan and Donald A. Walker (1990), "The Problem of Aggregation in Walras's General Equilibrium Theory," *History of Political Economy, 22* (3), Fall, 489–505; and in Walker 2001a, 2, 341–57.

van Daal, Jan and Albert Jolink (1989), "Léon Walras's Mathematical Economics and the Mechanical Analogies," *History of Economics Society Bulletin, 11* (1), Spring, 25–32; and in Walker 2001a, 1, 93–100.

van Daal, Jan and Albert Jolink (1993), "Walras's 'General' General-Equilibrium Model," in Robert F. Hébert (ed.), *Themes on Economic Discourse, Method, Money and Trade: Selected Papers from the History of*

Economics Conference 1991, Perspectives on the History of Economic Thought, *9*, Aldershot: Edward Elgar for the History of Economics Society, 121–36.

Wald, Abraham (1934–1935), "Über die Produktionsgleichungen der ökonomischen Wertlehre (II)," *Ergebnisse eines mathematischen Kolloquiums*, Heft 7; Leipzig and Wein: Frank Deuticke, 1936, 1–6; translated by William J. Baumol as "On the Production Equations of Economic Value Theory, Part 2," in Baumol and Goldfeld 1968, 289–93.

Wald, Abraham (1936), "Über einige Gleichungssysteme der mathematischen Ökonomie," *Zeitschrift für Nationalökonomie, 7* (5), 637–70; translated by Otto Eckstein as "On Some Systems of Equations of Mathematical Economics," *Econometrica, 19*, October, 1951, 368–403.

Walker, Donald A. (1970), "Léon Walras in the Light of His Correspondence and Related Papers," *Journal of Political Economy, 78* (4), July-August, 685–701.

Walker, Donald A. (1971a), "The Static Analysis of Disequilibrium Transactions Markets," *Indian Economic Journal, 18* (3), January-March, 305–327.

Walker, Donald A. (1971b), "The Determinateness of Equilibrium in Isolated Competitive Markets," *International Review of Economics and Business, 18* (12), December, 1158–1179.

Walker, Donald A. (1983), "William Jaffé, *Officier de liaison intellectuel*," in *The Craft of the Historian of Economic Thought,* vol. 1 *of Research in the History of Economic Thought and Methodology*, edited by Warren J. Samuels, Greenwich, CT: JAI Press, 19–39.

Walker, Donald A. (1984), "Is Walras's Theory of General Equilibrium a Normative Scheme?" *History of Political Economy, 16* (3), Fall, 445–69.

Walker, Donald A. (1987a) "Walras's Theories of Tatonnement," *Journal of Political Economy, 95*(4), 758–74.

Walker, Donald A. (1987b), "Walras, Léon (1934–1910)," in Eatwell et al., *4*, 852–63.

Walker, Donald A. (1987c), "Bibliography of the Writings of Léon Walras," 1st ed., *History of Political Economy, 19* (4), 667–702.

Walker, Donald A. (1989), "A Primer on Walrasian Theories of Economic Behavior," *History of Economics Society Bulletin, 11*, Spring, 1–23; reprinted in Blaug 1992, 214–36.

Walker, Donald A. (1990), "Commentary by Donald A. Walker" on "The Lausanne Tradition: Walras and Pareto," by Claude Ménard, in *Neoclassical Economic Theory, 1870 to 1930*, edited by Klaus Hennings and Warren J. Samuels, Boston, Dordrecht, London: Kluwer Academic Publishers, 137–50.

Walker, Donald A. (1991), Review of *"The Invisible Hand: Economic Equilibrium in the History of Science*, by Bruna Ingrao and Giorgio Israel," 1990, *History of Political Economy, 23*, no. 3, Fall, 560–65.

Walker, Donald A. (1996), *Walras's Market Models*, Cambridge, New York, and Melbourne: Cambridge University Press.

Walker, Donald A. (1997a), "The School of Lausanne," in *Encyclopedia of Keynesian Economics*, edited by Thomas Cate, with associate editors David Colander and Geoffrey Harcourt, Cheltenham, UK, and Brookfield, VT: Edward Elgar Publishing Limited, 361–65.

Walker, Donald A. (1997b), *Advances in General Equilibrium Theory*, Cheltenham, UK, Lyme, CT: Edward Elgar Publishing Limited; in French, translated by the author: *La théorie de l'équilibre général: De nouveaux éclairages*, Paris: Economica, 1999.

Walker, Donald A. (1998), "Léon Walras," in *The Handbook of Economic Methodology*, edited by John B. Davis, D. Wade Hands, and Uskali Maki, Cheltenham, UK, Northampton, MA: Edward Elgar Publishing Limited, 541–45.

Walker, Donald A. (ed.) (2000a), *Equilibrium*, 3 vols., in Kevin D. Hoover and Mark Blaug (general eds.), *Critical Ideas in Economics*, no. 2, Cheltenham, UK, and Northampton, MA: Edward Elgar Publishing Limited.

Walker, Donald A. (2000b), "La relation entre la Bourse au XIXe siècle et le modèle de Léon Walras d'un marché organisé," in Dockès et al. 2000, 443–57.

Walker, Donald A. (ed.) (2001a), *The Legacy of Léon Walras*, 2 vols., in Steven G. Medema, (series ed.), *Intellectual Legacies in Modern Economics*, Cheltenham, UK, and Northampton, MA: Edward Elgar Publishing Limited.

Walker, Donald A. (2001b), "A factual account of the functioning of the nineteenth-century Paris Bourse," *European Journal of the History of Economic Thought, 8* (2), 186–207.

Walker, Donald A. (2003), "Early General Equilibrium Economics: Walras, Pareto, and Cassel," in *A Companion to the History of Economic Thought*, edited by Warren J. Samuels, Jeff E. Biddle, and John B. Davis, Malden, MA, Oxford, UK, Melbourne, Berlin: Blackwell Publishing Ltd., ch. 18, 278–93.

Walras, Auguste (1831), *De la nature de la richesse et de l'origine de la valeur*, Paris: Alexandre Johanneau.

Weintraub, E. Roy (1983), "On the Existence of a Competitive Equilibrium: 1930–1954," *Journal of Economic Literature, 21* (1), 1–39.

Wicksell, Knut (1893), *Über Wert, Kapital und Rente, nach den neueren nationalökonomischen Theorien*, Jena: G. Fisher.

Wicksell, Knut (1898), *Geldzins und Güterpreise bestimmenden Ursachen*, Jena: G. Fischer; translated by R. F. Kahn as *Interest and Prices; A Study of the Causes Regulating the Value of Money*, London: Macmillan, 1936.

Wicksell, Knut (1901, 1906), *Vorlesungen über Nationalökonomie*; 2nd ed. 1911, translated by E. Classen as *Lectures on Political Economy*, 2 vols., London: Routledge & Kegan Paul, 1934.

Wicksell, Knut (1919), "Professor Cassel's System of Economics," in Wicksell 1934, appendix 1, 219–57.

Wicksell, Knut (1934), *Lectures on Political Economy*, vol. 1, *General Theory*, translated from the Swedish by E. Classen, London: Routledge and Kegan Paul.

Witteloostuijn, A. van and J. A. H. Maks (1988), "Walras: A Hicksian *avant la lettre,*" *Economie Appliquée, 41* (3), 595–608.

Wieser, Friedrich von (1891), "The Austrian School and the Theory of Value," *Economic Journal, 1,* March, 108–21.

Witteloostuijn, A. van and J. A. H. Maks (1990), "Walras on Temporary Equilibrium and Dynamics," *History of Political Economy, 22* (2), 223–37.

Wood, John C. (ed.) (1993), *Léon Walras: Critical Assessments,* 3 vols., London: Routledge.

Zatarin, Joseph de (1972), "La théorie des tâtonnements chez Walras," *Revue d'Economie Politique, 82* (6), 1222–28.

Zawadzki, Władyslaw (1914), *Les mathématiques appliquées à l'économie politique,* Paris: M. Rivière.

Zeuthen, Frederik L. B. (1928), *Den konomiske Fordeling,* Copenhagen: Busck.

Zeuthen, Frederik L. B. (1933), "Das Princip der Knappheit, Technische Kominatin und Ökonomische Qualität," *Zeitschrift für Nationalökonomie, 4,* 1–24.

Zylberberg, André (1988), "L'économie mathématique chez les actuaires français au temps de Walras (1820–1914)," *Oeconomia, 9,* 35–64.

Zylberberg, André (1990), *L'économie mathématique en France 1870–1914,* Paris: Economica.

References and Bibliography
for Chapter 11

I. Non-Virtual Walrasian models

A. Exchange models

Bottazzi, J.-M. (1994), "Accessibility of Pareto Optima by Walrasian Exchange Processes," *Journal of Mathematical Economics, 23* (6), November, 585–603.

Bronfman, Corinne (2000), "An Experimental Examination of the Walrasian Tatonnement Mechanism," *Bargaining and market behavior: Essays in experimental economics*, Cambridge, New York, and Melbourne: Cambridge University Press, 381–406.

Cordoba, Jose M. and Peter J. Hammond (1998), "Asymptotically Strategy-Proof Walrasian Exchange," *Mathematical Social Sciences, 36* (3), December, 185–212.

Grandmont, Jean-Michel (1992), "Transformations of the Commodity Space, Behavioral Heterogeneity, and the Aggregation Problem," *Journal of Economic Theory, 57* (1), June, 1–35.

Grodal, Birgit and Karl Vind (2000), "Walras Equilibrium with Coordination," Institute of Economics Working paper, University of Copenhagen.

Guesnerie, Roger (2002), "Equilibre général, coordination et multiplicité sur les marches au comptant," *Revue d'Economie Politique, 112* (5), September–October, 671–92.

Herings, Jean-Jacques (1997), "Equilibrium Adjustment of Disequilibrium Prices," *Journal of Mathematical Economics, 27* (1), February, 53–77.

Ma, Jinpeng and Fusheng Nie (2003), "Walrasian Equilibrium in an Exchange Economy with Indivisibilities," *Mathematical Social Sciences, 46* (2), October, 159–92.

Majumdar, Mukul and Vladimir Rotar (2000), "Equilibrium Prices in a Random Exchange Economy with Dependent Agents," *Economic Theory, 15* (3), May, 531–50.

Negishi, T. (1961), "On the Formation of Prices," *International Economic Review, 2*, 122–26.

Peters, Michael (1997), "On the Equivalence of Walrasian and Non-Walrasian Equilibria in Contract Markets: The Case of Complete Contracts," *Review of Economic Studies, 64* (2), April, 241–64.

for Chapter 11** 335

Uzawa, Hirofumi (1962), "A Walrasian Approach to Bargaining Games," *International Economic Review, 3*, 218–32.

B. Some structural characteristics of non-virtual exchange or production models

De Fraja, Gianni and Jozsef Sakovics (2001), "Walras *Retrouvé*: Decentralized Trading Mechanisms and the Competitive Price," *Journal of Political Economy, 109* (4), August, 842–63.
Kandel, Eugene and Avi Simhon (2002), "Between Search and Walras," *Journal of Labor Economics, 20* (1), January, 59–85.
Koutsougeras, Leonidas C. (2003), "Non-Walrasian Equilibria and the Law of One Price," *Journal of Economic Theory, 108* (1), January, 169–75.
Sertel, Murat R. and Muhamet Yildiz (1999), "Double-Edged Population Monotonicity of Walrasian Equilibrium – A Note on the Nature of Competition," *Mathematical Social Sciences, 37* (3), May, 235–51.
Starr, Ross M. and Maxwell B. Stinchcombe (1993), "Exchange in a Network of Trading Posts," University of California, *San Diego Department of Economics Working Paper*, 93–13, April, 1–14.

C. Non-virtual models in which there is production

Baigent, G. Glenn (2003), "Competitive Markets and Aggregate Information," *Eastern Economic Journal, 29* (4), 593–606.
Benetti, Carlo (2002), "Le problème de la variation de prix: Les limites de la théorie walrassienne," *Revue Economique, 53* (5), September, 917–31.
Bennardo, Alberto and Pierre Andre Chiappori (2003), "Bertrand and Walras Equilibria under Moral Hazard," *Journal of Political Economy, 111* (4), August, 785–817.
Berliant, Marcus and Sami Dakhlia (2002), "Sensitivity Analysis for Applied General Equilibrium Models in the Presence of Multiple Walrasian Equilibria," *Economic Theory, 19* (3), April, 459–76.
Borissov, Kirill (2004), "An Intertemporal General Equilibrium Model with Given Real Wage Rates," *Structural Change and Economic Dynamics, 15* (2), June, 207–33.
Brown, Donald J. and Chris Shannon (2000), "Uniqueness, Stability, and Comparative Statics in Rationalizable Walrasian Markets," *Econometrica, 68* (6), November, 1529–39.
Dore, Mohammed H. I. (1998), "Walrasian General Equilibrium and Nonlinear Dynamics," *Nonlinear Dynamics, Psychology, and Life Sciences, 2* (1), January, 59–72.
Fisher, Franklin M. (1983), *Disequilibrium Foundations of Equilibrium Economics*, Cambridge: Cambridge University Press.
Flaschel, Peter (1991), "Stability – Independent of Economic Structure? A Prototype Analysis," *Structural Change and Economic Dynamics, 2* (1), 9–35.

Funk, Peter (1995), "Bertrand and Walras Equilibria in Large Economies," *Journal of Economic Theory, 67* (2), December, 436–66.

Gul, Faruk and Ennio Stacchetti (1999), "Walrasian Equilibrium with Gross Substitutes," *Journal of Economic Theory, 87* (1), July, 95–124.

Hahn, Frank H. (1962), "On the Stability of Pure Exchange Equilibrium," *International Economic Review, 3*, 206–13.

Hens, Thorsten (1997), "Stability of Tatonnement Processes of Short Period Equilibria with Rational Expectations," *Journal of Mathematical Economics, 28* (1), August, 41–67.

Herings, Jean-Jacques (1997), "A Globally and Universally Stable Price Adjustment Process," *Journal of Mathematical Economics, 27* (2), March, 163–93.

Horiba, Yutaka (1998), "Gross Substitutability and the Laws of Comparative Statics: A Simultaneous Demand Shift," *Keio Economic Studies, 35* (2), 1–7.

Jensen, Bjarne S. (2003), "Walrasian General Equilibrium Allocations and Dynamics in Two-Sector Growth Models," *German Economic Review, 4* (1), February, 53–87.

Katzner, Donald W. (1999), "Methodological Individualism and the Walrasian Tatonnement," *Journal of Economic and Social Research, 1* (1), 5–33.

Majumdar, Mukul and Tapan Mitra (1997), "Complexities of Concrete Walrasian Systems," *Issues in economic theory and public policy: Essays in honour of Professor Tapas Majumdar,* 41–63, Oxford and New York: Oxford University Press, Delhi.

Podczeck, Konrad (2003), "Core and Walrasian Equilibria When Agents' Characteristics Are Extremely Dispersed," *Economic Theory, 22* (4), November, 699–725.

Rao, J. Mohan (1998), "A Leibenstein-Hobbes-Walras Model of Sharecropping," *Metroeconomica, 49* (1), February, 62–96.

Serrano, Roberto and Oscar Volij (1998), "Axiomatizations of Neoclassical Concepts for Economies," *Journal of Mathematical Economics, 30* (1), August, 87–108.

II. Uses and developments of special ideas of Walras's

A. Walras's law

Aiyagari, S. Rao (1992), "Walras' Law and Nonoptimal Equilibria in Overlapping Generations Models," *Journal of Mathematical Economics, 21* (4), 343–61.

Balasko, Yves (2004), "The Equilibrium Manifold Keeps the Memory of Individual Demand Functions," *Economic Theory, 24* (3), October, 493–501.

Bidard, Christian (1989), "Equilibrium with a Qualitative Walras' Law," *Journal of Economic Theory, 47* (1), February, 203–05.

Habibagahi, H. and J. Quirk (1989), "Hicksian Stability and Walras' Law," in John Cunningham Wood and Ronald N. Woods (eds.), *Sir John R. Hicks: Critical Assessments, 2,* in *Critical Assessments of Contemporary Economists,* London and New York: Routledge, 249–61.

Huang, Weihong (2001), "Statistical Dynamics and Walras' Law," *Journal of Economic Behavior and Organization, 46* (1), September, 57–71.

Lange, Oskar R. (1942), "Say's Law: A Restatement and Criticism," in Oscar Lange, *et al.* (eds.), *Studies in Mathematical Economics and Econometrics,* Chicago: University of Chicago Press, 49–68.

Rhodes, James R. (1984), "Walras' Law and Clower's Inequality," *Australian Economic Papers, 23* (42), June, 112–22.

Yeager, Leland B. and Alan A. Rabin (1997), "Monetary Aspects of Walras's Law and the Stock-Flow Problem," *Atlantic Economic Journal, 25* (1), March, 18–36.

B. Walras allocations

Armstrong, Thomas E. and Marcel K. Richter (1984), "The Core-Walras Equivalence," *Journal of Economic Theory, 33* (1), June, 116–51.

Armstrong, Thomas E. and Marcel K. Richter (1986), "Existence of Nonatomic Core-Walras Allocations," *Journal of Economic Theory, 38* (1), February, 137–59.

Herves-Beloso, Carlos and Emma Moreno-Garcia (2004), "El poder de veto de la gran coalición," *Investigaciónes Económicas, 28* (3), September, 489–513.

Manresa, Antonio (2002), "Can We Identify Walrasian Allocations?," *Review of Economic Design, 7* (1), June, 57–73.

Nagahisa, Ryo-ichi (1991), "A Local Independence Condition for Characterization of Walrasian Allocations Rule," *Journal of Economic Theory, 54* (1), June, 106–23.

Nagahisa, Ryo-ichi (1992), "Walrasian Social Choice in a Large Economy," *Mathematical Social Sciences, 24* (1), August, 73–78.

Nagahisa, Ryo-ichi (1994), "A Necessary and Sufficient Condition for Walrasian Social Choice," *Journal of Economic Theory, 62* (1), February, 186–208.

Nagahisa, Ryo-ichi and Sang-Chul Suh (1995), "A Characterization of the Walras Rule," *Social Choice and Welfare, 12* (4), October, 335–52.

Nouweland, A. van den, B. Peleg and S. Tijs (1996), "Axiomatic Characterizations of the Walras Correspondence for Generalized Economies," *Journal of Mathematical Economics, 25* (3), April, 355–72.

Serrano, Roberto and Oscar Volij (1997), "Abstract Equilibria, Interactive Choice Sets and Walrasian Allocations," Department of Economics Working Paper, April, Brown University.

Serrano, Roberto and Oscar Volij (2000), "Walrasian Allocations without Price-Taking Behavior," *Journal of Economic Theory, 95* (1), November, 79–106.

Tauman, Yair and Yan Chen (2000), "Acceptable and Walrasian Allocations," *Journal of Mathematical Economics, 34* (3), November, 415–38.

Tian, Guoqiang (2000), "Feasible and Continuous Double Implementation of Constrained Walrasian Allocations," *Annals of Economics and Finance, 1* (1), May, 19–32.

Yamazaki, Akira (1984), "Walras Degrees and Probability of a Blocking Coalition at Pareto Allocations," *Journal of Mathematical Economics, 13* (2), October, 105–21.

C. The Walras correspondence

Balasko, Yves (1975), "The Graph of the Walras Correspondence," *Econometrica, 43* (5–6), September–November, 907–12.
DeMichelis, Stefano and Fabrizio Germano (2000), "Some Consequences of the Unknottedness of the Walras Correspondence," *Journal of Mathematical Economics, 34* (4), December, 537–45.
Jouini, Elyes (1993), "The Graph of the Walras Correspondence: The Production Economies Case," *Journal of Mathematical Economics, 22* (2), 139–47.
Korthues, Bernd (2000), "Characterization of an Extended Walrasian Concept for Open Economies," *Journal of Mathematical Economics, 33* (4), May, 449–61.
Majumdar, Mukul and Bezalel Peleg (1997), "An Axiomatization of the Walras Correspondence in Infinite Dimensional Spaces," *International Economic Review, 38* (4), November, 853–64.
Saijo, Tatsuyoshi, Yoshikatsu Tatamitani and Takehiko Yamato (1999), "Characterizing Natural Implementability: The Fair and Walrasian Correspondences," *Games and Economic Behavior, 28* (2), August, 271–93.

III. Imperfectly competitive non-virtual general equilibrium models

A. Oligopoly, Cournot-Walras, and monopolistic models

Alos-Ferrer, Carlos (2004), "Cournot versus Walras in Dynamic Oligopolies with Memory," *International Journal of Industrial Organization, 22* (2), February, 193–217.
Benassy, Jean-Pascal (1976), "The Disequilibrium Approach to Monopolistic Price Setting and General Monopolistic Equilibrium," *Review of Economic Studies, 43*, February, 69–81.
Bobo, Robert J. Gary (1989), "Cournot-Walras and Locally Consistent Equilibria," *Journal of Economic Theory, 49* (1), October, 10–32.
Bobo, Robert J. Gary and Philippe Michel (1991), "Informative Advertising and Competition: A Noncooperative Approach," *International Economic Review, 32* (2), May, 321–39.
Codognato, Giulio (1994), "Cournot-Walras Equilibrium: A Reconsideration," *Economic Notes, 23* (3), 388–401.
Codognato, Giulio (1995), "Cournot-Walras and Cournot Equilibria in Mixed Markets: A Comparison," *Economic Theory, 5* (2), March, 361–70.
Codognato, Giulio and Jean J. Gabszewicz (1993), "Cournot-Walras Equilibria in Markets with a Continuum of Traders," *Economic Theory, 3* (3), July, 453–64.

Cordella, Tito and Manjira Datta (2002), "Intertemporal Cournot and Walras Equilibria: An Illustration," *International Economic Review, 43* (1), February, 137–53.

D'Aspremont, Claude, Rodolphe Dos Santos Ferreira, and Louis-André Gérard-Varet (1997), "General Equilibrium Concepts under Imperfect Competition: A Cournotian Approach," *Journal of Economic Theory, 73* (1), March, 199–230.

Huang, Weihong (2003), "A Naive but Optimal Route to Walrasian Behavior in Oligopolies," *Journal of Economic Behavior and Organization, 52* (4), December, 553–71.

Kaas, Leo and Paul Madden (2000), "Imperfectly Competitive Cycles with Keynesian and Walrasian Features," Institute for Advanced Studies, Vienna, Working paper, Economics Series, no. 83.

Kaas, Leo (2001), "Cournot-Walras Equilibrium without Profit Feedback," *Economics Bulletin, 4* (9), 1–8.

Morishima, Michio and Madhavi Majumdar (1996), "The Cournot-Walras Arbitrage, Resource Consuming Exchange, and Competitive Equilibrium," in *Dynamic Economic Theory*, Cambridge, New York, Melbourne: Cambridge University Press, 270–84.

Novshek, William and Hugo Sonnenschein (1978), "Cournot and Walras Equilibrium," *Journal of Economic Theory, 19*(2), December, 223–66, in Andrew F. Daughety (ed.) *Cournot Oligopoly: Characterization and Applications*, Cambridge; New York, and Melbourne: Cambridge University Press, 271–316.

Robert, Jacques (1994), "In the Cournot-Walras General Equilibrium Model, There May Be 'More to Gain' by Changing the Numeraire Than by Eliminating Imperfections: A Two-Good Economy Example: Comment," in Jean Mercenier and T. N. Srinivasan (eds.), *Applied General Equilibrium and Economic Development: Present Achievements and Future Trends*, Ann Arbor: University of Michigan Press, 225–31.

Schenk-Hoppe, Klaus Reiner (2000), "The Evolution of Walrasian Behavior in Oligopolies," *Journal of Mathematical Economics, 33* (1), February, 35–55.

Siebe, Wilfrid (1990), "General Equilibrium with a Continuum of Oligopolies," *Universitat Bonn Sonderforschungsbereich 303*, working paper, May, 176.

Wooders, John (1997–1998), "Equilibrium in a Market with Intermediation Is Walrasian," *Review of Economic Design, 3* (1), 75–89.

Yosha, Oved (1997), "Diversification and Competition: Financial Intermediation in a Large Cournot-Walras Economy," *Journal of Economic Theory, 75* (1), July, 64–88.

B. Nash-Walras, games and bargaining models

Allen, Beth and Heracles Polemarchakis (1994), "From Nash to Walras Equilibrium," in Jean-François Mertens and Sylvain Sorin (eds.), *Game-theoretic Methods in General Equilibrium Analysis, NATO Advanced Science Institutes Series D: Behavioural and Social Sciences, 77*, Dordrecht and Boston:

Kluwer Academic in cooperation with NATO Scientific Affairs Division, 225–41.

Alos-Ferrer, Carlos and Ana B. Ania (2001), "Local Equilibria in Economic Games," *Economics Letters, 70* (2), February, 165–73.

Bevia, Carmen, Luis C. Corchon and Simon Wilkie (2003), "Implementation of the Walrasian Correspondence by Market Games," *Review of Economic Design, 7* (4), February, 429–42.

Corominas-Bosch, Margarida (2004), "Bargaining in a Network of Buyers and Sellers," *Journal of Economic Theory, 115* (1), March, 36–77.

Dagan, Nir, Roberto Serrano and Oscar Volij (1998), "Comment on McLennan and Sonnenschein 'Sequential Bargaining as a Noncooperative Foundation for Walrasian Equilibrium,'" *Econometrica, 66* (5), September, 1231–33.

Dubey, Pradeep and John Geanakoplos (2003), "From Nash to Walras via Shapley-Shubik," *Journal of Mathematical Economics, 39* (5–6), July, 391–400.

Faias, Marta, Emma Moreno-Garcia and Mario Rui Pascoa (2002), "Non-manipulability in Walrasian Cost Games," *Review of Economic Design, 7* (1), June, 93–104.

Geanakoplos, John (2003), "Nash and Walras Equilibrium via Brouwer," *Economic Theory, 21* (2–3), March, 585–603.

Ghosal, S. and H. M. Polemarchakis (1997), "Nash-Walras Equilibria," *Research in Economics, 51* (1), April, 31–40.

Kunimoto, Takashi and Roberto Serrano (2004), "Bargaining and Competition Revisited," *Journal of Economic Theory, 115* (1), March, 78–88.

Minelli, Enrico and Heracles M. Polemarchakis (1999), "Nash-Walras Equilibria of a Large Economy," Université Catholique de Louvain CORE Discussion Paper, July.

Ponsati, Clara (2004), "Search and Bargaining in Large Markets with Homogeneous Traders," *Contributions to Theoretical Economics, 4* (1), 1st quarter, 1–25.

Sabourian, Hamid (1999), "Bargaining and Markets: Complexity and the Walrasian Outcome," Yale Cowles Foundation Discussion Paper, December.

Serrano, Roberto (2002), "Decentralized Information and the Walrasian Outcome: A Pairwise Meetings Market with Private Values," *Journal of Mathematical Economics, 38* (1–2), September, 65–89.

Sinha, Deepak K. (1997), "Diffusion of Innovations in Globally Stable Walrasian Equilibrium," *Journal of Economics (Zeitschrift für Nationalökonomie), 66* (1), 1–22.

Sonn, Sang-Young (2001), "Bargaining and Walrasian Equilibrium in Simple Production Economies," *Seoul Journal of Economics, 14* (4), Winter, 379–405.

Szymanski, Stefan (2004), "Professional Team Sports Are Only a Game: The Walrasian Fixed-Supply Conjecture Model, Contest-Nash Equilibrium, and the Invariance Principle," *Journal of Sports Economics, 5* (2), May, 111–26.

Trockel, Walter (1996), "A Walrasian Approach to Bargaining Games," *Economics Letters, 51* (3), 295–301.

Trockel, Walter (2000), "Implementations of the Nash Solution Based on Its Walrasian Characterization," *Economic Theory, 16* (2), September, 277–94.

Wooders, John (1998), "Walrasian Equilibrium in Matching Models," *Mathematical Social Sciences, 35* (3), May, 245–59.

Yildiz, Muhamet (2003), "Walrasian Bargaining," *Games and Economic Behavior, 45* (2), November, 465–87.

C. Fix-price models

Benassy, Jean-Pascal (2000), "Rigidités nominales dans les modèles d'équilibre général intertemporel stochastique," *L'Actualité Economique/Revue D'Analyse Economique, 78* (4), December, 423–57.

De Vroey, Michel (2004), "Théorie de déséquilibre et chomage involontaire: Un examen critique," *Revue Economique, 55* (4), July, 647–68.

Drèze, Jacques (1975), "Existence of an Exchange Equilibrium under Price Rigidities," *International Economic Review, 16*, June, 301–20.

Grandmont, Jean-Michel (1982), "Temporary General Equilibrium Theory," in Kenneth J. Arrow and Michael D. Intriligator (eds.), *Handbook of Mathematical Economics: Volume II*, Amsterdam: North-Holland Publishing Company, 879–922.

Herings, P. Jean-Jacques, Gerard van der Laan and Dolf Talman (1998), "Price-Quantity Adjustment in a Keynesian Economy," Tilburg Center for Economic Research Discussion Paper, November.

Herings, Jean-Jacques, Gerard van der Laan and Richard Venniker (1998), "The Transition from a Dreze Equilibrium to a Walrasian Equilibrium," *Journal of Mathematical Economics, 29* (3), April, 303–30.

Kades, Eric (1985), "New Classical and New Keynesian Models of Business Cycles," *Economic Review*, Federal Reserve Bank of Cleveland, Quarter IV, 20–35.

IV. Micro- and macro-economics: blending the ideas of Walras and J. M. Keynes

Allen, Ralph C. and Jack H. Stone (1998), "Walrasian, Non-Walrasian and Post-Walrasian Perspectives on the ADAS Model: Theoretical and Pedagogical Implications," *Aggregate demand and supply: A critique of orthodox macroeconomic modelling*, New York: St. Martin's Press; London: Macmillan Press, 67–81.

Backhouse, Roger E. (1998), "The Neo-Walrasian Research Programme in Macroeconomics," in *Explorations in economic methodology: From Lakatos to empirical philosophy of science*, in *Frontiers of Political Economy, 17*, London and New York: Routledge, 13–38.

Benassy, Jean-Pascal (2002), *The macroeconomics of imperfect competition and nonclearing markets: A dynamic general equilibrium approach*, Cambridge and London: MIT Press.

Citanna, Alessandro (2001), "Continua of Underemployment Equilibria Reflecting Coordination Failures, also at Walrasian Prices," *Journal of Mathematical Economics, 36* (3), December, 169–200.

Colander, David (1999), "A Post-Walrasian Explanation of Wage and Price Inflexibility and a Keynesian Unemployment Equilibrium System," *Growth, employment and inflation: Essays in honour of John Cornwall*, New York: St. Martin's Press; London: Macmillan Press, 211–25.

De Vroey, Michel (1999), "Keynes and the Marshall-Walras Divide," *Journal of the History of Economic Thought, 21* (2), June, 117–36.

Drèze, Jacques (1997), "Walras-Keynes Equilibria Coordination and Macroeconomics," *European Economic Review, 41* (9), December 1735–62.

Kaas, Leo (1998), "Stabilizing Chaos in a Dynamic Macroeconomic Model," *Journal of Economic Behavior and Organization, 33* (3–4), January, 313–32.

Kaas, Leo and Paul Madden (2000), "Imperfectly Competitive Cycles with Keynesian and Walrasian Features," Institute for Advanced Studies, Vienna, Working paper, Economics Series, no. 83.

Palley, Thomas I. (1998), "Walras' Law and Keynesian Macroeconomics," *Australian Economic Papers, 37* (3), September, 330–40.

Palley, Thomas I. (1999), "General Disequilibrium Analysis with Inside Debt," *Journal of Macroeconomics, 21* (4), Fall, 785–803.

V. Applied and computational general equilibrium models

Brown, D. J. and R. L. Matzkin (1996), "Testable Restrictions on the Equilibrium Manifold," *Econometrica, 64* (6), November, 1249–62.

Burniaux, Jean Marc et al. (1990), "Economy-Wide Effects of Agricultural Policies in OECD Countries: A GE Approach Using the WALRAS Model," in Ian Goldin and Odin Knudsen (eds.), *Agricultural Trade Liberalization: Implications for Developing Countries*, Paris: Organisation for Economic Co-operation and Development; Washington, D.C.: World Bank, 283–306.

Burniaux, Jean-Marc, François Delormé, Ian Lienert, and John P. Martin (1990), "WALRAS – A Multi-sector, Multi-country Applied General Equilibrium Model for Quantifying the Economy-wide Effects of Agricultural Policies," *OECD Economic Studies, 13*, Winter, 69–102.

Carvajal, Andres (2004), "Testable Restrictions on the Equilibrium Manifold under Random Preferences," *Journal of Mathematical Economics, 40* (1–2), February, 121–43.

Chang, S.-I. (1997), "The Effects of Economic Integration between North and South Korea: A Computable General Equilibrium Analysis," *International Economic Journal, 11* (4), Winter, 1–16.

Cheng, John Q. and Michael P. Wellman (1998), "The WALRAS Algorithm: A Convergent Distributed Implementation of General Equilibrium Outcomes," *Computational Economics, 12* (1), August, 1–24.

Delormé, François and Dominique van der Mensbrugghe (1989), "Assessing the Role of Scale Economies and Imperfect Competition in the Context of Agricultural Trade Liberalisation: A Canadian Case Study," *OECD Economic Studies, 13*, Winter, 205–36.

Dhillon, Upinder S., Dennis J. Lasser, and Taiji Watanabe (1997), "Volatility, Information, and Double versus Walrasian Auction Pricing in US and Japanese Futures Markets," *Journal of Banking and Finance, 21* (7), July, 1045–61.

Gottinger, H. W. (1998), "Greenhouse Gas Economics and Computable General Equilibrium," *Journal of Policy Modeling, 20* (5), October, 537–80.

Leontief, Wassily (1941), *The Structure of American Economy, 1919–1929*, Cambridge, MA: Harvard University Press.

Lienert, Ian (1989), "Quantifying Agricultural Policies in the WALRAS Model," *OECD Economic Studies, 13*, Winter, 103–30.

List, John A. (2004), "Testing Neoclassical Competitive Theory in Multi lateral Decentralized Markets," *Journal of Political Economy, 112* (5), October, 1131–56.

Martin, John P. (1989–1990), "Economy-Wide Effects of Agricultural Policies in OECD Countries: Simulation Results with WALRAS," *OECD Economic Studies, 13*, Winter, 131–72.

Noland, Marcus (2000), *Avoiding the Apocalypse: The Future of the Two Koreas*, Washington, D.C.: Institute for International Economics.

Mensbrugghe, Dominique van der, John P. Martin, and Jean Marc Burniaux (1989), "How Robust Are WALRAS Results?," *OECD Economic Studies, 13*, Winter, 173–204.

Piggott, John and John Whalley (1985), *New Developments in Applied General Equilibrium Analysis*, New York: Cambridge University Press.

Rao, J. Mohan (1998), "A Leibenstein-Hobbes-Walras Model of Sharecropping," *Metroeconomica, 49* (1), February, 62–96.

Scarf, Herbert E. (1973), *The Computation of Economic Equilibria*, New Haven: Yale University Press.

Scarf, Herbert E. and John B. Shoven (eds.) (1984), Applied General Equilibrium Analysis, New York: Cambridge University Press.

Yao, Shuntian (2002), "Walrasian Equilibrium Computation, Network Formation, and the Wen Theorem," *Review of Development Economics, 6* (3), October, 415–27.

Index

345

interest
  market/natural rates of, 282–283
  Walras on English theory of interest, 95
Interest and Prices (Wicksell), 282
intimate reality, in economic theory,
    87–88
inventory control/accounting, 93, 96–97
Isnard, Achylle Nicolas, 5
Israel, Giorgio, 312

Jaffé, William, 12
  on *Eléments*, 60
  on tatonnement, 149
  on Walras as idealist, 52, 113–114
  on Walras compared with other
      economist, 113–114
  on Walras legacy, 13
  on Walras growth model, 161
Jevons, W. S., 113–114
  business cycle theory of, 110
  creative years for, 9, 10, 14–15
  on human desires, 128–129
  trading bodies and, 95
Jolink, Albert, 27, 58

Kant, Immanuel, 46
Keynes, J. M., 9, 10, 169
Kirman, Alan, 267, 311, 312
Koopmans, Tjalling, 301
Koppl, Roger, 99, 113–114
Kurz, Heinz, 7

laissez-faire/laissez-passer, 98
Lallement, Jérôme, 66
land, Walras on state ownership of, 2–3,
    81, 109
land rents, 109
Lange, Oskar, 153, 288–289
last comprehensive model, 181–183
  markets in, 182, 183
  monetary theory in, 182–183
  reasons for poor quality of revisions in,
      183–187
  written pledges in, 181–182
Launhardt, C. F. W., 135
Laurent, Hermann, 279
Lausanne school, 279, 289
law of the variation of equilibrium prices,
    68
Lendjel, Eméric, 29, 270
Lengwiler, Yvan, 308–309
Lerner, Abba, 288
Lexis, William, 297
Lieben, Richard, 14–15

Locke, John, 26, 46, 47, 62
losses. *See* profits/losses

macroeconomic savings function,
    154–155
Maks, J. A. H., 149–150, 155, 167
Malthus, T. R., Walras on population
    theory of, 50, 51, 94
Manuale d' economia politica (Pareto),
    264
Marchionatti, Roberto, 280
Marget, Arthur W., 167, 279–280
marginal productivity theory, 143, 279
marginal utility functions, 107
marginal utility theory, 12, 13
  proportionality of prices to marginal
      utilties, 88
market demand curves,
  equilibrium price and, 303–305
  individual, 135
market/natural rates of interest, 282–283
markets
  assumption as purely competitive,
      302
  credit, 154–155
  oral pledges, 149
  problems with in written pledges
      sketch, 178, 179, 182, 183
  production/consumption sides of, 5
  rates of interest and, 155, 282–283
  stocks/bonds, 141–142. *See also* freely
      competitive markets
Marschak, Jacob, 289
Marshall, Alfred, 114, 141, 303
Marx, Karl, on economic theory scope,
    120, 121–122
mathematical model of exchange, of
    Isnard, 5
mathematics, use in theoretical work, 27
mathematization of economics
  dealing with exchange models, 3
  influence of Cournot on, 4
mature comprehensive model, 10–11
  absence of central price quoter in,
      150
  assumption of entrepreneur as
      sometimes price-taker in, 150
  Bourse incorporated into, 141–142,
      166
  consumer sovereignty in, 169–170
  entrepreneur in (*see* entrepreneur)
  equilibrium prices in, 154
  as growth model, 161
  legacy of, 170–171

For EU product safety concerns, contact us at Calle de José Abascal, 56–1°,
28003 Madrid, Spain or eugpsr@cambridge.org.